LOST BATTLES

Lost Battles
Reconstructing the Great Clashes of the Ancient World

Philip Sabin

hambledon
continuum

Hambledon Continuum is an imprint of Continuum Books
Continuum UK, The Tower Building, 11 York Road, London SE1 7NX
Continuum US, 80 Maiden Lane, Suite 704, New York, NY 10038

www.continuumbooks.com

First published 2007
Paperback edition published 2009

British Library Cataloguing-in-Publication Data
A catalogue record for this book is available from the British Library.

ISBN (HB) : 978 1 84725 187 9
ISBN (PB) : 978 0 82643 015 1

Typeset by Pindar NZ, Auckland, New Zealand
Printed and bound by MPG Books Ltd, Cornwall, Great Britain

New Orleans, LA.
June 2009

Contents

PART I: THE MODEL

PART II: THE BATTLES

Illustrations

(All the artwork was created by the author.)

Between pages 58 and 59

Between pages 138 and 139

Between pages 218 and 219

Acknowledgements

My first thanks must go to Tony Morris and Martin Sheppard of Hambledon for commissioning an ancient warfare book in the first place, and then for showing even more patience and tolerance than publishers normally display in the face of missed deadlines and the gradual evolution of the topic into something very different from what was envisaged in our initial discussions. I am also very grateful to Ben Hayes and his colleagues at Continuum for being so helpful and for getting the book into print so quickly when the boot was at long last on the other foot.

The dedication identifies two people whose inspirational writing has in different ways shaped the unique approach that this book adopts, but it would be invidious not to mention some others whose ideas and enthusiasm have been equally infectious over the years. I would particularly like to highlight Bernard Leather, Phil Barker, Richard Berg, Duncan Head, Peter Connolly, Nicholas Hammond, Ted Lendon, Barry Strauss and Adrian Goldsworthy in this regard. I am also indebted to Tim Cornell, Boris Rankov and Hans van Wees for their advice and encouragement during our various joint courses and projects over the years.

The book could never have come about without years of support from my many colleagues and friends within the Society of Ancients, who have helped me to publish and test each new variant of the model as it has gradually evolved since 1993. I would especially like to mention Phil Steele, Richard Jeffrey-Cook and John Graham-Leigh for their ideas and enthusiasm, and Eric Cruttenden and Alan Waller for becoming such wonderful partners in testing and presenting the system. There are dozens of others around the world whose suggestions and feedback have been invaluable, and I am very grateful to you all. Special mention must go to Dale Larson, whose simple but ingenious Cyberboard system has made it so much easier to produce and use the necessary diagrams and graphics.

Finally, and above all, I must thank my family for their unfailing support during the long gestation of this project. It has taken countless hours of study and design effort, and I simply could not have managed it without their constant love and encouragement.

To Charles Grant and John Lazenby
who inspired it all

1

Introduction

Ancient battles seize the modern imagination. Far from being forgotten, they have become a significant aspect of popular culture, prompting a continuing stream of books, feature films, television programmes and board and computer games. In our modern age, when war has become a dismal globalized continuum of suicide bombings, ethnic massacres, long-range bombardment, counter-insurgency operations and pervasive security restrictions, there is a certain escapist satisfaction in looking back to an era when conflicts between entire states turned on clear-cut pitched battles between formed armies, lasting just a few hours and spanning just a few miles of ground.[1] These battles were still unspeakably traumatic and grisly affairs for those involved – at Cannae, Hannibal's men butchered well over twice as many Romans (out of a much smaller overall population) as there were British soldiers killed on the notorious first day of the Somme.[2] However, as with the great clashes of the Napoleonic era, time has dulled our preoccupation with such awful human consequences, and we tend to focus instead on the inspired generalship of commanders like Alexander and Caesar and on the intriguing tactical interactions of units such as massed pikemen and war elephants within the very different military context of pre-gunpowder warfare.[3]

Unfortunately, there are severe limits to our understanding of these long distant engagements. Not only have transformations in the face of war left us with no personal experience of the dynamics of massed close quarter fighting, but the ancient evidence that has survived is lamentably thin – typically, just a few pages of often ambiguous or unreliable text on any individual battle. Hence, whereas the mass of secondary writing on more recent conflicts like the Second World War is based on an even larger mass of primary material such as archives and personal accounts, the situation for ancient military historians is exactly the reverse – an inverted pyramid in which modern scholarship teeters unsteadily above a narrow and unsatisfactory evidentiary base. Erich von Manstein famously wrote of the 'lost victories' in Hitler's campaign against the USSR, but the battles of antiquity are lost to us all in a much more pervasive sense of the word.[4]

One response to this problem would be to admit defeat, to acknowledge that scholars over the past two centuries have already wrung every ounce of useful information out of the surviving evidence, and to shift our enquiries to less well-studied and, hence, perhaps more fruitful topics. However, this goes against every instinct of scholarly endeavour, which strives to build upon and re-examine received wisdom so as to increase our understanding with each successive generation. Although there is certainly a sense of déjà vu when one finds the same detailed debates engaging historians today as preoccupied scholars such as Kromayer 100 years ago, it is undoubtedly the case that clever and novel approaches, or just better organized and more thorough study, have increased our understanding of ancient military history in recent years – one need only think of Hanson's work on Greek hoplite battle, Roth's examination of Roman logistics, and Austin and Rankov's study of Roman intelligence, to name but a few.[5] Imitating the proverbial drunkard by shifting our search for lost keys to an area with better light also neglects the fact that ancient battles are, as I said, intrinsically interesting to a wide modern audience. At a time when academic studies are under increasing scrutiny from an instrumental and utilitarian perspective, it would be a shame to neglect an area of ancient history where popular interest is such that a scholar like Adrian Goldsworthy can make a living purely as a commercial author, without any university post.[6]

So, is it possible to say anything really new about ancient battle, rather than taking the easier option of simply summarizing established wisdom in a more up-to-date package with fancier graphics? To my mind, the answer must lie in a process of synthesis. All the recent works to which I have referred advance our understanding of ancient military history because they adopt such a thematic approach, drawing together scraps of evidence from diverse sources to create an overall analysis that is greater than the sum of its individual parts. The two-volume *Cambridge History of Greek and Roman Warfare*, which I recently co-edited, embraced exactly the same stance, eschewing chronological narration in favour of providing thematic overviews of different aspects of warfare across four generic periods.[7] In the present volume, I will push this process of synthesis even further by building up a generic model of ancient battle in a more analytically rigorous way than in previous surveys of the topic. I will then use this model to cast new light on each individual battle in turn, thereby taking the whole process full circle and returning to the narrative details that are usually sacrificed within a purely thematic approach.

An example should help to illustrate what I mean. Alexander's defeat of Porus's Indians at the River Hydaspes in 326 BC is very difficult to reconstruct with any certainty because of pervasive ambiguity and contradiction within our surviving sources. Arrian (*Anab.* V.15–16) says that Porus had 200 elephants, which he posted 100 ft apart in front of his line, while Curtius (VIII.13.6) claims he had only 85 elephants, and Polyaenus (IV.3.22) says they were only 50 ft apart – figures that in combination could mean a line as short as 1.3 km or as long as 6 km. Arrian seems to imply that Alexander fought the battle with only the

5,000 cavalry and 6,000 infantry with which he made the surprise river crossing, but as Porus is credited by our various sources with between 23,000 and 55,000 troops, it has been suggested by some that there must have been many more than just 6,000 Macedonian foot. The Indian right wing horse are said to have transferred to the left wing and been pursued there by Alexander's left wing cavalry, but whether the latter moved behind their own infantry line, between the two infantry lines, or behind the rear of the Indian line is entirely unclear. In these circumstances, it is hardly surprising that existing scholarly reconstructions of this battle differ very significantly indeed, depending on which particular interpretations are deemed preferable.[8]

What I aim to contribute to this and to similar debates is to set each battle much more clearly within the context of the general run of other similar ancient engagements, and thereby to highlight which of the various conflicting interpretations are most in line with what we know from elsewhere. How long a frontage did other armies of similar size occupy, what sort of numerical odds was it feasible for armies like Alexander's to overcome, how many war elephants did it take to sway a battle and what kind of cavalry manoeuvres were practical as the infantry lines engaged? To give a scientific analogy, one might imagine plotting the differing interpretations of the Hydaspes as different x and y coordinates on a piece of graph paper. Without any further information, it is very difficult to determine which of the various plots is more valid, but if other battles are also plotted on the same paper, and if it is possible to evolve scaling principles to take account of differences that exist even between similar engagements, then it may be possible to discern a 'best fit' line that will link up the majority of points and thereby make outliers stand out as unlikely exceptions to the general rule. In Figure 1, I produce exactly such a graph plotting army size against army frontage and, on pp. 139–43, I use similar techniques to show that some of the diverse existing reconstructions of the Hydaspes, even by respected scholars like Hammond and Bosworth, are highly questionable, as they are so far out of line with comparative evidence from other engagements.

One obvious objection to this approach might be that comparing battles across centuries of history and across cultures ranging from Spain to India risks neglecting significant underlying variations that make the creation of a single generic model invalid. However, this was an era of relative technological stagnation and cyclical change, with devices such as pikemen and war elephants coming back into vogue centuries or even millennia after their earlier eclipse.[9] Ferrill's claim that Alexander's army might even have defeated Wellington at Waterloo is rather bizarre, but the fact that it can even be discussed is telling in itself – nobody would dream of suggesting that Napoleon's army could have prevailed on the Western Front just a century later.[10] Ancient writers themselves saw real continuities of military experience, as when the first century AD general Frontinus drew on the whole preceding history of Greece and Rome to furnish examples of good generalship for his *Stratagemata*, categorized entirely thematically rather than by date or culture. As long as we make some allowance for the distinctive characteristics of particular troops, such as Greek hoplites or Roman legionaries, the overarching commonality of human, equine and elephantine capabilities and limitations (both physical and psychological) suggests that a comparative approach to ancient land engagements is entirely defensible.

How can one 'model' an ancient battle in a way that will allow such systematic comparisons to be undertaken? Most scholars who have written overview works on the subject have approached it in almost entirely qualitative terms, as in Lloyd's 1996 edited book on *Battle in Antiquity*, Santosuosso's 1997 survey *Soldiers, Citizens and the Symbols of War*, Lendon's 2005 study *Soldiers and Ghosts* and Kagan's 2006 work *The Eye of Command*.[11] Montagu has recently tried to systematize examples of battle tactics and stratagems in a rather similar way to Frontinus, but with scant reference to other modern scholarship.[12] Writers such as Pritchett, Krentz, Gabriel and Metz have done some analysis of ancient statistics on issues such as casualty figures or formation depth, and authors like Goldsworthy and Daly have discussed similar figures in their analyses of Roman battle, but what has not so far occurred is any real attempt to model the processes of combat in anything like the systematic numerical manner used by Engels in his groundbreaking 1978 study of Alexander's logistics.[13] Engels used a variety of sources to underpin quantitative estimates of the carrying capacity of Alexander's troops and baggage animals, and of their march rate and their rate of consumption of such necessities as food, drink, fodder and firewood under various different conditions. He was thus able to comment critically on the logistic sustainability of particular moves of the army, and to choose the 'best fit' from among different hypotheses in a very similar way to what I attempt in this book for ancient battles.

Engels's book remains to this day an indispensable contribution to our under-standing of ancient logistics. However, the subsequent scholarly debate offers a very salutary illustration of the pitfalls of an overly prescriptive numerical model. Hammond objected early on that there were grounds for challenging Engels's assumption from the sources that Alexander made minimal use of carts, and he pointed out that the greater efficiency of carts compared to pack animals would seriously undermine Engels's strictures on the severe limits of Macedonian logistics.[14] More recently, Roth has published a more traditional source-based study of the wider canvas of Roman military supply arrangements, and has shown that Engels's logic about overland supply lines being limited to 100 miles or so is simply unsupportable in view of the number of contrary examples.[15] Clearly, any attempt at quantitative modelling of ancient warfare is highly vulnerable to erroneous assumptions, and the spurious precision that specific numbers bring should never obscure the enormous variation and margins for error that need to be borne in mind.

That being said, it is surely legitimate to apply some degree of logic and common sense to try to supplement (and sometimes even to challenge) the very limited and unreliable glimpses we gain from explicit indications in the ancient sources themselves. Some years ago, I used exactly this kind of logical analysis to discern what I called a 'battlefield clock', in which the large distances moved by other units during heavy infantry clashes like those at Cannae and the Metaurus indicated that such clashes could last hours rather than mere minutes, as in Hollywood and computer game representations.[16] I went on to suggest that the combination of this long duration with the very low fatality rates often suffered by the victorious army (sometimes less than 1 per cent of the troops engaged) made it hard to imagine the kind of continuous shoving or sword duelling that seemed to be assumed by other writers. Instead, I hypothesized a much more tentative 'stand-off' model, in which close quarter *mêlée* is only sporadic and neither side suffers many fatalities until one army breaks and the real one-sided slaughter begins.

In this book, I do not try to speculate any further about the contents of the 'black box' that mercifully conceals from us the horrendous experience of massed close quarter combat. Rather, I attempt to build on my 'battlefield clock' methodology by constructing a much more comprehensive and multi-dimensional analysis of deployment, manoeuvre and fighting at the level of ancient land engagements as a whole. In other words, this work is focused on a general's- rather than a soldier's-eye view – at the grand tactical rather than the tactical level. It is in that sense more traditional than other recent 'face of battle' literature, which (following John Keegan's inspirational lead) eschewed the previous focus on blocks of troops moving as if on a chessboard and focused instead on the activities and psychology of individual human beings at the front line.[17] Military units certainly are not inanimate chess pieces, but as long as one bears this all-important human dimension constantly in mind, the traditional focus on battlefield generalship remains just as valid as the soldier's-eye view, and also flows more directly from the evidence in the ancient sources themselves. The recent books by Kagan and Hutchinson take exactly this command-centred approach to ancient battle, and use eyewitness accounts by Caesar and Xenophon to reassert the importance of the 'big picture' in our understanding of the engagements concerned.[18]

Quantitative modelling of combat has become very common over the past century within the context of 'operational analysis', which seeks to use statistical techniques to discern the optimal employment of military resources.[19] Although the focus of this effort has understandably been on contemporary operations, analysts have made considerable use of historical examples to fill out their data sets and to help identify generic processes. A leading recent example is Biddle's 2004 book, *Military Power: Explaining Victory and Defeat in Modern Battle*, in which he employs case studies of Operations Michael, Goodwood and Desert Storm in 1918, 1944 and 1991 to argue that breakthroughs arise from greater mastery of the 'modern system' of force employment rather than through more superficial physical determinants, such as massed use of tanks.[20] Dupuy has pushed his own quantitative analysis of historical combat even further back to include data from the Napoleonic and American Civil Wars, but (unsurprisingly) the much more tenuous information on the distant battles of the ancient world has attracted hardly any interest from those whose primary concern is to understand warfare in the present day.[21]

One could, in principle, try to apply the same kind of approach as Biddle, Dupuy and others to the ancient evidence, but this has several disadvantages. Combat involves so many variables that attempting to model it through explicit formulae and equations will inevitably lead to impenetrable mathematical complexity. The resulting mass of symbols and calculations is actually self-defeating because it deters readers from engaging effectively with the arguments being developed – even when writing an article on Biddle's book, one eminent commentator confessed to having accepted the author's invitation to skip the denser theoretical chapters.[22] As I have said, such precise quantification is in any case particularly inappropriate for the ancient world, where the data are so uncertain and unreliable. Moreover, traditional mathematical modelling tends to shift the focus unduly towards local force ratios and advance rates, and away from the less quantifiable aspects of decision and command. Dupuy, for example, calculates that the numerically superior Allies could have prevailed in the West in 1940 if they had launched a concentrated counter-offensive similar to the German drive through the Ardennes, but this neglects the command asymmetries that historically made it so difficult for opponents of the *Blitzkrieg* to seize the initiative with any success.[23]

What we really need is a modelling technique that is sophisticated enough to accord command dynamics their historical importance alongside raw force-on-force comparisons, but that is also simple and broad brush enough to avoid the need for intimidating and misleadingly precise formulae. Previous scholars of ancient battles have found no systematic means of squaring this circle except by avoiding quantification altogether and producing entirely qualitative analytical frameworks.[24] However, popular interest in these battles revolves in part around 'refighting' them in simulated form, and the associated techniques actually offer an interesting and neglected avenue for academic study. People have been refighting ancient battles for decades using counters on a map or miniature figures on a tabletop, but it is only recently that the activity has acquired a higher public profile through the BBC television series *Time Commanders*, based on the 2004 computer game *Rome: Total War*.[25] The popularity of wargaming as a leisure activity brings a certain stigma that has hitherto deterred its employment by academics (even those who are themselves wargamers in their spare time), but the technique is actually of much wider application, and is employed extensively by military forces around the world for professional training, force development and strategic planning.[26]

All conflict simulations contain two essential elements. The first is an underlying mathematical model that provides the framework for troop manoeuvre and combat resolution, but which is easier to understand than the formulae of writers like Biddle and Dupuy because it is expressed more in verbal than numerical terms. The second, equally important element consists of constant decision inputs by the opposing players, which reflect the essence of war as a battle of wits as much as a blind collision of armed masses. It is this dual character of war as a set of physical realities in terms of force capabilities that is given life only by the interacting strategies of competing antagonists that led Clausewitz to make the surprising claim that, 'In the whole range of human activities, war most closely resembles a game of cards'![27] The dynamic and interactive competition inherent in conflict simulation methodologies offers its own unique insights in addition to those available from the comparative perspective that I have already outlined – not only is it possible to measure different scholarly reconstructions of any specific battle against the evidence from other engagements, but we can also judge whether the suggested actions by each side make military sense as part of an ongoing contest between opponents who had other tactical options available to them.

Clausewitz likened war to a game of cards rather than chess because he saw chance and uncertainty as being just as important as precise tactical calculation.[28] More recently, it has become popular for scholars like Culham and Kagan to apply modern scientific concepts of nonlinearity and 'chaos theory' to warfare, just as Clausewitz had appropriated earlier scientific ideas such as 'friction' and a 'centre of gravity'.[29] Although it might at first be thought that these notions of complexity and nonlinearity preclude any meaningful quantitative modelling of ancient battles, this is not in fact the case any more than the chaotic nature of individual weather systems precludes statistical generalizations about the climate in particular places and seasons. As Clausewitz insightfully recognized, certain kinds of games incorporate random elements that simply and quite effectively simulate the many unpredictable elements inherent in traumatic confrontations between thousands of individual combatants, without making the overall outcome a complete lottery independent of broader situational determinants such as the numbers, morale and generalship of the opposing armies. Purpose-designed conflict simulations are particularly good at capturing this blend of chaos and predictability, with the results obtained in individual trials varying very significantly due to differences in luck and player decisions, but with the overall pattern across a number of trials corresponding more closely to the designer's reasoned scholarly judgement of what factors most affected victory and defeat in the real engagements.

Many existing battle simulations produced for the popular market are compromised by inadequate research and historical documentation and by the sacrifice of realism in favour of entertainment value – in *Rome: Total War*, for instance, battles last just a few minutes but involve enormous mutual casualties rather than the one-sided losses attested by the sources. However, if properly grounded in the evidence, this technique of combining an underlying mathematical framework with random variation and human decision input offers a very good way of exploring past engagements.[30] Many thousands of more serious simulations aimed at smaller niche markets of historical enthusiasts have been produced over the past few decades, and they now cover virtually every past battle and campaign.[31] Indeed, some are based on a level of detailed research that would put many books to shame.[32] General Giap, the victor of Dien Bien Phu, was so taken with a recent simulation of that particular battle that he played it with his generals and ordered several more copies for inclusion in local museums and divisional archives.[33] I have been running an MA option course based on this academically neglected literature for several years now, with students studying and critiquing existing simulations and then designing their own simple model of a battle of their choice, thereby gaining much greater insight into the dynamics of the engagement than through the more traditional essay-based format.[34]

The best existing simulations of ancient battle are those designed by Herman and Berg since 1991 in their series on 'Great Battles of History'. These have been published mainly in map and counter format, but computerized versions were also produced in the late 1990s.[35] They are much more serious than *Rome: Total War*, as illustrated by the fact that combat inflicts abstract 'cohesion hits' rather than unrealistic mutual carnage. However, the designs are too detailed and complex for my own taste, incorporating the kind of fine-grained precision regarding orders of battle and battlefield geography that may be appropriate for later, better-documented periods but which in this case means that many evidentiary gaps and uncertainties are filled by sheer guesswork.[36] Design notes are also somewhat constrained due to commercial pressures, and, because each successive publication focuses on just a few individual battles, costs are high and the scope for a comparative overview is reduced.[37] Given how little we really know about these engagements, I think that a simpler, broader-brush treatment is more appropriate to the era – as well as being easier for non-wargamers to grasp and leaving more space for the all-important historical discussions that must underpin any academic reconstruction.[38]

I have been developing my own model of ancient battle for many years in conjunction with the Society of Ancients, and its evolution through several published iterations since 1993 has allowed me not only to improve its historicity but also to enhance its clarity and accessibility based on experience and feedback from a wide range of individuals (including my own students).[39] This book represents the culmination of that process, and gives me the scope to include a proper discussion of the historical evidence and of my own modelling and design decisions. Rather than simply presenting my own ideas, my aim is to give readers the intellectual tools to explore for themselves the dilemmas associated with ancient battles. By experimenting with different tactical choices, or by tweaking the orders of battle or the simulation system itself to accord with their own ideas, users of this book will achieve a much greater level of engagement with the issues than simply by reading yet another survey volume on the battles concerned.[40]

The book is divided into two parts. In Part I, I explain the development of the model itself, and how I have synthesized the ancient evidence to underpin a generic system that produces broadly similar patterns to those attested to historically. A key principle has been to avoid creating special rules for any individual battle, as this would undermine the comparative aim that I outlined above when discussing conflicting interpretations of the Hydaspes. The formal presentation of the system has been left until Appendix 1, not (as in Biddle's work) so that readers may skip it, but for precisely the opposite reason – to make it more accessible for reference purposes by disentangling the rules themselves from the underlying design rationales. As it is always easier to grasp a model through concrete examples than through abstract principles, Part I concludes with a step-by-step reconstruction of Cannae so that readers may see exactly how the system operates to simulate real events. I make repeated reference throughout this first part of the book to the dozens of individual battles that help to shape the development of the system, and instead of giving the dates, locations and other details at each point, I have provided in Appendix 3 and Figure 43 an alphabetical directory and map of engagements that show the relevant information.

In Part II, I develop detailed 'scenarios' for the 35 best-known ancient land battles from the last five centuries BC. This period, from the Persian invasions of Greece to the end of the Roman Republic, contains the highest concentration of such battles, thanks to the rivalry of numerous, fairly evenly matched powers. I exclude sieges and naval battles because of their very different character, and I also omit certain famous open field engagements, either because (as at Telamon with its surrounded Gallic army) they do not fit easily into the same pattern as other pitched battles, or more usually because, however large and significant the battle (as at Ipsus and Philippi), we simply do not have enough specific information about army composition, deployment and terrain to reconstruct it in the required detail. As my comments on each individual battle must necessarily be brief, I focus on what light the model casts on existing scholarly controversies, and I limit my references for the most part to fairly recent scholarship rather than tracing the repetitive debates all the way back to earlier authors like Kromayer, Veith, Tarn and Delbrück.[41] To save space, I also avoid constant repetition of explanations already given in the context of previous engagements, but I have included in Appendix 4 a glossary of key terms, such as troop types, to assist those who prefer to 'dip in' to the sections about whichever battles interest them most. In the Conclusion, I summarize in more traditional qualitative terms the key features of the model I have developed, and readers who find the earlier form of presentation unfamiliar may like to use the Conclusion to gain a clearer understanding of the underlying principles.

People today almost invariably associate the word 'simulation' with computer programmes, and most are not even aware of the older genre of map and counter products, even though they continue to be published at an undiminished rate.[42] Computers do have many advantages in terms of their ability to handle far more data and detailed calculations than is possible in manual simulations, but they also bring some disadvantages – the opacity and inflexibility of the underlying programme, and the tendency to become fixated on fancy graphics and realistic visual effects rather than on the accuracy of the model itself.[43] Because my programming skills are lamentable and because our knowledge of ancient battles is too limited to justify detailed data-crunching in any case, I prefer to use a more accessible multi-format approach that everyone can understand and where the model is entirely transparent and open to user modification, as well as being playable simply with pencil and paper if desired. The battles can still be refought on the computer screen using freely downloadable graphics and simple 'drag and drop' methods, as illustrated in the colour figures in this volume. Full details of the many ways in which the model may be used are given in Appendix 2.

My basic methodology is actually a very common one within social science, which routinely produces hypotheses that seek to explain the observed evidence better than other competing theories.[44] The wider the range and depth of evidence available, the more practical it is to test and refine complex, multi-dimensional theoretical models – Biddle and Dupuy use the mass of data from modern conflicts to tweak the many variables in their equations in order to get the best possible fit with the diversity of real-world experience.[45] Although the model I outline in Part I is presented as if derived from first principles, it is actually the product of exactly such iterative testing and refinement over a very long period. Variables such as the balance between infantry and cavalry and between numbers, troop quality and generalship are not just assumptions conjured out of the air, but are the result of years of systemic evolution to accord best with the real course and outcome of the various engagements. It is actually very hard to model even a single battle using decision-based conflict simulation, as not only should implementation of the actions taken historically produce a broadly historical result, but those actions should themselves appear at least as attractive to competing players as do alternative courses of action that the system makes available – otherwise, the simulation will never proceed along historical lines even if it is physically capable of doing so. If these demanding goals can be even partially achieved for three dozen different battles *using a single common system*, that is a powerful indication that the core concepts and the balance of variables within the system accord pretty closely with what mattered in reality. Hence, not only does modelling multiple ancient engagements help to overcome the evidentiary weaknesses associated with each individual one, but it also offers the range and diversity of evidence needed to help validate the model itself.[46]

There will undoubtedly be traditionalists who view such a methodology with disdain, and who are reluctant to acknowledge that anything other than direct exegesis of the sources can shed light on these battles, let alone a technique so apparently populist as conflict simulation.[47] My response is that limited and unreliable ancient sources can only take us so far, and that novel approaches such as modelling and reconstruction have already contributed significantly to our understanding of ancient warfare, with the building of the full-scale replica trireme *Olympias* in the 1980s being an obvious case in point.[48] Whatever their shortcomings, such novel contributions as Engels's study of Alexander's logistics or Luttwak's 1976 analysis of Roman grand strategy in terms of modern power politics did a great deal to stimulate thought and debate among more traditional ancient historians, to the benefit of our overall appreciation of the issues concerned.[49] Even the most respected classical scholars such as Hammond already routinely engage in the simulation of ancient battles by constructing scale diagrams showing their interpretation of the troop numbers, deployments and manoeuvres involved.[50] My own approach of comparative dynamic modelling simply makes this existing process of reconstruction more systematic, by introducing two vital checks on the plausibility of such individual depictions – how well they accord with what we know of other similar battles, and whether the suggested patterns make military sense as the product of deliberate choices by opposing commanders who had other tactical options available. Hence, far from being an unduly imaginative and speculative endeavour, my model is actually a useful complement to an existing tradition of scholarly reconstructions that is individualist and unsystematic, and that, not surprisingly, produces major disagreements serving only to bolster the despairing view that the battles are irredeemably 'lost' after all.

PART I

The Model

Sources

As the central purpose of the model that I develop in this book is to help (however slightly) in peering through the veil of ignorance and uncertainty that shields from us the 'lost battles' of antiquity, it is vital to start the process by examining what chinks already exist in the veil, and what techniques modern scholars have used to try to discern the reality beyond. I will begin by discussing the strengths and weaknesses of the different forms of evidence that survive from the ancient world itself. I will then explore the various 'aids' that historians have used to try to supplement and evaluate this ancient source material. In the final part of the chapter, I will lay the groundwork for the construction of our mathematical model by focusing on the two main forms of statistical evidence we have on the engagements concerned, namely claims by ancient authors as to the size of the armies involved and the number of casualties they sustained.

Ancient evidence falls into two broad types – literary and archaeological. I will deal with the latter first, as it is by far the least significant for our particular enquiry and so may be covered fairly quickly. Pitched battles in the open field are by their very nature evanescent phenomena, and leave little lasting archaeological record. Hence, we cannot hope to find anything like the same degree of surviving physical evidence as for sieges such as those of Paphos, Numantia and Masada, where (especially if the site has not been marred by later occupation) it may be possible to trace the works of both defenders and attackers in the soil to this very day.[1] For more recent open field engagements such as Towton and Naseby, battlefield archaeology may reveal actual remnants such as grave pits or musket shot, which can throw significant light on the course of the fighting, but ancient battles were so much longer ago that even the temporary camps of the two sides are usually impossible to trace.[2] Only the rare memorial structures like the Soros at Marathon or the Lion monument at Chaeronea tend to survive with their associated graves, and even these do not prevent continued disagreement over their precise relationship to the fighting lines.[3]

Much more common are indirectly relevant finds in the shape of armour, weapons and pictorial or sculptural representations of warriors and warfare in the general era concerned. These have contributed significantly to our image of the troops of the time, as long as one is constantly aware of the potential for artistic distortions – such as the portrayal of hoplites fighting naked or with their helmets raised, or the unrealistic uniformity of the Roman soldiers on Trajan's Column.[4] The evocative modern illustrations by experts such as Peter Connolly have built on this evidence and have done a great deal to popularize what might otherwise have remained a rather dusty and arcane academic subject.[5] However, understanding how troops were equipped is mainly of relevance at the tactical level, and tells us little about the conduct of battle at the grand tactical level that is the focus of the present volume. Even when equipment did have broader consequences for the overall shape of engagements, we learn about this not from remnants or depictions of the equipment itself but from literary accounts such as Thucydides's description (V.71) of how advancing hoplite lines drifted towards their shieldless right side, or Polybius's analysis (XVIII.28–32) of the weaknesses of Hellenistic pikemen compared to Roman legionaries. Hence, archaeological sources are peripheral at best to our present endeavour, and our understanding of the grand tactical nature of ancient battles stands or falls almost entirely on the quality of the literary evidence to hand.

The most important kind of literary evidence consists of historical accounts by ancient authors of a general period, a particular war, or the life of an individual general. There are around a dozen ancient historians and biographers such as Thucydides, Xenophon, Polybius, Livy, Plutarch and Caesar, whose surviving works provide most of our information about the battles of the last five centuries BC. They do this through the inclusion of more or less formulaic 'battle pieces', which vary in length from a few score to a few thousand words and aim to give readers at least some idea of the composition and deployment of the opposing armies and the course and outcome of the fighting itself. These accounts of specific battles are supplemented by a more generic kind of literary evidence, namely military theory. This comes in several forms, including compendia of historical 'stratagems' such as those compiled by Frontinus and Polyaenus, handbooks of drill and organization such as those by Aelian and Asclepiodotus, more focused works such as the cavalry manuals by Xenophon and Arrian, and advice on generalship such as that provided by Onasander and Vegetius.[6] The authors are sometimes the same as for the historical accounts, and occasionally the two genres are combined within the same work, as with Polybius's excursuses on generalship (IX.12–16), the Roman army (VI.19–42) and the phalanx (XVIII.28–32). (Basic reference information on the various ancient authors and their works is given in the first section of the Bibliography on pp. 285–7.)

Unfortunately, this literary evidence, vital though it is, has three major shortcomings. First, it contains too little detail on the aspects needed for reliable reconstruction of the battles concerned. Authors tend to focus instead on recounting impossibly long and high-flown speeches by the opposing commanders, and then concentrate on the personal conduct and perhaps the heroic death of individual generals and on 'novelties' such as the role of elephants or scythed chariots.[7] This preoccupation with dramatic anecdotes rather than technical overviews is entirely understandable, and we today are hardly in a position to complain given the routine amplification of anecdotal obsessions such as celebrity culture and child safety concerns within our own television-dominated societies.[8] However, the fact that many ancient authors were more concerned to tell a good story than to provide a complete technical reconstruction of the battles they describe makes the building of models challenging to say the least. Ipsus and Philippi were massive engagements with very significant political consequences, but I have not felt able to cover them in this book because Plutarch's few hundred words on the former (*Demetr.* 28–9) and Appian's few thousand words on the latter (*B Civ.* IV.88, 107–14 and 117–31) are frustratingly vague about how the armies were actually deployed.[9] Even when ancient writers give specific distances, this is clouded by the variability of the length of a 'stade' (600 ft) by several per cent up or down from the modern equivalent of 183 m that I shall use (for indicative purposes only) in this volume.[10]

The second problem with the literary sources is that there are real questions about whether and how the authors themselves knew or understood the details of the battles they describe. Although writers like Xenophon and Caesar were present in person at a few of the engagements, this did not in itself guarantee a clear overall perspective, as Wellington's famous comparison between the history of a battle and the history of a ball serves to illustrate.[11] Other authors such as Herodotus, Thucydides and Polybius had to rely on interviews with eyewitnesses some time after the event, while historians such as Arrian, Diodorus, Livy and Plutarch were writing centuries later and so were utterly dependent on earlier written sources (mostly now lost). This applies also to the military theorists, most of whom were writing under the Roman Empire even though they harked back to a long-obsolete Hellenistic precedent. The impact of this reliance on intervening sources is seen most clearly in the work of Diodorus, whose battle accounts from the early Successor era (when he is presumed to have relied on the now-lost eyewitness testimony of Hieronymus) are detailed and persuasive, but whose claims at other times are much more dubious.[12] It is obviously better to have lost writings preserved second hand than not at all, but one must always beware of distortions and misunderstandings, especially on the part of non-military authors such as Livy, Asclepiodotus and Polyaenus. My favourite example is when Livy (XXXIII.8) misunderstood Polybius's account (XVIII.24) of the Macedonian phalanx levelling their pikes at Cynoscephalae, and wrote instead that they discarded the pikes completely and relied on their swords![13]

This leads on to the third shortcoming of the literary sources, namely that their standards of scholarly technique and presentation fall far below what has become the norm today. Even the best and most rigorous writers such as Thucydides and Polybius rarely gave explicit citations of the multiple sources they employed, and less critical authors tended to 'hoover up' whatever was to hand without worrying much about its credibility. Livy, for example (XXX.33), tweaked Polybius's account of Zama (XV.11) by describing Hannibal's Italian veterans as unwilling conscripts and by adding in a 'legion' of Macedonians, both patent distortions by earlier Roman annalists stronger on patriotism than scholarship.[14] Some writers (or their sources) seem not to have been above sheer invention of entire battle accounts where real details were not available. Diodorus's battle pieces are sometimes suspiciously formulaic in their claims of cavalry contests followed by infantry duels, and Cornell suggests that Livy's account of Sentinum may be the first of his detailed battle descriptions to contain any element of authenticity.[15] Delbrück quoted the whole of Appian's long and highly dubious account of the Battle of Cannae (*Hann.* 19–26), as a salutary reminder that 'if, by chance, this were the only one that had come down to us, it would be absolutely impossible to gain from it an account having even the faintest resemblance to the truth'.[16] There are so many contradictions between different sources on the same engagements that one must constantly be on guard against putting too much trust in a single source simply because it is the only one that survives.

So how have modern scholars sought to overcome the manifold problems with the ancient evidence? Whatley presented a paper on the subject to the Oxford Philological Society in 1920, and it could almost have been written yesterday rather than nearly a century ago – a clear sign of how little has really changed in terms of our ability to penetrate the veil that conceals the reality of ancient battle.[17] Taking Marathon as a case study, Whatley argued that there were inescapable limits to our understanding given the limitations of the surviving evidence, but that our comprehension could be improved through the judicious use of five 'aids' to reconstruction. I will now discuss each of these aids in turn, highlighting their strengths and weaknesses as revealed by scholarship over the past century and more.

Whatley's first aid was to study the modern geography and topography of the battle area. The greatest exponents of this approach were Kromayer and Veith, who in the early twentieth century produced numerous studies of ancient battlefields based on personal inspection of the ground, and who tried to fit each engagement to a specific location and orientation.[18] Many modern scholars travel at some point to visit the supposed sites of the battles they describe, seeking to understand the engagements better by gauging the actual extent of the plain, the steepness of the hills, the width and depth of the rivers, and so on. Pritchett undertook such topographical study with his usual encyclopaedic thoroughness, and Hammond made this technique a key element of his battle analyses during his long academic career, devoting a lot of time to highly detailed arguments about exactly where the features and deployments described in the ancient sources must have been.[19] He then used this localization to shed new light on the courses of the battles themselves, as in his argument that Alexander's attack at Issus must have been at the head of his infantry guard rather than his Companion cavalry, in part because the riverbed that Hammond found during his 1976 survey formed such a significant obstacle to a mounted charge.[20]

Unfortunately, there are two problems with such topographical approaches to these long-distant battles. First, in the absence of definitive archaeological resolution like that provided by the finds at some more recent battle sites such as Naseby, scholars continue to disagree over their preferred localization of the battlefields, based on varying readings of the often ambiguous and problematic literary evidence.[21] Such disagreement is even the case with late medieval battles such as Bosworth, let alone the clashes of antiquity.[22] A telling map in Daly's recent study of Cannae shows no less than eight different sites along the River Aufidus that have been proposed by one writer or another as the locus of this famous ancient engagement.[23] Second, there has been ample time over the intervening millennia for rivers and shorelines to shift, so the ground as it appears today may give a misleading sense of what it was like in antiquity. Connolly's and Goldsworthy's proposed sites for Cannae assume that the Aufidus at the time followed a much more northerly course, because there is far too little space between river and hills at their suggested locations now.[24] Although Hammond and Devine agreed that the River Pinarus at Issus should be identified with the modern Payas, they criticized each other's suggestions about the ancient course of the stream and coast.[25] Bosworth, while opting instead for the more northerly Kuru Cay, noted that the changed hydrography meant that the whole vexed issue might never be resolved.[26] These two problems of inconclusive evidence and change over time thus interact perniciously to undermine the value of the topographical approach even in the minority of cases where distinctive terrain features make it possible and worthwhile to apply it at all. Too often (as at Pharsalus), the search for a precise location becomes almost an end in itself, absorbing massive amounts of scholarly effort in endless complex disputation without casting anything like commensurate light on the battle itself.[27]

Whatley's second aid involves the application of modern military wisdom to try to make sense of, and resolve ambiguities within, the ancient source material. It is this approach that has tempted so many military men such as du Picq, Dodge, Fuller, Hackett, Bagnall and Peddie to risk entering the intellectual minefield of ancient military history, counting on their own practical experience to help them make a distinctive contribution.[28] There are obviously advantages to having a military eye to spot absurdities in one's own source material, which is why Polybius (XII.25g and 28a) argued that such experience was essential and why we are often scornful of the unmilitary Livy despite his much more gripping literary style.[29] The problem is that the military wisdom of modern times does not necessarily correspond with that of antiquity. Although human beings themselves cannot have changed that much, and hence one may legitimately make comparisons between such things as march rates, sustenance requirements and how individuals may react to the stress and fear of combat, the technological advances that have transformed the face of war since pre-gunpowder times have made broader deductions increasingly dubious.[30] I will discuss this problem further shortly when I turn to the vexed question of relative army sizes and casualty statistics.

Whatley's third aid consists of the related technique of *Sachkritik*, a traditionally Germanic approach that basically entails the application of logic and 'common sense'. He cites what are still the most famous examples of this technique, namely Delbrück's illustration of the absurdity of Herodotus's figure of 5 million for Xerxes's army on the grounds that the rear of the column would only just be leaving Sardis when the front reached Thermopylae, and his similar scepticism about the Athenians being able to run 8 stadia (1.5 km) at Marathon without becoming completely exhausted before the battle even started.[31] The trouble, as Whatley points out, is first that this approach is better at destructive than constructive criticism (as it undermines ancient claims without having much positive to put in their place), and second that it depends crucially on what one considers 'common sense'. If one's initial assumptions are flawed, then the whole logical edifice constructed on them is undermined, as I discussed in the Introduction with regard to Engels's logistic model and the controversy over Macedonian use of carts.[32] Again, I will return to this issue shortly in the context of army numbers.

It is this third aid that best encompasses the use of physical reconstructions and practical experiments to help determine whether ancient claims really make sense. Whatley mentions Delbrück arming his students with pikes to test the viability of close-packed formations, and American scholars later used their students to gauge the feasibility of the run at Marathon.[33] The rise of numerous groups of historical re-enactors has given this approach a decidedly populist image, but writers such as Connolly, Junkelmann, Gabriel and Metz have made significant contributions to our understanding by constructing replicas of ancient weapons and equipment and then trialling them, sometimes with the help of such enthusiasts.[34] However, such techniques remain inherently limited as a means of gaining insight into battles themselves, partly because there are far too few ancient enthusiasts to get any real sense of the problems of manoeuvring and commanding armies tens of thousands strong, but mainly because the re-enactors are not struggling to kill and avoid being killed as were their ancient counterparts. Hence, land fighting, in which human factors played a much greater role than technology, is never likely to be as illuminated by physical reconstruction techniques as ancient naval warfare has been by the building and operation of the replica trireme *Olympias* 2 decades ago.[35]

Whatley's fourth aid, which he terms 'the Sherlock Holmes method', is rather a grab-bag of the previous three techniques, together with a discerning approach to contradictory literary evidence in which snippets from different sources are pieced together to create what appears to be a coherent overall picture. This is a very common scholarly technique for traditional ancient historians because it seems to give the most leeway for making an original and distinctive contribution, through an encyclopaedic knowledge of even the most obscure and fragmentary ancient text, and through the ability to bring diverse and seemingly unrelated passages to bear to cast some comparative light on the problem actually at issue.[36] The danger with this technique is that it can lead to a rather 'pick and mix' approach to sources, and to the creation of over-elaborate interpretations based on an artificial combination of unrelated passages. A classic example is the combining of Herodotus's silence on the role of Persian horsemen at Marathon with the story in a much later Byzantine text that what triggered the Greek attack was the news that the cavalry were absent. These elements have been used by scholars to underpin various fully fledged hypotheses, such as that the Persians were embarking their army (cavalry first) to sail to Athens itself, or that the horses were still being watered when the Greeks launched their surprise charge.[37]

Much more egregious was Green's attempt to reconcile the conflicting stories of Arrian and Diodorus regarding Alexander's crossing of the Granicus by arguing that the initial direct assault was a failure (covered up in later propaganda) and that success came only after a surprise crossing that night, in line with Parmenio's advice.[38] This ill-fated effort to straddle two clearly contradictory sources shows the pitfalls of the inclusivist approach that I once heard parodied by John Galbraith as holding that 'the truth lies somewhere about half way between right and wrong'! That being said, Whatley also criticizes the opposite stance of clinging to one ancient authority to the exclusion of the rest, as Hammond tends to do with Arrian's account of Alexander's campaigns.[39] The reality is surely that the less independent corroboration we have of the claims of any single source, and the more we have to piece together diverse fragments to reconcile contradictions or to create a coherent story, the less reliable and soundly based any resulting hypotheses are likely to be.

Whatley's fifth and final aid, and the one in which he places most of his (admittedly limited) faith, is the generic study of armies and navies as institutions to discern how they were likely to fight over the period as a whole rather than just in any specific battle. This has become a very popular approach over the past few decades, and a major feature of recent scholarship has been the development of a generic picture of particular military forces and their ways of fighting.[40] Hanson's work on Greek hoplites, Lazenby's analysis of the Spartan army, Head's study of the Achaemenid military, Spence's and McCall's works on Greek and Roman cavalry, Bar-Kochva's and Sekunda's books on Hellenistic forces and

Goldsworthy's examination of the Roman army all fall into this category.[41] Perhaps the main risk of this approach is that it may lead to an overemphasis on supposed tactical asymmetries as an explanation for the outcome of engagements, as in Samuels's analysis of Cannae where he argued that Roman forces before the middle of the Second Punic War were inflexible and had hardly evolved beyond the old phalanx tactics (despite the fact that they managed to perform much better in other engagements throughout the third century BC).[42] Greek, Hellenistic, Punic, Roman and Celtic armies all achieved sweeping victories or suffered crushing defeats while retaining much the same equipment and tactics, which suggests that generalship and the skill and morale of the soldiers themselves were more important determinants of success.

One additional aid to understanding that does not fit neatly into Whatley's five categories is detailed historiographical study of the sources, aims and methods of particular ancient writers. It has become *de rigeur* for encyclopaedic scholarly 'commentaries' to be produced on the various texts, such as Bosworth's two-volume work on Arrian or Walbank's three-volume accompaniment to Polybius.[43] Hornblower has even written a detailed study of Hieronymus, despite the fact that his work has been lost and is known to us only through references and summaries by other authors such as Diodorus.[44] Most modern studies of particular battles begin with a lengthy survey of the provenance and reliability of the various ancient accounts, and there are also more generic analyses of relevant overarching themes, such as Rubincam's examination of casualty figures in Thucydides and Lendon's comparative study of Greek and Roman perspectives on what made for success in battle.[45] This historiographical perspective is vital, but it does have two serious deficiencies. First, our actual knowledge of the sources and methods of ancient writers is inevitably limited given their much more haphazard bibliographical and scholarly conventions, and second, historiographical criticism (as with *Sachkritik*) tends to be more destructive than constructive – it can give us a better understanding of the writers themselves, but it usually serves to undermine rather than bolster their validity as objective sources of information on the battles they describe.

My own approach in this book fits most closely with Whatley's fifth Aid, given the focus on creating a generic and collective model of military capabilities that can then be used to cast light back onto individual engagements. I also bring in very important elements from elsewhere, notably the third Aid with its emphasis on logical analysis and practical reconstruction, and the second Aid with its concentration on what is militarily feasible and sensible in the context of an ongoing battle of wits between the opposing forces. In fact, this kind of dynamic model-building is a real innovation within the study of ancient military history, and it may therefore contribute some new insights despite the well-worn nature of the existing techniques and debates.[46] However, I cannot overemphasize the fact that my approach is designed to complement rather than replace the existing scholarly techniques, each of which has contributed very significantly to our understanding of the engagements concerned. This book aims to build on rather than to challenge existing scholarship, and if it can raise a few neglected questions and help a little in resolving some of the many outstanding controversies, it will have more than served its purpose.

Before proceeding with the development of the model, we need to focus on one aspect of the ancient sources that is of particular significance for the modelling process, namely their provision of specific figures for troop numbers and casualties in the opposing armies. More often than not, the ancient battle accounts do give such figures for at least one, and usually both, sides. A review of these statistics gives rise to three broad generalizations. First, the figures often vary significantly between different writers, or even within the same book when the author reports divergent claims among his own sources. Second, the victorious army is often said to have been outnumbered by its opponents, sometimes by a very considerable margin. Third, the victorious force is usually said to have suffered far fewer casualties than its adversaries, often by a factor of ten or more. The crucial question is, of course, whether these rather counterintuitive claims deserve credence, or whether they mainly reflect propagandistic distortion and exaggeration on the part of the victors – with the divergence among the sources indicating that few ancient writers had any clear idea in the first place of what the reality may have been.

Let me first give some examples of the degree of variation and asymmetry involved. Diodorus (XVI.77–9) claims that at the Crimisus, Timoleon, with just 11,000 troops, beat 70,000 Carthaginians with 10,000 cavalry and chariot horses. Arrian (*Anab.* I.14) says that the Persians at the Granicus had 20,000 cavalry and 20,000 infantry, while Diodorus (XVII.19) claims they had 10,000 cavalry and 100,000 infantry. At Gaugamela, Arrian (*Anab.* III.8 and 12) gives the Macedonians 40,000 foot and 7,000 horse against 40,000 Persian cavalry and an inconceivable 1 million infantry. At the Hydaspes, figures for the Indians range from 20,000 horse and 2,000 foot (Plutarch, *Alex.* 62) to 30,000 infantry and 4,000 cavalry (Arrian, *Anab.* V.15) or 50,000 infantry and 3,000 cavalry (Diodorus XVII.87). Polybius (III.113–14) says the Carthaginians had 40,000 foot and 10,000 horse at Cannae, compared to 80,000 Roman infantry and 6,000 cavalry. At Magnesia, Livy (XXXVII.39–40) describes how a Roman army with 27,000 foot and 3,000 horse beat a Seleucid force with 58,000 infantry and 12,000 cavalry. Plutarch (*Luc.* 26–7) says that at Tigranocerta, Lucullus's 11,000 troops overcame no less than 225,000 opponents. Caesar (*B Gall.* I.24 and 29) claims that a census of the Helvetii showed they had 92,000 warriors against his 6 legions and auxiliaries (perhaps 35,000 men). He later says that at Pharsalus his 22,000 infantry and 1,000 cavalry beat Pompey's 47,000 foot and 7,000 horse (*B Civ.* III.83 and 88–9).

As regards casualties, the most evenly matched figures are for the original 'Pyrrhic victories'. Plutarch (*Pyrrh*. 17 and 21) records Hieronymus's claims of 7,000 Roman and 4,000 Greek losses at Heraclea and 6,000 and 3,505 respectively at Asculum, whereas he says Dionysius gave around double these figures. The next closest claims relate to losses in Greek hoplite battles, which Krentz calculated to average out at 5 per cent for the victors and 14 per cent for the vanquished.[47] Sometimes both sides are said to have suffered greater losses – Livy (X.29) describes 8,700 Roman and 25,000 enemy casualties at Sentinum, while Polybius (III.117) claims there were 5,700 Punic and 70,000 Roman deaths at Cannae. Livy (XXVII.49) suggests an equally massive 8,000 Roman and 57,000 Punic dead at the Metaurus, but Polybius (XI.3) puts the losses there at only 2,000 and 10,000 respectively. The figures for other battles tend to be even more asymmetric, as at Marathon where Herodotus (VI.117) says there were 6,400 Persian and only 192 Athenian dead, and as at Gaugamela where Arrian (*Anab*. III.15) claims the Macedonians lost only 100 men and 1,000 horses compared to an unbelievable 300,000 Persians killed. Rome's later victories were said to be equally one-sided, with Livy (XXXVII.44 and XLIV.42) claiming they suffered only 350 dead at Magnesia and 100 at Pydna compared to 53,000 Seleucids and 20,000 Macedonians. Caesar (*B Civ*. III.99) put his losses at Pharsalus at 30 centurions and 200 rankers as against 15,000 Pompeian troops (with almost all the rest being captured).

So what are we to make of these and other similar figures? We clearly cannot accept them all, as the claims of different sources are often blatantly contradictory. Some numbers, like the several hundred thousand Persians said to be at Plataea, Cunaxa, Issus and Gaugamela, are so logistically impractical and so far out of line with the pattern elsewhere of armies numbering in the tens of thousands that they must surely be exaggerated. Round numbers are also rather suspicious, especially where (as at the Hydaspes) the estimates vary between different writers. We know from modern experience how difficult it is even with aerial observation to gauge the numbers of a mass of demonstrators, and how far estimates can vary depending on which side one supports – these factors must have operated to an even greater extent in the ancient world if the numbers we have come from simply looking across the plain at the opposing horde. By contrast, it would be going much too far to dismiss all ancient statistics as worthless inventions. At Paraitacene, Diodorus (XIX.27–31) bases his account on the contemporary testimony of Hieronymus, who was an intimate of Eumenes and later of his opponent Antigonus.[48] His claims that Antigonus fielded 28,000 infantry and 8,500 cavalry (of whom 3,800 were killed and 4,000 wounded) whereas Eumenes fought with 35,000 foot and 6,100 horse (of whom 540 died and 900 were wounded) seem eminently plausible, and if we discount such information we might as well give up studying these battles altogether.

The real question is where and on what basis we should strike the balance between scepticism and credulity. Considerations such as how detailed the figures are, how far they can be traced to an original source in a position to do more than guess, and how much trust we place in the critical faculties and scholarly integrity of the extant author, must all obviously play a major role. What is more difficult is to decide how to balance these factors against our own judgements of the plausibility of the absolute and relative numbers themselves. How suspicious should we be of alleged triumphs against the numerical odds? Should we always be inclined to favour the lower figures for the defeated side, even to the extent of 'cherry picking' among different sources (for instance, by accepting Diodorus's figure of 10,000 for the Persian cavalry at the Granicus but sticking with Arrian's 20,000 for the infantry total)? Similarly, should we be more persuaded by higher casualty figures for the victors (like Diodorus's casualty claims for Alexander's army), regardless of their provenance?[49] At what point should we abandon the ancient figures altogether and substitute our own more 'plausible' suggestions, as some modern writers do almost as a matter of routine?[50]

A century ago, Delbrück gave very clear answers to these questions, namely that the ancient claims are to be treated with enormous scepticism both on grounds of logistics and because of the natural tendency of the victors to exaggerate their achievement. Delbrück spent a lot of time discussing numbers, and produced some radical ideas of his own. At Plataea, he suggested that both sides had only some 40,000 men in all, rather than anything approaching Herodotus's figures (IX.29–32) of 38,700 hoplites, 69,500 Greek light-armed troops, and 350,000 Persians and allies not even counting the cavalry. At Gaugamela, he allowed the Persians at most 12,000 horsemen rather than Arrian's 40,000. He ridiculed Kromayer's acceptance of Livy's figures for Seleucid numerical superiority at Magnesia. At Bibracte, Delbrück suggested that Caesar, far from being outnumbered by 3:1, actually outnumbered the Helvetii by a similar ratio, and at Pharsalus, he allowed Pompey only a 4:3 superiority in infantry and a 3:2 superiority in cavalry instead of the 2:1 and 7:1 ratios that Caesar claims. However, he did accept Polybius's figures (III.113–14, V.65 and 79) of a total of 143,000 and 136,000 combatants respectively for the massive battles at Raphia and Cannae, showing that his main concern was with evening out what he saw as unrealistic numerical imbalances in favour of the losing side.[51]

Delbrück's stance may well reflect the misleading impact of the military wisdom of his own day (his work first appeared in 1900). In the nineteenth century, battles involved tremendous *mutual* attrition, because gunpowder weapons had invalidated the protection once offered by armour and shields and so allowed prolonged and very bloody firepower duels. This produced losses for the victors and vanquished, respectively, of around 28,000 and 50,000 at Borodino, 80,000 and 60,000 at Leipzig, 22,000 and 32,000 at Waterloo, 13,700 and 12,400 at Antietam, 12,800 and 16,800 at Chancellorsville, 23,000 and 28,100 at Gettysburg, 10,000 and 45,000 at Sadowa and 17,000 and 16,000 at Mars-la-Tour.[52] The result was that victory tended to go to the 'big battalions', with even military geniuses like Napoleon or Lee being ground down in the end by superior numbers. The greater articulation of large armies through the corps system also allowed them to conduct outflanking movements across a wider front, and it was precisely such encirclements that Delbrück argued that the Persians and Seleucids would have attempted at Plataea and Magnesia had they really enjoyed anything like the numerical superiority that the sources claimed.[53] If command arrangements in antiquity were too inflexible to give any practical option except piling superior numbers up in greater depth, and if clashes were decided more by moral confrontations than by mutual bloodbaths that would allow such reserves to come into play, then the objections to ancient armies triumphing through superior quality against significant numerical odds become far less potent.

Most modern scholars reject Delbrück's radical scepticism and are much more willing to give some credence to the ancient figures, especially as recent military experience has moved away from the mutual bloodbaths of the past and shown how small, high-quality forces such as the Israelis can indeed achieve sweeping triumphs (at least in 'conventional' operations) with remarkable asymmetries in the losses suffered by the two sides.[54] The image in the ancient sources of smaller armies prevailing with limited casualties is so pervasive that it is very hard to dismiss it altogether, particularly as it even appears in accounts written from the perspective of the defeated side (as at Leuctra, the Trebia, Cannae and Carrhae).[55] Everything is, however, a matter of degree, and it is difficult to believe an account such as Plutarch's tale (*Sull.* 15–19) of a Roman force of 15,000 infantry and 1,500 cavalry defeating a Pontic army of 100,000 foot and 10,000 horse at 2nd Chaeronea while losing only 12 soldiers, even if it does derive from Sulla's own memoirs![56] Massive body counts for the defeated side, such as Caesar's statement (*B Gall.* II.28) that only 500 out of 60,000 Nervii survived their defeat at the Sambre, are also treated with justifiable scepticism.[57] However, less fantastic claims in the sources are today given greater credence on the very reasonable grounds that if we reject the judgements of writers in the ancient world itself, we are hardly in a position to replace them with sounder judgements of our own after a passage of over 2 millennia.[58]

In my model building, I propose to adopt two responses to this controversy over how reliable the ancient statistics are. First, I will accept as broadly accurate the numbers given for better-documented battles such as Cannae, Magnesia and Pharsalus, and I will design my generic system so that it is eminently possible for the smaller army to win in these cases using something like the historical tactics. This should then provide a framework within which to gauge whether the numerical asymmetries claimed in other battles also make sense or whether they remain unsustainable – in some cases (such as the Granicus and Gaugamela), it may well be that the model suggests that modern scholars have actually been too ready to challenge the ancient figures, and that their own more 'credible' suggestions in fact swing the balance too far in favour of the historical victors.

Second, I will try to avoid making the model too sensitive to precise judgements of troop numbers or casualty levels, as neither of these factors seems actually to have been of decisive importance in shaping the real contests – armies won despite being outnumbered, and ran away for reasons other than the massive attritional losses suffered in the gunpowder era. Troop quality was clearly much more significant than either numbers or casualties, so if I introduce a trade-off whereby quality can substitute for quantity, then what matters is the overall fighting value of a given contingent – whether that force represents lower-quality troops in the numbers specified by the sources or somewhat higher-quality troops in lesser numbers becomes a second order question as far as the model is concerned. Similarly, the precise number of casualties that a contingent has sustained becomes a subordinate issue if one focuses instead on whether it is standing its ground or breaking into flight. Whatley rightly pointed out the risk of our becoming so preoccupied with detailed and controversial minutiae that we lose sight of the fairly clear story that the sources usually tell about the course of each individual battle. It is this 'big picture' that I want the model to illuminate, and if it can also cast some light on more specific issues such as 'the hunt for the Persian Cavalry', then so much the better.[59]

2

Armies

Because identifying the modern site of ancient battlefields is such a problematic endeavour, it is best to start our modelling not with the terrain but with the fighting forces themselves. The first step must be to find some means of subdividing the overall armies into a manageable number of individual elements that may be deployed and manoeuvred independently during our dynamic reconstruction. The smallest possible element is, of course, the individual soldier, but there are far too many of these to model each one separately – even simulations of ancient naval engagements do not distinguish each one of the many hundreds of galleys involved, and the number of soldiers in land battles runs not into hundreds but into tens of thousands.[1] Hence, we must find some means of grouping individual soldiers together into 'units' of one form or another.

The traditional approach used when creating static diagrams of the different stages of a battle is to draw blocks of varying dimensions, based on the widely varying sizes of the different contingents described in the ancient sources. Hence, to take an extreme example, Bar-Kochva's diagram of Magnesia has one small block showing the 4 turmae (perhaps only 120 horsemen) on the Roman left flank, faced by a larger block representing the 10,000 Silver Shields on the Seleucid right.[2] The number of separate blocks into which opposing armies are divided often varies greatly, depending on how detailed a breakdown the sources give of the respective sides – thus, Devine's plan of the Hydaspes breaks Alexander's small force down into 14 distinct units with named commanders, while showing the much larger Indian army just as a single, long infantry line with elephants in front and blocks of cavalry on either wing.[3] Clearly, such wide variations in representation, stemming mainly from limitations in the available evidence, are problematic when trying to move beyond these static 'snapshots' into the creation of a dynamic 'working model' of the engagements concerned.

An alternative approach would be to base our subdivision of the armies on the actual tactical organization and articulation of the historical forces. This is what is done in simulations of more recent land engagements, where a campaign such as Arnhem might be modelled at brigade, battalion or even company level depending on the degree of detail desired, with the number of units per side ranging from a couple of dozen in the former case to a few hundred in the latter.[4] The problem is that military organization in the ancient world was nothing like as standardized, with each army having its own system, and with unit sizes and nomenclature even within the same army changing significantly over time (as illustrated by the continuing scholarly debates over Spartan morai and lochoi, and over the shifting number and composition of Alexander's infantry and cavalry units).[5] Asclepiodotus's exposition of the minutiae of Hellenistic military organization smacks far more of schoolroom theory than of military practicality, and our understanding of the sub-unit structure within Greek armies other than the Spartans or within Persian, Indian, Celtic, Punic or Parthian forces is lamentable.[6] Only for the Romans do we have a fairly clear picture of small 'maniples' of around 100 infantry organized first into lines of hastati, principes and triarii and later into 'cohorts', and even here there are several areas of uncertainty, especially regarding the organization of Italian allied forces.[7]

A further problem with dividing armies into their historical sub-units for the purposes of our model is that the most prominent of such sub-units in armies of this period tended to have strengths in the hundreds rather than the thousands, and so handling each one separately in anything except the smallest battles would frustrate the aim of creating a simple grand tactical overview. The Roman legion or Italian ala containing several thousand soldiers offers a much more manageable level of unit differentiation for the larger engagements, but there were not always clear counterparts to these formations in other armies, and whole legions were not in any case the primary vehicle for grand tactical manoeuvres – Roman infantry more often redeployed by separating their 3 battle lines or by detaching groups of cohorts (as at the Metaurus, the Great Plains, Zama, Cynoscephalae, Aquae Sextiae, 2nd Chaeronea, Tigranocerta, Bibracte and Pharsalus).[8] The bottom line is that trying to subdivide armies based on a particular level of historical unit organization raises just as many problems as using the widely varying contingent sizes mentioned in the ancient accounts.

I think it is better to adopt a more utilitarian approach and to divide each army into around 20 abstract elements, each of broadly equivalent fighting power. This more generic and standardized subdivision makes it far easier to develop procedures for movement, combat and command than if the fighting power of different units varied by an order of magnitude or even more, as it would under either of the systems discussed earlier. Having more than around 20 units per side would make use of the model too time-consuming and impractical for all except committed wargamers, especially as (unlike in chess) players are not limited to acting with just 1 unit per turn. Conversely, having fewer units per army would make the model too coarse-grained even for the limited available evidence by preventing the representation of contingents or deployments involving just a few per cent of the army's fighting power, and by forcing troop numbers to be rounded up or down to an unacceptable extent.[9] Even with 20 units, some very small force elements such as the 4 turmae at Magnesia cannot be represented directly, as they can hardly be claimed to make up even 1 per cent of the fighting power of an army totalling some 30,000 men.[10]

This approach to army subdivision raises the obvious questions of equivalence between opposing units in the same battle and between units across different battles. As regards the first issue, I think it is important that the fighting power of opposing armies be weighed on the same scale, rather than handling each army in isolation. In other words, units of the same type and quality should represent roughly the same number of troops in any given battle, whichever side they are on. Differences between the fighting powers of opposing troops should be represented by explicit differences in categorization at the unit level, rather than through a more implicit approach of just dividing both armies independently into the same number of elements. This is especially important because the overall fighting power of opposing armies was obviously not equal, as in some artificial chess-like contest. It is vital that our model allows for a range of possible asymmetries between the fighting power of historical adversaries, and one key means of doing this is to standardize the potential of particular unit types while varying the overall number of units available to each side. In the scenarios developed in Part II, armies may have several units more or less than the average figure of 20 in order to reflect such differences in overall strength.

Arranging equivalence of unit fighting power across different battles is much more problematic, because army size varied so greatly – from less than 10,000 men per side in some Greek city state battles such as Delium and Leuctra to over 50,000 men per side in large engagements such as Raphia and Cannae. A constant unit scale would mean a several-fold variation in the number of units involved in different battles, which would entirely undermine my pragmatic approach of dividing each army into around 20 elements – either the smaller battles would involve only a handful of units or the larger ones would require hundreds. Hence, I propose instead to accept significant variation in unit scale across the range of battles covered, with units of the same type and quality representing up to eight times more troops in the largest engagements than in the smallest clashes. This obviously has significant consequences for comparisons between engagements and for the relationships between force, time and space in the battles concerned, and I will return to this issue in more detail in Chapters 3 and 4.

Now, how does one gauge 'fighting power' when comparing different troops within and between opposing armies? I argued on pp. 11–15 that the evidence for ancient armies triumphing against the numerical odds was so pervasive that Delbrück's radical scepticism cannot be upheld. This being the case, it seems to me that the first and most important measure of fighting power at the unit level, far ahead of any issues of equipment or fighting style, concerns the morale, discipline, cohesion, skill and reputation of the troops themselves.[11] Lendon has highlighted very well how Greek authors such as Polybius tended to ascribe military success to better tactics, techniques or equipment, whereas Roman writers like Caesar and Livy were more concerned with the superior bravery and *virtus* of the victorious soldiers.[12] The evidence from both Greek and Roman battles lends much more support to the Roman interpretation – how else can one explain the dominance of Spartan hoplites, or Eumenes's veteran Silver Shields, or of Caesar's legionaries over much larger numbers of similarly equipped opponents?[13] A key ingredient in such triumphs against the numerical odds seems to have been the intimidation of less-resolute adversaries. The Persian masses at Cunaxa fled from the 10,000 even before they had reached arrow range, and, by contrast, Xenophon has another very telling anecdote of how a small Spartan force with borrowed shields was massacred, in part because their more numerous opponents were misled by the shield blazons and did not realize they were fighting Spartans![14]

Clearly, we must have different categories of troop quality, and the principle of units having broadly similar fighting power suggests that the lesser-quality units should each represent more troops in order to compensate. To keep things simple, we can manage with just three different unit classes termed 'veteran', 'average' and 'levy'. More subtle variations between the fighting power of different armies may be encompassed by using a mix of units from different classes, such as a blend of veteran and average units for Roman infantry or a blend of average and levy units for Persian cavalry. The more difficult question is how great the 'quality premium' should be across the three categories. Even if one ignores altogether the tens of thousands of armed servants whose background presence is attested at battles like Plataea, Issus and Gaugamela, but who played no role in the actual fighting, I suggest that the quality premium between the three unit classes needs to be very significant if the enormous numerical imbalances reported in the sources are to be offset such that it is the smaller army that often has the greater fighting power. Not even a twofold ratio between adjoining categories will suffice – veteran troops need to be around three times more effective man-for-man than average soldiers, and average soldiers should in turn be around three times more effective than levies, if the necessary offsets are to be achieved.

One could simply rule that the troop ratio between veteran, average and levy units is 1:3:9, thereby accounting for the whole of this qualitative premium. However, having units represent such widely varying numbers of soldiers would make it difficult to handle force-to-space issues during movement and combat, so it is better to absorb part of the premium in a different way. Key to this is the fact that high-quality armies like those of Alexander, Scipio and Caesar tended to have much greater overall fighting power than their opponents despite their numerical inferiority. Rather than representing this advantage by giving them a larger overall number of units than their adversaries, it is better to have slight variations in the fighting value of the units themselves. If veteran units have a fighting value of 4, average units 3, and levy units 2, then the troop ratios between the three categories can be reduced to a more manageable 1:2:4 without sacrificing the quality premium (as it will take 2 levy units, representing eight times as many troops, to have the same fighting value as 1 veteran unit).

How can one decide to which class a particular contingent should be assigned? In part this is a matter of trial and error, by adding up the fighting values of opposing armies using a given set of judgements, and seeing how they compare. If the historically victorious army has a lower total fighting value, then something may be wrong with the assignments, as play of the scenario will tend on average to produce the opposite outcome. At the other extreme, if the total fighting values are hopelessly one-sided and differ by more than a ratio of 3:2, alarm bells should also ring because this was an era when battles tended to be fought only by mutual consent – hence Pericles's strategy of avoiding battle with the Peloponnesians, and Fabius Cunctator's similar approach against Hannibal.[15] If one assumes that the historical course of the engagement represents the average outcome that our reconstructions should aim to generate (a contentious stance, but one to which there is little reasonable alternative given the paucity of reliable evidence), then balanced and hard-fought battles should tend to produce broadly equal overall fighting values, while more one-sided clashes with highly asymmetric casualty figures should see the historical victors enjoying a superiority of up to 50 per cent.[16] If it is impossible to achieve the appropriate relative fighting values for the two armies, then it may be time to reconsider our assumptions about troop numbers, as discussed on pp. 14–15.

The other way of judging to which class particular contingents should be assigned is with reference to their own reported performance in the actual engagement. Ratings should not be seen as set in stone for specific troops whatever the occasion, as morale could vary significantly from battle to battle. Thus, in Gabiene, Eumenes continued to benefit from the terror inspired by his Silver Shields (despite their later betrayal), but most of his cavalry behaved dismally compared to their performance in Paraitacene a few months earlier.[17] Of course, there is a degree of circularity in assigning qualitative categories based on historical performance, but no more so than in Biddle's much more complex study, in which 'mastery of the modern system' becomes rather a vague catch-all explanation for military success.[18] Because the ancient evidence is so limited, there is no hope that a simulation will take us beyond existing speculations and somehow prove from first principles which intangible aspects of troop quality (such as morale, discipline, cohesion, skill and reputation) mattered most overall.[19] What my model can and does do is to place qualitative superiority in its proper perspective alongside other factors such as numbers, command, troop types and tactics, within a comprehensive framework that allows meaningful comparisons across the range of different ancient engagements.

This leads me neatly to additional means of categorizing troops within the unit system, other than as veteran, average or levy. The most obvious further sub-division is into infantry and cavalry. Although ancient horsemen did sometimes dismount temporarily while fighting (as at Cannae), there was nothing like the blurring of boundaries associated with the 'mounted infantry' of later eras, so the infantry/cavalry distinction is a very easy one to make.[20] More difficult is to decide what (if any) premium in overall fighting value should attach to mounted status, compared to infantry of similar quality. Ancient opinions run the gamut from Xenophon's understandable special pleading to the isolated 10,000 (*An.* III.2) that horses' only contribution in battle is to allow their riders to run away more safely, all the way to Polybius's comment after his account of Cannae (III.117) that cavalry superiority will bring victory even if the enemy infantry outnumber yours by 2:1. A surprising number of books have been published on ancient cavalry over the past 2 decades, and the general thrust of this scholarship is that both Greek and Roman horsemen have been underestimated as military assets due to a combination of ancient social prejudice and modern misconcep-tions about the role of the stirrup.[21] However, Gaebel takes a more balanced view and argues that victory always depended on successful combined arms tactics, with infantry retaining a decisive role even in the period from Alexander to Hannibal when mounted warfare was at its height.[22]

Polybius's generalization about the importance of cavalry superiority is in fact starkly at odds with the outcomes at Plataea, the Granicus, Gaugamela, Magnesia, and Pharsalus, where in every case the side with far more horsemen suffered a resounding defeat. That said, ancient armies clearly felt it well worthwhile to include at least a proportion of horsemen (averaging around 10 per cent) within their force, even though these troops were significantly more expensive and logis-tically demanding than the equivalent number of infantry. Some of the added value of cavalry lay in wider activities such as scouting, screening and pursuit, but conversely, they were much less useful than foot troops in difficult terrain and in the attack and defence of fortifications. On balance, it seems fair to suggest from the ancient evidence and the modern scholarship that the direct contribution of horsemen in pitched battle equated very roughly to that of twice as many infantry soldiers of similar calibre. This can be reflected in our unit system by making each cavalry unit represent half as many troopers as an infantry unit of the same quality, an approach that has the added advantage that it leaves the 4–3–2 system of unit fighting values unchanged and that it gives more flexibility to represent small cavalry contingents at the margin without increasing the number of units in the army as a whole.

We are now in a position to outline much firmer procedures for subdividing each army than in our initial focus on creating around 20 roughly equivalent elements. The crucial first step is to select a multiple from 1–8, which will define the troop ratio in that battle for all units on both sides. With a multiple of 1, each levy unit represents around 1,000 infantry or 500 cavalry, each average unit represents around 500 infantry or 250 cavalry, and each veteran unit represents around 250 infantry or 125 cavalry. With higher multiples, these figures are all increased by the factor concerned, so that an average infantry unit at a multiple of 5 would represent around 2,500 troops. Selection of the multiple depends on the number of troops in the historical armies and on the quality ratings or 'class' we judge should be used for each contingent. In order to give around 20 units per army, the total fighting value of its units (including the value of any generals as discussed on pp. 66–71) should lie between 50 and 100. To avoid units becoming unduly crowded or thinly spread, lower total fighting values within this range should generally be used for lower quality or infantry-dominated forces, while higher total fighting values should be used for better led and higher quality combined arms forces.

I will give a specific example in a moment of how the model may be applied, but first, one further categorization needs to be introduced. A minority of both infantry and cavalry fought in a more dispersed manner as skirmishers, evading combat with heavier troops and instead raining missiles from a distance. As Jones has pointed out, this distinction between heavy and light troops interacted with that between infantry and cavalry to create a classic 'scissors/paper/stone' relationship, only this time with four dimensions rather than three.[23] Heavy cavalry could catch and ride down light infantry, but were usually repulsed by a solid front of heavy infantry. Light cavalry could rain missiles on heavy infantry with impunity, but tended to be out-shot by light infantry due to the horsemen's lower numbers and more vulnerable mounts. This is a set of interacting strengths and weaknesses that may readily be simulated even at the broadest grand tactical level, and it offers a very important complement and corrective to what would otherwise be the unchallenged dominance of troop quality as the decisive element of the model. Hence, units will be categorized not just as infantry or cavalry and as veteran, average or levy, but also as heavy or light, with the latter distinction having no effect on their size or fighting value because of the 'swings and roundabouts' nature of the relationships involved.

Unfortunately, real life was much more complicated than this neat bipolar division might suggest, and the line between heavy and light troops was actually extremely blurred. Even Asclepiodotus (I.1–4) eschewed such a simple distinction, and instead identified three categories for infantry (hoplites, peltasts and psiloi), and an even greater variety for cavalry. Some troops such as Persian and Indian archers fought with missiles from close formations, while some dispersed skirmishers such as Roman velites were perfectly well equipped and motivated to fight at close quarters. Peltasts seem to have evolved from open order skirmishers into increasingly well-protected loose order troops (usually mercenary), used to complement the pikemen of the phalanx.[24] For cavalry, the blurring was even greater, with intermediate javelin-equipped troopers being much more common overall than either dedicated heavy lancers like Alexander's Companions or skirmishing horse archers like the Scythians or Parthians.[25] Hence, careful judgement will often be required when categorizing particular troops as heavy or light, with the latter appellation being applied only to dispersed skirmishers (including velites and early peltasts) while the former term is used to cover a broad range of intermediate troops in addition to those truly dedicated to close combat.

Hannibal's army at Cannae offers a convenient example of how the entire model developed so far may be applied in a specific case. Polybius (III.114) says that the Carthaginians fielded around 10,000 cavalry and 40,000 infantry. The precise breakdown of the various contingents is less clear, but deductions from earlier evidence suggest that roughly 8,000 of the infantry were Libyans in the famous concealed flanking columns, a similar number were skirmishers in front of the main line, and just under 6,000 of the cavalry were from the initial invasion force – of whom perhaps two-thirds were Numidians and the rest Spanish.[26] The Libyan heavy infantry (now re-equipped with captured Roman armour) should probably count as veterans, as should the Spanish cavalry who spearheaded Hasdrubal's drive by the river. All the other troops are better categorized as average, including the Numidians on Hannibal's right, who could not break an equal force of Roman allied cavalry until Hasdrubal threatened their rear.[27] If the maximum multiple of 8 is used, this produces an army of 4 veteran heavy infantry units (each representing 2,000 Libyans), 2 average light infantry units (each representing 4,000 skirmishers), 6 average heavy infantry units (each representing 4,000 Celts or Spaniards from the main line), 2 veteran heavy cavalry units (each representing 1,000 Spaniards), 2 average heavy cavalry units (each representing 2,000 Celts), and 2 average light cavalry units (each representing 2,000 Numidians). This makes 18 units, with a total fighting value of 60 ($6 \times 4 + 12 \times 3$), which will increase by a further 24 because of the generals as discussed on pp. 67–8. Using a lower multiple than 8 would probably breach the fighting value limit of 100, and the large numbers of the opposing Roman force argue strongly for the maximum multiple in this case.

Most existing simulations of ancient battles go into much more detail than this simple threefold categorization of troop types and classes, and they lay particular stress on equipment differences rather than the less tangible factor of troop quality – in this sense they are very 'Polybian' in their perspective.[28] As I hinted in the previous paragraph, it may be appropriate at the margin to take some account of superior armour or weaponry as part of an overall judgement of troop quality, especially where a contribution is specifically mentioned in the ancient sources, but human factors must surely form the overwhelming basis for the classification chosen. That said, there were some subtypes of troops whose particular strengths and weaknesses (based on socio-cultural as well as equipment differences) did have some impact beyond the purely tactical level, and it is worth incorporating such factors as additional elements into what would otherwise be a rather bland and generic set of categories. This applies particularly to heavy troops (especially heavy infantry), which will still form the lion's share of most armies, and which, as I discussed above, cover a wide range of specific fighting styles.

Five subtypes of heavy troops seem especially deserving of some special treatment to distinguish them from the general run of other heavy units. For cavalry, the fully armoured cataphract lancers that appeared in Seleucid and Parthian armies late in our period stood out in both protection and ponderousness from other medium and heavy horse.[29] For infantry, Greek hoplites clearly deserve special attention because of the distinctive fighting characteristics explored recently by Hanson and others, and so do the close-order archers of the Persians and Indians with their very different fighting style.[30] Later, the pike-armed phalangites who superseded hoplites in Macedonian and Hellenistic armies brought their own characteristics, as did Roman legionaries with their distinctive multi-line deployment – the confrontation between these two highly contrasting military systems became the focus for a classic Polybian tactical analysis (XVIII.28–32). I will leave until later any further discussion of the special provisions that may be applied to model the peculiarities of these five subtypes, with one exception – the issue of fighting value relative to other types of units. It seems to me that most of the subtypes had both strengths and weaknesses that broadly offset one another, but that Roman legionaries had greater net advantages, hence (at least in part) their ability to prevail and to dominate the Mediterranean world. To reflect this, I suggest a slight tweak to legionary fighting values, namely that average legionary units should have a value of 4 rather than 3 when assessing their overall contribution to an army, but *not* when assessing the impact of Roman losses. This latter refinement helps to reflect the strategic impact of Italian manpower reserves, which famously undermined the battlefield victories of Pyrrhus and Hannibal.[31]

It remains only to deal with two more exotic types of mounted forces, namely chariots and war elephants. By this era, chariots had largely been superseded by normal cavalry, but some were still used early in the period by Indian, Punic and Celtic armies. They seem to have been almost as effective man-for-man and horse-for-horse as ordinary cavalry, though with certain particular strengths and weaknesses that justify classifying them as a separate unit type. Hence, with a multiple of 1, an average chariot unit could have the standard fighting value of 3 and represent around 100 two-horse vehicles or 50 of the larger four-horse vehicles, compared to 250 horsemen within an average cavalry unit. There is little need to worry about veteran or levy chariots, because in the few battles of our era in which these vehicles appeared their quality seems to have been pretty average. However, we should certainly have a special subtype for the infamous scythed chariot, which was used sporadically by Persian, Seleucid and Pontic forces, with hardly any success. As the numbers employed were relatively few, it is worth halving the normal chariot ratio so that the single unit required represents very roughly 25 of these four-horse contraptions for every point of the current multiple. The fighting value must surely be only 1, and even this overstates the positive contribution of these devices.[32]

War elephants were a very different matter, and played a much more pervasive and important role in the battles of this era, even though they too sometimes proved to be a double-edged sword.[33] Here, the yardstick of troop numbers breaks down, and it would grossly understate the physical and especially psychological contribution of these beasts to equate their value merely to as many cavalrymen as there were elephant crew – as the number of elephants in an army was measured in dozens rather than thousands as for other troops, they would not even merit a single unit. However, the fact that elephants were often accompanied by a 'usual guard' of around 50 light infantry per beast offers a much more fruitful way forward.[34] As an average light infantry unit at a multiple of 1 contains around 500 troops, it seems reasonable instead to have a composite unit of 250 such skirmishers and 5 pachyderms. This allows armies to qualify for at least 1 elephant unit, and in many cases more, even in large battles with high multiples – hence at Raphia, with the maximum multiple of 8, the 102 Seleucid and 73 Ptolemaic elephants with their accompanying skirmishers translate fairly neatly into 3 and 2 units, respectively.[35]

Raphia also highlights the key distinction between Indian and African elephants, with the latter being intimidated and at a great disadvantage when facing the former. This relationship in itself would suggest giving Indian beasts the same threefold quality premium as veteran troops enjoy compared to average ones, but it is far from clear that the distinction between the two types of pachyderms mattered anything like as much in confrontations with men and horses, so it seems preferable to give Indian elephant units a fighting value of 4 and African elephant units a value of 3, while retaining the same representational ratios for both. Where the ratio does need modification is for disproportionately large elephant forces, in particular the 100 beasts fielded by Xanthippus at Bagradas as part of an army containing only 16,000 troops.[36] Here, the pachyderms seem to have formed a denser, unaccompanied line, with the light infantry being posted on the wings instead, so it is more appropriate to use pure elephant units, each representing 10 beasts for every point of the multiple.

This concludes my discussion of how the historical armies may be translated into standardized elements for use in the dynamic model of battle I am about to develop. Before proceeding, it is useful to round off the chapter with a summary table setting out the fighting values and troop ratios of all the possible units concerned.

Unit type and class	Fighting value	No. of troops/vehicles/beasts Multiple in use								
		1	1.5	2	2.5	3	4	5	6	8
Levy heavy infantry / Levy light infantry	2	1,000	1,500	2,000	2,500	3,000	4,000	5,000	6,000	8,000
Levy heavy cavalry / Levy light cavalry	2	500	750	1,000	1,250	1,500	2,000	2,500	3,000	4,000
Average heavy infantry / Average light infantry	3	500	750	1,000	1,250	1,500	2,000	2,500	3,000	4,000
Average legionaries	4/3	500	750	1,000	1,250	1,500	2,000	2,500	3,000	4,000
Average heavy cavalry / Average light cavalry	3	250	375	500	625	750	1,000	1,250	1,500	2,000
Veteran heavy infantry / Veteran light infantry	4	250	375	500	625	750	1,000	1,250	1,500	2,000
Veteran heavy cavalry / Veteran light cavalry	4	125	188	250	313	375	500	625	750	1,000
Average two-horse chariots	3	100	150	200	250	300	400	500	600	800
Average four-horse chariots	3	50	75	100	125	150	200	250	300	400
Scythed chariots	1	25	38	50	63	75	100	125	150	200
Indian elephants + light infantry	4	5 + / 250	8 + / 375	10 + / 500	13 + / 625	15 + / 750	20 + / 1,000	25 + / 1,250	30 + / 1,500	40 + / 2,000
African elephants + light infantry	3	5 + / 250	8 + / 375	10 + / 500	13 + / 625	15 + / 750	20 + / 1,000	25 + / 1,250	30 + / 1,500	40 + / 2,000
Unaccompanied Indian elephants	4	10	15	20	25	30	40	50	60	80
Unaccompanied African elephants	3	10	15	20	25	30	40	50	60	80

3

Movement

Now that we have the opposing armies converted into a standardized set of elements, the next step is to model the battlefield over which the units will move and fight. Existing static battle plans sometimes lay the armies onto an actual map of the suggested site of the engagement, and sometimes adopt a more diagrammatic approach that simply shows the armies in relationship to one another, with terrain either being omitted altogether or (as with the river on the Roman right at Cannae) being shown as a generic feature without any attempt at detailed localization.[1] As I discussed on pp. 6–7, uncertainties over the precise battle sites and over how features like rivers and shorelines have changed over the intervening 2 millennia make it fruitless to try to use detailed modern maps as the basis for reconstructing every battlefield required. Instead, I will use the more diagrammatic approach as a universally applicable 'lowest common denominator', and then bring in more specific geographical information for the small minority of battlefields where localization to a specific site appears more feasible.

Making the armies themselves (rather than specific terrain) the yardstick of the engagement is possible only because of the highly formulaic nature of battles in this era. Opposing forces generally formed up in battle lines several hundred metres apart before closing to engage, thereby forming an opening array with striking parallels to the array of pieces at the start of a game of chess. Such a formulaic approach to battle was not limited to the classical world – one need only think of the detailed contemporary engravings of early modern engagements such as Lützen and Naseby to see a similarly ordered initial deployment.[2] Clearly there were important practical reasons spanning all these eras for getting one's troops carefully in order before engaging, but one cannot dismiss the additional considerations of culture and psychology. Hanson, in particular, has written at length about the Western attachment to such 'fair and open' pitched battles as a way of deciding conflicts, and he sees their prominence compared to more pragmatic approaches such as raiding and ambush as a key characteristic of the Western way of war, stemming all the way from Homer and from the 'agonistic' ideology of the Greek poleis.[3] As I said at the outset, we remain fascinated by the concept of 'decisive battles', and this book is itself a symptom of that cultural preoccupation.[4]

The most important dimension of battle line plans is the lateral one, because this shows which troops faced which opponents and whether one army's line extended beyond that of its adversaries. The ancient sources do often describe such interrelationships, as they are key to the development of the battle. Where they are much less forthcoming is with regard to actual distances such as the length of the opposing lines or the width of each contingent. To try to estimate such distances, scholars have to resort to generic calculations of troop deployment patterns or to measurements from the suggested battle site – both techniques that were actually employed by Polybius himself (XII.17–22) in his critique of Callisthenes's account of Issus. I will return shortly to such methods of estimating frontages, but for the purpose of our model it may be better to use a more abstract approach, just as we did when dividing each army into units.

As previously mentioned, what the ancient authors do routinely describe is the differing outcome of the fighting at different points along the battle line. The clearest division is between the infantry battle in the centre and the cavalry duels on either wing, with the latter contests often being decided while the infantry fighting was still raging on (as at Cannae and Zama). Within the infantry battle itself, there are several instances in which fortunes differed between each army's right and left, as at Delium, 1st Mantinea, Nemea, 2nd Coronea, Sentinum and Cynoscephalae. Just as common, however, are cases in which a threefold distinction is made between the centre and the two wings of the infantry line. At Sellasia, Raphia, Magnesia and the Sambre, infantry deployments are clearly articulated in this tripartite way, and at Marathon, Trebia, Cannae and Ilipa, the contest in the centre took a very different course to that on the two infantry wings.[5] As a right–left split may be subsumed within this more detailed tripartite division, but not vice versa, an obvious generic way of dividing up the battlefield for the purposes of our model is into five lateral slices, representing the left and right flanks and the left centre, centre and right centre of the opposing lines.

These five sections of each army were obviously not of equal width in specific cases, though exact ratios are very hard to discern. Some modern plans show the cavalry wings in ancient battles only as narrow appendages to the infantry line, in accordance with the horsemen's contribution of only around 10 per cent of the overall troops, but other writers such as Connolly and Devine go to the opposite extreme and allocate half or more of each army's frontage to the cavalry, based on Polybius's remarks (XII.18) about the limited depth of cavalry squadrons and the wide intervals between them.[6] I will return to this controversy shortly, but the key issue for us at present is whether the five lateral slices should be of equal or variable width in each specific battle. To avoid serious complications with force-to-space ratios and lateral manoeuvre, I suggest that they must be of roughly equal width, and that major asymmetries between the frontages of different contingents should be reflected by splitting the units in a given contingent between different sectors. This is also the best way to handle asymmetries in the overall length of opposing battle lines, as at Cunaxa and Gaugamela – the five sectors should be set to accommodate the width of the longer line, and its adversaries will then occupy fewer sectors overall. In battles such as Leuctra, Tunis or Sellasia, where cavalry was scarcely present or operated in front of the infantry rather than on the wings, it may even be the case that neither side initially contests one or both flank sectors, and that the fighting is confined to the 3 central areas.

Is it possible to give a rough absolute width for each sector in a particular battle, in the same way as each average infantry unit represents around 500 troops for every point of the applicable multiple? Sadly, this is far from straightforward, because (as mentioned earlier) ancient figures for army frontages are very much rarer than those for troop numbers. To work out frontages from the troop numbers themselves, one must know or guess not only the depth of the soldiers' formations but also the distance between adjacent files of men and the width of intervals between sub-units, and (as I mentioned in the case of horsemen) these three variables are all the subject of significant scholarly debate.[7] The third variable is particularly uncertain and is often ignored altogether by ancient scholars, even though early modern comparisons suggest that the intervals between infantry as well as cavalry units could sometimes exceed the frontage of the units themselves (albeit in a context in which the intervals were usually covered by reserve units in successive lines).[8] Given all these imponderables, claims such as Marsden's that his calculated frontage of 3,800 yards for the Macedonians at Gaugamela 'is right to within 200 yards either way' deserve to be taken with a large pinch of salt.[9]

One pretty safe generalization is that the frontage of armies did not vary with the number of troops in a linear fashion. Larger armies seem to have formed up instead in significantly greater depth to avoid the command problems and terrain constrictions that would have hindered a thinner but longer line. Hence, at Marathon, the 10,000 Athenian hoplites are usually assumed to have formed up 8 deep on the wings and even shallower in their weakened centre, making for a total frontage of 1.5 km or more, while at Raphia, Bar-Kochva suggests that each side's infantry covered only twice that frontage, despite being around six times as numerous.[10] At Cannae, many scholars go even further by suggesting that the 70,000 Roman foot occupied only the same 1.5 km frontage as the 10,000 Athenians at Marathon, if not less![11] Thucydides (IV.94) explicitly says that the Athenians at Delium formed up 8 deep, while Livy (XXXVII.40) and Appian (Syr. 32) both claim that the Seleucid phalangites in the much larger army at Magnesia deployed no less than 32 deep. Polybius (XII.18) suggests that cavalry were of little use more than 8 deep and that the need for intervals between squadrons meant that 800 horse would fill 1 stade (180 m). However, his application of this yardstick to the large battle of Issus produced the absurd result that the alleged 30,000 Persian right wing horse would by themselves fill Callisthenes's total battlefront of 14 stadia (2.6 km) nearly three times over. Although this calculation certainly does give grounds to question Callisthenes's figures, it also casts some doubt on Polybius's own assumptions and suggests that, in such large engagements, cavalry probably did form up in multiple lines and so increased their effective depth just like infantry in order to maintain a manageable frontage.[12]

As there can be no simple equation between troop multiple and sector width, I will give for each scenario in Part II a very rough suggested scale in metres, based on my own readings of the ancient evidence and modern scholarship, and using 1 m per heavy infantry file as a broad rule of thumb that makes at least some allowance for unit intervals in addition to the 3 ft (0.9 m) file frontage mentioned in the sources.[13] My suggested sector widths for each battle range from 300 m to 1,200 m, with the larger distances obviously being more common in scenarios with higher troop multiples, but with the scale in different scenarios with the same multiple varying depending on individual circumstances. Although this does complicate use of the model to shed comparative light on the reconstruction of army frontages, it will already be evident that it helps discredit wilder possibilities such as Arrian's apparent implication (*Anab.* V.15–16) that the Indian infantry line at the Hydaspes (with a troop multiple of 3 in our model) was over 6 km long. The graph in Figure 1 plots zone width against troop multiple for all 35 battles in Part II, and clearly illustrates both the nonlinear nature of the relationship between army size and frontage (quadrupling the former only doubles the latter) and the operation of the comparative 'trend line' methodology described on p. xiii. By allowing the creation of such a graph (that takes into account troop quality as well as raw numbers thanks to the system of fighting values outlined in Chapter 2), the model offers a very useful yardstick against which to gauge the widely varying estimates that different scholars have often made of army frontages in individual engagements.

The combination of armies split into around 20 standardized elements of fighting power with a battlefront divided into five different lateral sectors already gives us the basis to undertake for ancient battles the kind of analysis performed by Dupuy of the 1940 *Blitzkrieg*, namely to model the impact of localized force concentrations like that amassed by the Germans in the Ardennes (or by Hannibal's left flank cavalry at Cannae).[14] However, one cannot take such analyses very far without running into the need for a second dimension (battlefield depth) to handle the resultant retreats and breakthroughs. As with lateral measurements, very few precise figures are given in the sources, but those that do exist suggest that the distances could be at least as great as the sector widths that I have already discussed. Plutarch's claim (*Cleom.* 28) that the

Macedonian left wing at Sellasia fell back 5 stadia (900 m) before rallying and pushing on to victory has attracted great scepticism, but Caesar (*B Gall.* I.25) has the Helvetii at Bibracte retiring about 1,000 paces (1.5 km) and then turning on their hilltop to renew the fight.[15] Sometimes the distances involved in such retrograde movements could be even greater – in Paraitacene, Diodorus (XIX.31) says that a new confrontation between the armies took place after nightfall on foothills 30 stadia (5.5 km) from the earlier battlefield, but this is better seen as outside the scope of the original engagement.

In line with the broad-brush approach that I have adopted throughout, what we need as a bare minimum is the facility for part or all of either army to be held back or pulled back from the main fighting line, either through a deliberate 'refusal' of one flank (as at Leuctra or Gaza) or through retirement in the face of enemy pressure (as at Cannae, Bibracte and the Sambre). This implies that both armies should have a 'forward' and a 'rear' position for their units within each of the five lateral sectors, with these two positions in a sector sometimes being occupied simultaneously (as with the Persians at the Granicus, who fielded a line of cavalry along the riverbank and a line of infantry on the hills behind).[16] It is a short step from this to the idea that our model battlefield should be divided into four longitudinal swathes, cutting across the five lateral sectors, to produce a 5 × 4 array of 'zones' that units will occupy like the squares on a chessboard. This has the inestimable advantage of flexibility in that the same rules of movement and combat can apply in all four orthogonal directions, allowing easy simulation of those instances in which victorious troops turned through 90 degrees to roll up the enemy flank or surge round behind the opposing line (as at 1st Mantinea, Nemea and Cannae). If each zone has roughly the same depth as width, our simulated battlefield will represent an area from 1.5 to 6 km across and from 1.2 to 4.8 km deep. The 20 zones can be divided longitudinally across the middle of the battlefield, and then named in terms of their position relative to the nearer army, as shown in Figure 2).

Now that we have a clearly defined battlefield, we can address the relative position of the opposing camps. Usually, these were outside the area covered by our board, with their distance and direction being highly variable – at the Trebia, for example, Hannibal's camp seems to have been just behind his rear zone whereas the Roman camp was around 6 km to their left rear, while at Cannae 2 years later Connolly suggests that Hannibal's camp was 3 km beyond his left flank and that the two Roman camps were (in our terms) just off their right wing and left wing zones respectively.[17] Camp locations are often highly speculative, and to avoid undue complication it seems best to ignore camps not on the actual battlefield and to treat all armies the same in terms of initial deployment, regardless of the length or direction of their approach march. The defeat of an army in the field was often immediately followed (as at Plataea, Sentinum, Ilipa and Pharsalus) by an assault on its fortified camp, but as with the attacks launched on off-board camps during the course of the main engagement (as at Cunaxa, Gaugamela, Asculum and Cannae), this is best seen as outside the scope of the simulation itself.[18]

In some cases, however, especially in larger battles with deeper zones, one or both camps were so close to the fighting line as to warrant being placed on the actual battlefield. Such nearby camps were sometimes attacked by victorious or raiding forces while the battle was still going on, as at 2nd Coronea, Magnesia and the Sambre.[19] In Gabiene this proved decisive, when the Silver Shields were persuaded by the seizure of their families and possessions to betray Eumenes to Antigonus.[20] Fortified camps were less vulnerable to such attacks, and fieldworks were sometimes even used to strengthen an army's main defensive line, as at Issus and Sellasia.[21] To reflect all this, the scenario may designate 1 of an army's 3 rear zones as containing an unfortified or fortified camp. The former will give the army a head start during deployment while the latter provides a useful defensive backstop, but both also represent a morale and victory point liability if the zone is captured by the enemy.

Most ancient battles are described as being fought on flat, open plains. We know from more recent engagements such as Naseby and Waterloo how much of a difference even minor terrain features such as low ridges, farm buildings, hedges, ditches and pits can make to the course of the fighting.[22] However, the ancient accounts make little or no reference to such minor terrain, so our model can reflect it only through abstract measures such as reducing average movement rates and making combat outcomes less predictable through a degree of random variation. Even our knowledge of more significant terrain features such as hills and rivers seldom justifies anything like the fine detail possible in simulations like those by Herman and Berg, which divide each battlefield into over a thousand individual grid cells.[23] My own much less fine-grained approach here comes into its own, as it corresponds pretty well with the level of terrain detail that we actually know. We may categorize any of the 20 zones as containing one or more generic terrain features, such as hills, woods, marshes, streams, rivers, or the shorelines of the sea or a wide river like the Euphrates. There may also be a town at the edge of some battlefields, though unlike camps this does not merit special provision within the model. Despite the small number of zones, it is surprising how well a judicious mixture and arrangement of terrain types can capture what we know of particular battlefields, as shown for example in Figures 18 (1st Chaeronea) and 20 (Issus).[24]

Now that we have come to grips with the unmanageable complexity of the real armies and the real battlefields by subsuming them within a small number of standardized units, unit types, zones and terrain types, the really hard work has been done, and providing for the movement of troops across the field is actually little more complex than regulating the movement of chess pieces across a board.

As movement is a matter both of space and of time, the first requirement is to systematize the temporal dimension as we have done the spatial ones. Computer games like *Rome: Total War* handle this by running the battle continuously while players struggle to react to the shifting challenges and opportunities, but in manual simulations, the usual approach is to divide up time, like space, into discrete intervals called 'turns', which are entirely disconnected from the real world pace at which the players operate the system and make their decisions. In some simulations, the amount of real time represented by each turn is variable, allowing play to be structured around action–reaction sequences like those that Kagan highlights in Caesar's battles.[25] However, it is much more common to standardize turn length so that movement, for example, can be regulated in terms of 'zones per turn' in exactly the same way as real movement speeds are measured in kilometres per hour.

If we employ this traditional system of turns, then the obvious basic movement rate is 1 zone per turn. Diagonal movement would complicate things, as it would cover ground 40 per cent faster and would introduce far more flexibility than is realistic for the unwieldy formations of the time, so it is better to prohibit it altogether and to rule that all movement must be orthogonal. Exceptions such as the involuntary rightward drift that Thucydides (V.71) ascribes to hoplite armies, and the more deliberate right incline that Arrian (*Anab*. III.13) mentions at Gaugamela, may be handled much better at this scale by arranging initial scenario deployments accordingly. The shallow rivers and streams represented in the model should not significantly inhibit movement, especially as they run within rather than between zones, and so troops may simply be moving along the bank. As the main asset of horsemen was their greater battlefield mobility, it seems appropriate for chariots and for cavalry other than cataphracts to be able to move 2 zones per turn, unless entering difficult terrain such as hills, woods, marshes or a fortified camp. Units that move into a camp zone (except during deployment) should not be able to leave or attack out of that zone on the same turn, to reflect the obstruction caused and the temptation to plunder the enemy baggage.

In chess, players are restricted to moving just one piece at a time, whereas in many wargames, they may move any or all of their units up to their maximum move allowance each turn.[26] Both of these extremes are in fact unrealistic. The pace at which different contingents moved in battle varied greatly with the circumstances and with the calibre of the troops and their commanders – in some cases they dashed along at full speed (as when Lucullus led 2 cohorts to seize a key hill at Tigranocerta, or when Labienus sent the 10th Legion hastening back to relieve Caesar at the Sambre) but more often they dawdled forward cautiously or even stopped altogether (as with most of the troops at Leuctra and Gaza, who apparently remained unengaged while the battle was decided on one wing).[27] I will outline in Chapter 5 the command provisions that will play the main role in reflecting this contrast, but for now it is enough to note that full-speed movement should be represented not by the allowances in the previous paragraph but by a special 'double move' of 2 zones per turn, rising to 4 zones for cavalry or chariots not moving through difficult terrain.

This modification is important because it bears upon the key simulation question of how much real time each turn represents. As mentioned on p. xv, my previous use of wide-ranging grand tactical manoeuvres like those at Cannae, the Metaurus and the Sambre to form a very basic 'battlefield clock' suggests that some Roman infantry combats must have lasted hours rather than mere minutes.[28] The methodology involved obviously depends on the simple equation that time equals distance divided by speed. As discussed earlier in this chapter, each zone in our model represents an area between 300 and 1,200 m across, depending on the specific battle. If we can estimate the maximum practical speed at which troops could move across the battlefield, then a very simple calculation will give us the rough period represented by each turn for any particular engagement.

Our knowledge of ancient movement rates comes not from battles but from marches on campaign. Engels suggests that Alexander's army averaged only some 21 km per day, though small, light detachments were capable of up to 80 km per day.[29] A key reason for this variation was that the larger the force (especially if accompanied by an extensive baggage train), the longer that those at the rear of the column had to wait before even leaving camp. The same applied in reverse, with the vanguard apparently finishing their march around noon so that the rest of the column could catch up (as at the Sambre) – a factor that helps to explain why the Roman practice of constructing a fortified camp after every march did not significantly reduce the distance they were able to cover.[30] Scholars usually assume that, when actually moving, troops on the march proceeded at around 4–5 km per hour. On the battlefield, terrain irregularities and the deployment of troops in unwieldy linear formations rather than march columns would have slowed things up significantly, as seen in the trade-off between line and column formations in Napoleonic times.[31] It seems reasonable to estimate that even the double movement rate outlined above should correspond to a speed of only around 4 km per hour for infantry and double that for cavalry. This means that each turn would equate to around 3 min for every 100 m of distance represented by each zone, producing turn lengths of 10 to 40 min in round figures, depending on the battle concerned.

The linearity of battlefield formations (with the units in a particular zone representing a battle line tens of times wider than it is deep) has a further consequence in terms of the orientation of the troops involved. It is clearly unrealistic to allow units (like rooks in chess) to move and attack without penalty in any of the four orthogonal directions. Instead, we must record which of the four directions they are 'facing' at any given time, and treat changes of facing as a form of movement. The obvious basic trade-off is that infantry should be able to turn or wheel to any other facing direction within their existing zone, in place of their normal move of 1 zone forward. Cavalry should be somewhat more manoeuvrable thanks to the intervals between the squadrons, so changing their facing should cost 1 zone of movement, allowing cavalry units to move 1 zone and turn or to turn and move 1 zone instead of moving 2 zones forward. On a similar basis, each facing change should reduce by 1 zone the move entitlement of 2 or 4 zones available to units using double movement, so that double moving cavalry could turn in place, move 1 zone forward, turn again, and then move 1 last zone in their new frontal direction. These provisions allow flanking cavalry that have beaten their initial opponents to sweep round behind an enemy infantry line, as happened most famously at Cannae.

In some circumstances, it seems appropriate to waive these costs for facing changes, and thereby give troops greater flexibility. Light troops are the most obvious candidates for such 'grace', and allowing 1 free facing change per turn for light infantry and 2 free facing changes per turn for light cavalry seems an ideal way of reflecting their greater manoeuvrability at the grand tactical level. It was also easier for troops to make a complete about turn (perhaps using one of the various forms of 'countermarch') than to wheel their long unwieldy lines through 90 degrees in either direction, so we may permit a free initial 180 degree turn to any units that have not been outflanked.[32] This has the merit of allowing even heavy infantry to turn and fall back in the face of the enemy and so trade space for time, as happened at Cannae, the Sambre and Bibracte. Greek hoplites seem to have lacked the flexibility to prolong battle in this way, so it is worth excluding them from this waiver, but phalangites (despite their ponderous pikes) were more flexible, judging by reports of the ordered withdrawals they conducted at Paraitacene, Gabiene, Sellasia and Magnesia.[33] Finally, there is a good case for allowing units with no enemy immediately in front to change their facing without cost before attacking nearby enemies to their flank or rear. This allows heavy infantry to react more quickly to such flanking threats, and means that they cannot be assailed with impunity from these directions unless they are pinned frontally as well.

With around 20 units per side and just 5 front line zones, there will usually be several units in each zone. As unit depth is only a tiny percentage of the depth of a zone, it would be feasible in principle to cram an entire army into a single zone, but this would require the use of far more ranks than are ever attested in the sources. Hence, it is worth imposing a limit of 12 units per zone to dissuade such unrealistic massing of troops, falling to 8 units in zones where terrain features like woods, marshes, rivers or shorelines further constrain the space available.

Where such limits should really become significant is with poor-quality troops, who already rely heavily on numbers and depth to try to offset their individually lower fighting value. As each levy unit represents twice as many men as an average unit, making levies count double towards the above stacking limits forces massive armies like the Persians at Cunaxa and Issus to spread out in long lines that become vulnerable to concentrated penetration and breakthrough by less numerous but higher-quality opponents.

Passing contingents through one another in a 'passage of lines' was highly problematic in this era, as illustrated at Zama when Polybius (XV.13) describes Hannibal's three lines actually coming to blows rather than cooperating effectively. To reflect this lack of grand tactical fluidity, it is worth ruling that all units in a given zone must face in the same direction, and that units that enter a zone already containing 1 or more friendly units must cease movement and turn to the same facing rather than proceeding on beyond that zone. The only troops who escaped these constraints to some extent were Roman legionaries, whose manageable sub-units and unique multiple line system gave them the flexibility not only to conduct line relief in a frontal engagement but sometimes also to move reserves laterally behind the front as at Sentinum, the Metaurus, the Great Plains, Zama, Cynoscephalae, 2nd Chaeronea and Bibracte.[34] To reflect this, veteran legionary units may be given an additional option of treble movement, which allows them (unlike other heavy infantry) to turn sideways, move into an adjacent friendly held zone, and still be able to turn forwards again to comply with the stacking restriction previously discussed. This special treble move capacity has the added advantage that it offers an even better way of simulating Roman forced marches like those at Tigranocerta and the Sambre mentioned on p. 35.

In what order should the various units be moved during any given turn? Some modern simulations use sophisticated interactive sequences in which each army activates only a handful of units before the enemy gets a chance to react, but it is much simpler to employ the more traditional approach of having the two armies alternate in moving and attacking with all their units at once (or as many as their command capacity permits).[35] However, there is no need to have separate movement and combat phases within each army's half of the overall turn – a system that all too often makes no distinction between the fighting capacity of units that start the turn right next to the enemy and those that use their entire movement allowance moving up into contact.[36] Instead, the units in an army can be activated in any order desired, with some using that opportunity to move and/or change facing, others to attack nearby opponents, and still others to do a little of both within a common overall limit on their capacity for action that turn.

Existing simulations of ancient battles tend to begin with the armies arrayed as they were historically, just like animated versions of the diagrams in more traditional scholarship. I have already shown how important such diagrammatic reconstructions are to the development of an appropriate dynamic model, but I consider it essential not just to take the historical deployments as read but rather to integrate the deployment process itself into the model so that we may experiment with alternative deployments and thereby gain greater insights into why the armies were actually arrayed as they were. Planning and the associated intelligence contest are often key to the success or failure of military operations – as I write this, I have just returned from leading a tour by senior British Army personnel of the Arnhem battlefields, and getting these staff officers to consider alternative drop zones for the Allied paratroops was an invaluable means of bringing to life the intractable dilemmas faced by their historical counterparts.[37] In ancient times, armies were so unwieldy and command arrangements so primitive that there was little scope for changing plans during battles themselves – this made insightful deployments and prior instructions to subordinates even more central to the overall outcome, as is clearly illustrated by engagements such as Cannae and Ilipa.

Fortunately, the zone system offers an ideal vehicle for simulating the deployment process as well as subsequent battlefield manoeuvres. If we assume that each army is camped just behind its rear zone, or has marched up to such a position from a more distant camp, then its units may enter the board via their left rear, rear or right rear zones using standard movement rules. The initial zone can simply count as 1 zone of movement, with cavalry discounting any difficult terrain in that zone to prevent their deployment being unduly hindered. Cavalry or chariots may choose to deploy in their left rear zone facing left or their right rear zone facing right, while other units must deploy facing directly forward (as shown by the arrows on the zone diagram in Figure 2). This allows horsemen to fan out sideways into the two zones on each wing using normal 2 zone moves, clearing the way for infantry to occupy the 3 rear zones using normal single moves. The movement cost for deploying into a zone with an unfortified camp can be waived, allowing infantry to move on right up to the centreline – this does not apply to fortified camps, as the defences themselves tended to hinder deployment (as at Sellasia).[38] If command capacity permits, some units may instead deploy through double or treble moves, allowing them to advance further and so seize the initiative. Light infantry and elephant units may be allowed to make such double deployment moves straight forward at a discounted command cost, thereby encouraging their historical employment as a forward screen for the main infantry line. Figures 8–42 show all the various armies after 1 turn of deployment along historical lines, illustrating how well such straightforward provisions can mirror the patterns described in the sources.[39]

This very simple and seamlessly integrated deployment system offers a surprisingly powerful lens through which to view the actual arrays of the contending armies. Rather than merely placing units in their historical starting positions as reported in the ancient sources, we can now view their deployment as part of a dynamic and interactive process of grand tactical choice, guided by clear constraints of troop capabilities, command capacity and enemy reaction. Placing elephants on the extreme wings is far harder than deploying them as a forward screen, which helps to explain why cavalry could usually ride around the flanks of elephant lines as at the Hydaspes, Paraitacene, Gabiene, Gaza, Raphia and Zama instead of having to face the beasts head-on. Even an unusual and enigmatic array like that of the Persians at the Granicus (with cavalry guarding the river and infantry on a hill behind) makes a little more sense when one is reminded of the command constraints on this ill-led army – it is far from clear what better options existed in the face of Alexander's incisive generalship.[40] By making deployment an integral part of the model, not only may users investigate such questions in a systematic fashion, but also uncertainties about the actual historical deployment of the opposing armies may be tackled by asking which of the contending interpretations appears more rational and achievable in terms of the generic system we have created.

Ancient tactical writers disagree about the merits of being the first army to deploy, with Vegetius (III.18) advocating seizing the initiative while Onasander (29–30) instead suggested waiting so one could tailor one's own array to that of the enemy. The system of alternating turns perfectly captures these offsetting benefits and disadvantages, as long as one takes the elementary precaution of banning newly deployed horsemen from double-moving forward into the enemy half of the field to pre-empt enemy deployment altogether. Sometimes, one or both armies did not form the usual battle array before engaging, but instead fed in troops piecemeal into an escalating confrontation (as at Plataea, Crimisus, Cynoscephalae, Pydna and the Sambre). One could simply exclude such surprise engagements from the model, but it would be a shame to lose them altogether given the detail in which some are described, and it is possible to simulate them without entirely battle-specific rules by a simple provision limiting to 4 per turn the rate at which new units may be deployed in these cases (with heavy infantry and elephants counting double on turn 1 as it was usually light troops and cavalry that engaged first). Where such surprises did not occur, it was very rare for troops to be left undeployed except to guard the camp, so it is worth restricting deployments by unsurprised armies after the first turn to the rear zone itself, lest units be held back as an ahistorically flexible reserve force. The first turn in regular engagements may be considered an exception to the standard timescale, as scholars often suggest that it may have taken hours for large armies to deploy into battle formation, and because skirmishing could continue almost indefinitely as long as each side's light troops had a safe point of refuge.[41] Not until turn 2, with the start of serious combat, does the notional timescale of 10–40 min per turn really begin to apply.

The grid and movement systems developed in this chapter remain resolutely broad brush, in line with the grand tactical focus of the model as a whole. With a much finer grid and more complex movement rules, it might be possible to explore those few instances of detailed tactical manoeuvring that the sources do actually describe. As it stands, subtle flanking manoeuvres by formations at the ends of the infantry line (as at the Nemea, Cannae and Ilipa) cannot be represented directly, but only indirectly through the advantages that the veteran troops involved gain in straightforward frontal combat between the overall zones concerned.[42] Not only is this outcome-oriented approach much simpler, but it also avoids having to generate entirely speculative tactical reconstructions of the great majority of battles for which the sources contain no such fine details. The model still offers a great deal of insight into deployments and manoeuvres at the broader grand tactical level, as the reconstruction of Cannae in Chapter 6 amply illustrates. Before proceeding with that reconstruction, we need to develop systems to handle the two main outstanding elements of the simulation, namely fighting and command.

4

Fighting

Modelling the processes and outcomes of actual combat is invariably the most challenging part of conflict simulation, as the behaviour of thousands of individual soldiers in the face of mortal danger is far more complex and enigmatic than the relatively straightforward calculations of time and space associated with deploying and moving these soldiers on the battlefield. That is why the equations of analysts like Biddle and Dupuy are so detailed and impenetrable. One can, of course, fall back on simple rules of thumb such as the old chestnut that attackers should outnumber defenders by at least 3:1 to have a good chance of success, but such simplistic and unidimensional yardsticks can often be highly misleading. This applies especially in ancient battles, where raw numbers were such a poor predictor of success that there are probably nearly as many cases of victorious attacks at odds of 1:3 as at odds of 3:1!

Trying to construct a combat system based on detailed modelling of inputs such as weapon lethality seems doomed to failure in this case. This is clearly demonstrated by considerations of missile fire. Gabriel and Metz undertook practical trials and ballistic calculations that suggested that over 20 per cent of a salvo of arrows would strike individual targets within a densely packed infantry formation.[1] Wheeler came at the same issue from his own preferred basis of source exegesis, and made much of a little-noticed ancient claim that 1 javelin hit out of 10 shots represented poor marksmanship.[2] All of these authors remarked on the contrast between such relatively high hit ratios and the much lower figures for musket fire in more recent battles.[3] The problem, of course, is that in the ancient world the perennial contrast between theoretical weapon lethality and the degraded performance produced by the strains and stresses of combat was compounded by the lower penetrative power of the missiles used, meaning that a very high proportion of them could be stopped by armour and shields.[4] These same two factors operated to an even greater extent when it came to the effectiveness of close combat weaponry, and I have argued elsewhere that the visceral mutual dread of 'cold steel' that one finds in more recent engagements probably made ancient *mêlées* a much more tentative affair than Holywood epics would have us believe.[5] Given such yawning uncertainties, it seems hopeless to base our combat system on any form of casualty rate calculation grounded in the number and lethality of the weapons being brought to bear.

I suggest instead that we focus on the *effects* of combat as described in the battle accounts themselves. As discussed on p. 12, these accounts do often give figures for how many were killed on each side in the engagement as a whole, but these figures are usually highly asymmetric and include losses inflicted during the subsequent pursuit as well as during the fighting itself. Much more significant are the descriptions of the behaviour of individual contingents as the battle proceeded. By far the most common such description is of units breaking and fleeing in disorder. This could happen after a bitter and protracted struggle or (as at Cunaxa) at the first onset, without the unit having suffered a single casualty.[6] Flight was not confined to one side, and both armies often had troops flee in one sector while other contingents put the enemy to flight elsewhere. Sometimes broken troops rallied while still on the battlefield, and were able to put up renewed resistance – at Cannae, Hannibal's centre even went on to prevail over its opponents, but at Bibracte and the Sambre the stands were decidedly temporary affairs.[7] More usually, fleeing troops did not rally until they reached their camp or the shelter of distant hills, and often not even then. For the purposes of our model, it seems simplest just to remove broken units permanently from the board, and to simulate the rare instances when they rallied on the battlefield through a different mechanism, namely the voluntary retirement of units at risk of breaking, using the about turn provisions that I discussed on p. 37.

The battle accounts also make clear that good troops could sustain quite high levels of depletion and trauma without actually breaking and fleeing. Although the casualty figures suggest that fatalities among unbroken troops were very limited compared to the mutual bloodbaths of gunpowder-era battles, wounds seem to have been much more common (though actual figures are frustratingly scarce).[8] Physical and moral exhaustion was a further progressive drain on fighting fitness, and Roman writers in particular stress this aspect and extol their multi-line system as a means of relieving tired troops with fresh ones.[9] Ammunition depletion added to the mix, and eroded the effectiveness even of skirmishers who could not be caught or out-shot by their opponents – Plutarch (*Crass.* 25) has a lovely tale of how the Romans at Carrhae were at first quite sanguine and expected the opposing horse archers to withdraw after emptying their quivers, only to be cruelly disappointed when they realized that the enemy had had the foresight to bring a camel train laden with spare arrows. Caesar's eyewitness description of the parlous state of his 12th Legion at the Sambre (*B Gall.* II.25) nicely illustrates the progressive loss of resilience even among good troops after protracted combat, with almost all the centurions killed or wounded, and with the tired men huddling together in a vulnerable mass while some at the rear slipped away. At Pharsalus, Caesar's claimed losses of 30 centurions but less than 200 rankers (*B Civ.* III.99) indicate a sevenfold higher casualty rate for the former than the latter, showing how a force could lose its 'cutting edge' even without suffering crippling casualties overall.[10]

Clearly, we need to reflect such depletion within our combat system, and the simplest way seems to be to have all units start off 'fresh' but to allow each of them to become 'spent' through the process of combat, thereby making them more vulnerable to breaking and being removed altogether. How much fighting it takes to make troops spent should vary greatly, depending on the quality of the forces concerned. Good units could endure considerable punishment (as at the Sambre), whereas poor-quality troops could become spent simply through demoralization in the face of an advancing enemy (as at Cunaxa). It is this enormous variation in resilience that helps to explain why veteran troops deserve nearly a tenfold advantage in fighting value man-for-man.

Some simulation systems go further by having multiple levels of cohesion loss, tracking ammunition expenditure separately from combat strain, and allowing troops to recover if they are able to escape from immediate enemy pressure.[11] There might be a case for such greater sophistication if we were trying to simulate the preliminary skirmishing between cavalry and light infantry forces, which could last for hours or even days (as at Ilipa) as each side's troops withdrew to the safety of their main line to rest and regroup before sallying forth once more.[12] However, we are more concerned with the climactic contest between entire armies, and we are excluding later confrontations between regrouped forces like that in Paraitacene. Within a single battle, the main lines did not usually have the opportunity to regroup, except in the case of a prolonged stand-off like that created much later at Hastings between the Norman cavalry dominating the plain and the English shield wall on Senlac hill.[13] Hence, it seems best to avoid unnecessary complication and to have just the two conditions of fresh and spent for units that remain on the field, with the latter state being irreversible within the timescale of the simulation.

The next task is to define what relative positioning of opposing units constitutes 'combat'. Here, the coarse-grained nature of our simple 5 × 4 grid is actually problematic compared to the usual approach of having several hundred much smaller grid cells. As each zone represents an area several hundred metres across, it could be argued that opposing units should occupy the same zone to be considered in combat. However, this would introduce significant complications, especially when units are assailed from two or more directions. Therefore it is simpler to have units attack from their present zone into the one they are facing without actually entering that zone until all the enemy units therein break. Combat can thus proceed in the same way as movement, with activated units attacking into their forward zone instead of moving into it. This system has the advantage that it includes within 'combat' the intimidating effect of the mere approach of enemy troops, as at Cunaxa where the Persian infantry dropped their shields and fled even before the Greeks came within arrow range.[14] There is a case for compelling attacking units to advance into a zone if the occupants flee, but this might encourage excessive use of sacrificial units to draw enemies forward into a trap, so it is better to make advances voluntary for successful attackers.

Some units may be able to turn and/or move before launching an attack, though they should suffer a penalty compared to units that are in a position to attack from the outset. Horsemen should not be able to move before attacking into hills, woods, marshes or fortified camps, and the same should apply to attacks on zones containing enemy elephants because of the problem of getting horses to approach such beasts (as at Ipsus).[15] It is also desirable to prevent victorious cavalry turning in at once against the flanks of the enemy infantry rather than spending at least some time pursuing their erstwhile opponents (as at Zama).[16] This could be handled through complex provisions for pursuing off, and returning to, the board, but it is much simpler to reflect it more abstractly by preventing units in board edge zones attacking any of the 3 enemy centre zones if they have changed facing that turn. Newly deployed units and those using double or treble movement should also be prohibited from attacking, because otherwise it would be too easy to charge in from a distance and engage before the enemy has a chance to react.

The other key issue concerns how many units should be able to attack from a single zone. This is basically a question of force-to-space ratios and the value of formation depth. What makes it very difficult to tackle is the fact that the presence of several units in a zone actually represents a wide variety of real-life situations. It could signify a single deep battle line where each unit holds its own 'slice' of the front, or at the other extreme it could represent several successive shallower lines, as with Hannibal's deployment at Zama that had elephants and light infantry in the lead, then Celts and Ligurians, then Punic and Libyan levies and finally Hannibal's veterans from Italy.[17] Because battle line frontages did not vary anything like as much as army size, the number of extra ranks added by each average heavy infantry unit in a zone could range from just 1 rank at Marathon (500 m zones, 500 men per unit) to 5 ranks at Cannae (800 m zones, 4,000 men per unit). When one adds in variations of troop type and class that could at least double the frontage per file as well as doubling or halving or quartering the number of soldiers per unit, the sheer complexity of the problem becomes apparent.

A crucial offsetting consideration is that the duration of turns increases linearly with the distance across each zone, in order to maintain the rough equivalence of movement speeds discussed on p. 36. If combat proceeded at a constant rate, it might hence be expected to last for more turns in small battles and fewer turns in large battles. However, no such pattern is evident from the historical record – if anything, it was more common in smaller battles like Marathon and

1st Mantinea than it was in large engagements such as Cannae and Pharsalus for frontal contests to be decided before outflanking forces could intervene.[18] The explanation is presumably that the increased depth that larger armies usually adopted made combat last significantly longer, and so offset the greater time it took for grand tactical manoeuvres to take effect across the wider battlefields. By far the simplest way of handling this is to let the various offsetting factors cancel one another out, and to allow the same number of units per zone to attack in large as in small battles, so that combats take roughly the same number of turns in each case. However, we do need to reflect variations in zone width between different battles with the same troop multiple, and this is best achieved by varying slightly the number of units allowed to attack from each zone.

The combination of around 20 units per army with a 5 zone frontage gives an average of 4 units per zone, so attack limits of broadly this level seem to offer the best abstract reflection of the historical density in which armies deployed. If we divide the width of each zone in metres by 100 times the square root of the troop multiple (as army frontage and depth both varied roughly with the square root of army size as in Figure 1), then rounding to the nearest whole number will yield a figure between 3 and 5 for each scenario, as shown on the table below.

Zone width	Attack limit at the indicated troop multiple								
	1	1.5	2	2.5	3	4	5	6	8
300 m	3								
400 m	4	3	3	3					
500 m	5	4	4	3	3	3			
600 m		5	4	4	3	3	3		
800 m				5	5	4	4	3	3
1,000 m						5	4	4	4
1,200 m							5	5	4

This formula offers an ideal way of determining the maximum number of attacking units per zone for any particular combination of ground and troop scales. The limit can be increased by 1 if the attackers have other adjacent enemies (to reflect the increased length of diagonal rather than orthogonal battle lines), but this increase should not apply to attackers who have enemies to both left and right or front and rear, as such all-round threats would make it harder rather than easier to thrust in any given direction. The limit can be halved (rounding halves up) if fighting along the constrained banks of a stream, river or shoreline, as on the wings at Delium, in the centre at Sellasia or on the Roman right at Cannae.[19] We should also give the first attacking unit in each zone more chance of success, as there needs to be a system of diminishing returns so that attack effectiveness does not increase linearly with depth, and so that it matters which unit is selected to take the lead. Because combat was as much a psychological as a physical phenomenon, this system of having 1 lead unit followed by 1–5 supporting units attack from each zone provides a simple broad-brush alternative to keeping track of the detailed tactical positioning of the individual units within the zone concerned.

Now that we have a basic system of attack limits, we can introduce variations to reflect the differing type and quality of the troops involved. There were usually fewer cavalry units on the flanks than infantry units in the centre of the line (despite each cavalry unit representing only half as many men), so it seems appropriate that each mounted unit (other than the more densely packed cataphracts) should count as 2 units towards the attack limit, in line with Polybius's remarks (XII.18) about how wide a frontage they took up. Light infantry and elephant units with their looser formations should also count double unless they are the first attacking unit in their zone, with the latter exception encouraging their use as a thin screen along the front of the battle line. Conversely, veteran infantry or cavalry should count only half as much as other troops towards the attack limit, thus allowing them to concentrate their limited numbers more effectively to achieve a local breakthrough, as Alexander often did with his Companions, Hypaspists and Agrianians. Levy troops could in theory count as 2 units each on the same basis, but as they routinely formed up in great depth it seems better to count them normally towards the attack limit but to increase their own fragility when attacked.

Polybius's famous claim (XVIII.29–30) that Hellenistic phalangites fought in formations twice as dense as Roman legionaries has prompted considerable debate about the routine frontage per file of these two types of heavy infantry. At the tactical level, the explanation is probably that both troop types had variable frontages, with pikemen occupying 1.5–3 ft per file while legionaries took up 3–6 ft per file, these being the three standard infantry frontages identified by Asclepiodotus (IV.1–4).[20] The difference may be reflected at our grand tactical level by giving even average phalangites the ability to launch massed attacks in excess of the normal limits (hence encouraging their concentration in great depth as at Raphia) while depriving even veteran legionaries of this concentration bonus (thereby prompting Roman armies to use their unengaged rear lines for outflanking movements as at the Great Plains and Cynoscephalae). Average hoplites deserve the same ability as average phalangites to mass for attacks, to reflect their frequent use of deep formations (especially the Theban employment of columns 25 or 50 deep to break through shallower lines of even veteran Spartan opponents, as at Delium, the Nemea, Leuctra and 2nd Mantinea).[21]

If we are to base our combat system on units attacking into the enemy-held zone in front, we must decide if combat results should be mutual or should affect only the defenders. More detailed simulations often distinguish between missile fire (affecting only the target) and *mêlée* (causing mutual losses), but such a distinction is inappropriate at our grand tactical level. Not only was the difference extremely blurred, with missiles continuing to play a major role even after the onset of 'close combat', but (as mentioned above) ammunition depletion meant that even one-sided missile fire placed some strain on the firers themselves.[22] Hence, it is simpler just to fold all the enigmatic and controversial processes of tactical combat into one abstract mechanism, and to focus on the observed outputs in terms of units spent or broken. As regards whether attack results should be mutual, there are strong arguments for requiring both sides to attack to cause damage to their opponents, as otherwise troops could play for time and reduce their rate of loss simply by sitting idly in place near the enemy without absorbing any command resources. However, making attacking units entirely immune to losses would make launching the first attack unduly important, and so would risk creating too many 'stand-offs', with infantry facing each other across an intervening zone that neither side wished to occupy as the enemy would then get to attack first. Hence, a balanced approach seems more appropriate.

The obvious way to proceed is to give the attacker some discretion over the impact of each unit's attack. He can either inflict a certain degree of damage without suffering any ill effects, or inflict up to double the amount of damage by an all-out attack at the expense of having his own unit suffer some damage itself. The latter option would represent troops expending their missiles at a faster rate or charging boldly to close quarters in an attempt to achieve a quicker breakthrough in the sector concerned. Only fresh troops may choose an all-out attack (and thereby become spent), as it is unreasonable for already spent units to push themselves voluntarily to the point of breaking into flight. This system has the added advantage that it may be tweaked to reflect the nuances of certain troop types. Hoplites must always launch all-out attacks whenever possible because of the ferocity with which they charged in an attempt to reach a rapid result, while only light troops may launch all-out attacks against light cavalry, because other opponents lacked the speed and counter-fire capability to frustrate their delaying tactics and so could be kept in check – as was the Roman allied cavalry at Cannae.[23]

Differences in the pace at which combat was resolved were of fundamental grand tactical significance, and require much more than just a few tweaks to the option of all-out attacks. Cavalry combats tended to be decided a lot quicker than contests between heavy infantry other than hoplites, and many battles in the Punic Wars assumed the character of a race, with one side striving to win in the centre before being encircled and defeated by the superior enemy cavalry. At Cannae and Zama, the enemy infantry line held long enough for such a complete double envelopment to take effect, but at Bagradas and the Trebia some of the

Roman infantry were able to break through their frontal opponents and escape, showing how close-run the race could be.[24] Attacks by heavy cavalry on enemy heavy cavalry clearly need to cause around three times as much damage per turn as attacks by heavy infantry on enemy heavy infantry if the cavalry are to have time to beat the opposing horsemen, envelop the enemy centre, and make their presence felt in the continuing infantry struggle despite the abstract pursuit delay mentioned on p. 46.

What the *absolute* rate of damage per turn should be is harder to assess. Heavy infantry contests sometimes lasted long enough for other heavy infantry to intervene even after marching for several kilometres, as at the Metaurus and the Sambre.[25] Plutarch (*Aem.* 22) says that Pydna was decided very rapidly after only an hour's fighting, while Vegetius (III.9) says that battles lasted 2 or 3 hours, and Livy gives times generally ranging from 2 to 4 hours.[26] Caesar (*B Civ.* I.45–6) describes one infantry combat at Ilerda lasting 5 hours, but it was restricted to a narrow front and both sides were constantly sending up fresh cohorts to replace the weary. With each turn in the larger battles representing 20 to 40 min, this suggests that, in each army, roughly 1 infantry unit per zone per turn should become spent (or broken, if already spent). However, hoplite combat seems to have been much quicker; when Spartan hoplites defeated their immediate opponents at Nemea and 2nd Coronea, and began to roll up the enemy army from the flank, the other enemy contingents had already broken the Spartan allies and were caught returning to their own camp.[27] This suggests that hoplite attacks on zones containing enemy hoplites should receive a further bonus (except initially, lest the benefits of striking first encourage undue stand-offs), but that hoplites should be prohibited from advancing after combat if still adjacent to any enemy heavy infantry (thereby leaving them vulnerable to attack by any enemies who have already advanced onto their flank).

Combat is clearly the aspect of our model that most requires the inclusion of a random element to reflect the many unquantifiable details that could allow theoretically outmatched contingents to break through or hold out 'against the odds' in line with Culham's and Kagan's non-linear interpretation.[28] The easiest way to incorporate such random variation is to give each attack an appropriate percentage chance of inflicting a hit, thereby removing the need to record partial hits. Although this makes individual attacks something of a lottery, the large number of attacks during a battle allows luck to even out, reducing the overall amount of variation and making it easier to 'play the odds' based on local superiority in fighting values. Dice rolls are the simplest way of incorporating chance, and using two dice at once gives greater flexibility than using just one. The all-out attack option can be included by ruling that total rolls exactly equal to the number required either have no effect or cause both units to be hit (at the attacker's option), while higher rolls hit only the defending unit. To ensure that the odds of success increase by comparable proportions in the faster combats between cavalry or hoplites, a similar provision can be made for much higher dice scores than that required, with the attacker inflicting 2 hits if he exceeds the required number by 4 or more, or if he rolls 3 higher and chooses to make the attacking unit spent. The percentage chances of these different outcomes would then vary with the required dice roll, as shown on the following table.

Required two-dice roll	Chance of the indicated outcome			
	No effect or both units hit (%)	Defender hit (%)	Defender hit, or hit twice if attacker also hit (%)	Defender hit twice (%)
12	3	0	0	0
11	5	3	0	0
10	8	8	0	0
9	11	14	3	0
8	14	19	5	3
7	17	25	8	8
6	14	31	11	17
5	11	31	14	28
4	8	25	17	42
3	5	19	14	58
2	3	14	11	72

It is obviously appropriate that the first attacking unit in each zone becomes the lead unit that must absorb any hit from subsequent enemy attacks. However, once a lead unit is hit, including through its own all-out attack, it would be unrealistic to force it to stay in place and be broken by a subsequent hit while other units in the zone remained fresh. The beauty of using such large zones is that we can simulate the gradual weakening of whole sectors of the line by allowing players to replace their lead unit after each hit, thereby avoiding any units breaking altogether until all units in the zone have taken the lead and become spent. This abstractly simulates the usual situations in which each unit holds its own slice of the front or forward troops, such as light infantry skirmishers or Roman hastati, fall back through their supports once they have become spent. Players can still choose to leave spent units in the lead to become broken if they prefer – this would reflect unusual tactics like those of Hannibal at Zama, where Polybius (XV.16) tells us that he allowed his elephants and his mercenary and levy infantry to fight until they collapsed in order to weaken the Romans as much as possible before his own fresh veterans engaged. Only if a lead unit of fresh levies suffers

2 hits from a single attack is there a case for *forcing* it to absorb both hits and become broken rather than being relieved, as this reflects the rapidity with which poor-quality troops could collapse, and stops levies gaining unrealistic resilience simply by piling men up in enormous depth.

As with all-out attacks, this lead unit system can be tweaked to simulate the nuances of particular troop types or tactical situations. To reflect the use of light infantry as a skirmish screen that would retire through the main battle line once spent, we may rule that only 1 hit can ever be scored against fresh light infantry (even levies) as long as they are accompanied by at least 1 heavy infantry unit and every unit in their zone is still fresh. We can complement this by ruling that spent light infantry can never take the lead unless there are enemies directly behind them, in which case they *must* do so to simulate the vulnerability of sheltering skirmishers to cavalry encirclement – this softens the artificiality of having the same lead unit absorb attacks from whatever direction for simplicity's sake.[29] Scythed chariots can be forced to take the lead and can be removed automatically when subjected to a single attack, to reflect their use as an expendable screen in front of the battle line.

Elephants were more flexible and usually fought in a more integrated fashion with other troops, as at Magnesia where they were posted in the intervals of the phalanx, or at Bagradas where the Punic heavy infantry cut down those Romans who managed to force their way through the elephant line.[30] When elephant forces were defeated, this usually coincided with the defeat of the other troops with whom they had become intermingled, as at the Hydaspes, Gaza, Beneventum, the Metaurus, Ilipa, Magnesia and Thapsus.[31] Hence, there seems little reason to treat elephant units specially from a lead unit perspective, except to rule that dice rolls 3 greater than that required automatically inflict 2 hits when attacking elephants (without any need for an all-out attack), because of the well-documented phenomenon of panicking beasts getting out of hand and trampling their own men as well as the enemy. This penalty might seem rather weak, but anything more draconian would risk discouraging players from putting elephants in their usual lead position, and would unduly privilege the literary *topos* of pachyderms as a double-edged sword whose presence dominated battles for good or ill – at Paraitacene, Gabiene and Raphia, the large-scale elephant contests seem to have had only limited impact on the overall outcome of the engagements.[32]

Resolving combat as a succession of attacks, each by 1 individual unit on another, has the great advantage that it facilitates easy integration of the tactical strengths and weaknesses of each troop type against various possible opponents, as discussed on p. 23. To make heavy infantry combat proceed at the historical pace, each attack should require a dice roll of 9 to succeed, thereby giving each of the 3 to 5 attacks per zone a 17 per cent chance of inflicting a hit (rising to a 31 per cent chance if using all-out attacks). This in turn suggests that heavy cavalry should require a roll of 7 against other heavy cavalry, if such combats are to be resolved around three times as quickly. Light infantry and light cavalry fighting seems to have proceeded at closer to the pace of heavy infantry. There seems little justification for different factors in contests between heavy and light infantry, as the more open order of the skirmishers is already reflected in terms of attack limits per zone. However, heavy cavalry deserve a slight combat advantage over light cavalry to offset the latter's ability to change facing more easily and to avoid all-out attacks.

Heavy cavalry should be able to ride down light infantry, but should face significant disadvantages in frontal combat against heavy infantry (including, of course, their higher cost against attack limits). Conversely, light cavalry should be out-shot by light infantry but should have more of a 'stalemate' relationship with heavy infantry, being able to stay out of reach but not able to do significant damage given their limited missile supplies and the large shields of their opponents – a required dice roll of 10 seems appropriate in this context. Elephants should enjoy a huge advantage over heavy cavalry and a lesser one over heavy infantry, whereas chariots should be less capable than ordinary horsemen against light troops (due to their unwieldiness and vulnerability to missiles), but possibly fare a little better against heavy cavalry (to judge by their performance at Sentinum and Crimisus and against Caesar's horsemen in Britain).[33] The table below shows how these many possible tactical confrontations may be simulated by means of variations in the basic dice roll required for the success of each attack.

Attacking unit	Defending unit					
	Heavy infantry	Light infantry	Heavy cavalry	Light cavalry	Elephants	Chariots
Heavy infantry	9	9	8	9	9	8
Light infantry	9	9	8	8	8	8
Heavy cavalry	9	7	7	8	9	8
Light cavalry	10	9	9	9	9	9
Elephants	8	8	7	8	8	7
Chariots	9	8	7	9	9	8

To represent the many other tactical circumstances that could affect the outcome of combat, the actual dice roll for certain attacks may be modified up or down before comparing it to the required score shown on the table above. As I discussed earlier, the first attacking unit in each zone deserves a +1 modifier to reflect its front line role (except for the notoriously ineffective scythed chariots). Conversely, the last attacking unit in a zone can voluntarily suffer a –1 modifier in return for counting at half its normal rate towards the attack limit (to stop a unit that cannot quite fit in being left out altogether). Units that have moved or changed facing (even at no cost) before their attack should also suffer a −1 modifier compared to units already in attack position at the start of the turn. This plays a key role in offsetting the 'first strike advantage' in heavy cavalry combat, as a force charging from 2 zones away will get in the first blow, but this blow should be less effective than the impending enemy counter-attack. Differences in troop quality are mainly counterbalanced by the widely varying number of troops that each unit represents, but it is also appropriate to give a +1 dice roll modifier to all non-levy units attacking a levy unit, as otherwise there would be a strong incentive to place levy units in the lead wherever possible as expendable 'spear fodder', especially as they would in any case be the first to panic as army morale declines.

Modifiers can also be used to add more detailed nuances to the relationships reflected in the table itself. A lead unit of cavalry or chariots can suffer a −1 penalty if attacking elephants facing towards the attack, to make this option even more unattractive without one's own elephant or light infantry screen. Conversely, cavalry and chariots deserve a +1 modifier against heavy infantry if they are in the lead and are attacking from the rear, or if both units are in board edge zones, or if there are fresh cavalry, chariot or light infantry units in the attacked zone. This reflects the impact of horsemen attacking the rear of an infantry line as at the Trebia, Cannae and Zama, and it also penalizes heavy infantry that try to 'shield' more vulnerable troops, that anchor their flank on the board edge, or hang back in their rear zones to frustrate encirclement.

Attacking the enemy in flank or rear is often felt to justify massive combat bonuses, but this may in fact be exaggerated. At Ibera, the Romans easily dealt with encirclements on the flanks after putting their frontal opponents to flight, and at Telamon and Ruspina, troops fought for a long time despite having enemies to both the front and rear.[34] Insisting that all units in a zone face in one orthogonal direction is a simulation abstraction, and troops who have enemies to their front and on one flank may simply have formed their battle line at an angle to cope with this. Allowing a single zone to be attacked at full strength from 2 or more enemy zones while its occupants can only counter-attack in one direction (albeit perhaps with 1 more unit than normal) is already a significant advantage for the attackers. However, certain subtypes of heavy troops do seem to have bought their extra strength in frontal combat at the expense of added vulnerability to attacks from other directions. Several hoplite contingents were rolled up by the Spartans from their unshielded flank at 1st Mantinea, the Nemea and 2nd Coronea, even after defeating their frontal opponents.[35] Polybius (XVIII.32) and Livy (XLIV.41) emphasize the vulnerability of phalangites with their unique pike hedge to flank or rear attacks, and the same was probably true of close-order archers if the enemy could evade the 'beaten zone' of their arrows. Hence, attacks by heavy infantry (of whatever kind) on hoplites, phalangites or archers not facing the attack should receive a +1 dice roll modifier. Units with adjacent enemies to their front and rear or their left and right should also lose their lead unit bonus, to reflect the disruptive impact of having enemies on both sides. Xenophon (*An.* IV.8.9–19) exploited this to deter infiltration between the attacking columns used by the 10,000, and the same effect operated on a much larger scale at Ilipa, where Polybius (XI.22–4) describes how the Libyan troops were unable either to come to grips with Scipio's refused Spanish centre or to wheel against the Roman wings.

Other modifiers may be used to reflect the impact of terrain. A non-infantry unit, or a lead heavy infantry unit not in its own fortified camp, can suffer a –1 modifier if attacking into or from a wood, marsh, hill or fortified camp zone, because of the disruptive impact of these obstacles on anything except light infantry. Cavalry that started their turn in such a zone should suffer the same penalty even if they charge out into a clear zone before attacking. Conversely, there can be a +1 modifier for a lead infantry unit attacking downhill, and for any lead unit attacking into a river zone from a non-river zone (because the river impedes troops trying to cross or to fight with the water at their backs). These are fairly mild bonuses, but anything stronger (such as +1 for all units rather than just the lead unit) would tend to deter engagement and create unrealistic stand-offs – especially where the hill and river bonuses are combined, as at the Sambre.[36] Even fortifications do not deserve to give greater benefits in the context of an open battle, because hiding behind them surrendered the initiative and could encourage one's opponents, as at Issus. Therefore good troops usually sallied forth and fought in front of their fieldworks, as at Thermopylae, Sellasia and Magnesia.[37]

Modifiers are also the best way to reflect the characteristics of particular sub-types of troops. Archers should get a +1 modifier against light troops because of their ability to fight fire with fire, whereas African elephants should suffer a –1 penalty if attacking a zone containing Indian elephants because of their intimidation by the larger beasts. The faster pace of hoplite combat can be reflected by giving +1 to all hoplite attacks on a zone containing enemy hoplites (not just to attacks on hoplites themselves, because this would encourage players to spread them out in support of other lead units rather than deploying them separately as the Persians did the Boeotians at Plataea).[38] Fresh average hoplites and phalangites can attack with more units per zone by having non-lead units of this type attack in pairs, each counting as just 1 unit towards the attack limit but getting a +1 modifier against heavy infantry. A lead unit of fresh hoplites or phalangites also deserves +1 when attacking heavy infantry, unless the pikemen have been outflanked or are fighting in broken terrain, in which case Polybius's criticisms of the formation's flexibility (XVIII.31–2) come into play. Roman combat advantages are better represented by a –1 penalty for a lead infantry unit attacking fresh legionaries, thereby making Roman infantry contests last longer and encouraging opponents to lead instead with horsemen or elephants as was often done historically. Defending cataphracts deserve a similar –1 modifier unless attacked in flank or rear, as they were at Tigranocerta.[39]

Finally, there are certain special conditions that warrant reflection within the modifier system. The sources sometimes describe an army as suffering from progressively increasing fatigue due to its prior exertions, a lack of sleep or nourishment, or lower preparedness for extreme heat or cold (as at Sentinum, Trebia, the Metaurus, Ilipa and Vercellae).[40] This is easily simulated by imposing a –1 modifier on attacks by that army's units once they become spent. On other occasions (and sometimes the same ones), battles were affected by wet weather ranging from thunderstorms to morning mist. These conditions were not constant but could come and go, so it is worth identifying two generic weather states – 'wet' and 'overcast' – and having certain scenarios start with one or the other and toggle between the two on a single die roll of 6 at the start of any turn after the first. In wet weather, chariots, archers and spent light troops should suffer a –1 modifier because of the bogging down of wheels and the soaking of bowstrings (as at the Hydaspes and Magnesia), while the lead unit in a stream or river zone should suffer the same penalty because of the flooding of such watercourses (as at Crimisus and the Trebia).[41] These numerous dice roll modifiers make up what is perhaps the most complex single part of the entire model, but only a minority of them apply in most individual scenarios and they play a key role in making the combat system subtle and nuanced enough to channel player choices and battle outcomes along historical lines.

It was not just direct confrontations with opposing troops that caused forces to break and run. Panic could prove infectious (especially in the later stages of an engagement), and it was rarely necessary to defeat every enemy contingent individually in order to prevail. Such escalating panics were the clearest instance of the non-linear 'butterfly effect' to which Kagan alludes.[42] Some existing simulations of ancient battle go to the extreme of testing the morale of each unit separately, whereas others opt for a much simpler approach such as defining a 'panic threshold' of around 50 per cent and ruling that, when this many troops have already broken, the entire army will flee.[43] The latter approach is rather too simple for accurate simulation, as there were several instances (as at Cunaxa, the Granicus and Magnesia) in which large parts of an army fled in panic but other contingents in different parts of the field fought on.[44] Hence, we need a more nuanced but still quick and straightforward way of testing the morale of different units as the battle proceeds.

The best approach is probably to see every instance in which a unit breaks and runs in combat as a potential trigger for wider panic. The resulting test can be a two-stage process – first checking the morale of the army as a whole due to its overall situation, and then examining variations to that morale at the local level, which might prompt individual units to join the flight. There must clearly be a random element in each test to reflect detailed imponderables and to prevent players calculating in advance when panic will occur, and the simplest way of incorporating this is to roll a single die and halve the result, rounding halves up, to produce a basic army morale that is poor (1), average (2) or good (3). This value can then be reduced by 1 for every 4 friendly units that have been broken in combat, to reflect the demoralizing impact of accumulating losses. There should also be a gross measure of the shifting balance between the two sides, which can take the form of a –1 modifier if there are at least twice as many enemy as friendly units on the field, and a corresponding +1 modifier if the reverse is the case (to stop units panicking when their army seems on the brink of victory).

The other influence on overall army morale should be territorial. Hanging back in a cautious defensive posture could be demoralizing for one's troops, and this helps to explain Pompey's strategically unnecessary acceptance of battle on the plain at Pharsalus.[45] To dissuade inferior armies from staying back in their rear zones, and to avoid overuse of the tactic of pulling back and creating a pocket in front of concentrated enemy forces, there needs to be a morale penalty for enemy occupation of an army's 3 centre zones. This is best achieved by imposing a –1 on morale if at least 2 more friendly centre zones contain enemy units than there are enemy centre zones containing friendly units. We can also designate one of each side's 3 centre zones as a 'key zone' that counts double for this purpose, so that enemy occupation of that single zone will trigger the penalty if no enemy zones have been taken. Conversely, river zones should count at only half the normal rate, to allow for the defence of the friendly bank, as at Issus. This territorial morale penalty should be triggered permanently as soon as the enemy occupies a zone containing an army's camp, thereby penalizing too heedless an advance.

Designating key zones in each scenario helps to simulate a contrast I have remarked on elsewhere, namely that between asymmetric Greek and Hellenistic deployments (with one wing – usually the right – leading the attack) and the much more symmetrical deployments of Persian, Punic and Roman armies (with the best troops usually being in the centre and other troops being divided equally between the two wings).[46] A very simple way of reflecting this contrast is to make the centre zone itself the key zone for most Roman, Punic and Persian armies, while for most Greek or Hellenistic armies the left centre or right centre zone is chosen instead, depending on what best fits the deployment used in that particular engagement. This straightforward variable helps encourage players to use something like the historical grand tactics in each case, and reflects the contrast between battles like Leuctra and Gaza (where two opposite wings clashed head-on) and those such as Delium, 1st Mantinea, Nemea, 2nd Coronea and Raphia (where the right wing of both armies prevailed, giving a 'revolving door' effect in the battle as a whole).[47] It could be argued that Hellenistic armies, at least, should have some choice over their key zone when not using historical deployments, but this would give an undue advantage to the side moving second as their opponents would have no idea at all where they were likely to deploy, so it seems better to retain the existing assignments.

Once the overall army morale has been worked out, it can be modified to find the morale of each individual unit, though obviously only those units most at risk need to be checked in the first instance. Unit quality is naturally a key consideration, and modifiers of +1 for veterans or Indian elephants and −1 for levies need little further explanation. It is also worth having a generic +1 for heavy infantry, as they tended to stand their ground even after their flanking cavalry had fled (perhaps because they were so much more vulnerable to enemy pursuit). Legionaries were particularly stubborn and resilient, even in the face of calamities like those at Cannae and Carrhae, so average legionaries deserve the same +1 given to veteran troops. Hoplites, by contrast, could flee much sooner if intimidated by enemy hoplites such as the Spartans (as at 2nd Coronea), so it is worth denying them the usual morale bonus for being heavy infantry if there are enemy hoplites in an adjacent zone.[48] Turning to less intrinsic determinants of unit morale, having already become spent is a clear occasion for a −1 penalty, as is having enemy units to both front and rear or right and left. Conversely, being 3 or more zones away from where the unit that triggered the test was broken warrants a +1 to unit morale, as the panic effect would clearly diminish with distance.

This procedure will fairly quickly produce a numerical morale rating for as many individual units as might be at risk of joining the initial unit in flight. We now need to decide what the threshold should be below which these other units panic and run. As panic is infectious, there are good grounds for having troops flee more easily if they actually occupy the zone where a unit was broken, or if another friendly unit in their own zone flees due to that morale test. This may produce a 'chain reaction' in which the flight of some units causes others in the same zones to flee as well. However, the breaking or panic of light infantry should not have this knock-on effect except on other light infantry in their zone, as otherwise, spent skirmishers would be a severe morale liability and would have to be pulled much further back from the main line than they appear to have been in reality. Having units flee with a morale of −1 or less, or with a morale of 0 if another unit in their zone has just broken or fled, seems to give roughly the right balance of solidity and fragility to match historical experience. It means that, once all the units in a zone containing average cavalry or levy heavy infantry have become spent, each unit broken in combat will have a 1 in 3 chance of carrying all the others away in rout, and this chance will double after 4 units in the entire army have broken. To avoid 1 or 2 units hanging on unrealistically when the rest of the army has fled, we can rule that everyone automatically withdraws or routs as soon as that side has less than 3 units on the field or undeployed, counting levies as only half a unit each.

What one must remember is that the combat outcomes themselves may be largely morale-driven, and that attacks do not necessarily represent the actual use of weapons but may also reflect intimidating charges like that of the 10,000 at Cunaxa. Morale tests merely provide a means of amplifying combat results and spreading them to other units, including those not actually in the zone attacked. However, although the distinction between combat damage and morale collapse is extremely blurred, it is still worth differentiating between the causes of unit removal from the field. Units broken in combat may be termed 'shattered', while units that panic through failing a morale test or that move voluntarily off a board edge may be described as 'routed' if they were spent or 'withdrawn' if they were still fresh. One impact of these distinctions is that shattered troops will count more, and withdrawn and routed troops less, in the victory calculations that I will discuss in the next chapter, but equally important is the fact that only shattered units count towards the progressive morale reductions for every 4 units lost (to stop the early panic of masses of poor-quality troops from unduly discouraging the better-quality units that remain). These factors help to offset the impact of bad luck in early morale tests, and there will even be cases where players *want* units to panic rather than staying around to be shattered by subsequent attacks. In an earlier simulation, I included elaborate procedures for checking unit escape paths so as to reward complete encirclements like that at Cannae, but the added complexity did not seem justified in the present model given the unimportance of raw casualty figures as an index of victory (for reasons discussed on pp. 71–2).[49]

As I said at the outset, modelling the tangled physical and psychological interactions of opposing troops is necessarily the most complex part of conflict simulation. Even using abstractions and simplifications such as dice rolls, an irreversible 'spent' status and a standard attack limit of 3–5 units per zone, the resulting system will be difficult at first for non-wargamers to grasp. However, by focusing on generic grand tactical effects rather than on specifics such as casualty numbers or the precise location of opposing units, I have tried to keep the model as simple as possible while still retaining the differentiation between troops and armies that is key to understanding the varying course of the historical engagements. With morale being at least as important as physical factors in determining whether troops stood or fled, this more qualitative and broad-brush approach seems amply justified. It is now time to move on to the final, even less easily quantifiable, dimension of the battles: namely command and control.

Command

As I discussed in the Introduction, what makes conflict simulation such a useful tool for studying warfare is its combination of a mathematical model with continuous tactical choices by opposing players, a combination that mirrors the way in which real military capabilities are deployed by real commanders in an interactive battle of wits. Over the last three chapters, I have built up a model of the military capabilities of ancient armies, by defining the ability of different types and classes of troops to move and fight one another across a simulated battlefield. It is now time to 'give life' to this model by adding the element of command and control that determined how the armies were actually deployed and what manoeuvres and attacks they made in order to make the most of their theoretical potential. If we are to model this process, we must first seek to understand how command and control operated in the real engagements.[1]

One key consideration is that ancient armies were not animated by a single guiding hand, in the same way as inert chess pieces or playing cards are deployed by a single individual. Instead, the armies were composed entirely of animate entities in the form of individual human beings, and were distinguished (if at all) from mere 'crowds' only by the presence of a hierarchy of junior and senior officers who sought to exercise some degree of influence over the actions of their subordinates. How extensive these hierarchies were seems to have varied enormously – we know little of early Athenian officers below the level of the tribal regiments, each roughly 1,000 strong, whereas most Roman centurions commanded less than 100 men, and Thucydides (V.66) famously remarked that the Spartan hierarchy was so pervasive that almost their entire army seemed to consist of officers serving under other officers. These differences clearly had an impact on the command flexibility of the various armies, but even the most basic hierarchy contained many separate officers, all of whom shared responsibility for directing the actions of the army as a whole.

Although most hierarchies had at their apex a single man who in theory exercised overall authority, this was in practice heavily circumscribed by physical constraints. In the dust and noise of battle, no individual could be aware of what was going on outside his immediate vicinity, nor could he communicate orders, except by the use of signals or messengers or by travelling himself to the point in question.[2] This produced significant delays, as at 2nd Coronea, Gaugamela and Raphia, where generals leading the victorious right wing of their armies only learned belatedly of the problems occurring elsewhere, or as at 2nd Chaeronea, where Sulla spent most of the battle hastening back and forth behind the line rather than being on the spot when a crisis occurred.[3] Hence, it was necessary for generals to delegate considerable authority to their subordinates who were in a better position to exercise local command. Even when generals did despatch orders to such subordinates, they were not always obeyed, as at Plataea and 1st Mantinea when Spartan officers ignored instructions to redeploy because these manoeuvres seemed to them unwise or cowardly.[4] Sometimes there was not even a single authoritative voice in the first place, as in the coalition army at the Nemea, where the Thebans ignored the agreed common depth of 16 ranks and formed up considerably deeper.[5] What all this means is that the 'real-time' direction of armies during a battle was more of a collective than an individual endeavour.

This leads on to a second key point about ancient command, namely that pre-planning seems to have played a significant role in shaping what happened during the battle itself. The sources tell us frustratingly little about this pre-planning process, aside from several rather stereotypical and hindsight-driven accounts of debates between commanders over whether to engage at all.[6] However, associated snippets such as the discussions at Marathon and Nemea over how deep to make the line to stop it being penetrated or outflanked show that armies did seek to overcome the constraints on real-time command by pre-planning deployment and battle tactics during councils of war held in camp beforehand.[7] Hannibal's carefully calculated deployment at Cannae can hardly have been improvised on the spur of the moment but must surely have been planned at least to some extent before the battle, based on assumptions or advance intelligence about how the Romans would form up.[8] We know that gaining intelligence on the enemy army played a key role in the decision of whether to engage at all (hence the attempt to conceal Nero's reinforcements during the Metaurus campaign to tempt Hasdrubal into battle on unfavourable terms), so it is reasonable to suppose that second-guessing the enemy battle plan was also part of this intelligence contest.[9] Scipio's stratagem at Ilipa offers an excellent illustration of how this could work in practice, with the Carthaginians becoming accustomed over several days of confrontation to the Romans deploying with their best troops in the centre, only to rush out one morning in their usual array in response to a Roman advance and find that Scipio had reversed his deployment and strengthened his wings instead.[10]

Despite such evidence of prior planning, we should not assume that battles consisted solely of the working through of pre-conceived orders, as there was plenty of scope for unplanned actions and reactions to occur even within the deployment process itself. At both Issus and the Hydaspes, Alexander's opponents moved large bodies of horsemen from one wing to the other, with the Macedonians matching this shift with their own horsemen as they moved forward to engage.[11] At Pharsalus, Caesar (*B Civ.* III.89) says that it was only when he saw Pompey's cavalry massed against his right flank that he ordered several cohorts from his third line to move across to counter the threat. Such last-minute redeployments could be dangerously disruptive, as the Spartans found at 1st Mantinea, but it was certainly feasible to attempt them.[12] Indeed, as I discussed on p. 40, there were several occasions (such as at Plataea, Crimisus, Cynoscephalae, Pydna and the Sambre) in which one or both armies had to arrange their battle lines entirely on the spur of the moment, without having planned to deploy for battle that day at all. Once engagements were under way, such improvisations became even more common, and were sometimes initiated by junior officers rather than generals, as at Cynoscephalae and Magnesia.[13]

A direct simulation of this mixture of pre-planning, limited intelligence and local delegation of authority would require the use of several players per side, each with their own particular 'agendas', who might be allowed to concert together in an initial 'council of war', but who would then be separated and given information and command only over their own small part of the field, with orders and messages between them being subject to realistic delay and disruption. This would require equally complex and manpower-intensive umpiring arrangements within a 'mega-game' format, and so would take the whole system way out of reach of the individual users at whom it is aimed.[14] The only way of squaring this circle would be to use a computer-based system and to have artificial intelligence routines mimicking the decisions of everyone except the player himself, and this has usually proved a very poor substitute for real human inputs as well as embodying all the problems of opacity and inflexibility that I discussed on p. xx.[15]

As with the combat model discussed in Chapter 4, we should focus instead on creating a more abstract and output-based command system that is not only simpler but that requires far fewer players to operate. Indeed, it should even be possible for a single user to reconstruct the battles, by the simple expedient of playing each side in turn. Such 'solitaire playability' is a key issue for conflict simulations, because their users tend to be interested less in competitive play than in exploring for themselves the dynamics of the historical conflict concerned.[16] Just as academic game theorists are able to study situations like 'chicken' or the 'prisoners' dilemma' without needing another person to help, so it is important that users of our model be able to reconstruct ancient battles as dispassionate observers, interested far more in how the various capabilities interact and what this means for our understanding of the real engagement than they are in which side does better in any given 'refight'.[17]

Rather than taking as a starting point armies with prominent and capable generals, it is better to begin with forces whose overall commanders (if any) were so unimportant that we are not even told their names. Such armies (like the Argives at 1st Mantinea, the coalition forces at Nemea, 2nd Coronea, 2nd Mantinea and 1st Chaeronea, and the Helvetii at Bibracte) still managed to deploy and fight with some success, showing that it was the collective command capacity of the officers as a whole that provided the basis on which capable individual generals could build. The player's input should represent this collective command capacity, and the main role of the command system should be to *constrain* the player from using all of an army's capabilities to their maximum individual potential. This is best achieved by having inaction as the 'default state' for all troops, and giving players a limited number of 'commands' that they may use to activate particular units for movement or attacks. The resulting tensions over command allocation will tend to focus each army's efforts on what is most important and achievable in any given turn. There are clearly drawbacks to the player having such a 'god-like' overview when choosing priorities in this way, but he does after all represent a collective command structure rather than the viewpoint of any single individual, and it is far better to have human tactical input at every point rather than having the armies fight as mindless automata, as in models that do not incorporate this decision element.

The obvious starting point for the command system is to have each individual unit cost 1 command to activate that turn. However, this simple tariff would not in itself reflect the pressures that impelled large armies to deploy in considerable depth rather than extending themselves across an impractically wide frontage. Hence, there is a case for providing a 'group discount' for units that start in the same zone and make exactly the same moves or attacks. If it costs just 2 commands to activate any such group (whatever its size), then there is a real incentive to mass 3 or more units together rather than using each of them independently. The simplest 3-zone infantry line would then require a total of 6 commands to activate, and this would rise by 1 command for every cavalry unit on the wings (unless either wing had 3 or more units of horsemen, in which case the group discount would again come into effect). Because even poorly commanded armies could generally manage to advance and fight in a 3-zone line, this suggests that each side should have at least 6 commands available per turn. It should also be possible to activate any group to change facing and/or have just 1 unit of its total force attack for a discount cost of 1 command, to avoid whole sections of an overextended line becoming unnaturally passive and helpless.

Command availability should be greater for armies with higher fighting values (to reflect the greater flexibility of high-quality troops with better command structures), and there is also a case for significant random variation to reflect the many mischances of war (such as the insubordination at Plataea and 1st Mantinea). This suggests that each army should roll one die per turn for its commands, and add 1 to the total for every full 10 points of its fighting value still intact (hence yielding the desired minimum of 6 commands, even for 50 point armies which roll a 1). As surprised armies can only bring on a few units per turn, the fighting value of their undeployed units should be ignored for this calculation, thereby encouraging them to deploy higher-quality units first (as happened at Crimisus and elsewhere) so as to boost their future command availability.[18] In wet or dusty conditions, the command die roll can be halved to reflect the impact of visibility being even more limited than usual.

It should not be compulsory to activate all the units in a zone as a single group, as it may be preferable (if commands are available) to activate them individually or in 2 groups or more so they may move in different directions or at a different pace. However, to avoid major complications with attack limits, units should only be allowed to attack if they are part of an activated group including all the friendly units in the zone at that instant. This means that each zone can only be attacked by 1 group per turn from any given neighbouring zone. The system still allows a mixed force of cavalry and infantry to activate the cavalry alone, move them 1 zone, launch an attack from there, and then activate the infantry as a separate group to move up and reinforce the horsemen (though the initial lead unit in the zone will have to be the cavalry unit that attacked first, unless it became spent through an all-out attack).

As discussed on pp. 35–6, units should be capable of double (that is, full speed) movement if the commands are available. Activation for double rather than normal movement should cost 2 commands per unit, with no group discounts. However, light infantry and elephants that make a double deployment move directly forward as a screen should cost only 1 command each. Veteran units like Spartan hoplites or Alexander's Companions should also be able to make double moves at any time for just 1 command because of their lower troop numbers and superior command structure, as the variation of commands with fighting value would not otherwise be enough to reflect their increased flexibility of manoeuvre. To fit in with this veteran bonus in double movement, it should be possible to activate a group of 2 veteran units for normal movement or attacks for just 1 command, while treble movement by veteran legionaries should cost 2 commands per unit.

This system of varying movement rates is particularly helpful in allowing an abstract simulation of the second-guessing of enemy battle plans as part of the deployment process. Units may deploy either through group moves ending in the same zone or individually through normal or double moves. Having one army move first allows its adversaries to tailor their deployment better at the expense of letting the enemy strike the first blow in combat, but differences in command capacity modify this by allowing the superior army to rush more troops forward to its flank or centre zones on turn 1, so shifting the dynamic balance in its own favour. With key zones thrown into the mix to give the army moving first at least some idea of likely enemy deployment, the system offers a very effective indirect simulation of pre-planning and the intelligence contest. Units left undeployed on turn 1 are restricted (except in surprised armies) to entering the rear zone itself because keeping a grand tactical reserve so far to the rear was very uncommon in this era, no doubt due to the command problems involved in calling up such uncommitted troops in a timely fashion when communications were so primitive and no officer knew much about events outside his own immediate area.[19] As undeployed units would also have to be activated as a separate group from those already on the field, thereby diluting command availability, there are strong incentives for following the usual historical course and deploying everyone at the outset instead.

Once the armies close for battle, any spare commands should be able to increase the effectiveness of unit attacks by providing a +1 dice roll modifier, reflecting the inspiration provided by a greater commitment of the army's officers to that sector of the front. We do not want such bonuses to become routine lest they speed combat up unduly, so a cost of 2 commands per unit in addition to the normal cost of activation seems appropriate. Veteran units and Indian elephants deserve cheaper bonuses costing 1 command each if they are the lead attacking unit, as otherwise there would be no incentive to put them in front and risk losing extra points because of their higher fighting value. Light cavalry deserve to pay only 1 command for bonuses in all circumstances because their normal attack effectiveness is so low compared to other troops that it would not otherwise be worthwhile to allocate bonuses to them at all. These opportunities for faster movement or more effective attacks give players far more ways to spend commands than there are commands available, thereby fuelling the allocation tensions that I mentioned while also allowing most armies to manage full basic activation on most turns. They also create another dimension for player decisions to add to the existing stream of choices over lead units and all-out attacks, and so they help to prevent battles degenerating into mere dice-rolling exercises if the fighting bogs down for a while along a particular line. The various command costs are summarized on the opposite table.

Now that we have developed a basic command system to reflect the collective leadership structure within each army, it is fairly straightforward to add provision for individual generals. Most armies had just a single commanding general, but it was not uncommon for there to be a second leading figure, such as Alexander's deputy Parmenio, or a second Roman consul when the consular armies were combined. Hence, each army can have 1 or 2 generals in addition to its combat units. In some instances, we know the names of several other senior officers, but it is not reasonable to model them separately from the army's normal officer structure just because the evidence is available in these cases to do so. We may even want to refrain from including *any* of the known leaders in an army as distinct generals, as at 1st Chaeronea and the Granicus, where the sources record several named senior individuals in the Greek or Persian forces, none of whom necessarily deserve separate representation from the officers who are already integral to every army.[20] Conversely, where 2 generals are present we need to penalize their use in the same or adjacent zones, to encourage them to take charge of different wings of the army as happened historically.

Activity	Command cost
• Single unit activated for normal movement/attack • Group of 2 veteran units activated for normal movement/attack • Group activated for facing change and/or single unit attack • Veteran unit activated for double movement • Light infantry or elephant unit activated for a double deployment move with no free facing change • Attack bonus for an activated light cavalry unit • Attack bonus for an activated lead unit of veterans or Indian elephants	1 Command
• Any other group activated for normal movement/attack • Average, levy or elephant unit activated for double movement • Veteran legionary unit activated for treble movement • Attack bonus for any other activated unit	2 Commands

As with the troops themselves, the most important attribute of generals must be their quality, so as to distinguish between geniuses like Hannibal and nonentities such as Varro. Some simulations leave such distinctions to be reflected by the strengths and weaknesses of the players themselves, but I have already shown that the players need to embody a much more collective role.[21] From this perspective, the generals are 'assets' just like the units, and asymmetries in their capabilities should be a key element when trying to simulate a battle such as Cannae. Four classes of general should suffice, termed 'uninspired', 'average', 'inspired' and 'brilliant'. If the fighting value of an uninspired general (reflecting his overall contribution to an army) is 3, the same as an average unit, then an average general could have a value of 6, an inspired general one of 12, and a brilliant general one of 18 (not 24, because there are limits to what any single individual could contribute given the command constraints discussed earlier).

Giving one person a fighting value equivalent even to 6 average units each representing up to 4,000 troops might seem ridiculously excessive, but Wellington did famously remark that Napoleon's presence on a battlefield was worth 40,000 men![22] I showed on p. 24 how reconstructing the Punic army at Cannae with the maximum multiple of 8 gave a total fighting value of 60 for the troops themselves. If we add Hannibal as a brilliant general, and also include as an average general

Hasdrubal who led the crucial cavalry encirclement, the army's overall fighting value rises to 84 (60 + 18 + 6). The Romans, by contrast, deserve only uninspired generals to represent the 2 consuls, with an added value of just 3 each. This allows the massive Roman army to have a higher fighting value of 64 for its troops alone (as I discuss on pp. 77–8), while still giving the Carthaginians an overall lead of 14 points (84 – 70) to reflect their historical grand tactical superiority. It could be argued that the contribution of individual generals should be less in larger armies, but as the width of zones did not vary anything like as much as troop numbers, and as generals gave a 'force multiplier' effect rather than a separate absolute bonus, it is simpler (as with unit attack limits) to stick with a single common system.

Generals will marginally increase their army's available commands simply by increasing the overall fighting value, but this is nothing like enough of a positive impact. Their main contribution must be to give command bonuses at the local level to units that start in the same zone. The simplest way of handling this is through exemptions from the normal command costs of unit or group activation. Uninspired generals can give an exemption worth 1 command per turn, average generals one worth 2 commands, and inspired and brilliant generals one worth 4 commands. Generals can also give similar and separate exemptions from the command costs of attack bonuses for a group to which they are attached. Hence, an average general could both activate a group and give the lead unit an attack bonus for free, allowing the 2 commands that would normally have been spent on activation to be used for a further attack bonus or to activate another group elsewhere instead. The resulting increases in an army's ability to manoeuvre and/ or fight offer a very appropriate reflection of the tactical and moral leadership that generals were able to provide, as at Cannae where the Carthaginian tactics of holding against overwhelming numbers in the centre while extending their wings to envelop the Romans were only possible through the command flexibility that Hannibal and Hasdrubal gave.

Brilliant generals should also contribute something more, namely the ability to throw the enemy off balance by clever grand tactics at the level of the battlefield as a whole. Examples would include Alexander's drive into a gap in the Persian line at Gaugamela, Hannibal's use of Mago's ambush forces against the Roman rear at the Trebia, and Caesar's use of reserve infantry against Pompey's cavalry at Pharsalus.[23] Such strokes of genius are inevitably unique and *sui generis*, but if there is any common factor it is the ability of these generals to seize an opportunity and exploit it before the enemy could react. A good way to simulate this is to have brilliant generals start off moving second in each turn, but let them reverse this at any one moment of their choice so that they go first in every turn thereafter. This gives them the best of both worlds, allowing them to react to the enemy deployment while also seizing the initiative and getting in the first blow, as Scipio did so effectively at Ilipa. Having 2 activation opportunities in a row allows troops to move up from a distance and then attack, or to break through and then exploit into the enemy rear, as at the Trebia and Cannae. A similar 'flip-flop' mechanism can be used to reflect the *mutual* opportunities for surprise when the battlefield was enveloped in unusually dense clouds of dust as at Gabiene or Vercellae – here, the order of movement can be decided by a random die roll at the start of every turn, thereby creating pervasive and continuing uncertainty.[24] However, to stop such 'flip-flops' in either context becoming unduly devastating in straightforward frontal combat, we should rule that attacks cannot be launched from the same zone in 2 successive turns if the enemy has had no chance to react in between.

A continuing tension throughout this period was between the Homeric ideal of the general as 'heroic warrior' and the later image as espoused by Onasander (33) of the general as 'battle manager' who should stay away from combat and focus on providing tactical direction. Actual practice tended to shift from the former towards the latter model as the era progressed, but there was plenty of blurring of the boundaries as commanders sought to have (or at least to convey the image of having) the best of both worlds.[25] Alexander judiciously directed the initial engagement of his forces before plunging into the maelstrom of personal combat (as at the Granicus), Pyrrhus pursued a similar dual approach at Heraclea, and even Sulla and Caesar offered personal inspiration at the front line in times of crisis.[26] Clearly, we need some means of giving every general the option of such front line intervention if circumstances warrant, while also reflecting the gradual trend away from routine leadership by example as time went on.

A useful starting point is to divide generals into two broad types – 'leaders' like Alexander or Antiochus III, who were accompanied by a significant body of guard troops, and 'commanders' such as Sulla or Caesar, who could range the battlefield more independently (as at 2nd Chaeronea or the Sambre).[27] The distinction is not always easy to make, and sometimes a category may be chosen partly to reflect the historical course of a given battle – hence, Ptolemy at Raphia is best classified as a commander because he was able to escape and join his infantry centre after the rout of his cavalry on the left wing, while Varro at Cannae the following year is better portrayed as a leader, as he was carried away with the routing horsemen in very similar circumstances.[28] Leaders may be considered attached to a specific guard unit. When in the lead, the unit receives 2 attack bonuses rather than 1 (as long as both are covered by the leader's exemption) to reflect the enormous moral power of a charge led in person by someone like Alexander. Commanders may accompany any units, either joining a particular group so it may benefit from their attack bonus exemptions that turn, or being redeployed independently to any other friendly zone. Leaders are lost if their guard unit withdraws, routs or is shattered, while commanders are lost if every unit in their zone withdraws, routs or is shattered. Lost generals are mostly assumed to have fled the field, though they may instead have been captured like Porus at the Hydaspes or Regulus at Bagradas, or even given way to suicidal despair like Decius at Sentinum, Paullus at Cannae, Hasdrubal at the Metaurus or Cassius at Philippi.[29]

The potential risks and benefits of personal involvement in combat may be simulated by allowing players the option of using a general to try to cancel any hit inflicted on that zone except one sustained through the unit's own all-out attack. This gamble may be resolved by rolling two dice. On a high total score (ranging from 10 or more for uninspired generals to 8 or more for brilliant generals), the rally attempt succeeds and the hit is cancelled. However, on a roll of 2 or 3, the general himself is killed (though inspired or brilliant leaders who roll a 3 escape with just a temporarily disruptive close shave, like that of Alexander at the Granicus or Pyrrhus at Heraclea).[30] These odds have been chosen so that the net victory point consequences as discussed below are roughly balanced (a 28 per cent chance of an average leader saving 3 points by rallying an average unit, versus an 8 per cent chance of losing 12 points by getting himself killed), and also so that the likeliest outcome is for there to be no effect either way. Leaders should be forced to attempt a rally if their own guard is hit, and hoplite leaders should be forced to try to rally any other hoplite unit in their zone (because leadership from the front was so routine in this era that even *victorious* generals like Callimachus, Brasidas and Epaminondas sometimes paid for their triumph with their own lives).[31] Conversely, commanders (as distinct from leaders) should be prohibited from trying to rally units unless they would otherwise be shattered altogether, and the chances of a commander dying in such a 'last ditch' effort should be doubled because of the absence of a dedicated guard unit. This system adds yet another dimension of player choice to the combat model, and the increased element of luck that it introduces directly mirrors the risks that the real generals ran when they prejudiced their personal safety in order to inspire their men.

This leads us directly to the final issue concerning generals, namely their impact on army morale. The positive aspects have already been covered in terms of attack bonuses and rally attempts, and there seems little case for further generic benefits except perhaps to give units in the same zone as an inspired general or within 1 zone of a brilliant general a +1 morale modifier. The latter provision helps to simulate how Hannibal, in the centre of his infantry line, held his men together for so long in the face of fierce Roman attacks at both Cannae and Zama.[32] The death of a general during a failed rally attempt should trigger a morale test just like the shattering of a unit, and there is a clear case for deducting 1 point from the morale of an army if its general has been lost or killed. The exception is that the loss or death of a single uninspired general should not trigger this modifier, because such generals (like Callimachus at Marathon, Hanno at Tunis, Decius at Sentinum, Varro at Cannae and Publius at Carrhae) would not be risked by players of the simulation as much as they were historically if their loss had such a serious overall consequence.[33] Average generals were a different matter, and a good way of representing a significant but timid figurehead such as Darius III at Issus or Gaugamela, Perseus at Pydna or Tigranes at Tigranocerta, is as an average leader of an average cavalry unit, but with a morale penalty to reflect the general's own lack of resolution.[34] Such a timid general can be banned from trying to rally even his own guard, and he is likely to flee the field far earlier than a comparable leader of heavy infantry or veteran cavalry, thereby causing the wider morale collapse on which Alexander historically relied. These weaknesses can be offset by halving the leader's fighting value. The following table summarizes the attributes of the various kinds of generals.

Class and type	Fighting value	Command exemption	Rally success	Rally risk	Morale bonus	Loss penalty
Uninspired leader	3	1	10–12	2,3	0	0
Uninspired commander	3	1	(10–12)	2,3,4	0	0
Timid average leader	3	2	–	–	0	−1
Average leader	6	2	9–12	2,3	0	−1
Average commander	6	2	(9–12)	2,3,4	0	−1
Inspired leader	12	4	9–12	2,(3)	Own zone	−1
Inspired commander	12	4	(9–12)	2,3	Own zone	−1
Brilliant leader	18	4	8–12	2,(3)	Adj. zone	−1
Brilliant commander	18	4	(8–12)	2,3	Adj. zone	−1

Just as game theory relies fundamentally on the varying pay-offs attached to the possible player choices, so any conflict simulation that has the opposing forces governed by human decisions rather than artificial directives must include 'victory conditions' to channel player choices along historically plausible lines.[35] As discussed on pp. 12–15, actual battle outcomes in terms of casualties tended to be highly asymmetric, with the victors often escaping amazingly lightly while the losers suffered horrendous attrition in the ensuing pursuit. This is why the most important grand tactical decision of all was whether to accept battle in the first place. The modern science of operational analysis was expressly developed to make such tactical choices more rational and less based on preconceptions and wishful thinking, and an inescapable artificiality in our mathematical model is that (despite the inclusion of a significant random element) battle outcomes and probabilities are more calculable than they would have been to the real ancient generals.[36] If we were to base player rewards on the most obvious and 'realistic' yardstick of the number of simulated casualties received and inflicted, then by far the most rational choice for an army with significantly inferior fighting value would be not to engage at all.

Fortunately, the very artificiality of our model makes it possible to offset this unrealistic degree of calculability by imposing a different set of reward criteria, more reflective of the fact that the fateful decision to engage has already been taken. The best way forward is to avoid making victory points directly proportional to casualties suffered, and to penalize voluntary withdrawal such that even an utterly outclassed army cannot win simply by retiring out of reach. This must be accompanied by the creation of a handicap system that allows an inferior army to win a 'game victory' even if it is driven from the field, as long as it inflicts greater damage on the enemy in the process than it managed to do historically. Although these measures are rather artificial, they are infinitely preferable to the alternative of creating a balanced contest by giving both armies the same chance of winning a real battlefield victory.[37]

Each army should receive victory points at the end of the battle for damage inflicted on the enemy. Awards equal to the fighting value of all spent, withdrawn or routed enemy units and lost enemy generals plus twice the fighting value of all shattered enemy units and killed enemy generals offer an obvious starting point, and mean that there is no victory point incentive to absorb hits with spent rather than fresh units or vice versa, because either option costs the same number of points. The fact that the shattered units have probably suffered at least 10 times as many casualties as those that are only spent is immaterial for this purpose, as 'spent' status offers an ideal means of tracking the wearing down of a superior army by wounds and exhaustion, even if its fatalities have been minimal and none of its units have fled. Armies should gain 1 additional victory point for each enemy unit routed. This is a far less draconian penalty than for units that retire while still fresh, thereby giving inferior armies an incentive to inflict as much mutual attrition as they can manage before breaking altogether. The losing army should also get 5 victory points if it managed to raid the enemy camp before withdrawing, as at 2nd Coronea. If one army suffered from fatigue or surprise, this can be compensated by awarding that side an extra 20 or 30 victory points respectively.

The army with the lower initial fighting value should receive twice the difference as a handicap bonus. Even with such a substantial handicap, the superior army is likely to gain slightly more victory points because of cascading losses during a morale collapse, but there is always a chance that an army that is only moderately inferior will upset the odds and drive its enemies from the battlefield instead, thereby achieving a far higher victory point margin because the better army has more points to lose and the handicap bonus will add to the difference rather than reducing it. To reward such success, and to encourage players to do their best to limit the scale of defeat even when game victory seems out of reach, we should have a gradation of victory levels, ranging from a narrow victory if the margin is less than 25 to a stunning victory if it is 100 or more.

Trying to fix a maximum number of turns for each battle based on estimates of how early or late in the day the battle started, when the sun set in that season and location, and how long a period each turn represents, would be a challenging endeavour in itself. However, there is no real need to attempt this, as refights will usually conclude after several turns with the collapse of one side's morale. Hence, we can arbitrarily fix a maximum duration of 10 turns for the simulation (representing between 1.5 and 6 hours of fighting, based on the timescale derived on p. 36). If both sides still have units on the board at that point, the battle is assumed to have had the kind of equivocal result seen at 2nd Mantinea, Paraitacene or Carrhae, but game victory can still be judged using the standard victory point system. This is the final element needed to complete the model, and we should now be in a position to reconstruct and refight most open field land battles in antiquity for which a certain minimum amount of information survives. The system developed and explained over the last four chapters is set out in a more concise and precise form in Appendix 1, and readers are encouraged to review this now to remind themselves of the key details. In the next chapter, we will reinforce this review process through practical example, by exploring on a step-by-step basis how the model can simulate the historical course of the Battle of Cannae.

Zone Width (metres)
1200
1000
800
600
400
200
1
2
3
4
5
6
7
8
Fig.1
Troop Multiple

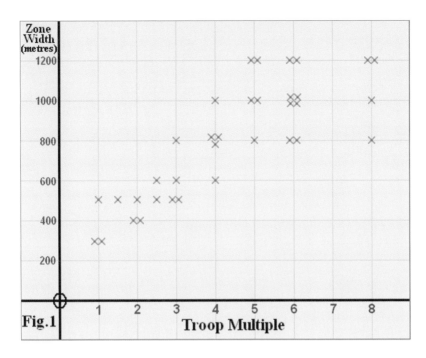

Figure 1: Graph showing how army frontage in the 35 battles increased only in proportion to the square root of army size – see pp. 31–2.

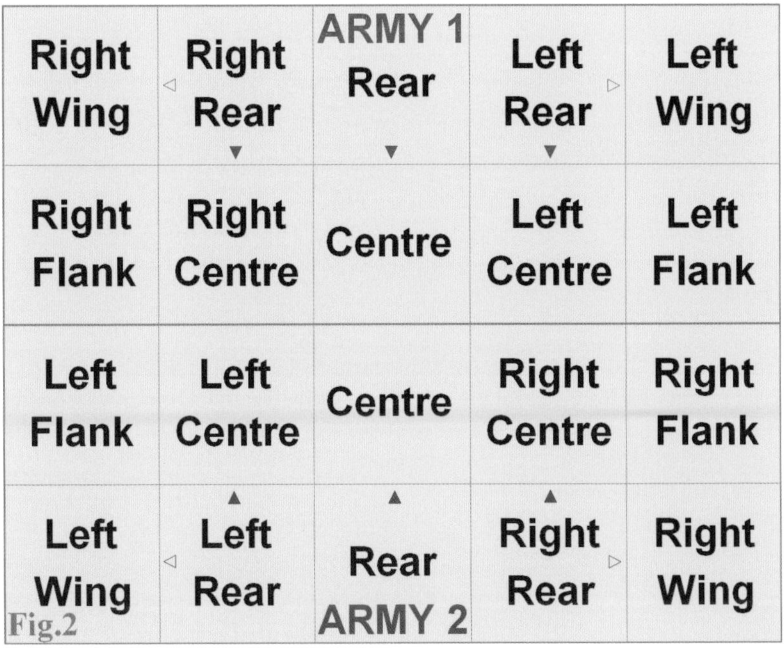

ARMY 1
Right Wing
Right Rear
Rear
Left Rear
Left Wing
Right Flank
Right Centre
Centre
Left Centre
Left Flank
Left Flank
Left Centre
Centre
Right Centre
Right Flank
Left Wing
Left Rear
Rear
Right Rear
Right Wing
ARMY 2
Fig.2

Figure 2: The 5 × 4 array of zones into which battlefields are divided for the purposes of the model, as discussed on pp. 30–33.

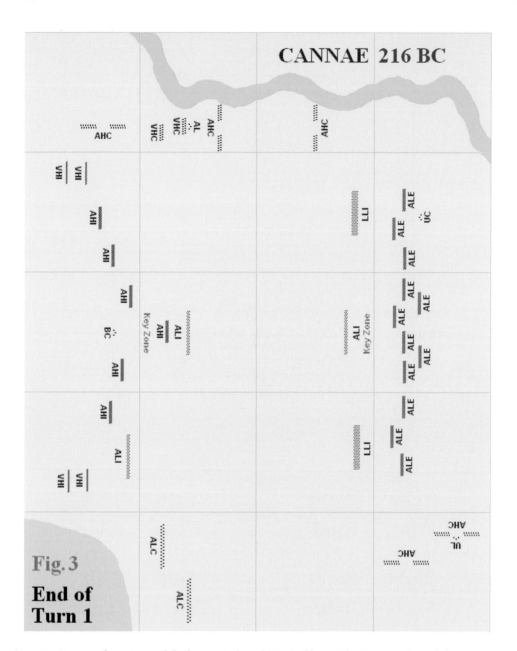

Figure 3: Cannae after 1 turn of deployment along historical lines. The Romans (in red) have massed their numerous legionaries for a central breakthrough, while Hannibal has concentrated his superior cavalry by the river and plans to play for time with the rest of his line – see pp. 77–81, and the key in figure 7.

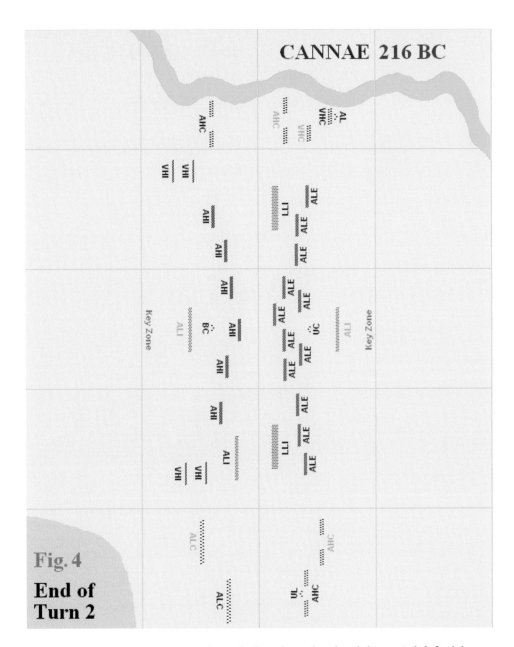

Figure 4: One turn (about 25 minutes) later, the lines have closed and the Punic left flank horsemen have prevailed after a hard fight – see pp. 81–3. Units which have become 'spent' are indicated by lighter text (requiring only a simple mouse click in the PC version). This reflects the progressive exhaustion of both sides without inflicting the unrealistic mutual carnage seen in some other simulations.

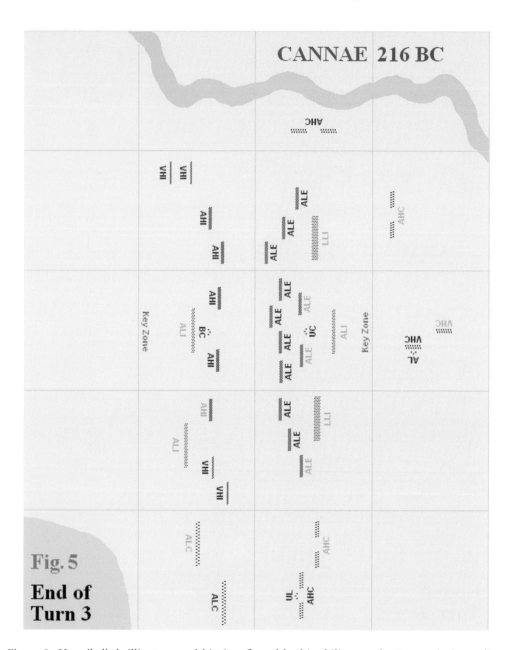

CANNAE 216 BC

Fig. 5

End of
Turn 3

Figure 5: Hannibal's brilliant generalship is reflected by his ability to take 2 turns in immediate succession, allowing his victorious cavalry to curve round into the Roman rear before they can react. The Numidian light horse on the Punic right flank are fighting a successful delaying action, but in the centre the Celtic and Spanish infantry are suffering at the hands of the massed legions – see pp. 83–4.

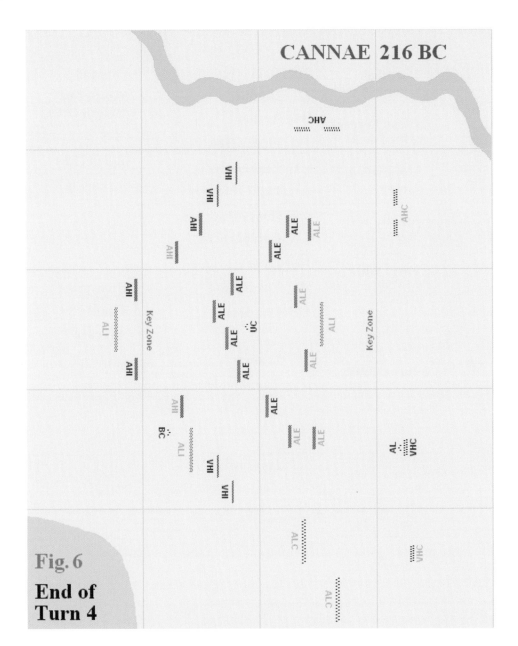

Figure 6: The weakened Punic centre pulls back to trade space for time, while Varro's horsemen on the Roman left finally flee as their rear is threatened. The legions are now well and truly encircled, but it will still be a struggle for Hannibal's cavalry and veteran African spearmen to turn the tide. As discussed on pp. 84–8, modelling and refighting the battle in this way provides numerous insights not readily available from traditional scholarship.

Fig.7 MAP KEY

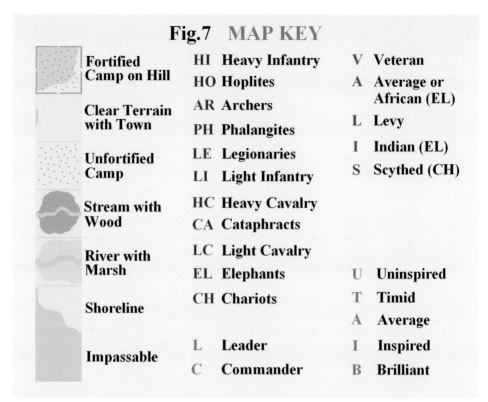

Fortified Camp on Hill	HI Heavy Infantry	V Veteran
	HO Hoplites	A Average or African (EL)
Clear Terrain with Town	AR Archers	
	PH Phalangites	L Levy
Unfortified Camp	LE Legionaries	I Indian (EL)
	LI Light Infantry	S Scythed (CH)
Stream with Wood	HC Heavy Cavalry	
	CA Cataphracts	
River with Marsh	LC Light Cavalry	
	EL Elephants	U Uninspired
Shoreline	CH Chariots	T Timid
		A Average
Impassable	L Leader	I Inspired
	C Commander	B Brilliant

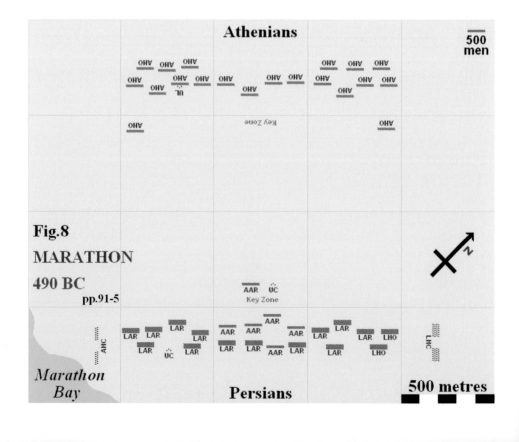

Athenians

500 men

Fig.8

MARATHON

490 BC

pp.91-5

Marathon Bay

Persians

500 metres

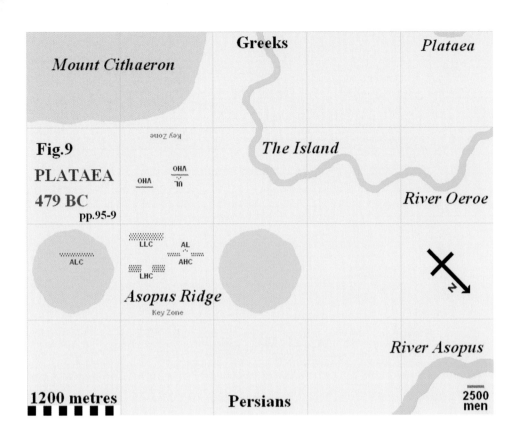

Fig.9
PLATAEA
479 BC
pp.95-9

Mount Cithaeron

Greeks

Plataea

The Island

River Oeroe

Key Zone

OHA   OHA
    UL

LLC   AL
ALC   AHC
    LHC

Asopus Ridge
Key Zone

N

River Asopus

1200 metres

Persians

2500
men

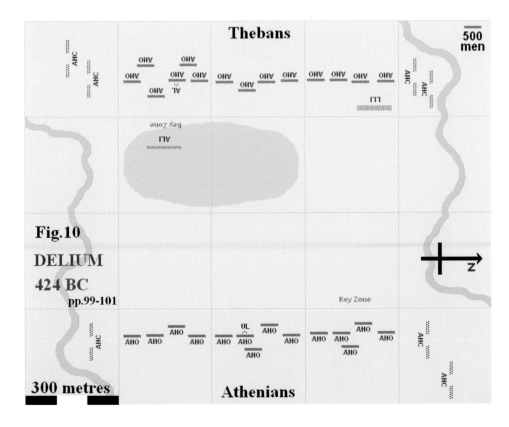

Fig.10
DELIUM
424 BC
pp.99-101

Thebans

500
men

AHC
AHC

OHA   OHA
OHA   OHA OHA OHA   OHA OHA OHA OHA OHA OHA
    OHA   AL OHA   LLI

AHC
AHC

Key Zone
ALI

N

Key Zone

AHC

AHO
AHO AHO   AHO

UL   AHO
AHO AHO   AHO   AHO AHO   AHO
    AHO   AHO

AHC

300 metres

Athenians

AHC

Argives

750 men

Fig.11
1st MANTINEA
418 BC
pp.101-5

500 metres

Spartans

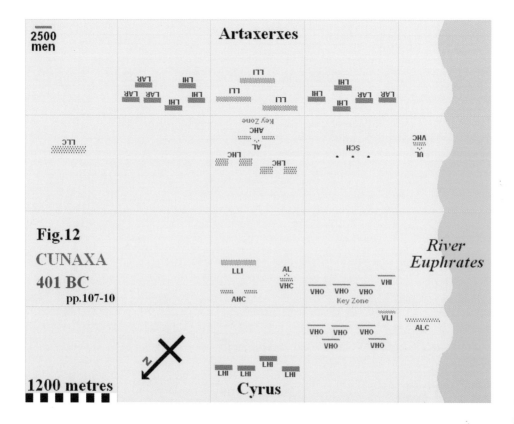

2500 men

Artaxerxes

Fig.12
CUNAXA
401 BC
pp.107-10

River Euphrates

1200 metres

Cyrus

The Model in Operation

In Part II, I develop full 'scenarios' for 35 individual battles by interpreting the evidence we have in terms of the model created in Part I. Each scenario has a map (Figures 8–42) that shows any terrain features within the various zones, as discussed on p. 34. Where possible, these terrain features are named to show their correspondence to those identified within the ancient sources or apparent from the modern topography. Each map is oriented so that the army moving first enters from the top edge, and I indicate on the map roughly which direction is north (if known). I also give an approximate scale width for each zone, based on the actual topography or on calculations and scholarly estimates of army frontage as discussed on pp. 31–2. The 2 'key zones' that affect morale as outlined on pp. 57–8 are indicated, as are rear zones containing an army's camp. Fortified camps have darker zone borders to distinguish them from unfortified ones. Figure 7 provides a comprehensive key to show how these various pieces of information are conveyed within individual maps.

The other element of each scenario is the reconstruction of the armies and their generals. The first key factor is the troop multiple (M), which determines roughly how many actual troops each unit represents (as shown in the table on p. 27), and that combines with the ground scale to produce an attack limit (AL) of 3, 4 or 5 units per zone. I then list how many units of each type, subtype and class the army contains, starting with the army moving first. I give an illustrative attribution for each unit, to link it in with the real army composition as given in the sources. These attributions can only be approximate, because the artificial breakdown of each army into standard-sized units very rarely corresponds exactly with the specific numbers given by the sources for individual contingents, and because the use of a mix of units of different classes cannot always be linked to clear distinctions in fighting value between the actual troops. For example, in a Roman army with a mixture of veteran and average legionary units, to call the veteran troops 'Roman' and the average ones 'Allied' is convenient, but significantly exaggerates the actual difference in fighting power – the main thing is that the overall mixture should give the army as a whole something like its historical effectiveness. Generals are shown either separately (if commanders) or with their guard unit (if leaders), the overall fighting value (FV) of each army is calculated, and a note is made of any initial weather conditions or if either army is surprised or fatigued. For convenience, the listings use straightforward acronyms, as shown in the table below.

Unit class	Unit type/subtype	Generals
V: Veteran	HI: Heavy infantry	UL: Uninspired leader
A: Average (or African EL)	HO: Hoplites (HI)	UC: Uninspired commander
L: Levy	AR: Archers (HI)	TL: Timid average leader
I: Indian (EL)	PH: Phalangites (HI)	AL: Average leader
S: Scythed (CH)	LE: Legionaries (HI)	AC: Average commander
	LI: Light infantry	IL: Inspired leader
	HC: Heavy cavalry	IC: Inspired commander
	CA: Cataphracts (HC)	BL: Brilliant leader
	LC: Light cavalry	BC: Brilliant commander
	EL: Elephants	
	CH: Chariots	

The map and the army listings between them give all the information required to refight the battle using free initial deployment, with each army entering the field on turn 1 using the standard movement and command systems discussed in Chapters 3 and 5. However, it is also worth modelling the actual historical disposition of the armies, to see if it is attainable and makes sense within the free deployment system, and to check whether the subsequent fighting proceeds along broadly similar lines to what took place in reality. Hence, each map shows not just the terrain but also a proposed historical deployment for the two sides after a putative first turn. These dispositions assume an average initial command die roll of 3 or 4, so as to ensure maximum compatibility with the free deployment system. The lateral positioning of the units accords as far as possible with historical precedent, but double moves are used to advance as many units in appropriate sectors as the available commands allow, thereby capturing the dynamic character of the deployment process (as discussed on pp. 65–6). Units are shown by their acronyms, with the orientation of the text showing which way the units are facing, and lead units being pushed slightly further forward in this facing direction. Units are also shown by an array of dots which give a visual impression of the type and number of troops they contain. This is accompanied by a reminder on each map of how many troops an average heavy infantry unit contains at the appropriate multiple for that battle. Generals are indicated in a similar fashion. In those few cases where unsurprised armies left any troops undeployed, this is shown at the end of the army listing as a reminder.

It cannot be emphasized too strongly that the scenarios that I provide represent just one interpretation of the often ambiguous and unreliable ancient evidence. As I make clear in the historical analysis accompanying each scenario, there are different scholarly theories about army size, deployment and battlefield terrain, as well as various possible ways of categorizing troops and generals within the model itself, and users are encouraged to experiment with their own modified scenarios to explore these different interpretations. The beauty of the model is that it is flexible enough to accommodate such changes, as the fighting value system tracks the worth of any combination of forces, the attack limit system allows for tweaks to the army frontage, and the handicap system should offset all but the grossest asymmetries between the two sides. However, although a wide range of different versions of a scenario should produce balanced *games*, only a few of them are likely to approximate the actual historical course of the engagement concerned. The point of experimenting with different interpretations is to see which ones tend to produce player choices and battle outcomes that most closely parallel the reported reality. Because the model is a generic one rather than being based just on that engagement, those interpretations that work best in reproducing actual events in any particular case deserve somewhat enhanced credence, in accordance with the comparative methodology outlined in the Introduction.

Cannae offers perhaps the ultimate test of this methodology, as it is obviously a challenge for any model to replicate the complete double envelopment of one army by another force with only two-thirds as many men. Indeed, some scholars have doubted Polybius's explicit statements about the size of the Roman army, largely due to their incredulity that such a feat could be achieved.[1] I will devote the rest of this chapter to a detailed account of a refight of Cannae using our model. This not only shows that Polybius's account is entirely plausible, but it illustrates the kind of more detailed grand tactical insights that one may gain about any battle through such a modelling and reconstruction process. The refight also serves as an example of play that should make it a lot easier for readers to grasp the abstract principles within the model by observing their operation in a specific case.

I discussed on p. 24 how Hannibal's army of 40,000 infantry and 10,000 cavalry could be represented by 18 veteran and average units using a troop multiple of 8. I built on this on pp. 67–8 by showing that both sides at Cannae deserve 2 generals, but that the much higher quality of the Carthaginian generals gives them a distinct advantage in overall fighting power even if the Romans are ahead in terms of the fighting value of the troops themselves. The 6,000 Roman and Allied cavalry translate neatly into 3 average heavy cavalry units. The force of nearly 70,000 Roman infantry (not counting those guarding the camps) is harder to reconstruct, but as I discuss on pp. 184–5, there were probably around 20,000 light infantry and around 50,000 legionary heavy infantry. Given the rapid mobilization of this massive army, the impact of earlier catastrophic losses at Trebia and Trasimene, and the apparent failure as yet to bring the skirmishers up to the standard of the later velites, it seems appropriate to categorize all the legionaries as average and the light infantry as either average or levy.[2] This yields a total force of 18 average and levy units, but with the troops themselves having a fighting value of 64 compared to 60 for the Carthaginians because average legionary units are worth 4 rather than 3 each, except when counting losses.

The scholarly controversy over the location of the battle site was mentioned on p. 7. We know that the Roman right rested on the bank of the river, but it is unclear whether the other flank was bounded by hills as Connolly and Goldsworthy suggest.[3] However, the fact that Hannibal chose to mass his heavy cavalry on the constrained river flank suggests that there may well have been some similar obstacle on the opposite wing, so it is worth placing a hill in the Punic right wing zone to explore what effect it might have. Estimates of the army frontages differ widely as I discuss on pp. 183–4, but the comparative process that I outlined on p. 32 suggests a scale of at least 800 m per zone, and when this is divided by 100 times the square root of the troop multiple of 8, the result rounds up to an attack limit of 3 units per zone. We are now in a position to run through each turn of a sample refight to study the pros and cons of each side's historical tactics, and how they work out within the model. I will illustrate with a diagram the state of play at the end of each turn, with the Punic army being in black and the Romans in red (Figures 3–6). Lead units are pushed forward as usual, and spent units are shown in lighter text. The key zones for these two symmetrically disposed armies are their centre zones as illustrated on the maps. We will have the armies begin off the field, but both sides will choose to implement the historical deployments given in the scenario, so that the refight is compatible with both forms of play.

TURN 1

The Romans go first, and a command die roll of 4 adds to the 7 from the initial Roman fighting value of 70 (1 for every 10) to give 11 commands – enough with the 2 exemptions from the 2 uninspired generals to make a few double moves in addition to the basic deployment. The Roman player knows that his army is comprehensively outgeneralled, and to achieve a game victory he must bring his strong and stubborn legionary forces to bear in a battle of attrition before they are surrounded by the superior Punic cavalry – hence, he must attack rather than waiting to be defeated in detail. The centre is the obvious place for the main effort because it contains both sides' key zones, and hence the Carthaginians will pay a price in morale if they fail to contest it. The role of the infantry and cavalry wings will be to shield this main effort for as long as possible while inflicting as much attrition as they can in the process. Any fancier or more subtle plan such as concentrating on one wing while 'refusing' the other faces the problem that Hannibal's forces can react to counter whatever the Romans do, evading their attack while sweeping round the flank of their refused wing to encircle them just the same.

As the attack limit is 3 units per zone on the Roman left but only 2 units per zone on the right by the river, the most efficient deployment of the cavalry (that count as 2 units each towards the limit) is to put 2 units on the left and 1 on the right. By using Paullus's and Varro's exemptions together, the right-hand unit may make a double move without expending any of the 11 commands. It is deployed in the right rear facing right, then moved into the right wing zone, turned forward, and moved into the right flank zone by the river, having used all 4 moves available. The other 2 cavalry units (including Varro's) could make similar double moves on the other flank, but this would cost 4 commands and leave too few commands to advance the skirmish screen in the centre, so the horsemen are instead activated normally as a group for 2 commands, being deployed in the left rear zone facing left and then moved into the left wing zone still in that facing.

Three commands are now available to activate all 3 light infantry units for the special double deployment moves costing just 1 command each, allowing them to reach the 3 centre zones and so be ready to get in the first blow in combat. The remaining 6 commands are exactly what is required to activate the 12 legionary units in 3 groups to occupy the 3 rear zones. The obvious approach would be to spread them evenly with 4 units per zone. However, this would leave two-thirds of the Roman infantry exposed to encirclement on three sides, while depriving the centre of the reserves needed to achieve a frontal breakthrough, as at the Trebia 2 years earlier. Hence, the Roman player instead opts for a shorter but deeper infantry line, represented abstractly in the model by a 3–6–3 distribution of legionary units (with the light infantry and flanking cavalry being assumed to fill in the gaps on either side). The role of the infantry on the left and right is to guard the flanks of the central mass, even once the cavalry are defeated. Finally, Paullus is deployed in the right rear, because it would be too dangerous to place him with one of the lone frontal units, lest Hannibal conduct a 'flip-flop' on turn 2 and shatter the unit, removing him at the outset.[4] This overall Roman deployment deliberately matches the historical one, and shows how (even with the advantage of hindsight) it is difficult for the Roman player to find a better approach once the fateful decision to engage in the first place is assumed to have been made.

It is now the Punic part of the turn, and a command die roll of 4 like that of the Romans gives a total of 12 commands when added to the 8 from the initial Carthaginian fighting value of 84. There are also no less than 6 exemptions

(4+2) because of the superior quality of the Punic generals. With the Romans having adopted a fairly symmetrical deployment, the issue for their opponents is whether to match this or to concentrate their forces on one wing or the other. The obvious place to concentrate is on the more open flank away from the river, but here the hill is an impediment because it stops the Carthaginian heavy cavalry from reaching the right flank zone facing forwards, even after a double move. On the river flank, by contrast, there is only 1 Roman cavalry unit to break through rather than 2 units, and the 2 veteran units of Spanish horse can still both attack because they only count as 1 unit each towards the reduced attack limit. It would be possible to divide the Punic horsemen fairly equally between the wings and to rely on their overall numerical superiority to achieve success on both, but there is also a case for having a striking wing of heavy cavalry and a holding wing of light cavalry, as at Hellenistic battles such as Gabiene and Gaza.[5] The Carthaginian player opts for the latter approach, and decides to strike on the river flank where there is greater chance of a rapid breakthrough, while holding on the opposite flank where the foothills may be used to impede attacks and slow down the combat further should the need arise.

The 2 Numidian units first make double moves into the right flank zone, using up Hannibal's 4 exemptions, and expending only 3 moves each as they can bypass the hill via the right centre zone and, as light cavalry, their 2 facing changes are free. Hasdrubal now leads the 2 Spanish cavalry units into the left flank zone by double moves, costing only his 2 exemptions as they are veterans. A Celtic cavalry unit also double moves into the same zone for 2 commands, and is placed in the lead to shield the costlier veterans from damage. The remaining Celtic horsemen could make a similar double move, but as the Punic player already has more cavalry by the river than can attack, he prefers to spend just 1 command activating the unit for a normal move into the left wing.

In the infantry contest, the challenge is clearly how to counter the central Roman juggernaut. There are 12 Carthaginian infantry units compared to 15 Roman ones, and rather than directly matching the weighting of the Roman centre, the Punic player opts for a more balanced deployment of 4 units per sector, intending to encircle and defeat the Roman infantry wings with the help of his cavalry, while holding in the centre for as long as possible. The Libyan veterans will be deployed on the left and right to sharpen the cutting edge of these flanking attacks while protecting the veterans from the costly attrition in the centre, whereas the Celts and Spaniards will be concentrated more thickly in the centre to absorb the Roman thrust. The 9 remaining commands allow 1 light infantry unit and 1 Celtic heavy infantry unit to be double moved forward to protect the Punic key zone and tempt the Romans forward to attack, while the remaining infantry occupy the 3 rear zones through group moves costing 6 commands. Hannibal himself is placed in the rear zone where his morale bonus extends to every Punic infantry unit, and lead units are designated as shown. This deployment again broadly mirrors the famous historical reality described by Polybius (III.113) of a forward-facing crescent, thicker in the centre, with the Libyan veterans held back in column on either side and with the Celtic and Spanish cavalry on the left and the Numidians on the right. When using the historical deployments given in the scenario, it would be at this point rather than at the start of turn 1 that the refight would actually begin (Figure 3).

TURN 2

It is not worth the Carthaginians reversing the turn order at this point with only 4 units in a position to attack adjacent enemies, so the refight proceeds with the second Roman turn. Another die roll of 4 again yields 11 commands. Varro could use his exemption to turn the Allied cavalry to face the enemy at the special discount rate, and then leave it at that to give the Numidians a penalty for having to move forward before attacking, but the player decides instead to add in 1 command for a normal activation and to use the horsemen's second move to enter the left flank zone, ready to press on with this fairly even cavalry contest before nemesis arrives from the other wing. The light infantry in the centre are now activated for 1 command, and attack the Punic light infantry. There is a +1 for being the lead unit, and a further +1 comes from an attack bonus bought for 2 more commands. The subsequent two-dice roll of 7 hence rises to 9, which exactly equals the score shown on the combat table for infantry attacking infantry. As he wants to make progress in the centre, the Roman player opts for an all-out attack, and so both units become spent. The 9 legionary units in the rear and left rear are now activated as 2 groups for 4 commands and moved forward to join the line. It would be suicidal for the levy light infantry in the left centre to move forward into the pocket in front, and it would require a double move costing 2 of the remaining 3 commands to move them sideways to reinforce Varro's horsemen (because the second turn would not be free), so they are instead left in place without being activated, to continue their role as a skirmish screen.

The real dilemma for the Romans is how to respond to the threat posed by Hasdrubal's cavalry on their right. They could pull their own horsemen and light infantry back to join the legionaries in their right rear and form a strong refused flank. However, this could be attacked from two sides by the Carthaginians, who could get in the first blow after reversing the turn order, and whose cavalry would receive a major bonus against the legionaries by attacking from another board edge zone. Alternatively, the Punic forces could use their superior command to transfer units to their right and defeat the Romans there, so outflanking the central mass of legionaries on both sides. Hence, the Roman player decides to stick with his original plan and advance his legionaries on the right to stay level with the rest of the infantry line. This absorbs Paullus's exemption plus 1 command more, with Paullus himself relocating to the centre where combat is already going on and where he is still not adjacent to Varro. The right flank cavalry are activated for 1 command, but the 1 command remaining is wasted because it is not enough to provide an attack bonus. The combat dice roll is 8, with +1 for being the first attack, so still easily hits the Celtic horsemen (because heavy cavalry only need a 7 against enemy heavy cavalry). Hasdrubal could attempt a rally, but the Punic player decides that it is not worth the risk at this stage. Finally, lead units are selected by the Roman player, with the average light infantry no longer being eligible due to being spent from their own all-out attack.

The Carthaginian command roll is only 2, giving 10 commands, but the Punic player decides to focus on setting his army up for a turn reversal on turn 3 thanks to Hannibal's brilliant generalship. The left flank cavalry are activated with Hasdrubal's exemption, and he attacks first with his own veteran Spanish unit, using his 2 extra combat exemptions to give it a double attack bonus in addition to its lead unit bonus. A roll of 5 thereby rises to 8 and scores a hit. The other Spanish horsemen now attack with a single bonus that costs 2 commands (as veterans need to be in the lead to receive attack bonuses at the lower rate). Their roll of 6 (rising to 7) allows an all-out attack, and the Punic player accepts this so as to shatter the Roman horse, even though it costs him more victory points than he gains (4 as against 3). The Roman morale roll is a 3, so there is no chance of panic as even the neighbouring light infantry have a morale of 1 (army morale of 2, –1 for being levies). The Carthaginian player chooses to advance all of his 3 cavalry units in the attacking group into the Roman right flank zone. The remaining Celtic horsemen are activated normally for 1 command so they can turn and follow up into the Punic left flank zone.

The infantry in the Punic centre are not activated, as the player does not want to pre-empt a larger attack from that zone after reversing the turn order. Instead, the whole following infantry line is moved forward for 4 commands plus Hannibal's exemption (half of which is wasted because it can only be used in his initial zone). The Numidian horse are activated for 2 commands, and the 1 remaining command is used to give the first unit an attack bonus (which is cheaper for light cavalry than for other units). Its roll of 5 (rising to 7) nevertheless misses, and the second unit's roll of 10 (reduced to 9 because it must attack at half rate to fit within the attack limit) only succeeds through an all-out attack that the Carthaginian player decides to accept. Varro attempts a rally, but fails on a roll of 5, and so takes over the lead with his own attached horsemen. Punic lead units need not be designated as turn reversal is imminent, except in the right centre where the light infantry need to start the next Punic turn in the lead if they are to count as only a single unit against the attack limit (Figure 4).

TURN 3

The Carthaginian player declares the flip-flop and rolls a 5 to get 13 commands. Now is the time to exploit the breakthrough by the river before the Romans can react. The veteran Spanish cavalry again make double moves using Hasdrubal's exemption, and curve round as far as they can into the Roman rear. The spent Celtic cavalry double move into the Roman right rear for 2 commands and change facing ready to attack, while the fresh Celtic cavalry move up and turn onto the Roman flank for 1 command. The Numidians on the other flank are not activated, as they cannot attack again from this zone after turn reversal, and because there is no need to play safe and pull back to the foothills now that Hasdrubal has broken through and is galloping to support them. The Punic infantry, by contrast, are in a perfect position to exploit the flip-flop by getting in the first attack despite having only just moved up into contact.

The Carthaginian left centre is activated for 2 commands, and a further 2 commands give an attack bonus to the lead average unit. The roll of 10 increases to 13 because of the bonus, the first attack, and the levy status of the defenders. This would normally inflict 2 hits and shatter the levies outright, but because they are accompanied by heavy infantry and everyone in the zone is still fresh, the second hit is negated. However, as there are enemies facing the zone from behind, the spent skirmishers must remain in the lead. The other 3 units attacking (with the veterans counting as half each) roll 4, 7 and 6, so the levies survive for now. In the right centre, the light infantry lead the attack, and the first 2 attacking units receive bonuses, with this plus the activation of the group costing all of the 6 remaining commands. Scores of 6 (rising to 9), 6 (rising to 7), 10 and 3 make the Roman skirmishers and 1 legionary unit spent, but at the cost of the Punic light infantry being hit in an all-out attack as the Carthaginians race to defeat the enemy infantry wings before their own centre gives way. In the centre, Hannibal activates his group and joins it himself to give free bonuses to the first 2 attackers from his own combat exemptions. The lead unit has its bonus offset by the penalty for attacking fresh legionaries, but its score of 10 (rising to 11) still inflicts a hit. (The Roman skirmishers do not take over the lead, because Hasdrubal's horse are not facing the zone.) The other 2 attackers score 5 (rising to 6), and 9, with the light infantry being surplus to the attack limit. The highest roll could have succeeded through an all-out attack, but the Punic player rejects this chance in order to play for time against the Roman juggernaut. Finally, lead units are selected as required.

After this protracted onslaught, the Romans now at last have the chance to fight back. A lucky roll of 6 gives 12 commands (the Roman fighting value having fallen to 67 with the loss of the cavalry). Varro's Allied horse fight on valiantly in the slim hope of saving the left wing from the encirclement already suffered on the right. Four commands plus Varro's exemptions for activation and combat allow both units to receive attack bonuses, but the scores of 6 (rising to 8) and 5 (with the bonus cancelled out by the half rate penalty) still have no effect, because all-out attacks are prohibited against the elusive Numidians. In the left and right centres, the 3 legionary units attack without bonuses at a total cost of 4 commands. The spent light infantry cannot attack first even if they have enemies behind, and the presence of enemies to the rear cancels the attack limit increase that the Roman right centre would otherwise receive, as well as penalizing the attack by the lead unit itself. The pay-off is hence only 1 unit in the Punic right centre hit.

It is in the centre where the Romans make their greatest effort, and the remaining 4 commands plus Paullus's exemptions allow the first 2 of the maximum of 3 legionary attacks to be given bonuses. The lead unit rolls an 8 that rises to 9 (as the bonus is offset by having enemies behind) and so scores a hit through an all-out attack. The Punic player decides to leave the spent unit in the lead so as to keep the others fresh. The two following Roman attacks inflict another hit and so shatter the unit. Hannibal would have a 42 per cent chance of negating the hit through personal intervention, but the 8 per cent chance of dying is a powerful deterrent because of the catastrophic impact this would have, so the Carthaginian player decides not to take the risk. The morale roll of 2 gives an army morale of 1 and means that the light infantry in the zone only just avoid being carried away as well, their spent status being offset by Hannibal's charisma. A fresh legionary unit is put in the lead as the turn ends (Figure 5).

TURN 4

A roll of 3 gives the Carthaginians 11 commands, as their fighting value is still 81. Their first priority is to prevail on the right. The spent Spanish cavalry unit uses 1 of Hasdrubal's 2 exemptions to make a double move into the rear of Varro's horse, so as to reduce the morale and effectiveness of the Allied cavalry. The Numidians then attack with bonuses for both units, at a total cost of 4 commands. The fresh unit scores 7 (rising to 9) and chooses an all-out attack. Varro's compulsory rally attempt fails, so he switches the other spent unit back to the lead. The spent Numidian unit is also lucky to hit with a roll of 10 (the bonus cancelling out the half rate penalty), and when Varro's rally attempt again fails, the unit is shattered. The morale roll is 4, so Varro's unit routs with a morale of

0 (thanks to the penalties for being spent and having enemies to front and rear), carrying him away with it. The nearby levy light infantry also have a morale of 0, but they stand because nobody in their zone has routed or been shattered. The Numidians advance into the Roman left flank zone, though they will not be able both to change facing and to attack the enemy infantry next turn, as an abstract reflection of their pursuit of the Roman horse. Hasdrubal himself now need not reinforce the encirclement of the Allied cavalry, and so he can use his remaining exemption to turn in behind the Roman left centre.

The infantry in the Punic left and right centres are activated for normal attacks for a total of 4 commands. One legionary unit in both zones is hit, and the sheltering skirmishers must be moved into the lead because of the cavalry facing them from behind. The Celtic horse surrounding the Roman right centre can now attack for 2 commands, and they easily shatter the exposed light infantry. The morale roll of 1 carries away the now encircled levies on the other wing whose morale is –2, but the average skirmishers in the centre manage to stand with 0, and the spent legionaries in the left and right centre survive comfortably with a morale of 1 because of Roman stubbornness and the non-transmissibility of light infantry panic. In the centre, Hannibal could simply press on with the fight, but the Carthaginian player is worried that he now faces odds of over 2:1 and so could be overwhelmed before the Roman infantry wings collapse. Hence, he decides instead to trade space for time, even though this means abandoning his key zone. As they have not been outflanked, all 3 units could make a free about turn and retire to their rear zone using a normal group move, but Hannibal's 4 exemptions plus the 1 remaining command allow the retirement to be made by double moves for the heavy infantry and a normal move by the light infantry so that they may all turn back to face the enemy. As Hannibal has not had to stay with the units to contribute attack exemptions, he takes the opportunity to relocate to his still engaged right centre in case the Romans do not take the bait. Hasdrubal's cavalry is no longer in the Roman rear, which is a good thing as otherwise the legionaries could turn and attack it now they no longer have enemies immediately in front.

A roll of 2 gives the Romans just 7 commands, as their fighting value is now down to 56, but at least their forces are compressed into 3 groups compared to the 8 Punic ones. The left centre attacks with 1 bonus for 4 commands, and the right centre attacks for 2 commands, hitting the leading unit in the Punic left centre despite the penalty for being surrounded. In the centre, the Roman player uses Paullus's exemption plus the 1 remaining command to move his 4 fresh legionary units into the Punic key zone, while leaving his 3 spent units to guard his own key zone. Hence, both sides have secured some success – the Roman cavalry have been broken and the Punic double envelopment has been achieved but the Carthaginian infantry line that was convex has become concave under the relentless pressure and the Romans dominate the centre of the field with over half of their legionary units still fresh (Figure 6).

We will leave the refight at this point, with game victory still very much in the balance. Although almost every Roman unit is now surrounded on three sides, the legionaries are stubbornly resilient and there is still everything to play for given the tenuous nature of the outnumbered Punic cordon and the morale penalty they suffer for losing their key zone and not yet having seized one of the enemy centre zones. The Romans currently have 59 victory points (25 for spent Punic units, 6 for the shattered unit and 28 for the handicap bonus), while the Carthaginians have only 44 (26 for spent and routed units and the lost general, an extra 2 for the routed cavalry and skirmishers, and 16 for shattered units), so it will take hard fighting and good command for the dispersed and exhausted Punic troops to hold the ring and inflict the historical massacre. It should take a few more turns (each representing around 25 min at this ground scale) before the Romans are either reduced to a milling mass of fugitives incapable of effective resistance, or burst through the Punic centre and escape as 10,000 of them did at Trebia – this corresponds well with the reported duration of around 3 hours for similar engagements.[6] Readers might like to continue the refight for themselves to see how the battle develops, or go back to an earlier point to explore alternative tactics and outcomes.

Cannae is one of the best-known and most heavily studied engagements of antiquity, and there are even entire modern books that take this single battle as their principal focus.[7] This being the case, one might expect that our own necessarily broad-brush treatment would have little insight to add, and that Cannae would be far more of a net contributor to the generic model than a beneficiary of this analytical approach. However, even with a battle less 'lost' than most of the others that I will attempt to reconstruct, the process of modelling and refighting the engagement and allowing a variety of player choices does still throw up several worthwhile grand tactical insights that are not readily available in other ways. These include the following observations:

- It is not clear that the Romans would have done much better by arraying their numerous infantry in a shallower but longer line, as long as Hannibal had been able to adjust his own deployment accordingly. The real enigma is how he knew in advance what formation the Romans would adopt in order to counter it so effectively.
- It is difficult to understand Hannibal's approach of massing all his heavy cavalry on just one flank, and moreover on the flank nearest the river that Livy (XXII.47) emphasizes was very confined. This suggests that the other flank was not as open as some have tended to assume, and so it may have implications for the debate over the location of the battlefield (as I discuss further on pp. 183–4).

- Polybius's account (III.116) of Hasdrubal leading his squadrons to the relief of the Numidians before turning into the rear of the Roman infantry should not necessarily be interpreted as meaning that all 6,000 or so horsemen from the Punic left flank galloped back and forth in this way.[8] The model suggests that it may be more realistic to imagine the cavalry gradually forming a curtain along the back of the Roman line, with only the leading squadrons proceeding all the way to the opposite wing.

- There are real problems in interpreting Polybius's account (III.115) of the Roman infantry being trapped in a pocket by the Libyan columns. The usual image of the Libyans flanking the entire legionary line raises the question of how on earth they could help to stop Romans fighting and winning in the centre, several hundred metres away from either column. Goldsworthy has an intriguing and little-known alternative suggestion that only the centre of the Roman line burst through and that the Libyan columns charged against its exposed flanks by moving inwards *behind* the screening Celts and Spaniards still holding on the wings of the Punic infantry line.[9] Our model suggests that either this was what occurred or that the Roman wings were quickly 'rolled up' by the Libyans and fled in towards the centre to create a milling mass. The more common image of the whole Roman infantry line remaining straight and intact while being enclosed in an essentially rectangular box of Carthaginian troops seems far less plausible.[10]

- Whatever form the fighting took, it is clear from our model that the Punic infantry, and particularly the Celts and Spaniards, played the most important role in defeating the Roman legions. Polybius's judgement (III.117) about the overwhelming importance of cavalry superiority is misleading in this regard. The cavalry encirclement did surely demoralize the Romans, sap their forward momentum and (above all) prevent them from escaping the subsequent massacre, but the hard fighting was done by the infantry, as indicated by Polybius's claim that the Carthaginian dead numbered 5,500 infantry and only 200 cavalry. The achievement of the Celts and Spaniards in the centre was particularly impressive. If they had failed to rally from their retreat in the face of the Roman juggernaut, neither the Libyan columns nor Hasdrubal's cavalry would have been of much avail. One might be tempted to praise Hannibal for ensuring that 4,000 of his losses fell among his relatively 'expendable' Celts, but had he not been able to inspire them to endure such sacrifice by his personal presence at this point in the battle line, then the entire Punic plan could have fallen apart as happened to his brother at Ibera the following year.[11]

The modelling process thus provides ample recompense for the necessarily rather involved preliminaries that I have outlined over the last few chapters. Once one gets down to specifics and starts modelling and refighting a particular engagement, numerous insights and questions appear that do not become obvious simply from reading the sources themselves. Ideally, I would be able to describe and analyse refights of every other battle in the same way as I have just done for Cannae, but there is obviously far too little space to do this for the other 34 engagements to be covered in Part II. I will therefore offer as much detailed commentary as I can to build upon and supplement the existing scholarship, but it must be primarily for readers themselves to use the model to explore in greater depth whichever engagements interest them most. In that sense, this book is far less about offering conclusions than about developing a tool that readers can use for themselves to generate insights that altogether could fill many volumes. Now that the model has been developed and explained, it is high time to get on with creating the specific scenarios that are the vehicle for this process of study and exploration.

PART II

The Battles

7

Athens and Sparta

The fifth century BC saw two great conflicts in the Mediterranean – first the successful resistance and counter-offensive of the mainland Greeks in the face of invasions by the vast Persian Empire, and then the internecine struggles that split the Greek world into rival camps led by Athens and Sparta during the Peloponnesian Wars. In both of these conflicts, naval fighting was as important as clashes on land. However, there were a few open field land battles that the sources describe in sufficient detail for us to attempt their reconstruction. One is obviously Marathon, where the Athenians smashed the force sent by Darius to punish the Greeks for their support of the Ionian rebels a few years earlier. The second is Plataea, where the Greek coalition routed the much larger invasion force left by Xerxes when he himself returned home after his naval defeat at Salamis. Similarly climactic land battles were uncommon during the prolonged Peloponnesian Wars, because of Pericles's strategy of avoiding a direct confrontation with the much larger enemy army. However, at Delium the Athenians did sally out against the Thebans in an attempt to defeat their opponents in detail, while at 1st Mantinea, Sparta's traditional adversaries the Argives emerged from neutrality and confronted them once again, with some Athenian support despite the fragile truce embodied in the Peace of Nicias. In both cases, Athens was defeated, though these land battles were far from decisive and it took 14 more years of bitter fighting, including the disastrous Sicilian expedition and the rise of a Persian-financed Peloponnesian fleet, before the Athenians finally succumbed.

MARATHON, 490 BC

Marathon is perhaps the clearest case of the 'inverted pyramid' described in the Introduction, with the battle being the focus of prolific modern scholarship including some entire books, even though our evidence on the actual fighting comes mainly from just a few hundred words of Herodotus (VI.111–17).[1] We know that the battlefield lay somewhere on the Marathon plain, but debate rages over how the area has changed since antiquity, as well as over where in the surrounding hills the Athenians were initially deployed, and where and in what orientation the battle lines met. Hammond's very thorough study in 1968 placed the Greeks on Mount Kotroni and the Persians near the *Soros* mound with their backs directly to the sea, whereas Lazenby argued that the Athenians started from Mount Agrieliki and that the battle lines were instead perpendicular to the coast.[2] Pritchett, Burn and Doenges opted for an intermediate option with the Greeks coming from the intervening Vrana valley and the battle lines at an angle to the shore, while Sekunda has recently espoused the perpendicular alternative but has shifted the confrontation along the plain to the northeast, away from the Soros and towards the Great Marsh.[3]

The key consideration for our present purpose is one of scale. Herodotus (VI.112) says the Athenians charged for 8 stadia (1.5 km), and most modern scholars estimate that the Athenian infantry line was of a roughly similar width as they think the wings were 8 deep and the centre 4 deep.[4] This strongly suggests that each of our zones should represent around 500 m, making our overall battlefield some 2.5 by 2.0 km. The plain as a whole is currently nearly 3 km wide between the mountains and the sea, and nearly 6 km long between Mount Agrieliki and the Great Marsh. Hence, there is less need to fix the battle lines precisely, as most of the surrounding terrain features will be off the board in any case. The Charadra stream currently bisects the plain, but we have no real idea of its ancient course, and it made no recorded difference in the actual battle. Similarly, we are not even sure that the present Little Marsh on the coast near Mount Agrieliki existed in antiquity. The only terrain feature that may deserve some representation is the shoreline itself. I have opted in Figure 8 to show it on the Persian left wing as per the angled reconstructions by Pritchett, Burn and Doenges, but one could equally well argue for extending it into the Persian left and Greek right flank zones if one prefers the more perpendicular model. As the Athenians had no cavalry at all, and as the opposite flank is open in any case, this should make little difference to the refight.

The Greek army is by far the easier of the two sides to reconstruct. Herodotus gives no specific figures, but Justin (II.9) says there were 10,000 Athenians and 1,000 Plataeans, while Nepos (*Milt.* 5) says there were 10,000 including the 1,000 Plataeans. These claims are of very dubious reliability, but they do broadly tally with the 8,000 Athenian and 600 Plataean hoplites that Herodotus (IX.28) says were at Plataea 11 years later, so most scholars accept the round figure of 10,000.[5] Pausanias (I.32) mentions some slaves who fought and were buried at Marathon, but (unlike at Plataea) Herodotus says nothing of their contribution, so there seems little case for including them as a distinct light-armed unit.[6] There is no sense of any of the Greek hoplite contingents being especially good or bad, so they can all be classified as 'average', which at the minimum multiple of 1 translates into exactly the desired number of 20 units, each of around 500 men. Herodotus (VI.109–11) portrays Miltiades as convincing the nine other tribal strategoi to engage after a finely balanced vote, but the closest thing the Athenians seem to have had to an overall general was the polemarch Callimachus who led the right wing and who was killed during the later fighting at the Persian ships.[7] It is worth including him as an uninspired leader, bringing the Greeks to a total fighting value of 63.

The Persian army is much more of an enigma. Again, Herodotus gives no figures, and claims such as Nepos's 10,000 cavalry and 100,000 infantry (*Milt.* 4) or Justin's 600,000 (II.9) are patently absurd. Most modern scholars tend to argue for a total of 20–25,000, on the grounds that this fits in with Herodotus's claim of 600 triremes (at 30–40 troops per vessel) and that it also accords with his figure of 6,400 for the Persian dead (VI.95 and 117).[8] Doenges instead suggests 12–15,000 troops, arguing that 'A larger force no matter how poorly equipped and led would surely have overwhelmed the Greeks'.[9] Sekunda combines both hypotheses, proposing that the entire Persian army numbered 25,000 but that only half of these fought the battle, with the rest having been embarked on the fleet to attack Athens itself.[10] These claims of a smaller numerical imbalance carry some credibility, as the Greeks had not yet established their later psychological dominance over the Persians – if anything, the reverse was the case, as Herodotus (VI.112) explicitly asserts. The native Persian troops in the centre surely deserve the same 'average' classification as the Athenians, and even if we make all the other nationalities 'levies', too large a force would have an ahistorically high fighting value relative to the Greeks. Any detailed reconstruction is necessarily highly speculative, but the scenario below assumes a 10,000 strong force of Median infantry bolstered by smaller contingents of Persians, Saka and Ionians (all of which are mentioned by Herodotus) totalling some 8,000 foot.[11] The Ionians (if in the fighting line at all) would surely have been hoplites, while the Asiatic infantry would have been the enigmatic combination of bowmen and spearmen best classified as heavy infantry archers.[12]

The most famous uncertainty about Marathon concerns the Persian cavalry. Most scholars think there were around 1,000 horsemen in the expedition, though Evans and Doenges put the number at under 200.[13] As I discussed on p. 9, some writers follow the Byzantine *Souda* and argue that the cavalry did not take part in the battle, while others (like Lazenby) believe that Herodotus's silence on the matter implies otherwise.[14] If the horsemen did take part, they clearly did not make much difference, so there is certainly no case for giving the Persians 4 average cavalry units each representing around 250 troopers. In the scenario below, I have given them 1 average and 1 levy unit, totalling around 750 horsemen but making up only 8 per cent of the fighting value of the Persian units as a whole. We are not told what role the Persian generals, Datis and Artaphernes, played in the battle, but Herodotus (VI.118–19) says they both survived the rout (unlike the victorious Athenian polemarch), so I have made them both uninspired commanders to increase the likelihood of this.[15] This gives the Persians a fighting value of 59, just 4 less than their opponents.

The Athenians should clearly move first, to reflect their seizure of the initiative. The historical Greek deployment is easily reproduced, with the thinned Athenian centre simulated by an 8–4–8 unit split, though the key zone should be in the centre to reflect the unusual symmetry of the Greek array and to persuade the Athenians to advance all along the line as they did historically. Stacking limits force a more even distribution of the Persian infantry, with the best troops in the centre to contest the key zones, and with the cavalry on the wings (rather than in the centre, which would be tactically senseless). The placing of the Ionians on the Persian right is entirely hypothetical. An attractive tactic for the Persians might be to 'refuse' one of their infantry wings while using their centre and flanking cavalry to create a pocket, reflecting the use of combined arms to pin enemies in the beaten zone of their arrows.[16] To pre-empt this, the Athenians should probably double move their 2 advanced hoplite units outward onto their flanks to confront the enemy horsemen directly, neatly simulating the extension of the Greek line to prevent outflanking as Herodotus (VI.111) describes.

Most refights should resolve themselves into a race between the Persians trying to break through in the centre and the Athenians trying to do the same on the wings. Scholars have long debated Herodotus's description (VI.113) of the victorious Athenian wings breaking off their pursuit and joining together to attack the successful Persian centre. The apparent implication that they turned entirely about and rejoined battle on a reversed front does not explain Herodotus's assertion that the Persians then fled to their ships whereas the Athenian centre, in a similar position, fled inland.[17] Hammond tries to resolve the problem by placing the battle lines parallel to the coast and having the Plataeans on the eastern flank do less well in this second phase, thereby leaving the Persians an escape route to the Great Marsh.[18] Burn and Lazenby suggest instead that what happened was an attack in both flanks, with the Athenian wings pivoting inward to catch the Persian centre in a pocket.[19] Our own zone-based model clearly favours this latter interpretation, but if *both* armies succeed in breaking their frontal opponents and advancing into the enemy half of the field (with the Greeks advancing first because of the prohibition on advances by hoplites who have already been outflanked), then it is entirely conceivable that the Athenian wings could indeed end up joining together during the subsequent manoeuvring.

The persistence of so many different theories about Marathon amply bears out Whatley's scepticism of nearly a century ago.[20] Every modern scholar has his own pet hypothesis, and it is only by comparing these impressively argued but radically divergent claims that we realize how little we really know. What distinguishes the following reconstruction is that one may easily modify contentious details such as the course of the coast, the number of Persian infantry or the presence and composition of the cavalry, while still making use of the basic model. Such variations suggest that it is actually Persian *infantry* numbers that have the greatest impact on the outcome – an aspect on which there has been too little detailed debate, because scholars have been preoccupied instead with more marginal issues like the role of the horsemen and the location and orientation of the battle lines. The initial triumph of the Persian centre showed that Greek hoplites did not enjoy unqualified superiority regardless of the odds, and for ordinary Athenian militia to overcome odds of 2:1 or even 3:1, as they are routinely assumed to have done, is in fact highly problematic.[21] It would be difficult to make the Persian army any larger than in the following scenario without giving them too much chance of an outright victory, and the actual recorded casualties of 6,400 Persians as against just 192 Athenians could well imply a Persian force that was several thousand smaller still.[22]

MARATHON, 490 BC (Figure 8)

M: x1. AL: 5.

Athenians: UL + AHO (Callimachus + Athenians), 19 AHO (17 Athenian, 2 Plataean). FV: 63.

Persians: 6 AAR (Persian), 13 LAR (10 Median, 3 Saka), 2 LHO (Ionian), 1 AHC (Persian), 1 LHC (Asiatic), 2 UC (Datis and Artaphernes). FV: 59.

PLATAEA, 479 BC

Plataea was a much larger battle than Marathon, involving as it did the entire Greek coalition and a land-based rather than amphibious Persian invasion force. Herodotus is once again our main source, and he describes the 2 weeks of tangled preliminary manoeuvres and skirmishing at some length, with around 2,000 words (IX.56–71) on the climactic final day of fighting. However, military details are still frustratingly scarce or uncertain, and scholars continue to debate the vexed issue of troop numbers and the precise location of the geographical features to which Herodotus refers.[23]

The best place to start is with the Greek army. Herodotus (IX.28) gives a detailed numerical breakdown of the forces from each city, amounting in total to 38,700 hoplites. Delbrück was sceptical, but most modern writers accept these figures as broadly in line with what we know of later armies fielded by the individual cities concerned, even though they do represent the largest hoplite force ever assembled on the same side.[24] The 5,000 native Spartans and 1,500 associated Tegeans surely deserve veteran status given Herodotus's repeated praise (IX.28 and 61), and at an appropriate multiple of 5, the army then translates into

5 veteran and 13 average hoplite units, each representing around 1,250 and 2,500 troops respectively. Herodotus (IX.29) goes on to calculate the presence of no less than 69,500 Greek light-armed troops, based on 1 servant for each non-Spartan hoplite and the remarkable figure of 7 helots for each Spartan. Hunt has recently made the radical suggestion that these helots formed the 7 back ranks within an 8 deep phalanx, but he then has to question Herodotus's overall numbers to make such a single rank of hoplites appear even remotely feasible.[25] Because (as I will illustrate) the length of the hoplite line is already highly problematic, and because the contribution of this mass of servants is as opaque as in later battles when similar hordes are enumerated but then forgotten, I go along with the majority of scholars who ignore them as fighting troops, although it is worth including 2 light infantry units as a nod to Herodotus's claims (IX.22, 60 and 85) of helot casualties and of a useful force of Athenian archers. There seem to have been no loyal Greek cavalry, and the overall leader Pausanias warrants no more than 'uninspired' status given the confusion into which the army fell during the retreat preceding the battle, so the Greek fighting value comes to 67.

As at Marathon, Persian numbers are much more problematic. Herodotus's figures (IX.32) of 300,000 Asiatics and 50,000 allied Greeks, not even counting the cavalry, are universally rejected. Modern scholars have attempted to divine the truth by such means as hypothesizing a systematic tenfold inflation of Herodotus's claims, or by employing Roman comparisons to calculate how many men the reported 10 stadia (1.8 km) square Persian camp could hold, or by using the initial Greek battle line as a yardstick to estimate the strength of the enemy forces opposite each hoplite contingent. Guesses as to the overall size of the Persian army nevertheless range from Green's 40,000 foot and 10,000 horse through Head's 45,000 infantry and 15,000 cavalry to Burn's and Lazenby's 80–90,000 troops, Santosuosso's 100,000 and Connolly's 120,000 men.[26] Head interprets Herodotus (VIII.113) as meaning that only 11–12,000 Persian guard infantry and a similar number of Medes formed the core of Mardonius's Asiatic foot, but Lazenby thinks that regular Persian infantry remained as well (or even instead).[27] Herodotus (IX.62) praises the spirit and strength of the Persian foot in the actual battle but criticizes their skill, training and lack of armour compared to the Spartans, so a rating of 'average' rather than 'veteran' seems best for the 10,000 Immortals. The rest of the Asiatic infantry should surely be levy archers as at Marathon, and I have included around 35,000 of them in the suggested scenario as this seems to give a better balance relative to historical performance than do the higher or lower suggestions – as usual, this is one of the many areas in which users may experiment for themselves.

As for the medising Greeks, Herodotus (IX.67–9) highlights the role of the Boeotians in standing up to the Athenians with their hoplites while their cavalry routed a Megarian and Phliasian column and then screened the overall retreat.

The Boeotians thus certainly deserve to be classed as average, while the other medising Greeks can be represented by 2 levy infantry units. The Asiatic cavalry, despite their greater numbers, seem not to have contributed decisively during the final battle, and so (as at Marathon) deserve mainly to be classed as levies. Exceptions can be made for the Saka horsemen and the 1,000 Persian guard cavalry, whom Herodotus (IX.63 and 71) singles out for praise. His descriptions (IX.20–3 and 49) of earlier skirmishes like that in which the Persian cavalry leader Masistius was killed suggest that the horsemen fought with bows and javelins at least as much as at close quarters, so some of them may be classed as light rather than heavy cavalry, further reducing their ability to contribute during a climactic infantry *mêlée*.[28] The Persian leader Mardonius seems on the whole to have been a better general than Pausanias, and Herodotus (IX.63) says that his death at the head of his cavalry guard triggered the collapse of Persian resistance, so he is best classed as average, bringing the overall Persian fighting value to 58.

The main battle was preceded by a stand-off for several days across the shallow River Asopus. Most scholarly reconstructions of the opposing battle lines have been based on the assumption that the hoplites were arrayed 8 deep, producing a Greek line some 4.5 km long stretching all the way from the Pyrgos hill to the Asopus ridge, with the light troops deployed even beyond that on the flanks.[29] Connolly goes still further by having the Lacedaemonians and Tegeans just 4 deep, extending the hoplite line to 6 km.[30] A significant contribution of my comparative model is to cast doubt on such assumptions. As I pointed out in Chapter 3, there was a clear tendency for larger armies to deploy in greater depth rather than just greater width, no doubt due in large measure to the command problems that I discussed on pp. 61–4. At the Nemea, Xenophon (*Hell.* IV.2.13–18) describes how a coalition force of just 24,000 hoplites formed up 16 deep, with the Theban contingent deploying even deeper.[31] If the initial hoplite line at Plataea did indeed stretch for 4.5 km, let alone 6 km, this would make it by far the longest infantry line in any of my 35 battles, even though it contained by no means the largest or the best-commanded infantry force. As the Persians were still quite able to send cavalry round the flank to choke the spring and interrupt supply convoys, and as the 'island' to which Pausanias attempted to withdraw offered a much narrower refuge, I suggest that the Greeks may actually have formed up significantly deeper than most scholars propose.[32] Even a line 12 deep (like that used by a much smaller force of the vaunted Spartans at Leuctra) would bring the overall width back within more common bounds.[33]

Terrain played an important role at Plataea, with streams like the Oeroe and hills like the Asopus ridge and the slopes of Mount Cithaeron to the south helping to protect the Greeks from the Persian cavalry. The main battle took place between the Asopus ridge and Mount Cithaeron, after a bungled night-time withdrawal from the ridge left the Greek army scattered and exposed, prompting

Mardonius to abandon his previous caution and rush forward to seek a rapid victory. If we use the maximum scale width of 1,200 m for each zone, overlaying the resulting 6 km by 4.8 km grid at an appropriate angle on a map of the overall battlefield produces a board like that in Figure 9, with the River Asopus lying just behind the Persian board edge and with the Pyrgos hill just off their right flank. Both armies were caught very much 'on the hop', with the initial clash occurring between the Persian cavalry and the Lacedaemonians, and with the other Persian and Greek forces marching into action as the fighting progressed. In our generic model, this is best simulated by treating both armies as 'surprised', as discussed on p. 40. Placing the key zones opposite one another on the Greek right encourages the historical focus on this flank, and giving the Greeks the first move offsets their lack of cavalry and reflects the greater distance from the Persian camp north of the Asopus.

This scenario should produce a wild battle, with the Greeks having a higher chance of victory due to their superior fighting value. Historically, it was the contest between the Lacedaemonians and the Persian infantry on the Greek right that proved decisive, with Herodotus (IX.61–3) giving a vivid description of the hoplites suffering under a prolonged barrage of arrows before surging forward and tearing down the barricade of shields to defeat their opponents in a bitterly fought *mêlée*. Meanwhile the Athenians beat the Thebans in a similarly hard-fought contest. Herodotus (IX.67–70) records only 767 Greek dead (600 from among the routed Megarians and Phliasians), while claiming that 300 Boeotians and no less than 257,000 of his massive Persian horde also fell, mostly after the capture of their camp. Later ancient writers put the Greek losses at 1,360 or even 10,000, but certainty is obviously impossible.[34] The model presented here is far too generic and broad brush to cast light on the continuing uncertainty about exactly where the various Greek contingents ended up after their confused withdrawal, and debates on how Herodotus's numerous geographical references correspond to the battlefield as it is today will no doubt continue in the future as they have for generations.[35] Where our model *can* provide some new insights by setting this battle much more clearly within the context of other similar engagements is over the vexed question of Persian numbers and over the practicality of maintaining supposedly 'standard' formation depths in a coalition force many times larger than those fielded by individual city states.

PLATAEA, 479 BC (Figure 9)

M: x5. AL: 5.

Greeks: UL + VHO (Pausanias + Spartans), 4 VHO (3 Spartan, 1 Tegean), 13 AHO (3 Athenian, 2 Lacedaemonian, 2 Corinthian, 1 Sicyonian, 1 Megarian, 4 Allied), 1 ALI (Archers), 1 LLI (Helots). FV: 67. Surprised.

Persians: 4 AAR (Immortals), 3 AHO (Boeotian), 7 LAR (3 Median, 2 Persian, 1 Bactrian, 1 Indian and Saka), 1 LHI (Macedonian), 1 LLI (Thessalian), AL + AHC (Mardonius + Persians), 1 AHC (Boeotian), 1 LHC (Median), 1 ALC (Saka), 1 LLC (Bactrian). FV: 58. Surprised.

DELIUM, 424 BC

Athens and Thebes clashed again (as they had at Plataea) during a bungled multi-pronged attack on Boeotia several years into the Peloponnesian War. Our main source is, of course, Thucydides, who describes the battle in under a thousand words (IV.93–6), but still conveys the key military details. The Athenians had fortified Delium across the Boeotian border, and had marched back just over a mile towards Attica when the Theban army came up from Tanagra to the west.[36] Thucydides (IV.93 and 96) mentions two terrain features that affected the fighting – the presence of a hill behind which the Thebans formed up before cresting it to engage, and the impeding of both wings by watercourses that prevented troops at the very ends from making contact at all. Pritchett found a site that he felt met these conditions, but the identification is unavoidably speculative, and I have included the terrain features in a more generic fashion on Figure 10.[37] Thucydides claims (IV.94) that the roughly 7,000 Athenian hoplites formed up 8 deep, which would produce a line of up to 900 m, so each zone should clearly represent around 300 m across. Because each turn hence represents only about 10 min (as discussed on p. 36), there is plenty of time for a decision to be reached, even though we are told (IV.93) that the battle only started late in the day.

Thucydides (IV.93) gives the Boeotians 7,000 hoplites, 1,000 cavalry, 500 peltasts and over 10,000 light troops, and these forces seem not to include those he says were detached to mask the Delium fort. The famous 300 strong Theban Sacred Band is usually assumed not to have existed until the following century, but Diodorus (XII.70) does describe a select group of 300 'charioteers and sidesmen' forming the front rank at this battle, and it is an interesting coincidence that Herodotus (IX.67) should speak of the 300 best and bravest Thebans falling at Plataea.[38] There might thus be grounds for postulating that such an elite force already existed, but I have not included it as a veteran unit in the scenario because it does not seem to have fought separately and the Boeotians have enough of an advantage as it is. The 10,000 light troops raise exactly the same problems as those at Plataea, and as they do not seem to have contributed anything significant during the battle despite not being matched by similar Athenian forces, I have represented them by just 1 token levy unit. All the other Boeotian troops seem best classified as average. Pagondas was apparently only one of 11 generals serving in rotation, but he seems to have displayed inspirational leadership and tactical flair, so he probably deserves an average rating.[39]

Thucydides (IV.94) says that the Athenians had about as many hoplites as the enemy, but that the horde of ill-armed light troops that had accompanied the expedition had already mostly left for home. It is not clear how many cavalry Athens deployed. Thucydides does not mention their contribution beyond saying (III.93–4) that they were stationed on each wing and that 300 troopers had been left to guard the Delium fort. Diodorus (XII.70), however, claims that the Athenian cavalry fought brilliantly and at first routed the Boeotian horse. This may simply be another instance of his invented stereotypes of a cavalry clash followed by an infantry fight, but the initial triumph of the Athenian right does not appear to have been affected by enemy cavalry superiority on that wing, so we may postulate the presence of as many as possible of the 1,200 horsemen recorded in 431, as modified for plague losses and the Delium detachment.[40] Hippocrates seems not to have been an outstanding leader, so is best rated as uninspired. At a multiple of 1, this gives the army a fighting value of 54, which is significantly less than the 65 of the Boeotians.

The Thebans should surely move first, given what both Thucydides (IV.96) and Diodorus (XII.70) say about the Athenians being engaged before they were entirely ready (with Hippocrates having got only halfway along the line making his address). Thucydides (IV.93) describes the native Theban contingent on the right as forming up in 25 ranks in what would become their characteristic tactic of a deep attacking column. The *Hellenica Oxyrhynchia* (XVI.3–4) says the Thebans made up 4 of the 11 districts of Boeotia, with the Haliartians and others around Lake Copais (whom Thucydides places in the centre of the line) having 2 districts between them, and the Thespians, Tanagreans and Orchomenians on the left having the remaining 5 districts. Each district in theory provided 1,000 hoplites and 100 cavalry, but it is not clear what the respective contributions were to this force of just 7,000 (rather than 11,000) hoplites. Both sides' key zones are in their right centre, to encourage the historical anticlockwise turning movement.

The actual battle was hard fought, with the deep Theban column pushing back the Athenian left, but with the Boeotian left giving way except for the Thespians who stood firm and were cut down in a confused encirclement in which some Athenians mistakenly killed their own men. The decisive stroke came when Pagondas sent 2 squadrons of cavalry from his right wing round behind the hill and panicked the hitherto victorious Athenian right. Thucydides (IV.96 and 101) says that 500 Boeotians and 1,000 Athenian combat troops fell, with losses among the vanquished being reduced by nightfall and by the availability of refuges at Delium, Oropus and Mount Parnes. The Athenian dead included Hippocrates, but not Socrates who was famously able to escape by keeping his head and deterring potential attackers.[41] There is not as much scholarly controversy about this battle as there is about some others, but the model does highlight the fact that, given all the advantages that the Boeotians enjoyed (a better general, an uphill position, cavalry superiority and an overwhelming advantage in light troops) the Athenians were lucky to do even as well as they did. If they had even fewer horsemen, then some enemy hoplites would have to count as levies to give the Athenians any chance at all.

DELIUM, 424 BC (Figure 10)

M: x1. AL: 3.

Thebans: AL + AHO (Pagondas + Thebans), 13 AHO (5 Theban, 2 Thespian, 2 Orchomenian, 1 Tanagrean, 1 Haliartian and Lebadean, 1 Coronean and Acraephnian, 1 Copaean and Chaeronean), 1 ALI (Peltasts), 1 LLI (Psiloi), 4 AHC (2 Theban, 2 Boeotian). FV: 65.

Athenians: UL + AHO (Hippocrates + Athenians), 13 AHO (Athenian), 3 AHC (Athenian). FV: 54.

1ST MANTINEA, 418 BC

Seven years after Delium came perhaps the most famous hoplite battle of all, between the two traditional rivals of the Peloponnese – Sparta and Argos. Thucydides (V.66–74) devotes nearly 2,000 words to this encounter, but despite his efforts, there remain very significant uncertainties, especially about troop numbers. At least terrain is less of an issue than at Delium, as there is no indication that the battle was fought on anything other than the flat plain south of the city of Mantinea. Some scholars have suggested that the Pelagos wood may have played a part in the preliminaries to the engagement, and that it was not until the Spartans emerged in column from the wood on their way north from Tegea that they saw the Argives deployed for battle close at hand.[42] However, this only affects the issue of surprise (that I will discuss below), and there is no suggestion that the wood played any tactical role in the battle itself.

The central issue for this battle reconstruction (and for some of those in the next chapter) concerns the size of the Spartan army. Thucydides (V.68) says that Spartan secrecy made it hard to know their numbers, but he tried to estimate their strength by calculating that they fielded 7 lochoi, each of 4 pentekostyes, each in turn made up of 4 enomotia deployed in 4 files with an average depth of 8 ranks. He works this out at 448 files, or 3,584 troops if we assume 8 ranks throughout. In addition, he notes the presence of 600 Sciritae, who seem to have been more flexible hoplites from the hills north-west of Sparta, used especially

to guard the vulnerable left wing.[43] Sadly, almost every aspect of this account
has triggered bitter scholarly controversy, as Anderson discussed in detail a
generation ago.[44] Debate rages over how Thucydides's model relates to the four
other Laconian contingents that he mentions – the remnants of Brasidas's force
(that numbered 700 freed helots and 1,000 Peloponnesian mercenaries in 424),
a further group of freed helots, the 300 Hippeis guarding King Agis, and the 'few'
Spartans he says were on the right wing.[45] Some writers argue that Thucydides's
alleged organization is itself fundamentally flawed, and that he is hopelessly
confused about the size and number of the lochoi and should instead have
spoken of morai as in later Spartan armies. There is no space here to rehash the
many highly complex arguments, but modern estimates of the Spartan hoplites
present at the battle (excluding the Sciritae, Brasideioi and freed helots) range all
the way from Sekunda's figure of 2,560 to Lazenby's suggestion of up to 6,500.
Even the identity of 'Spartan' troops is a matter of dispute, with many scholars
suggesting the incorporation at some point in the later fifth century of perioikoi
from elsewhere in Laconia to offset the rapidly dwindling numbers of 'pure'
Spartiates, while others like Lazenby postulate an intermediate category of lesser
Spartan citizens.[46]

What our model can contribute to this vexed debate is a more structured
framework within which to compare the fighting values of the various suggested
Spartan forces with those of their opponents in this and other related battles. If
the relative Spartan fighting values are too low, then it is hard to explain their
continued victories, while if they are too high, the resulting contests would be
so one-sided as to make it irrational for enemies to accept battle and impractical
for them to achieve even such initial successes as they often did. The process is
complicated by the fact that two distinct dimensions are in play – the size of
the Spartan forces, and their quality as reflected in the composition of the units
concerned. Before we can gauge the impact of these interacting elements, we must
establish a yardstick by reconstructing the opposing army at this engagement.

The only definite figure that Thucydides gives for the enemy army (V.72)
is for the 1,000 picked Argives, who should surely count as veterans. Modern
estimates of the overall strength of the army, based on the likely size of the
different contingents, range from 8,000 to 11,000.[47] Both Thucydides (V.61)
and Diodorus (XII.79) mention an Athenian contribution of 1,000 hoplites and
2–300 cavalry, and Diodorus (XII.78) puts the Mantinean levy at nearly 3,000
hoplites. There were also small Arcadian, Cleonean and Ornean contingents that
probably totalled several hundred between them. The main uncertainty concerns
how many other Argives were present. Xenophon (Hell. IV.2.17) claims there were
7,000 Argives a generation later at the Nemea, so there must surely have been at
least 5–6,000 in this engagement as it seems to have involved the full levy. At a
multiple of 1.5, a total force of 10,500 troops brings the allied fighting value to

51. Thucydides (V.68 and 71) says that the Spartan army appeared larger than its opponents, so our reconstruction should aim for a Spartan force that has at least 10,000 men but whose fighting value is not so much greater than 51 that the Argive decision to offer battle and the initial success of their right wing become totally implausible.

If Thucydides's 7 lochoi included the Brasideioi and freed helots as many scholars think, then it is very hard to see how the army could come anywhere near 10,000 troops unless his calculations are grossly in error, as the Tegeans and other allies seem unlikely to have contributed more than 3,000 hoplites.[48] By contrast, if Thucydides has miscalculated Spartan numbers by a factor of 2, then Lazenby's rejection of the widespread incorporation of perioikoi into the army becomes equally questionable, as this would suggest making most of the troops veterans as at Plataea, which would give an overall fighting value of around 90.[49] The only thing that would make this enormously powerful Spartan army at all plausible in our model would be if it were caught by surprise. Thucydides (V.66) does emphasize how shocked the Spartans were to find the Argives ready to engage them, but ironically it is Lazenby himself who minimizes the impact of this and points out that the Spartans nevertheless had time to form a full battle line before the clash.[50] The Argives should clearly get the first move, but there is no case for subjecting the Spartans to the full rigours of a surprise deployment, as at Plataea.

The idea that there were twice as many Spartan hoplites as Thucydides suggests becomes more plausible if we accept the view of Cartledge and others that the perioikoi who had formed a separate 5,000 strong contingent at Plataea were now integrated alongside the Spartiates.[51] Thucydides (IV.38) says that only 120 of the 292 Spartans taken prisoner at Pylos in 425 were Spartiates, so if we take this proportion as broadly representative, and if we classify only the Spartiates themselves as veterans, then the army's fighting value would fall to around 70 – still high compared to the Argives' total of 51, but not impossibly so. However, as Thucydides (V.72) describes the Argives and their allies fleeing as soon as they were charged, and trampling one another in their anxiety to escape, there is little evidence that the Spartans had become any less fearsome and more reliant on numerical superiority in order to prevail. It is also distinctly hubristic for us to assert so readily that Thucydides's careful and detailed calculation of a frontage of 448 shields for the Spartan main body is out by a factor of two, as we are certainly in no better position to make such estimates than he was at the time.[52]

Van Wees has recently taken a refreshingly different tack, by avoiding a direct challenge to Thucydides's figures and focusing instead on those areas where he is vague, tentative and ambiguous. Van Wees makes a strong case that the Brasideioi and freed helots were not counted in Thucydides's 7 lochoi after all and that the right wing contained not just 'a few' but at least 1,000 extra Spartans, as this was the only logical source of the 2 lochoi that Thucydides (V.71–2) describes Agis abortively trying to redeploy to strengthen his weak left.[53] This brings the total of Spartan hoplites to at least 4,600, and if we add in the 600 Sciritae, well over 1,000 Brasideioi and freed helots, up to 3,000 allied hoplites and several hundred cavalry, the Spartan army comes close enough to the suggested opposing total of 10,500 to explain Thucydides's uncertainty about which army was larger, especially if the Spartans actually had the longer line. Van Wees thinks that the majority of Spartan hoplites were now perioikoi, but we need only make a third of his 4,600 men average rather than veteran to bring the army's fighting value down to a more reasonable level, and even this reflects the specific confusion and disruption at this battle as much as it does any systemic dilution of Spartan combat effectiveness.[54] The 600 Sciritae can be represented as an average heavy infantry (rather than hoplite) unit, to reflect their greater resilience if outflanked, while the notoriously poor Spartan cavalry deserve just 1 levy unit.[55] With Agis as an uninspired general, the army's total fighting value comes to 64, giving it a clear edge without precluding some localized success for the other side.

The most famous aspect of the battle is surely Thucydides's description (V.71) of the tendency of hoplite lines to drift right as they advanced, so that each side's right tended to overlap the enemy left. He goes on (V.71–2) to detail Agis's attempt to offset this tendency by a last-minute redeployment of 2 Spartan lochoi to bolster the Sciritae, Brasideioi and freed helots on his left wing, and tells how this had to be abandoned when the unit commanders refused to comply. As I discussed in Part I, our model is too generic and broad brush to capture such elements directly, but the key zone system encourages both sides to strengthen their right, and the free deployment variant captures very well the Spartan dilemma over how far to bolster their left at the expense of reducing their advantage elsewhere, while the random element within the model gives ample scope for the confusion that historically hastened the left's collapse. At an average of 8 deep, the nearly 10,000 Spartan and allied hoplites would cover around 1,200 m, so a scale of 500 m per zone leaves ample scope for the gap that developed on the left due to the abortive redeployment. Parts of the Argive army may well have used deeper formations of around 12 ranks, and so they could easily have had a shorter line even if numbers were roughly equal.[56] Units in Figure 11 have been pushed forward during deployment as far as average command availability permits, and the Spartan cavalry have been placed on the right wing opposite the Athenian horse, as it is not possible to split a single unit between both flanks.

Like Delium, 1st Mantinea was a classic 'revolving door' battle, with the Mantineans and picked Argives breaking the Sciritae, Brasideioi and freed helots on the Spartan left, while the Tegeans on the right swept round the Athenians who retreated under the cover of their horsemen. The decisive clash came in the centre, where Agis broke the main body of the Argives (most of whom fled at the first shock) and then turned to see off the Mantineans and picked Argives as well. Thucydides (V.74) says the Spartans lost about 300 men and their enemies a total of 1,100.[57] The scenario below should on average produce just such an outcome, with both sides tempted to hold back their weaker left while pushing forward with their stronger right to create the historical anticlockwise twist, but with the prohibition on advances by outflanked hoplites exposing both the Mantineans and Spartans to flank attack if the others can turn first.

This does not mean that the fine details of the reconstructed armies are correct – far more likely they are not. The contribution that our model makes is much broader – to draw on other instances where good troops like the Spartans fought and won against great odds, and to use this experience to cast systematic light on Thucydides's contradictory claims that the Spartan army was the larger and that there were only a few thousand Spartan hoplites. If he has indeed miscalculated Spartan numbers by a factor of two, then our model suggests that their troop quality must have been very seriously compromised and that hoplites outside the core of 'pure' Spartiates must have been indistinguishable in fighting ability from the militia of other states, despite their integration into joint units. As we shall see, subsequent battles from the Nemea to Sellasia cast grave doubt on this dilution of Spartan fighting quality, so it seems preferable to place greater faith in Thucydides's calculations and to seek other means of squaring the circle, perhaps along the lines that van Wees has proposed. We will never know the truth, but our approach of comparative dynamic modelling may at least add something useful to the continuing debate.

1ST MANTINEA, 418 BC (Figure 11)

M: x1.5. AL: 4.

Argives: 3 VHO (Picked Argives), 12 AHO (6 Argive, 4 Mantinean, 1 Athenian, 1 Arcadian, Cleonean and Ornean), 1 AHC (Athenian). FV: 51.

Spartans: UL + VHO (Agis + Hippeis), 7 VHO (Spartan), 8 AHO (3 Tegean, 2 Spartan, 1 Brasideioi, 1 Freed Helots, 1 Heraian and Mainalian), 1 AHI (Sciritae), 1 LHC (Spartan). FV: 64.

8

The Age of Xenophon

Just as Herodotus dominates our perspective on Greek history up to 479 BC, and Thucydides is our main source for the period from 479 to 411, so the 50 years from 411 to 362 are known primarily through the writings of Xenophon.[1] The end of the Peloponnesian War produced a glut of Greek mercenaries – in 401 over 10,000 of these troops (including Xenophon himself) fought for Cyrus at Cunaxa as he tried to win the Persian throne, and after his death they escaped from Persia in an epic fighting retreat. In Greece itself, the ensuing period saw a series of challenges to the dominant power of Sparta. The Corinthian War broke out in 395 BC, and the following year witnessed two of the biggest ever hoplite clashes, one at the Nemea River and the other at Coronea. The anti-Spartan coalition was defeated on both occasions, but resentment continued to fester, and the Thebans in particular were determined to end Spartan hegemony. In 371 at Leuctra, under the inspired leadership of Epaminondas, they finally managed to break the spell of Sparta's invincibility in pitched hoplite battle. Sparta herself held out, despite her lack of walls, and when Epaminondas fought a Peloponnesian and Athenian coalition at Mantinea 9 years later, he himself was killed at the moment of victory. Theban dominance was thus even more short-lived than that of Sparta or Athens beforehand, and the constant internecine fighting left the Greek cities vulnerable to the rise of an external hegemon in the shape of the northern kingdom of Macedon.

CUNAXA, 401 BC

Cyrus's attempt to seize the Persian throne from his brother Artaxerxes came to a head at Cunaxa, north of Babylon. Xenophon (*An.* I.8 and 10) provides an invaluable eyewitness account nearly 3,000 words long. Plutarch (*Artax.* 6–13) and Diodorus (XIV.22–4) give their own descriptions, drawing on lost authorities including Ctesias, who was Artaxerxes's personal physician. As usual, the sources sometimes conflict, and their figures for Asiatic numbers are as absurd as those of Herodotus. At least the battlefield terrain is fairly clear, consisting of an open plain on the east bank of the River Euphrates down which Cyrus had been advancing. Xenophon (*An.* I.10.12–14) and Plutarch (*Artax.* 11) both record a hill behind Artaxerxes's line, but as this was later occupied by the king's cavalry, it was probably neither steep nor rough, so does not seem to warrant special representation. Reconstructing the size, deployment and manoeuvres of the contending armies is more problematic, and has been the subject of some scholarly debate.[2]

Our most reliable figures are for the Greek and Thracian mercenaries, whom Xenophon (*An*. I.2.9 and 7.10) numbers just before the battle at 10,400 hoplites and 2,500 peltasts (including some 200 Cretan archers).[3] They clearly enjoyed massive psychological dominance over the Asiatics, so they should all be classed as veterans. Our figures for Cyrus's cavalry are surprisingly restrained, with Diodorus (XIV.19 and 22) putting the total at just 3,000 in 3 equal divisions, and Xenophon (*An*. I.8.5–7 and 9.31) mentioning Cyrus's personal guard of 600 armoured horsemen as well as 1,000 Paphlagonian cavalry and an unspecified number of horse led by Ariaeus. This relative shortage of cavalry is confirmed by the enemy superiority in scouting before the battle, and it makes Rahe's arguments about the military benefits of combining hoplite infantry with powerful cavalry perhaps a little premature.[4] Where matters become problematic is with regard to Cyrus's Asiatic infantry, which Diodorus (XIV.19) numbers at nearly 70,000 and Xenophon (*An*. I.7.10) at almost 100,000. Modern scholars suggest 20–30,000 as a more reasonable figure, and as the troops made no discernible difference in the battle, this sounds about right as long as they are classed as levies.[5] Cyrus should clearly be an average leader at the head of his guard, but there is no case for boosting the army's command resources further by representing Ariaeus or the mercenary 'leader' Clearchus as an additional general. The fighting value of Cyrus's force in our model thus adds up to 66, with the mercenaries contributing 60 per cent of this in line with their major impact on the fighting.

The size of Artaxerxes's army is even more a matter of educated guesswork. Xenophon (*An*. I.7.12) describes 3 satraps each commanding 50 scythed chariots and no less than 300,000 troops, even though he had earlier claimed (I.2.4) that one of the three (Tissaphernes) left his province with just 500 horse! Diodorus (XIV.22) and Plutarch (*Artax*. 13) cite Ephorus and Ctesias as giving the scarcely more reasonable figure of 400,000 for Artaxerxes's host. Modern writers reduce this to around 60,000, though Cawkwell does mention 120,000 as an unlikely maximum possibility.[6] Xenophon (*An*. I.8.9) says the infantry included men with wicker shields (gerrhophoroi), Egyptian hoplites with long wooden shields, and more bowmen. The gerrhon was described by Herodotus (VII.61 and IX.61–2 and 99) as the palisade from behind which Persian close-order archers shot and fought, so it is probably safe to assume from this and from the repeated references to arrows at Cunaxa that the bow remained the main Persian infantry weapon.[7] However, Asiatic infantry was in transition at this period with the rise of peltast-type troops not armed in the old fashion, so it is probably best to give both sides some generic heavy and light infantry in addition to the close-order archers still fielded by Artaxerxes.[8]

Besides Tissaphernes's 500 white-armoured horsemen, Xenophon (*An.* I.6.1 and 8.24–5) mentions just the 2,000 cavalry who earlier screened Cyrus's advance and the 6,000 horse led by Artagerses who defended the king himself. As these 6,000 were allegedly routed by Cyrus's 600, they surely deserve only levy status except for 1 average unit to guard Artaxerxes, who does not seem to have been as timid as his successor Darius III. Tissaphernes probably warrants representation as an uninspired leader in his own right, given the prominent role he is accorded in this battle and later in the campaign. If everyone except Tissaphernes's and Artaxerxes's guards counts as levies in line with their dismal failure to stand up to the Greeks, then even an army of 80,000 only has a fighting value of 51, which should give Cyrus's men an overwhelming advantage, but which also means that killing Cyrus and routing his Asiatic troops should bring a handsome game victory for the king's forces even if the mercenaries end up roaming the battlefield unscathed and unopposed as happened historically.

Xenophon (*An.* I.8.1–17) describes how news of the king's proximity came only in the late morning when the head of Cyrus's column was nearing the planned camp site, and he records how Greek troops continued to trickle in to the hastily formed battle line throughout the next few hours as Artaxerxes's host steadily advanced until it was just 3 or 4 stadia (6–700 m) away. Anderson and Nelson both suggest that Cyrus's Asiatic troops were still coming up at the rear of the long and disorganized column (*An.* I.7.19–20) when the battle began, and that this helps to explain Xenophon's otherwise enigmatic claims (*An.* I.8.13 and 21–4) that Cyrus's whole line hardly stretched from the river to the centre of Artaxerxes's line, but that Cyrus himself charged the king even though both were in the centre of their respective lines.[9] However, Xenophon (*An.* I.8.5, 9.31 and 10.1) and Diodorus (XIV.22–4) do repeatedly mention Ariaeus's Asiatic forces on the left, and it is probably going too far to have Cyrus's army count as surprised, given the severity of this penalty within our model. Artaxerxes should certainly move first, and the historical deployment in Figure 12 (with Cyrus's mercenaries concentrated on the right, his cavalry thrown forward in the centre and the Asiatic infantry in the rear) should help reflect the initial course of the fighting.

Xenophon (*An.* I.2.14–18) famously described the 10,000 as forming up just 4 deep for the earlier review and mock charge at Celaenae, and it is often assumed that they used a similar shallow formation at Cunaxa itself.[10] However, this would make the hoplite line alone some 2.5 km long, not even counting the peltasts and Paphlagonians by the river, and it is very doubtful that this entire force covered such a small proportion of Artaxerxes's frontage. The 10,000 later formed up 8 deep (*An.* VII.1.23), and some modern writers suggest they did so in this battle.[11] Our comparative model very strongly supports this latter interpretation, because even this would suggest zones with the maximum scale width of 1,200 m. Xenophon (*An.* I.8.12–13) claims that Cyrus wanted the mercenaries to head straight for Artaxerxes in the enemy centre, but that Clearchus was concerned about exposing his flanks and so stuck closer to the river instead. This tactical dilemma is easily explored in our model, with the free deployment option allowing the Greeks to concentrate in either the right or centre zones or to cover both by extending themselves in a shallower 4 deep line, at the risk of suffering the same fate as the Athenian centre at Marathon.

According to Xenophon (*An.* I.8–10), the king's left infantry wing fled as soon as the Greeks charged, with the scythed chariots proving typically ineffectual. However, Tissaphernes broke through the peltasts by the river, while Artaxerxes began to wheel his overlapping right wing round to outflank the enemy.[12] Cyrus charged with his guard to forestall this, but after initial success (that may have included wounding the king) he was overwhelmed and killed, triggering the flight of his Asiatic troops. The pursuing Greeks were now some 30 stadia (5.5 km) away from their baggage that Artaxerxes's men were plundering – the distance suggests that the camp should not be on the board, where it would give an unrealistic boost to Cyrus's initial deployment. Both forces marched back towards one another and, after some tangled preliminary manoeuvring, the mercenaries again charged and the Persians again fled, with the Greeks pursuing them until sunset without making contact. Diodorus (XIV.24) claims that 3,000 of Cyrus's Asiatic troops died and that the Greeks killed 15,000 of Artaxerxes's men in close combat and pursuit without suffering any losses themselves, but this contradicts Xenophon's image of the Persians fleeing long before contact, and Bigwood suggests that it represents the same kind of stereotypical invention as in some of Diodorus's other battle pieces.[13] By focusing on morale and cohesion rather than physical combat and casualties, our model provides an ideal vehicle for exploring this contest in which qualitative differences were extreme and in which the Greeks' ability to overawe all nearby resistance by no means guaranteed strategic success.

CUNAXA, 401 BC (Figure 12)

M: x5. AL: 5.

Artaxerxes: 6 LHI (3 Egyptian, 3 Asiatic), 5 LAR (Gerrhophoroi), 3 LLI (Archers and Slingers), UL + VHC (Tissaphernes + Guard), AL + AHC (Artaxerxes + Guard), 2 LHC (Persian), 1 LLC (Asiatic), 1 SCH. FV: 51.

Cyrus: 8 VHO (10,000), 1 VHI (Peltasts), 4 LHI (Asiatic), 1 VLI (Peltasts and Cretans), 1 LLI (Asiatic), AL + VHC (Cyrus + Guard), 1 AHC (Asiatic), 1 ALC (Paphlagonian). FV: 66.

NEMEA, 394 BC

The largest battle of the Corinthian War saw the Spartans and their Peloponnesian allies facing a coalition of most of the other major Greek states near the Nemea stream west of Corinth. Xenophon (*Hell*. IV.2.13–23) describes the engagement in about 1,000 words, and includes a number of interesting details, though in a rather careless fashion. Diodorus (XIV.82–3) gives a much briefer and more problematic statistical summary. The only terrain feature of any relevance is the dry streambed behind which Xenophon (*Hell*. IV.2.15) says the allies camped, and that they presumably crossed to give battle to the Spartans camped some 10 stadia (1.8 km) to the west. Anderson presumes this was the Nemea stream itself, but Pritchett and Lazenby suggest on good evidence that it was the Rachiani, a few kilometres further east.[14] Fortunately, the identification makes no difference to the stream's representation in our model within the allies' rear zones. Xenophon (*Hell*. IV.2.18–19) says the Spartans did not at first notice the allies' advance because of the amount of natural cover. This certainly provides grounds for the allies to move first, but it would be going too far to include more than a token zone of woods along the stream, even though the whole area today is heavily covered with vegetation.[15]

Xenophon (*Hell*. IV.2.16) lists hoplite contingents on the Spartan side that total 13,500, but he does not include the Tegeans, Mantineans or Achaeans (apart from Sicyon) whom he mentions elsewhere as contributing to the force. Diodorus (XIV.83) gives an overall total of 23,000 infantry, which most scholars are inclined to accept, but Lazenby suggests that the missing hoplites numbered only around 5,000, bringing the total to 18–19,000.[16] Six thousand of Xenophon's total were said to be from Sparta and the surrounding area, but as at 1st Mantinea, scholars disagree widely over the composition of this force. It is thought that 5 of the 6 citizen morai were present, but how many and what kind of troops each mora contained are matters of dispute. Some writers think their strength was around 600, in line with Xenophon's figure (*Hell*. IV.5.12) for a mora that was mauled by light infantry at nearby Lechaeum 4 years later, but Lazenby cannot believe that Spartan hegemony rested on only around 4,000 citizen troops, so he argues that each mora contained 32 rather than 16 enomotiai, giving it a maximum strength of 1,280 men. He thus suggests that almost all of Xenophon's 6,000 at Nemea were Spartan citizens of one kind or another, whereas other scholars think that only a minority of them were, and that the remainder consisted of Sciritae, freed helots or perioikoi. Cartledge believes in larger morai that themselves incorporated perioikoi, while Anderson and Sekunda think that even the smaller morai now consisted largely of perioikoi, with Spartan citizens reduced to less than 1,500 Spartiates.[17] Here again is exactly the kind of controversy on which our model may be able to cast some light.

According to Xenophon (*Hell*. IV.2.17), the allied army contained some 24,000 hoplites, including 7,000 Argives, 6,000 Athenians, 5,000 Boeotians and 3,000 each from Corinth and Euboea. He does express some uncertainty about the Argive figure, and Anderson has suggested that the total may have been slightly lower, but Xenophon's detailed breakdown is given far more credence than Diodorus's bald claim (XIV.82) of just 15,000 allied infantry.[18] Xenophon (*Hell*. IV.2.16–17) says the Spartans had 600 cavalry and 700 archers and slingers, whereas the allies fielded 1,550 horsemen and an unspecified number of light infantry.[19] There is no indication that their cavalry superiority gave the allies any advantage, or indeed that these troops played any role in the battle, but this may simply reflect one of the many careless omissions for which Xenophon is renowned.[20] There seems to be little case for making non-Spartan troops on either side anything other than average, so at a multiple of 3, the allies have a total fighting value of 57. Leaving aside for a moment the 6,000 Lacedaemonians, and using Hammond's intermediate figure of 20,000 for the hoplites as a whole, the rest of the Spartan army has a fighting value of 33.[21] Unlike Pagondas at Delium, the regent Aristodemus is not described as making much personal contribution to the decisive battle-winning manoeuvre, so deserves only an 'uninspired' rating. The 6,000 Lacedaemonians could be represented by anything from 2 veteran and 3 average hoplite units to 8 veteran units, depending on one's assumptions about their composition and quality. This would produce total fighting values for the Spartan army of anything between 53 and 68, as against 57 for the allies. To see which interpretation is most plausible, we must look more closely at the course of the engagement and at deductions from related battles.

Nemea was a classic instance of one contingent on both sides pursuing its own advantage with little thought for the welfare of its allies. The Spartans concentrated on winning on the right, with no attempt (as at Mantinea) to bolster the resistance of their centre and left, now made up of non-Spartan troops. In the other army, Xenophon (*Hell*. IV.2.13 and 18) tells a fascinating story of the coalition partners debating how deep to form up so as to avoid the twin perils of encirclement or of frontal breakthrough, and he then describes how the Boeotians delayed battle until it was their turn to be on the opposite wing from the dreaded Spartans, at which point they ignored the agreement and made their own formation very deep as they had at Delium, compounding this by inclining to the right to outflank the Achaeans. On the other wing, Xenophon (*Hell*. IV.2.19–21) says that the Spartan right extended so far beyond the allied left that only some 3,600 Athenian hoplites faced the Lacedaemonians themselves. As the agreed allied depth was 16 ranks, the 24,000 allied hoplites probably had a front of up to 1,400 m.[22] The Spartan army was most likely drawn up 12 deep as at Leuctra, though some of their allies may have used 16 ranks.[23] A scale of around 600 m per zone gives scope for a longer Spartan line and for the overlaps on both right flanks. If the camps were only 1.8 km apart, the Spartan camp should be on the board, and it seems best to place it in the right rear zone as this reduces its vulnerability and gives the Spartan right a very historical head start.

Anderson argues that the Spartan contingent used its superiority in drill to turn into a rightward-facing column that then marched round into a position to roll up the entire enemy army.[24] However, it is hard to see how this would work without leaving a yawning gap in the line, and Lazenby's image of the unengaged part of the Spartan line wheeling forward to take the Athenians in flank seems equally compatible with Xenophon's narrative.[25] I pointed out on p. 41 that our model is too broad brush to reconstruct such detailed manoeuvres in any case, and that the main thing is to reflect the *outcome*, namely a rapid and one-sided Spartan triumph over the 6 Athenian tribes they faced. Meanwhile, all Sparta's allies, including the neighbouring Tegeans, had been beaten by their opponents, though the Pelleneans on the left did put up more of a fight. What saved the Spartans is that they themselves were able to roll laterally across the battlefield, catching successive enemy contingents in their shieldless flank as they marched back victorious to their camp.[26] In our model, the special hoplite rules should help to simulate this course of events, because if the Spartans can quickly dispose of the outnumbered Athenians in front, then even if the Argives in the centre are victorious on the very next turn, they will be prohibited from advancing by the Spartan flanking threat, and so will be exposed to a devastating flank attack that may well rout them and perhaps also panic the Thebans and Corinthians due to the fragility of hoplite morale if the Pelleneans are still hanging on nearby.[27] The model also neatly captures the role of the Spartan allies in wearing down their opponents during the initial frontal combat, making most of them 'spent' and so reflecting their lack of residual fighting capability against the Lacedaemonians themselves. For what it is worth, Diodorus (XIV.83) puts allied losses at 2,800 compared to 1,100 for the Spartan army, though Xenophon (*Hell.* IV.3.1) says the Spartans themselves lost just 8 men.

The battle may actually have been more evenly balanced than these figures suggest, with two-thirds of the troops in the Spartan army fleeing, and with both sides returning to their existing camps and the allied forces recovering to confront Agesilaus shortly afterwards.[28] Although there is a strong case for making all the Lacedaemonians veterans in line with Lazenby's interpretation, I have already shown how difficult it is within our model to accept his claims as regards 1st Mantinea, and I will demonstrate shortly that they pose even greater problems at Leuctra, when the Spartans were finally defeated despite apparently having the larger army. That being said, the Lacedaemonians did perform exceptionally well in winning the present battle single-handed after their allies had fled, so it is surely legitimate in this case to use an intermediate representation of 6 veteran and 1 average hoplite units, giving the Spartan army a definite edge with 6 more points of fighting value than their opponents, and making it harder for the allies to attain the sweeping morale benefits of having twice as many units left on the field. This suggests that restricting veteran status to the dwindling core of Spartiates is inappropriate, and that, whatever the provenance of the other Lacedaemonian troops may have been, at least some of them continued to perform significantly better man-for-man than their counterparts from other states.

NEMEA, 394 BC (Figure 13)

M: x3. AL: 3.

Allies: 16 AHO (5 Argive, 4 Athenian, 3 Boeotian, 2 Corinthian, 2 Euboean), 1 ALI (Locrian, Malian and Acarnanian), 2 AHC (1 Boeotian, 1 Athenian and Euboean). FV: 57.

Spartans: UL + VHO (Aristodemus + *Hippeis*), 5 VHO (Spartan), 10 AHO (2 Mantinean, 1 Lacedaemonian, 1 Tegean, 1 Elean, 1 Triphylian, Acrorian and Lasionian, 1 Sicyonian, 1 Pellenean, 1 Epidauran, 1 Troezenian, Hermionan and Halieian), 1 ALI (Cretan, Marganian, Letrinian and Amphidolian), 1 AHC (Spartan). FV: 63.

2ND CORONEA, 394 BC

Soon after the contest at the Nemea, the renowned Spartan king Agesilaus arrived back from his campaign in Asia and was confronted in Boeotia by forces from the reconstituted allied army. Xenophon was with Agesilaus, and describes the battle in several hundred words both in his biography of the king (*Ages.* II.6–16) and in his general history (*Hell.* IV.3.15–21). We also have shorter accounts by Plutarch (*Ages.* 18–19) and Diodorus (XIV.84). The plain of Coronea had witnessed an earlier engagement between Athenians and Boeotians in 447 BC, but now the two states were united against the Spartans. Xenophon (*Hell.* IV.3.16–19) says that Agesilaus came down from the River Cephissus in the north while the allies advanced from and then fled back to Mount Helicon. There is no sense that terrain played any role in the actual battle, wherever on the plain the exact site may have been, but the high ground around Coronea narrows the gap between the mountains and Lake Copais to the northeast, so it may be worth placing hills in the allied left wing zone to reflect this slight constriction.[29]

Our sources are frustratingly vague about the numbers involved in this engagement, so we have to fall back on educated guesswork. Xenophon (*Hell.* IV.3.16) says the allied forces consisted of the Boeotians, Athenians, Argives, Aenianians, Euboeans, and both tribes of Locrians. Lazenby guesses that there were around 20,000 hoplites, based on losses at the Nemea and on the suggestion that nearby states like the Boeotians, Athenians and Euboeans may have sent at least as many troops as at that battle whereas Argos and Corinth were now further off and concerned to defend their own territory against the other Spartan army.[30] Pritchett suggests a similar total, but Cartledge is more cautious and estimates overall allied strength at 15–20,000.[31] The main contribution from our sources is relative rather than absolute, with Xenophon (*Ages.* II.7–9) emphasizing the exact match of strength between the two armies, and also (*Hell.* IV.3.15) saying that the two cavalry forces were about equal but that Agesilaus had a great superiority in peltasts. His horsemen were of unusually good quality, having just defeated the vaunted Thessalians, though (as at the Nemea) we hear nothing of their contribution or that of the peltasts in this battle.[32]

Most scholars are content to assume from Xenophon's statements that the two sides were roughly equal in numbers.[33] Lazenby puts forward a different view, and suggests that the Spartan army was smaller, with less than 15,000 hoplites compared to the 20,000 he gives the allies.[34] Xenophon (*Hell.* IV.3.15) says that Agesilaus's army consisted of the freed helots he had led in Asia, the survivors of Cyrus's Greek mercenaries, allies from Greek cities in Asia and on the route back, local allies from Phocis and Orchomenos, half of the mora that had been garrisoning Orchomenos, and a whole mora that had been shipped across the Gulf of Corinth from the other Spartan army. He does not mention the many thousands of Peloponnesian allied troops sent to Asia since 399, so these may have returned earlier or formed the bulk of the garrison left behind with Euxenos.[35] There is the usual disagreement over how many troops the 1.5 morai contained, with Lazenby estimating 1,680 and Anderson only 850, but this is somewhat overshadowed in the present case by uncertainty over how many Cyrean veterans were present.[36] As at 1st Mantinea, the problem that our model highlights is that, if Agesilaus's army is given roughly the same numerical strength as that of the allies, then the higher the proportion of veterans it contains, the more imbalanced the fighting values will become. To see how much of a problem this presents, we must review the course of the actual engagement to determine how evenly matched or one-sided it was.

The sources are somewhat vague on the respective deployments, but this was clearly yet another 'revolving door' battle, with the Argives on the allied left fleeing from Agesilaus and his men even before contact, and with the Cyreans and the Ionian, Aeolian and Hellespontine contingents routing the allied centre, but with the Thebans on the allied right shattering the Orchomenians and going on to plunder the Spartan baggage containing all the booty from Asia. When Agesilaus heard the news, he countermarched his phalanx and led it against the Thebans, who were returning themselves to rejoin their allies on Mount Helicon. It is not clear whether the term 'Thebans' here does or does not include the rest of the Boeotians, but it probably does, as otherwise the odds would have been enormous. Xenophon (*Hell*. IV.3.19) criticizes the king for not letting the enemy go past and then attacking them in flank and rear as at the Nemea, but instead launching a frontal charge on a reversed front. The result was a bitter and hard-fought contest, which some sources claim ended with the Spartans opening their ranks to let the Thebans through before attacking them in flank after all, but which Xenophon simply says led to some Thebans breaking through and many others being killed, with Agesilaus himself being wounded.[37] Diodorus (XIV.84) records total casualties of 600 for the allies and 350 for the Spartan army – if at all reliable, these figures are more balanced and also proportionally lighter than for other hoplite battles.[38] They certainly do not suggest that the Thebans were trapped and massacred as Agesilaus may have hoped to achieve to prevent the kind of recovery seen after the Nemea, and Plutarch (*Ages*. 18) says that the Thebans withdrew in good order and took pride in remaining undefeated.

Any reconstruction based on these flimsy sources is necessarily highly speculative, and this battle is on the verge of being too ill-documented to be modelled effectively at all. The course of the engagement certainly suggests that the Boeotians, on their home ground, numbered significantly more than the 5,000 they sent to the Nemea, as they held up so well alone against almost the entire Spartan army. Conversely, the other allied contingents may all have been weaker than at the earlier battle, given their losses and the need to fight on two fronts – this casts some doubt on Lazenby's estimate of 20,000 allied hoplites. On the Spartan side, the main issue we must consider is whether more than a few units really deserve classification as veterans. My analyses of 1st Mantinea and Leuctra pose serious challenges to Lazenby's figures for Spartan citizens within the morai. Similarly, even though the surviving Cyreans must have been incredibly experienced and 'grizzled' after their many ordeals, we must remember that their experience had been mainly against Asiatic opponents rather than other Greeks. Xenophon (*Hell*. IV.2.5) explicitly tells us that most of the troops would have preferred to stay in Asia, and his criticism of Agesilaus's head-on confrontation of the Thebans is a telling echo of the mercenary caution and calculation that Machiavelli would later parody.[39] Hence, the majority of the Cyreans should probably count as average rather than veteran in this case, as with similar mercenaries in Macedonian and Successor engagements.

If we give the allies around 20,000 troops overall, then at a multiple of 2.5 this gives them a fighting value of 51. On the other side, Agesilaus should surely count as an average leader given his extensive command experience, but the allies can move first to offset the deployment boost from the Spartan camp. We can give the Spartans almost as many troops as their opponents (in line with Xenophon's claim), while sticking to Lazenby's maximum estimate of 15,000 for the hoplite force. We do not know how deep either side's formations were, but 12–16 ranks as at the Nemea and Leuctra would suggest a scale of around

500 m per zone for armies of this size. The overall Spartan fighting value of 64 produces a superiority of 13 points as at 1st Mantinea, making it unlikely that more than a few of the army's units will flee, but giving a significant handicap penalty that may even allow the allies to win a game victory if the Thebans can ransack the enemy baggage and then fight as well as they did historically before they eventually withdraw.

2ND CORONEA, 394 BC (Figure 14)

M: x2.5. AL: 3.

Allies: 14 AHO (5 Boeotian, 3 Athenian, 3 Argive, 2 Euboean, 1 Corinthian), 1 ALI (Locrian and Aenianian), 2 AHC (1 Boeotian, 1 Athenian and Euboean). FV: 51.

Spartans: AL + VHO (Agesilaus + Spartans), 3 VHO (2 Mercenary, 1 Spartan), 10 AHO (3 Mercenary, 2 Freed Helots, 1 Ionian, 1 Aeolian, 1 Hellespontine, 1 Phocian, 1 Orchomenian), 1 AHI (Peltasts), 1 ALI (Peltasts and Archers), 2 AHC (1 Allied, 1 Mercenary). FV: 64.

LEUCTRA, 371 BC

When Cleombrotus of Sparta attacked a now-isolated Boeotia from the same direction a generation later, he outflanked the blocking position at Coronea so the two armies met at Leuctra, about 30 km to the southeast.[40] Xenophon (*Hell.* VI.4.8–15) describes the battle in several hundred words, but is clearly influenced by his pro-Spartan perspective. Among later writers, Diodorus (XV.54–6) gives an account of equal length but of dubious provenance, while Plutarch (*Pel.* 23) and Pausanias (IX.13.3–4) have shorter treatments. This time, the Boeotians came from the north while the Spartans advanced from and later retreated to the hills in the south, but this was such a small engagement that there is no case for any battlefield terrain.[41] As in so many other cases, the real problem is in reconstructing the armies themselves, as Xenophon gives no figures for either side and the other sources are contradictory and sometimes utterly implausible. Diodorus (XV.54), for instance, claims that the Boeotians were joined by 2,000 troops under Jason of Pherae and that Cleombrotus was bolstered by another large army under Agesilaus's son Archidamus, whereas Xenophon (*Hell.* VI.4.4, 20–2 and 26) makes it plain that neither reinforcement arrived until after the battle had been fought.[42]

It is best to start with the Boeotian side. Frontinus (*Str.* IV.2.6) says they had just 4,000 troops including 400 cavalry, while Diodorus (XV.52–3) gives them 6,000 troops under 6 Boeotarchs before a seventh joined them at Leuctra and cast the deciding vote for action. Lazenby combines these figures and assumes the overall totals actually refer to hoplites alone, so he suggests there were 7,000 hoplites and 700 cavalry, of which 4,000 hoplites and 400 cavalry came from Thebes itself.[43] This basic principle seems in accordance with the *Hellenica Oxyrhynchia* (XVI.3–4), which claims that Thebes should contribute 4 Boeotarchs each with 1,000 hoplites and 100 cavalry while the other districts should add a further 1 each. However, we know from Delium (7,000 Boeotian hoplites and 1,000 cavalry) and from the Nemea (5,000 hoplites and 800 horsemen) that these neat proportions of 10:1 were not usually manifest in practice. Pausanias (IX.13.3) does describe the arrival of a seventh Boeotarch with his contingent that had been guarding the route across Mount Cithaeron, but he then says that the Thespians withdrew to their nearby home just before the battle, which would cancel out this accretion of strength. The truth is that there is no real way of accurately discerning Boeotian numbers at Leuctra, and modern scholars have made estimates ranging from 6,000 to 9,000, with some hypothesizing the presence of light troops in addition to the hoplites and horsemen.[44]

The scenario below is based on an overall force of some 7,000 men. It is generally agreed that the famous Theban Sacred Band of 300 homosexual lovers, under its leader Pelopidas, made an important contribution, but it is not clear that any other Thebans warrant veteran status despite some recent successes, as their trademark deep formations are hardly a tactic associated with the highest-quality troops.[45] What made the Thebans so effective in this case was the inspirational leadership of Epaminondas. Although Xenophon does not even mention him, and Hanson has questioned his tactical originality, his successful deployment and motivation of his troops to face and overcome the dreaded Spartan main force surely earn him classification as an inspired general, especially as Pelopidas cannot really be represented separately in our system because he fought in such close proximity.[46] At a multiple of 1, the fighting value of the Theban army therefore comes to a total of 61.

The Spartan army is even harder to reconstruct, though at least we now have a yardstick in terms of fighting value against which to measure its overall effectiveness. Plutarch (*Pel.* 20) gives the strength of Cleombrotus's forces as 10,000 infantry and 1,000 cavalry, which are suspiciously round numbers but certainly preferable to Frontinus's 24,000 foot and 1,600 horse (*Str.* IV.2.6), or Polyaenus's even more ridiculous total of 40,000 men (II.3.12). Most modern scholars accept Plutarch's figures as the best available estimate, even though they mean that Epaminondas was outnumbered overall by around 3:2.[47] In addition to Lacedaemonians, Xenophon (*Hell.* VI.4.9) mentions mercenaries, Phocian peltasts and Heraclean and Phliasian cavalry, while Pausanias (VIII.6.2) says there were Arcadians from the Peloponnese – Hammond suggests there were around 6,600 allies and probably the complete levy of the Phocians.[48] However, Sparta's exploitation of its allies as 'spear fodder' at the Nemea and elsewhere had clearly taken its toll, as both Xenophon (*Hell.* VI.4.15) and Pausanias (IX.13.4) stress how discontented and unmotivated the allies were, to the point of being secretly pleased by Sparta's humiliation in this engagement. This suggests that they should all count as levies, thereby helping greatly to explain how Epaminondas was able to overcome such daunting quantitative and qualitative odds.

As usual, it is the Lacedaemonian contingent that arouses most controversy. Xenophon (*Hell.* VI.4.12–17) tells us that 4 of the 6 morai were present, that each enomotia had 3 files of up to 12 men, that 35 of the 40 age classes had been called up, and that there were 700 Spartiates. Lazenby, with his belief in 32 enomotiai in each mora, calculates that there were 4,480 citizen hoplites plus another 300 Hippeis.[49] Other scholars think that the morai were only half that size and that they included the Hippeis, so they postulate a force of 700 Spartiates and 1,600 others, with some (such as Anderson and van Wees) believing the others to be perioikoi.[50] Cartledge also thinks the 700 Spartiates were accompanied mainly or entirely by perioikoi, though he considers there were roughly as many Lacedaemonians as there were Thebans.[51] There is no reference to Sciritae or freed helots in addition to the morai, though this does not prove that they were absent. Cleombrotus deserves classification only as an uninspired leader, and the Spartan cavalry should count as levies as Xenophon (*Hell.* VI.4.10–11) emphasizes their poor quality.

Lazenby's suggested figure of 4,800 citizen hoplites seems very dubious according to our model, as this force would translate into no less than 19 veteran units, bringing the fighting value of the army as a whole to nearly 100. If we make only the 700 Spartiates veterans then the balance becomes much more reasonable, but I have already argued in relation to the Nemea and 1st Mantinea that there is no case for dismissing the fighting quality of integrated perioikoi. Our model hence casts grave doubt on the claims by Lazenby and Cartledge that there were over 4,000 Lacedaemonians. The alternative total of only around 2,300 Spartans makes much more sense, because even if they are all counted as veterans, the army's fighting value of 60 would still be very slightly less than the 61 for the Boeotians. It could be argued that the real battle was so evenly balanced that this classification should be adopted, but Xenophon (*Hell.* VI.4.8–9) does say that some of the Spartans were rather the worse for drink, so (as with the confusion at 1st Mantinea) there is a case for downgrading a small minority of their troops in order to give Epaminondas a clearer edge by cutting the overall Spartan fighting value to 55.

Cleombrotus deployed in the usual manner, with the Spartans themselves on the right, and he should probably move first to allow Epaminondas to tailor his own deployment accordingly. In 12 ranks, over 9,000 hoplites would have a frontage of around 750 m, so the smallest scale of 300 m per zone is clearly appropriate.[52] Epaminondas broke with tradition by massing his Thebans on his left, directly opposite the Spartans, with his centre and right being 'refused' to avoid initial contact. Polyaenus (II.3.15) claims Epaminondas explained this with the evocative analogy of crushing the head of a snake, and it clearly justifies placing both key zones on this wing to encourage such a head-on clash. Diodorus's tale (XV.55) of the Spartans responding by attacking on both wings in a crescent formation has been widely disbelieved as stemming from his erroneous belief that Archidamus was also present, but Xenophon (*Hell.* VI.4.9) does say that the Spartan light troops and allied horse cut off the withdrawing Boeotian camp followers just before the engagement, and as the outnumbered Boeotian right must have been widely overlapped by the Spartan allies on the left, it is not impossible that some tentative efforts were made to exploit this.[53] On the other wing, Xenophon (*Hell.* VI.4.13) tells us that the Theban and Spartan cavalry clashed and that the fleeing Spartan horsemen fell foul of their own hoplites just as the Theban infantry attacked. Most modern scholars interpret this as meaning that the cavalry were directly in front of the infantry rather than in the more usual position on the flank.[54] This makes some sense in our model as an opening gambit to seize the initiative and screen the hoplites from damage, but Epaminondas is likely to move his horsemen onto the flank once his infantry move up, and the Spartans will probably detach at least 1 hoplite unit to guard against encirclement, thereby creating some interesting tactical interactions.

There has been very extensive scholarly debate about the nature of the 50-deep column that the Theban contingent formed, as well as about what (if any) outflanking manoeuvres the Spartans attempted, and whether the Sacred Band simply acted as the 'cutting edge' of the Theban column or played a more independent flanking or penetration role.[55] As I explained on p. 41, our own model is resolutely grand tactical, and so does not even attempt to resolve such vexed tactical issues. Whatever the precise details, we know that there was a bitter fight between the two main forces, with Polyaenus (II.3.2) famously claiming that Epaminondas prevailed only after asking for one last effort from his hard-pressed troops. When the Spartans gave way, their allies fled, probably without even having engaged the oblique Boeotian line. Xenophon (*Hell.* VI.4.13–15) says that Cleombrotus and nearly a thousand of his army fell, including no less than 400 of the 700 Spartiates. Theban losses are given as 300 by Diodorus (XV.56) but as only 47 by Pausanias (IX.13.4). Our model should reproduce this finely balanced struggle fairly well, with the special hoplite rules accelerating the pace of mutual exhaustion, but with the Spartans' veteran status and Epaminondas's morale boost keeping both sides in the fight, and with forces elsewhere sometimes being left out of command to maximize attack bonuses in the main contest. However, the combat itself is simulated only in a fairly abstract fashion, and the main contribution of the model in this case is to cast comparative light on the forces involved, and to show that certain scholarly suggestions about army size and composition carry significantly more credibility than others when modelled in this way.

LEUCTRA, 371 BC (Figure 15)

M: x1. AL: 3.

Spartans: UL + VHO (Cleombrotus + Hippeis), 6 VHO (Spartan), 1 AHO (Spartan), 7 LHO (Allied), 1 ALI (Mercenary and Phocian), 2 LHC (1 Spartan, 1 Heraclean and Phliasian). FV: 55.

Thebans: 1 VHO (Theban Sacred Band), IL + AHO (Epaminondas + Thebans), 10 AHO (6 Theban, 4 Boeotian), 1 ALI (Peltasts), 3 AHC (2 Theban, 1 Boeotian). FV: 61.

2ND MANTINEA, 362 BC

Nine years after Leuctra, a civil war within the Arcadian League gave rise to a major coalition engagement that was among the largest ever hoplite battles. Sadly, it is no better documented than 2nd Coronea, so many details must remain highly speculative. Xenophon (*Hell.* VII.5.18–27) describes it in around 1,000 words at the very end of his Greek history, but his account is lamentably vague on the overall shape of the engagement, and could scarcely form the sole basis of any serious reconstruction. Diodorus (XV.84–7) has a longer description that seems to do greater justice to the scale of the battle. Unfortunately, his principal source here was the lost contemporary writer Ephorus, whose inventions and rhetorical excesses were pilloried by Polybius (XII.25f) in the specific context of this engagement. Diodorus's information must clearly be treated with great caution and scepticism, but where his account tallies with Xenophon's much more vague picture it may perhaps be used to supplement our understanding of what actually occurred.[56]

Epaminondas had just tried unsuccessfully to seize Sparta itself, but had been forestalled by Agesilaus, now over 80 years old.[57] He then marched back north via his ally Tegea to try to surprise Mantinea, but the newly arrived Athenian cavalry held up his own horsemen long enough for the allied army to deploy.[58] Pausanias (VIII.11.5–10) locates the battle near the Pelagos wood some 6 km south of Mantinea astride the road to Tegea, and Xenophon (*Hell.* VII.5.21–2) says that the Thebans threw the enemy off guard by pretending to camp at the foot of the mountains to the west of Tegea. Modern scholars hence think that the allied line occupied the obvious blocking position where the mountains close in between the Mantinean and Tegean plains.[59] There is surprising confusion about the width of the gap, which some writers put at just 1 mile, but which Pritchett measures at 2.1 to 2.4 km.[60] He also casts some doubt on the usual assumption that the wood filled the northern part of the gap at the time of the battle.[61] The terrain in Figure 16 captures the key features, with a scale of around 600 m per zone allowing the Mytikas and Kapnistra hills to be represented along with the western part of the wood, but with the orientation of the board being skewed to reflect the north-easterly direction of the Theban advance. The hills are so steep that they are best treated as impassable.

Xenophon gives little clear idea of the forces engaged, but Diodorus (XV.84) at least gives some round figures (for what they are worth) – 20,000 infantry and 2,000 cavalry for the allies, as against 30,000 foot and 3,000 horse for Epaminondas. He says (XV.84–5) that there were 6,000 Athenians on the allied left, Eleans and Achaeans in the centre and Mantineans, Arcadians and Lacedaemonians on the right. Xenophon (*Hell.* VII.5.10) reports that the Lacedaemonian detachment with this army earlier in the campaign included all their cavalry and mercenaries, and 3 of the 12 lochoi that now made up the Spartan forces. Buckler suggests that Agesilaus brought up the rest of the lochoi that had defended Sparta itself, but most scholars think that only the detachment was present for the battle.[62] If they are right, there can scarcely have been more than 1,000 Spartan hoplites, based on the small, high-quality interpretation of their forces that we have used at Leuctra and hitherto, and it is difficult to imagine the whole army reaching as many as 20,000 infantry if comparisons with contingent sizes from these regions at the Nemea and elsewhere are anything to go by, especially as the stronger Arcadian states seem to have been on the Tegean side.[63] Diodorus (XV.85) says the Athenians had only a few outclassed and heavily outnumbered foot skirmishers, and both he and Xenophon (VII.5.23–4) highlight the lack of such infantry support as the key weakness of the allied cavalry, which Stylianou thinks numbered less than 2,000.[64] At a multiple of 2.5, a total force of around 20,000 foot and horse gives the allies a fighting value of 59.

If Epaminondas did have as many as 30,000 infantry and 3,000 cavalry, and if all these troops counted as average, the army's fighting value would reach nearly 100. Both Xenophon (*Hell.* VII.5.4) and Diodorus (XV.84–5) do give long 'laundry lists' of the states from all over Greece that contributed to this large force, but whereas Hammond and Pritchett accept Diodorus's figures, Stylianou thinks there were no more than the 1,600 horse mentioned by Polyaenus (II.3.14), and Buckler suggests there were only 25–30,000 troops in all.[65] Xenophon (*Hell.* VII.5.23) makes it plain that Epaminondas adopted the same kind of oblique formation as when he had the smaller army at Leuctra, leaving his weaker troops far behind lest their flight encourage the enemy and discourage his own troops. This is a clear indication that most of his allied hoplites were no more enthusiastic than the Spartan allies had been at Leuctra, and it is striking that he fought the battle mainly with his cavalry and light infantry as well as with his Boeotian hoplites. How many of the latter were present is very hard to say. Pelopidas is said to have had 7,000 troops when he was killed in 364, but Boeotia allegedly fielded 13,000 against Phocis a decade later.[66] Because the Arcadians, whom Diodorus (XV.85) says were in support of the Boeotians, would surely have been as motivated as their Mantinean adversaries, our model strongly supports the lower figure, for otherwise the odds against the allied right would be overwhelming. If only around 11,000 hoplites were reliable Boeotians or Arcadians, and if we use intermediate figures of 16,000 other infantry and 2,500 cavalry, then (excluding Epaminondas himself) the army would have a fighting value of 59, exactly the same as its opponents.[67] With Pelopidas now dead, there is a strong case for making Epaminondas an average rather than inspired leader, as this greatly increases the chance of him being killed as happened historically, and as the difference of only 6 between the two sides' overall fighting values accords better with the equivocal outcome of the actual engagement. Those who believe (like Buckler) that the rest of the Spartan army was present after all may like to add 3 veteran hoplite units to the allied army but to make Epaminondas inspired as at Leuctra, thereby yielding fighting values that are exactly equal at 71 each.

Although Xenophon (*Hell.* VII.5.21–2) does emphasize how surprised and unprepared the allies were in the face of Epaminondas's advance, their established blocking position means that it is better to give them the first move as at Leuctra. Epaminondas can then focus his attack where he chooses, and use his superior command to reach the centreline first while the allies are still coming back into their battle positions from the wood where Hammond suggests they had been sheltering from the sun.[68] As at Leuctra, the Thebans concentrated against the enemy right wing, so both key zones should again be on this side of the field to dissuade the Mantineans and Spartans from hanging back in the face of the Boeotian juggernaut. The allied cavalry on this wing were quickly driven back into the phalanx by the more numerous Boeotian and Thessalian horse.[69] Xenophon (*Hell.* VII.5.24–5) recounts what followed very sparely, saying only that Epaminondas's attack succeeded but that he himself fell, prompting his victorious troops to withdraw. Diodorus (XV.86–7) has a much longer rhetorical account of the back and forth struggle between Thebans and Spartans and of Epaminondas's heroic death, which is plainly mostly invention as indicated by the anachronistic references to missiles in this hoplite combat. If there really were only 3 lochoi of Spartans, our model suggests that the contest was probably less hard fought than at Leuctra, and Epaminondas's death was an unlucky mischance.

On the other wing, Xenophon (*Hell.* VII.5.24–5) describes the posting of cavalry and infantry on some hills opposite the Athenians so as to threaten their rear if they advanced, and he later says that a victorious body of horse and foot (presumably from the left wing) attacked the Athenians at the end of the battle but were defeated. Diodorus (XV.85 and 87) again has a more detailed account in which the Athenian cavalry are routed early on by Theban and Thessalian horsemen and skirmishers; the Theban cavalry outflank the Athenian hoplites, who are only saved when Elean horsemen arrive from the rear to turn the tide, and the Athenians overrun a force of Euboeans and mercenaries sent to seize the nearby hills. Pritchett and Buckler dismiss Diodorus's claims, and suggest that the cavalry and infantry shadowing the Athenians were on a slight rise in the plain just to the south of our battlefield and played no active role in the engagement.[70] Hammond and Stylianou, by contrast, think there really was active fighting on the allied left, as Diodorus asserts.[71] Our model allows dynamic exploration of these competing hypotheses, as it is possible either for the Thebans to try to deter an Athenian advance using a 'force in being' in their right flank zone, or to push forward more actively, and to operate at the foot of Kapnistra itself as Kromayer thought.[72] This is a perfect illustration of how our system can give new insights into what would otherwise be a straightforward impasse over whether an unreliable source is or is not to be believed.

The compulsory nature of rally attempts for hoplite generals in our model means that Epaminondas will often be placed at risk in the frenzied head-on clashes at Leuctra and 2nd Mantinea. If he does die, the resulting morale penalty for already exhausted and fragile hoplite forces could indeed trigger mass panic, even among troops on the brink of victory. Both Xenophon (*Hell.* VII.5.25–7) and Diodorus (XV.87) emphasize the indecisiveness of this battle, with each side claiming victory due to its success in one part of the field. Our model not only helps us to explore the many uncertainties of this ill-documented engagement, but it also highlights the increasingly sophisticated grand tactical handling of the forces involved, including the use of terrain and of combined arms. The battle thus sets the stage very well for the even more complex and multidimensional interactions and trade-offs in the contests of the Alexandrian and Hellenistic eras.

2ND MANTINEA, 362 BC (Figure 16)

M: x2.5. AL: 4. Hills count as impassable.

Allies: 2 VHO (Spartan), 13 AHO (5 Athenian, 2 Mantinean, 2 Elean, 2 Achaean, 1 Arcadian, 1 Allied), 1 ALI (Mercenary), 3 AHC (1 Athenian, 1 Spartan, 1 Elean, Achaean and Arcadian). FV: 59.

Thebans: AL + VHO (Epaminondas + Sacred Band), 8 AHO (2 Theban, 3 Boeotian, 2 Tegean, 1 Megalopolitan, Asean and Pallantian), 5 LHO (2 Argive, 1 Euboean, 1 Thessalian, 1 Messenian and Sicyonian), 3 ALI (1 Locrian, Malian and Aenianian, 1 Thessalian, 1 Euboean and Mercenary), 4 AHC (2 Thessalian, 1 Theban, 1 Boeotian). FV: 65.

9

Alexander the Great

Philip II of Macedon fought for 20 years to establish his dominance in Greece, but the climax came in 338 when he and his 18-year-old son Alexander shattered a coalition army led by Athens and Thebes at Chaeronea. Philip was assassinated 2 years later, but after whirlwind campaigns to secure his inheritance, Alexander at last began his father's long-planned invasion of the Persian empire in 334. Disregarding the caution urged by the Greek mercenary commander Memnon, the local Persian satraps gave battle straight away at the River Granicus, and were defeated. While Alexander conquered Asia Minor, King Darius III gathered a much larger army and managed to cut in behind the Macedonians as they marched round into Syria at the end of the following year, but Alexander turned back north and won a sweeping victory at Issus. He then focused on securing the rest of the Mediterranean coast including Egypt and the recalcitrant fortress of Tyre, so that when he headed inland across the Euphrates and Tigris late in 331, Darius faced him at Gaugamela with another massive host, only to be defeated yet again. Alexander conquered the Persian heartland and spent the next 4 years in difficult campaigns subduing the eastern satrapies, but then he invaded India and in 326 he beat one of its most powerful kings, Porus, at the River Hydaspes. His exhausted men finally forced him to turn back, and 3 years later he died of fever, but his incredible conquests had transformed the ancient world and meant that the ensuing Greek internecine conflicts would be played out on the much larger canvas of the whole of the eastern Mediterranean and south-west Asia.

1ST CHAERONEA, 338 BC

Philip's gradual rise to dominance in Greece had come as much through shrewd diplomacy as military conquest, but his inveterate opponent, the Athenian orator Demosthenes, finally helped to spur the development of an anti-Macedonian coalition that brought together Achaea, Corinth, Megara, Euboea, Acarnania, Leucas and Corcyra in addition to its principal members, Athens and Boeotia.[1] Sadly, our sources for Philip's reign are far weaker than for that of his more famous son, and the ensuing battle at Chaeronea in Boeotia, despite being the largest inter-Greek engagement yet fought, is very poorly recorded. Only

Diodorus (XVI.85–6) has a connected account, with just a few hundred words of vague and pro-Athenian text on the battle itself. We must supplement this with snippets from Plutarch (who was a native of Chaeronea) and with references in Polyaenus (IV.2.2 and 7) and Frontinus (*Str.* II.1.9) to Philip's alleged battle-winning manoeuvre. For once, we also have archaeological evidence in the shape of two mass graves presumed to be from this engagement, one beneath the famous Lion monument just east of Chaeronea, and the other (the Polyandrion) 3 km further east on the bank of the River Cephissus.[2] Even then, much remains uncertain, and hence 1st Chaeronea is the very embodiment of the 'lost battles' we are seeking to understand.

Terrain is obviously crucial, given the size of the forces and the relatively limited extent of the plain. Hammond disputed Kromayer's earlier suggestion that the Greek line ran north-north-west from the Kerata valley to the river, blocking the narrowest part of the plain where it was only around 1.5 km wide. He argued instead throughout his extensive career that the Greek line was longer and ran west-north-west from just south of the Lion monument to the Polyandrion (both of which he thought were Macedonian graves from the heavy fighting on the two wings).[3] Other scholars have followed Pausanias (IX.10.1 and 40.10) in seeing the 254 bodies under the Lion monument as members of the Theban Sacred Band, but there has been little major disagreement with Hammond's orientation of the battle line.[4] This suggests a scale of around 800 m per zone, and terrain features as shown on Figure 18. Plutarch (*Dem.* 19) mentions the Haemon stream of his own day as perhaps having got its name from the blood that filled it after the battle – Hammond identifies this stream as that currently flowing past the Lion monument, and Pritchett and Griffith agree, even though the slight rise to which Polyaenus (IV.2.2) claims Philip withdrew is difficult to identify.[5] The Greeks should move first because of their established defensive position, and placing both key zones on the side nearest Chaeronea is the best way to tempt both armies to advance into the killing ground along the Haemon.

Diodorus (XVI.85) gives the Macedonians over 30,000 infantry and 2,000 cavalry, including some allies who arrived shortly before. As he says (XVII.17) that in 334 there were 24,000 native Macedonian foot, it is usually assumed that all of these were present and that the remaining infantry were allies and mercenaries (mostly peltasts and skirmishers).[6] This may somewhat underplay the non-Macedonian element in the army, but several states had remained neutral, and Hammond even came to question the usual assumption of a Thessalian cavalry contribution.[7] Most of the Macedonian infantry were the new sarissa-armed phalangites that Philip had created to bolster the fighting capability of his peasantry, but Diodorus (XVI.86) says that Philip himself led picked troops, who were probably the 3,000 Hypaspists who later formed Alexander's infantry guard. Their equipment at this time has been the subject of endless debate – it may simply have been pikes like the other infantry, but there are enough indications to the contrary (including the Alexander sarcophagus, the finds in Philip's tomb, and the alleged feigned retreat at Chaeronea itself) to warrant classifying the Hypaspists as generic heavy infantry instead.[8] Markle has even suggested that *no* Macedonian infantry yet used the long sarissa, but this has been widely dismissed, and he himself admits that the central phalanx at Chaeronea may have been sarissa-armed, because the terrain there was more favourable.[9] Philip must surely rank as an inspired leader like Epaminondas, and it is also appropriate to include Alexander as an average cavalry leader on the other wing, as Diodorus (XVI.86) says he was stationed there along with Philip's most seasoned generals (probably including Parmenio). At a multiple of 4, this gives the Macedonian army a fighting value of 83.

Diodorus (XVI.85) claims the Greeks were outnumbered as well as out-generalled, but Justin (IX.3) contradicts the former claim, and modern scholars agree. Plutarch (*Dem.* 17) says the allies hired 15,000 mercenary infantry and 2,000 cavalry to supplement their citizen forces, but 10,000 of these were later overwhelmed while detached to guard Amphissa.[10] It is usually assumed that the allies fielded up to 35,000 infantry at the battle itself.[11] DeVoto suggests there were 10,000 Athenians, 7,000 Boeotians, and 15,000 allies and mercenaries.[12] Hammond proposed 30,000 hoplites and 5,000 light troops, but his breakdown of hoplite numbers was confused for many years until he finally settled on 10,000 Athenians, 12,000 Boeotians, 2,000 mercenaries and 2,000 each from Corinth, Megara and Achaea.[13] The Greek cavalry is even more of an enigma, as one would have expected strong contingents from both Boeotia and Athens in addition to any mercenary force, but they played no recorded role in the battle. Judging by precedents such as the Nemea and 2nd Coronea, this probably reflects the inadequacy of our sources (and the constrained terrain on both flanks) rather than the complete absence of allied horsemen – Hammond suggests there were 2,000.[14] We are told the names of some Athenian and Theban generals, but in each case the references are derogatory, so it seems best not to include any in the scenario.[15] The troops themselves have a fighting value of 61, so the Macedonians enjoy an overwhelming advantage, mostly through superior generalship.

Diodorus (XVI.86) does not even make clear on which wing Philip and Alexander or the Athenians and Boeotians were deployed, and just about the only solid claim that emerges from his brief account of the fighting is that Alexander broke through before Philip did so. Fortunately, Plutarch (*Alex.* 9) helps to resolve the confusion by claiming that Alexander beat the Sacred Band near the Macedonian grave mound by the Cephissus. It is usually assumed that all the Macedonian horsemen were on Alexander's wing, and modern scholarship about the fight there revolves mainly around the (in)effectiveness of cavalry against the front of formed hoplites (and hence the role of the infantry phalanx in achieving the breakthrough), with a tangled sub-debate about whether Macedonian cavalry were also equipped with the long sarissae that Plutarch (*Pel.* 18) says defeated the Sacred Band.[16] Hammond argues that the Athenian advance on the other wing dragged the rest of the Greek line with it and opened a gap in the Boeotian front into which Alexander's cavalry charged to get at the hoplites' vulnerable flank and rear, but this goes well beyond the meagre evidence.[17] The main contribution of our model is to give a sense of perspective. The Sacred Band made up only a few per cent of the troops on the Greek right, forming less than a third of a veteran unit in our system. The deployment in Figure 18 poses an interesting tactical choice of whether to use the unit to reinforce the cavalry by the river or to push it forward against the phalanx, but in either case the contest on this wing will be decided by the overall correlation of forces and command capacity, and especially by the struggle between the phalanx and the Boeotian hoplites as a whole.

On the other wing, the presence of the Greek key zone helps to foster the same tense and highly unstable stand-off as may develop across the Cephissus marshes. Polyaenus (IV.2.2 and 7) describes how Philip withdrew his men gradually to draw out the eager Athenians, then turned and broke his exhausted opponents once he reached some rising ground.[18] As at Hastings 14 centuries later, this may have been less of a planned stratagem and more of an improvised reaction to the failure of the initial attack.[19] There is certainly a strong case at first for the command-strapped Athenians to hold back in their uphill position to draw Philip into a pocket formed by the allied centre and by their light infantry on the hills near Chaeronea. Philip may well take the bait in order to seize the Greek key zone and to avoid standing idle with his command potential wasted. If he starts to lose, he may indeed pull back to limit his exposure, and the Athenians may well at this stage be tempted to move forward to secure their key zone and keep up the pressure, rather than waiting idly for their left flank to be turned or for panic to spread due to Alexander's victory on the other wing. If they do advance, their shortage of commands and the prohibition on free about turns by hoplites means they will be well and truly committed even if things go wrong, so the model could very faithfully simulate the historical course of events. Diodorus (XVI.86) says that 1,000 Athenians were killed and 2,000 captured, and Plutarch (*Dem.* 20) records Demosthenes himself fleeing in panic.

This scenario creates difficult tactical choices for both sides, and provides an ideal vehicle for exploring different possibilities such as that the Greeks had fewer or no horsemen or that more or fewer of the Macedonians were phalangites. Above all, it is an antidote to the excessively 'Polybian' tone of the scholarship and its preoccupation with sarissae and with the theoretical limitations of cavalry, when everything we know about better-documented Greek battles suggests that it was the quality of the troops and leaders themselves that made much more of a difference.

1ST CHAERONEA, 338 BC (Figure 18)

M: x4. AL: 4.

Greeks: 1 VHO (Theban Sacred Band), 15 AHO (5 Athenian, 4 Boeotian, 2 Mercenary, 1 Corinthian, 1 Megaran, 1 Achaean, 1 Euboean, Leucasian and Corcyran), 2 ALI (1 Locrian, Phocian and Acarnanian, 1 Mercenary), 2 AHC (1 Boeotian, 1 Athenian and Mercenary). FV: 61.

Macedonians: IL + VHI (Philip + Agema), 2 VHI (Hypaspists), 10 APH (Foot Companions), 2 AHI (1 Allied, 1 Mercenary), 2 ALI (1 Allied, 1 Mercenary), AL + VHC (Alexander + Companions), 1 VHC (Companions), 1 AHC (Thessalian). FV: 83.

GRANICUS, 334 BC

Soon after Alexander crossed the Hellespont, the local Persian satraps made a stand behind the River Granicus. Our principal source is the much later writer Arrian, whose battle account (*Anab.* I.13–17) consists of around 2,000 words, probably based mainly on the lost testimonies of Alexander's officer Ptolemy and his engineer Aristobulus. Plutarch (*Alex.* 16) has a shorter description, while Diodorus (XVII.18–21) has a long account that contains some interesting supplementary details but contradicts the other two descriptions by claiming that the battle was fought not as an assault crossing of the river in the afternoon, but on the far side the following morning after a surprise initial crossing at dawn. I mentioned on p. 9 the ill-fated attempt by Green to reconcile the contradiction by postulating two successive battles, with the first being hushed up after a headstrong direct assault failed – he has since abandoned this confection in the face of trenchant criticism.[20] However, there is a much more balanced scholarly debate about whether the single real engagement was more akin to Arrian's or Diodorus's version. Badian, Hammond and Devine largely believe Arrian, while Bosworth and Lane Fox are more persuaded by Diodorus.[21] Can our model cast any light on this enduring controversy?

Arrian and Plutarch both mention two significant terrain features – the river itself, which they describe as deep, fast flowing and with steep banks, and a range of hills some way away on the Persian side on which the Greek mercenaries made their ill-fated stand. There is the usual debate among modern scholars over exactly where along the modern river (generally identified as the Kocabas Cay) the battle was fought, and over whether and how its course may have changed since antiquity. However, visitors to the site have concluded that the sources significantly exaggerate the river's depth and intractability, especially in the summer, with only the banks in some places posing a significant obstacle.[22] Bosworth suggests that the low hills were around 1.5 km east of the river

– close enough to be on our battlefield, but not so close as to leave no room for cavalry manoeuvring on the Persian side.[23] If we discount Green's unsupported suggestion that Alexander crossed further downstream as at the Hydaspes and that the eventual battle lines were perpendicular to the river, then we can actually create a terrain layout that is compatible with both Arrian's and Diodorus's account, with the river running laterally across the 5 Macedonian frontal zones, and with hills in the 3 Persian initial deployment zones. The fact that rivers in our system run *within* the large zones rather than along their borders has the advantage that there is no need to distinguish between troops fighting their way across a transverse river and those who are already on the far side but whose room for manoeuvre is critically constrained by the obstacle immediately at their backs. This is very helpful, because even Badian thinks the Persians formed up further back from the river than Arrian suggests, to give themselves room to charge.[24] As I will discuss shortly, our model handles the different interpretations of the Granicus battle much more in terms of who gets to attack first, making it far easier to experiment with alternative assumptions.

Diodorus (XVII.17) says that Alexander crossed the Hellespont with 12,000 Macedonian infantry, 7,000 Thracian infantry, 7,000 allied Greek infantry, 5,000 mercenary infantry, 1,000 archers and Agrianian javelinmen, 1,800 Companion cavalry, 1,800 Thessalian cavalry, 600 Greek cavalry, and 900 Thracian and Paeonian horsemen. This broadly tallies with Arrian's overall totals (*Anab.* I.11) of 30,000 infantry and over 5,000 cavalry.[25] One problem is that an advance guard of around 10,000 troops had been sent to Asia earlier and may have boosted these totals, but a greater offsetting factor is that, of the infantry, only the Macedonians, archers and Agrianians are listed in the battle line at this engagement. Modern scholars generally accept that Alexander deployed just his best 13,000 infantry in the battle line, and broke with previous Greek tradition by placing greatest reliance on his 5,100 cavalry.[26] The Companions and the 3,000 Hypaspists certainly warrant 'veteran' classification, as do the archers, Agrianians and some of the Thessalians, given their fighting performance against great odds in this and later battles. Parmenio deserves inclusion as an average commander, and Alexander himself must clearly be an inspired or brilliant leader. This choice is actually the best way of exploring the different interpretations of the battle, as if the Persians move first to reflect their established defensive position, then their cavalry will get in the first blow against a merely 'inspired' Alexander while his forces are vulnerable crossing the river, whereas a brilliant Alexander will be able to reverse the turn order to simulate the kind of surprise strike that Diodorus alleges. At a multiple of 4, the Macedonian army will have a fighting value of 74 or 80, depending on how Alexander is rated.

Persian numbers are much more in doubt. Arrian (*Anab.* I.14) says they fielded 20,000 cavalry and nearly 20,000 Greek mercenary infantry, while Diodorus

(XVII.19) claims there were only 10,000 cavalry (he mentions several specific contingents) but no less than 100,000 infantry. Hammond and Bosworth accept Arrian's figures, while Devine goes with Diodorus's lower cavalry total and proposes an even lower figure of 4–5,000 Greek mercenaries based on the force earlier attributed to Memnon by Diodorus (XVII.7) and Polyaenus (V.44.4).[27] Our own model suggests that it would have been crazy for the Persians to have made a stand with just 10,000 horse, as even 20,000 cavalry still only have a fighting value of 40 if half are classed as average and the rest as levies. By contrast, the idea of nearly 20,000 Greek mercenaries being present sits very uneasily with their negligible role in the battle and with Arrian's other claims (I.12 and 16) that the Macedonians had many more infantry and that only 2,000 Greeks survived the subsequent massacre. Green and Ashley agree with Devine that there were only 5–6,000 Greeks, and Badian suggests that the native Persian infantry mentioned by Plutarch (*Alex.* 16) as fighting the phalanx may have contributed the majority of Arrian's 20,000.[28] Three units of Greeks are just enough to make a stand as they did historically, even if everyone else has fled. Whether or not there was an overall commander within the welter of Persian nobles listed by Arrian (*Anab.* I.12), command was clearly a key weakness as shown by the neglect of the Greeks, so there is no case for including a distinct Persian general.[29] The army's fighting value hence works out at just 55.

Alexander used what would become his standard front line, with the Companions, archers, Agrianians and some light cavalry on the right under his own command, then the Hypaspists and the 6 brigades of the phalanx, and finally the Thessalians and the rest of the cavalry on the left under Parmenio. In 8 ranks, the heavy infantry would have a frontage of around 1,500 m, and the cavalry would cover a further 1,200 m using the yardstick in Polybius (XII.18).[30] The Persian deployment with the cavalry guarding the river and the mercenaries in the rear is much more enigmatic, but the command constraints in our model certainly help to reflect it, as the only way the Persians can man the river line quickly with their horsemen is to leave their infantry undeployed at first, ready to reinforce the centre (if the cavalry survive that long). The free deployment option allows users to experiment with different approaches, but as Alexander can react to counter whatever the Persians do, it is far from clear that there are many better alternatives unless there really were 20,000 Greeks.[31] Scholars usually give the Persian cavalry the same overall frontage as the Macedonian line, with Hammond and Ashley assuming up to 16 ranks of troopers while Devine instead uses Polybius's 8 ranks for his force of only 10,000 horse.[32] Polyaenus (IV.3.16) does mention Alexander outflanking the enemy left, but this sits uneasily with Arrian's claims (*Anab.* I.14 and 16) that the Persian line was very long and that it collapsed when the centre (rather than the left flank) was broken. Figure 19 hence uses a scale of around 800 m per zone, allowing for an intermediate density of

Persian cavalry deployment and a longer line that overlaps Parmenio's refused left.

Understanding the overall course of the battle is complicated by the fact that the sources focus so much on the fighting around Alexander himself, just as Hollywood films zoom in on the personal duels around the central characters. Arrian (*Anab.* I.15) does mention the use of a spearhead force of mixed cavalry and infantry units to lead the cross-river attack on the right wing, and this may be reflected in our model by which units are put in front to absorb the initial Persian attacks.[33] When Alexander himself joined the battle, he was nearly killed in the frenzied *mêlée*, but the death of several Persian leaders, along with the advantages that the Macedonian horsemen gained from their longer lances and their supporting light infantry, soon turned the tide. Arrian (*Anab.* I.16) says that only 1,000 Persian horsemen fell, though Diodorus (XVII.21) and Plutarch (*Alex.* 16) increase this to 2,000 or more. Arrian and Plutarch also differ about how hard-fought the ensuing encirclement and massacre (as 'traitors') of the isolated Greek mercenaries was, but they both still give very low figures for the Macedonian dead, with Arrian putting these at just 85 cavalry and 30 infantry.

The Granicus was actually the first ancient battle that friends and I tried to refight over 30 years ago. We based our scenario on that of Grant, who chose to model Green's hypothetical second battle, since an assault river crossing did indeed seem doomed to failure given the rules then in use.[34] However, our simulated Alexander was still roundly defeated because of the greater numbers of Persian cavalry, providing an early object lesson that simulation systems must be constantly tested against real historical patterns and outcomes if they are to give any sort of valid representation of the factors actually making for success and failure. Our present model cannot entirely resolve the many scholarly disputes about this battle, but by providing a generic framework based on many other ancient engagements (including Alexander's successful cross-river assault against a much larger Persian host at Issus the following year) it allows experimentation that can throw significant light on issues such as Persian numbers and the enigmatic Persian deployment. The following scenario shows Alexander as merely 'inspired', and so accords with the majority view of an immediate Macedonian attack, but the systemic Persian disadvantages in command and troop quality should still more than outweigh the limited benefits they receive from defending the river line, and their only real hope is if Alexander suffers the same fate as Epaminondas while trying too hard to minimize the cost of victory.

GRANICUS, 334 BC (Figure 19)

M: x4. AL: 4.

Persians: 3 AHO (Mercenary), 3 LLI (Asiatic), 8 AHC (4 Persian, 2 Hyrcanian, 2 Median), 3 LHC (Asiatic), 2 ALC (1 Bactrian, 1 Paphlagonian), 2 LLC (Asiatic). FV: 55. (3 AHO and 3 LLI undeployed.)

Macedonians: 3 VHI (Hypaspists), 5 APH (Foot Companions), 1 VLI (Agrianian and Cretan), IL + VHC (Alexander + Companions), 3 VHC (2 Companions, 1 Thessalian), 2 AHC (1 Thessalian, 1 Greek and Thracian), 1 ALC (Prodromoi and Paeonian), AC (Parmenio). FV: 74.

ISSUS, 333 BC

At Issus, the Persians defended another river, this time astride Alexander's line of communications after an impressive encircling manoeuvre that allowed the massacre of the wounded he had left behind.[35] Arrian (*Anab.* II.7–11) is again our main source, and has over 2,000 words on the ensuing battle. We also have an equally detailed but rather confused and rhetorical account by Curtius (III.8–11), a brief and dubious summary by Plutarch (*Alex.* 20), and a ridiculously stereotypical tale by Diodorus (XVII.32–5) of exactly the sort that gives him such a bad name. Polybius does not cover this era, but fortunately he used the now-lost account of Issus by Alexander's official historian Callisthenes as an object lesson (XII.17–22) in the application of exactly the kind of analyses of force and space we are employing in this volume. Polybius's criticisms are themselves questionable as I mentioned on pp. 31–2, but it is very helpful that the information survives. Nevertheless, the battle is difficult to reconstruct because of contradictory details.

I mentioned on p. 7 the continuing scholarly disagreement over which modern river corresponds to the ancient Pinarus, and over how the river and coastline may have changed since antiquity.[36] This is despite (or perhaps because of) the significant geographical information we are given by our sources. Arrian (*Anab.* II.8) describes a coastal plain that gradually widened as it went north, with the hills receding further to form a kind of 'bay' out of which the Pinarus flowed. Polybius (XII.17) reports Callisthenes's claim that it was 14 stadia (2.6 km) from the sea to the foot of the hills, with the river running obliquely across this space and having steep banks except near the mountains. None of the proposed sites are this narrow today, and even Hammond, who suggests the ancient coastline was up to 1 km further inland, makes his river some 4 km long after leaving the hills because of its oblique course.[37] For our purposes, it is enough to have a broad-brush representation of the terrain, as shown in Figure 20. A scale of 1,000 m per zone still almost fits with Callisthenes if his 14 stadia are measured directly to the coast rather than along the river itself. Arrian (*Anab.* II.10–11) confirms that the river had steep banks and that these broke the formation of the phalanx, but he describes both sides' cavalry charging across the stream without apparent hindrance.[38] Hammond and Devine have tried to use the modern characteristics of the Payas to make topographical deductions about the tractability of different stretches, but for our purposes, the inclusion of a fortified camp to reflect the stockades that Arrian describes should suffice to simulate the greater defensibility of the Persian centre.[39]

Alexander's army is harder to reconstruct than at the Granicus, because of uncertainty over the numbers of reinforcements, losses and troops detached elsewhere. Polybius (XII.19) estimates that he now had 42,000 foot and 5,000 horse, but this calculation (based on Callisthenes's total of 40,000 foot and 4,500 horse for the initial invasion force) is hard to reconcile with Arrian and Diodorus. The other ancient sources do not give figures for the army at Issus. Hammond suggests Alexander deployed 5,300 cavalry but only 26,000 infantry for this engagement, and this is probably about right as the 7,000 allied Greeks seem again to have been left in the rear.[40] However, Arrian (*Anab*. I.29) records 3,000 new Macedonian infantry levies having joined the army at Gordium, so it is possible that there were rather more phalangites than at the Granicus.[41] The Thracian and mercenary infantry now played a more active role, and it is surely appropriate to class more of the Thessalian cavalry as veterans given how well they performed against the mass of Persian horse. Similarly, Alexander must surely now count as 'brilliant' if he is to have the appropriate chance of triumphing against such great numerical odds. At a multiple of 5, this gives a Macedonian fighting value of 89.

Arrian (*Anab*. II.8) gives Darius 30,000 Greek mercenary infantry, 60,000 Cardaces, 40,000 light infantry, 30,000 cavalry, and a mass of other troops bringing the overall total to 600,000! There has been much scholarly debate about who and what the Cardaces were, but it seems clear enough from Arrian's term 'hoplites' that they were close-order troops best classified in our model as levy heavy infantry.[42] Curtius (III.9) says Darius's bodyguard had 3,000 horse, and that his front line infantry included 30,000 Greeks, 26,000 skirmishers and 60,000 others – he earlier (III.2) lists a variety of contingents totalling 250,000 foot and over 60,000 horse. Polybius (XII.18) cites Callisthenes's claims of 30,000 cavalry and 30,000 mercenaries, so these may be the source of some of the other figures. Polybius's purpose in citing these troop numbers is to show that they could not possibly all fit within the distance claimed, and this is equally true of the zones in our model, quite apart from the fact that the army's fighting value would be well over 100. Few scholars have ventured to suggest lower figures, though Devine has made some tentative proposals that are around half of Curtius's front line numbers, and Ashley has guessed at 12,000 mercenaries, 10,000 Cardaces, 12,000 light infantry and 24,000 horsemen.[43] Here, our model comes into its own as a means of giving a very broad-brush indication of what might be more reasonable forces. If we classify everyone except the Greeks and half of the cavalry as levies, then with Darius as a timid average general, an army of 15,000 mercenaries, 30,000 Cardaces, 20,000 light infantry and 15,000 cavalry (exactly half of Arrian's totals) would have a fighting value of 68, and would just fit within the available zones.

The sources give two versions of the Persian deployment. Arrian (*Anab.* II.8) has the Greeks in the centre flanked by two equal bodies of Cardaces, with almost all the cavalry by the coast and half the light infantry sent onto the hills to threaten the Macedonian flank. Curtius (III.9) and Callisthenes (in Polybius XII.17–18) differ in having the mercenaries on the right and the Persian infantry (along with Median and Hyrcanian cavalry) on the left of the main line. Hammond as usual believes Arrian, while Devine and Bosworth prefer Curtius.[44] Our model can be used to test either interpretation, but the scenario in Figure 20 uses Curtius's battle line because it fits better with the Persian tactic of attacking on their right while defending in the left and centre. Key zones are in the Persian centre and Macedonian right centre as normal, but this is less important here because of the intervening river. Alexander employed his usual formation, with the phalanx in front switching from 32 to 16 and then to 8 ranks deep as the plain widened during the advance, and with the Thessalians being sent to the left wing to match the Persian shift of their own cavalry to the coast. The enemy flanking force on the hills was countered by detachments of infantry and cavalry and withdrew higher up the mountainside, allowing all but 300 horse to be reassigned to help outflank the main Persian line (best simulated by use of turn reversal).[45]

Arrian (*Anab.* II.10) says that Alexander's charge quickly shattered the Persian left. Hammond suggests that he must have led the Hypaspists because cavalry could not successfully attack heavy infantry across a broad river, but this was clearly a combined assault by foot and horse, and our model suggests that the decisive factor must have been the enormous gulf in troop quality, morale and command – it is perfectly conceivable that the whole Persian infantry force gave way rather than just the extreme left.[46] Meanwhile, the phalanx was engaged in a bitter and bloody struggle with the Greeks across the river, and the Persian cavalry were attacking the Thessalians in an equally prolonged and hard-fought contest. Sources and scholars differ over how soon Darius panicked and fled, but Alexander's outflanking of the mercenaries and the news of Darius's flight were enough to trigger a general rout.[47] Macedonian losses had clearly been higher than at the Granicus – Arrian (*Anab.* II.10) says 120 phalangites died, while Curtius (III.11) and others speak of 150 cavalrymen killed. Persian casualties were doubtless vastly greater, but the sources' figures of 100,000 or more are impossible to verify.[48]

The main contribution of our model in this battle is as a laboratory for users to test different hypotheses about Persian troop numbers and deployment. It certainly suggests that Darius had far fewer troops than the sources claim, as well as that the mass of Persian cavalry took up much more space than most scholars allow, and that Alexander's Thracian and Greek mercenary infantry played a more important role on each wing than is widely recognized.[49] The model also shows the importance of the time dimension, as too careful and methodical an approach by Alexander to the reduction of the enemy left and centre may expose his own left to defeat by the Persian horse, whereas an overly 'gung ho' attitude may bring unacceptably high friendly casualties.

ISSUS, 333 BC (Figure 20)

M: x5. AL: 4.

Persians: 6 AHO (Mercenary), 6 LHI (Cardaces), 4 LLI (Archers and Slingers), TL + AHC (Darius + Guard), 6 AHC (3 Persian, 1 Median, 1 Hyrcanian, 1 Armenian), 2 LHC (Asiatic), 1 LLC (Asiatic). FV: 68.

Macedonians: 2 VHI (Hypaspists), 4 APH (Foot Companions), 4 AHI (2 Thracian, 2 Mercenary), 1 VLI (Agrianians and Archers), 1 ALI (Cretan and Illyrian), BL + VHC (Alexander + Companions), 4 VHC (2 Companions, 2 Thessalian), 1 AHC (Greek and Thessalian), 1 ALC (Prodromoi and Paeonian), AC (Parmenio). FV: 89.

GAUGAMELA, 331 BC

When Darius next faced Alexander 2 years later between Gaugamela and Arbela, it was on an open plain that gave much greater scope than the confined terrain at Issus for him to use his superior numbers. Unfortunately, command remained a serious constraint, and the Persians no longer had many solid infantry, so they were just as reliant as at the Granicus on their cavalry forces. Arrian (*Anab.* III.8–15) has a long and detailed account, with over 2,000 words just on the deployments and the course of the fighting. Curtius (IV.13–16) provides another detailed but highly rhetorical treatment, while Plutarch (*Alex.* 32–3) has some propagandist anecdotes from Callisthenes, and Diodorus (XVII.57–61) gives a sensationalist overview focusing on the scythed chariots and the Persian success against Alexander's camp. Arrian (*Anab.* III.9 and 13) says that Alexander camped on a ridge some 30 stadia (5.5 km) from Darius's forces, and that his rightward advance threatened to drag the Persians away from the ground specially levelled for their chariots, but neither of these warrants the inclusion of any terrain features, nor does examination of the possible modern site suggest any.[50] The scale should clearly be the maximum of 1,200 m per zone, as estimates of the Macedonian frontage range from Hammond's 3.3 km and Marsden's 3.5 km to

Judeich's and Devine's 4.8 km, and we know that the Persian line was significantly longer.[51]

Unlike at Issus, Arrian (*Anab.* III.12) does give a total for the Macedonian army at this battle, namely 40,000 infantry and 7,000 cavalry. Alexander seems to have used all the contingents with which he crossed the Hellespont, plus reinforcements (especially of mercenaries) that had joined him since then.[52] Scholars differ over the fine details of the contingent sizes, but for our broad-brush purposes, the general picture is fairly consistent.[53] The Hypaspists, Companions, Agrianians and Thessalians should again count as veterans, while the allied Greeks are best classed as levies as they seem to have been hostages for the good behaviour of their states and were never given a prominent role.[54] At a multiple of 6, this gives the army a fighting value of 94. Less than half of the 70 points of combat units come from Macedonian troops, showing how important the allied and mercenary contribution was in this engagement. The phalanx and Hypaspists formed the usual line, with strong flank guards of infantry and cavalry and a second line of infantry behind to guard against encirclement. The whole formation advanced obliquely, with Alexander's right wing in the lead and Parmenio's left flank refused to make outflanking even harder.[55] Marsden thinks the main infantry line was 16 deep and covered only 700 m, while Hammond suggests it was 8 deep and over 1,700 m long but that the flank guards were much more compressed. Devine has both an 8 deep phalanx and extended flank guards, which is why his proposed line is so much longer overall.[56] Our model allows these different hypotheses to be explored, by investigating the relative merits of concentrating the Macedonian forces in just 3 zones or spreading them across 4 zones as shown in Figure 21.

Persian numbers are, as usual, more problematic. Arrian (*Anab.* III.8) gives Darius 40,000 cavalry and 1,000,000 infantry, Curtius (IV.12.13) suggests 45,000 horse and 200,000 foot, and Diodorus (XVII.53) claims there were 200,000 cavalry and 800,000 infantry. It is generally agreed that most of the foot made no more contribution than did the mass of men in the rear at Issus, but scholars still disagree significantly over the number of effective troops. Marsden and Devine think that the only infantry that counted were the 1,000 foot guardsmen, 2,000 Greek mercenaries and a few thousand Asiatics, and they also limit the cavalry total to 34,000 (Marsden) or even 25,000 (Devine).[57] Hammond, by contrast, suggests that there were 6,000 Greeks, that the Asiatic foot played a more significant supporting role, and that Arrian's figure of 40,000 horse is by no means inconceivable.[58] Lane Fox and Head suggest an intermediate figure of 4,000 Greeks.[59] It is here where our model has most to contribute. Even if we make half the horsemen average, Marsden's army would have a fighting value of just 54, and Devine's army would give only 41. Hammond's force, by contrast, would come to 69, making Darius's offer of battle much more credible while still giving Alexander a decisive advantage. Having the Persians count as fatigued because they spent the previous night under arms would again make the disadvantage too overwhelming, so this is better reflected through Alexander's contribution as a brilliant general.[60]

Both Arrian (*Anab.* III.8 and 11) and Curtius (IV.12) give detailed accounts of the different Persian contingents and their deployment, thanks in the former case to a captured order of battle recorded by Aristobulus. A higher proportion of the cavalry than at the Granicus or Issus was light horse from the eastern satrapies, spearheaded by smaller contingents of armoured heavy cavalry as was characteristic of these peoples.[61] The battle array was fairly balanced, with strong cavalry wings under Mazaeus and Bessus and a centre of mixed horse and foot led by Darius himself. The 200 scythed chariots that so fascinated Diodorus (XVII.53 and 58) were no more effective than at Cunaxa, but more problematic is Arrian's claim (*Anab.* III.8 and 11) that Darius had around 15 Indian elephants in front of his centre. Even with a light infantry guard, this would translate into only half a unit at this troop scale, and the beasts were probably not in fact deployed at all as there is none of the loving attention to such a novelty that one would have expected from the sources, and Arrian later says (*Anab.* III.15) that the animals were captured in the Persian camp.[62]

The battle began with an escalating cavalry contest on the Macedonian right, which drew in far more Persian than Greek horse thanks to the backstop provided by Cleander's mercenary infantry, and which was soon followed by the famous but ineffectual charge by the scythed chariots. Alexander then led his Companions and Hypaspists into a gap that emerged in the Persian front due to the ongoing cavalry duel, and he turned left to attack Darius himself, prompting him once again to flee. This is reflected in our model by Alexander's ability as a brilliant general to break through and advance on one turn, then reverse the turn order and attack again from his new zone before the Persians can react. Meanwhile, Parmenio's wing was under pressure from the expected encirclement by Mazaeus's forces, and the Macedonian baggage was raided by a small detachment of horse that either rode around Parmenio's flank or galloped through a fleeting gap that opened in the phalanx.[63] Alexander led his victorious forces to help Parmenio, and faced the heaviest cavalry fighting of the battle as the enemy tried to escape as the Thebans had at 2nd Coronea. There has been much scholarly speculation about the tactical details of these various episodes, but our model focuses more on the big picture and especially on helping to resolve the disagreements about Persian numbers and the length of the Macedonian battle line.[64] Figures for Alexander's losses range from 100 to 500 killed, with Arrian (*Anab.* III.15) giving the lowest figure but also saying that 60 Companions died in the final struggle on the left and that more than 1,000 horses perished overall. Claims of Persian fatalities range from 40,000 to 300,000, with the reality being impossible to discern.[65]

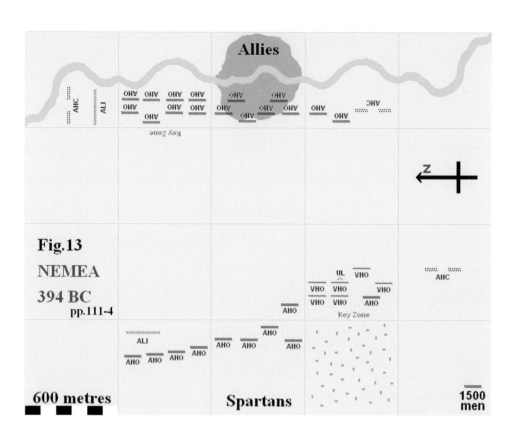

Fig.13
NEMEA
394 BC
pp.111-4

Allies

Key Zone

Key Zone

Spartans

600 metres

1500 men

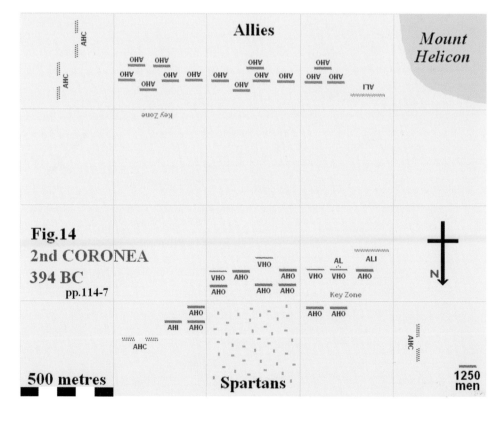

Fig.14
2nd CORONEA
394 BC
pp.114-7

Allies

Mount Helicon

Key Zone

Key Zone

Spartans

500 metres

1250 men

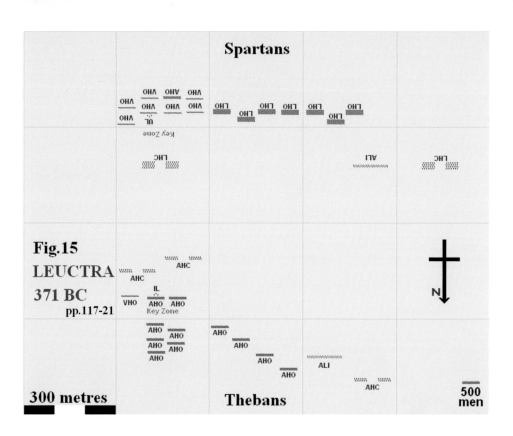

Spartans

Key Zone

Fig.15
LEUCTRA
371 BC
pp.117-21

Key Zone

N

300 metres

500 men

Thebans

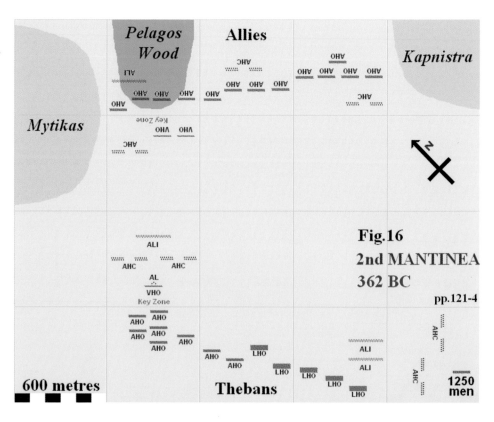

Pelagos Wood

Allies

Kapnistra

Mytikas

Key Zone

N

Key Zone

Fig.16
2nd MANTINEA
362 BC
pp.121-4

600 metres

1250 men

Thebans

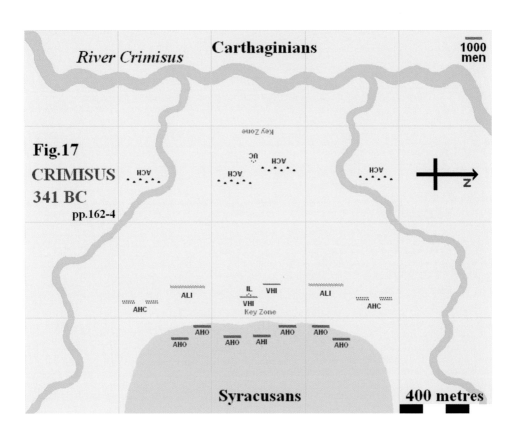

Carthaginians

River Crimisus

1000
men

**Fig.17
CRIMISUS
341 BC**
pp.162-4

Key Zone

UC
ACH
ACH
ACH
ACH

Z

ALI
IL VHI
ALI
VHI
AHC
VHI
Key Zone
AHC

AHO
AHO
AHO
AHO
AHO
AHI
AHO

Syracusans

400 metres

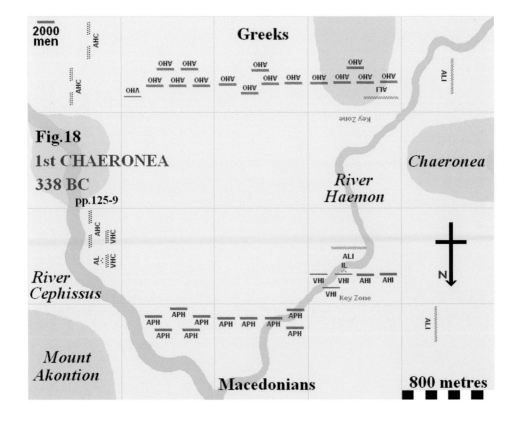

2000
men
AHC

Greeks

AHC
OHA
OHA
OHA
OHA
OHA
OHA
OHA
OHA
OHA
OHA
OHA
OHA
OHA
OHA
OHA
OHA
OHA
ALI
OHA
ALI

Key Zone

**Fig.18
1st CHAERONEA
338 BC**
pp.125-9

Chaeronea

*River
Haemon*

AHC
VHC
AL
VHC

ALI
IL
VHI
VHI
AHI
AHI

*River
Cephissus*

VHI
Key Zone

N

APH
APH
APH
APH
APH
APH
APH
APH
APH
APH

ALI

*Mount
Akontion*

Macedonians

800 metres

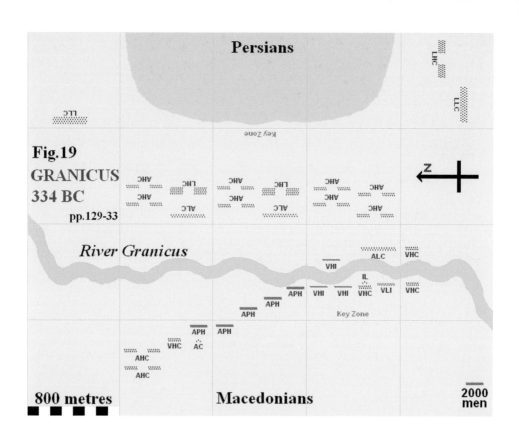

Persians

LHC

LLC

LHC

LLC

Key Zone

Fig.19
GRANICUS
334 BC
pp.129-33

N

AHC
AHC
LHC
AHC
ALC
AHC
LHC
AHC
AHC
ALC
AHC

River Granicus

ALC   VHC
VHI
IL
APH   VHI   VHI   VHC   VLI   VHC
APH
APH   Key Zone
APH

APH   APH
VHC   AC
AHC
AHC

800 metres

Macedonians

2000 men

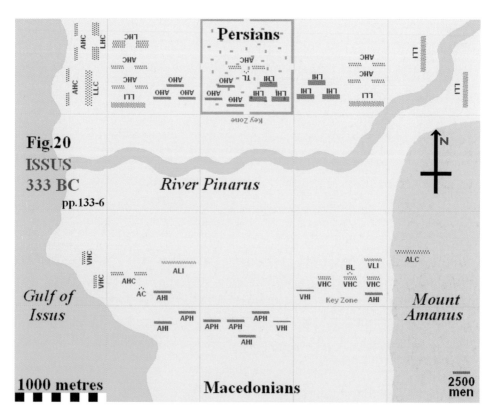

AHC   LHC
AHC
LHC   AHC   AHC
LLI
AHC   LLC   AHO   AHO   AHO   AHO   LHI   LHI   AHC   LLI
LLI   AHO   LHI   LHI   AHC
AHO   TL   LHI   LHI   LHI
Persians   AHC
Key Zone

Fig.20
ISSUS
333 BC
pp.133-6

N

River Pinarus

VHC
ALI   VLI   ALC
VHC   AHC   BL
AC   VHC   VHC   VHC
AHI   VHI   Key Zone   AHI

Gulf of Issus   APH   APH   APH   APH   VHI   *Mount Amanus*
AHI   AHI

1000 metres   **Macedonians**   **2500 men**

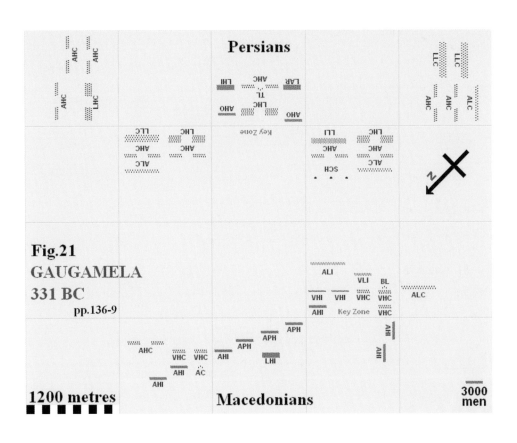

Persians

Key Zone

**Fig.21
GAUGAMELA
331 BC**
pp.136-9

1200 metres

Macedonians

**3000
men**

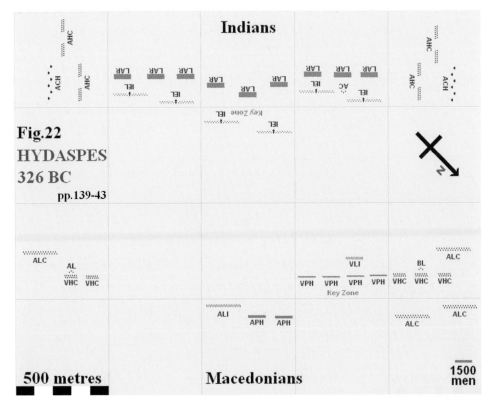

Indians

Key Zone

**Fig.22
HYDASPES
326 BC**
pp.139-43

Key Zone

500 metres

Macedonians

**1500
men**

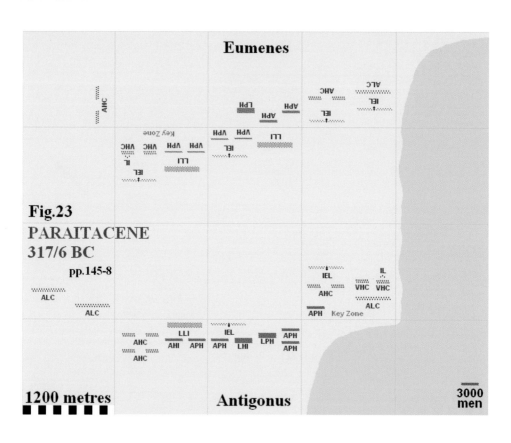

Eumenes

Fig.23
PARAITACENE
317/6 BC
pp.145-8

1200 metres

Antigonus

3000 men

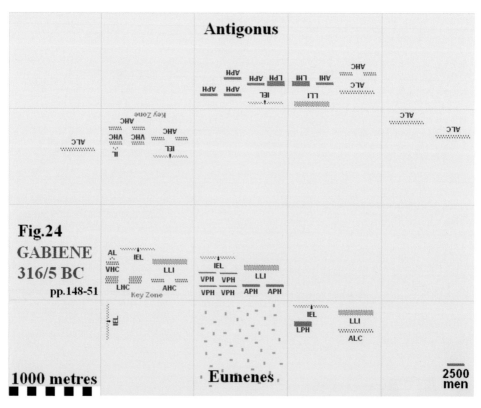

Antigonus

Fig.24
GABIENE
316/5 BC
pp.148-51

1000 metres

Eumenes

2500 men

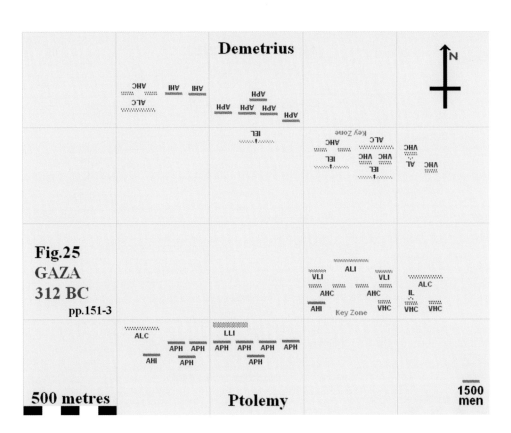

Demetrius

N

Fig.25
GAZA
312 BC
pp.151-3

500 metres

1500 men

Ptolemy

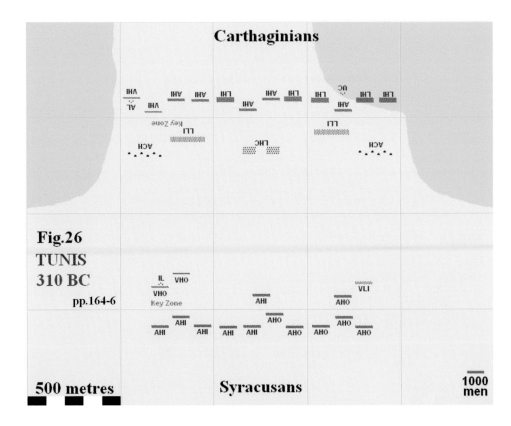

Carthaginians

Fig.26
TUNIS
310 BC
pp.164-6

500 metres

1000 men

Syracusans

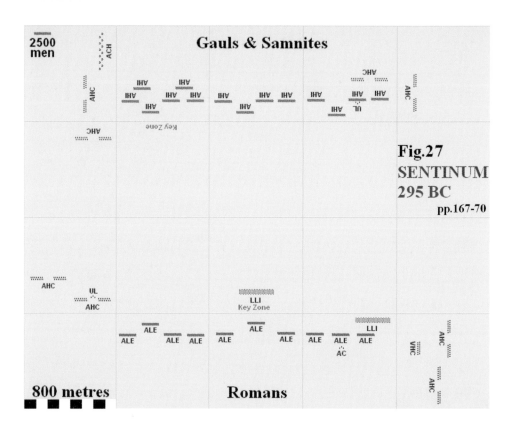

Gauls & Samnites

2500 men

Fig.27 SENTINUM 295 BC

pp.167-70

800 metres

Romans

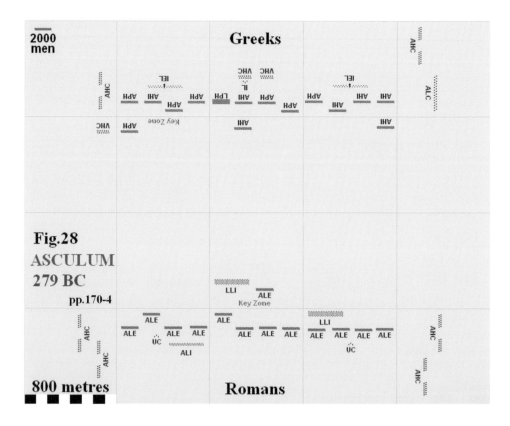

Greeks

2000 men

Fig.28 ASCULUM 279 BC

pp.170-4

800 metres

Romans

GAUGAMELA, 331 BC (Figure 21)

M: x6. AL: 5.

Persians: 2 AHO (Mercenary and Guard), 1 LHI (Carian, Red Sea and Sitacenian), 1 LAR (Mardian, Uxian and Babylonian), 1 LLI (Persian, Indian and Cadusian), TL + AHC (Darius + Guard), 9 AHC (2 Persian, 1 Armenian, 1 Cappadocian, 1 Median, 1 Hyrcanian, 1 Tapurian, 1 Massagetae, 1 Bactrian), 4 LHC (1 Syrian and Mesopotamian, 1 Albanian and Sacesinian, 1 Indian and Cadusian, 1 Susian and Arachosian), 3 ALC (1 Saka, 1 Dahae, 1 Bactrian), 3 LLC (2 Bactrian, 1 Parthian), 1 SCH. FV: 69.

Macedonians: 2 VHI (Hypaspists), 3 APH (Foot Companions), 6 AHI (4 Mercenary, 2 Thracian), 1 LHI (Allied), 1 VLI (Agrianians and Archers), 1 ALI (Cretan and Illyrian), BL + VHC (Alexander + Companions), 4 VHC (2 Companions, 2 Thessalian), 1 AHC (Greek, Thracian and Mercenary), 1 ALC (Prodromoi, Paeonian and Mercenary), AC (Parmenio). FV: 94.

HYDASPES, 326 BC

The River Hydaspes was much wider than the Granicus or the Pinarus, so when he encountered Porus's Indian army on the other side, Alexander had to undertake a surprise dawn crossing 150 stadia (27 km) upstream.[66] He then smashed a force of cavalry and chariots led by Porus's son, and marched back down the river to meet Porus himself. As I said on pp. xii–xiii, this engagement is plagued by ambiguous and contradictory sources and scholarly disagreements, and is an archetypal 'lost battle'. Arrian (*Anab.* V.15–18) is again our principal source, with some 1,500 words on the battle itself, based mainly on Ptolemy and Aristobulus. Diodorus (XVII.87–9), Plutarch (*Alex.* 60), Curtius (VIII.14) and Polyaenus (IV.3.22) have shorter and more anecdotal accounts that nevertheless contribute something, though often by challenging the details in Arrian.

There is the usual scholarly controversy over exactly where on the modern Jhelum the engagement took place, with the shifting course of the channels posing familiar complications.[67] Fortunately, this is immaterial for our purposes as there are no indications that terrain (even the riverbank) impinged on the actual battle. A more important issue concerns the weather conditions. The sources describe a thunderstorm during the night, and Arrian (*Anab.* V.15) tells how the soft mud made the chariots under Porus's son useless. Curtius (VIII.14.4–8 and 19) confirms this story, and also claims that the slippery ground hindered the Indian archers during the main battle. However, he runs the two engagements into one, when in fact a number of hours must have passed before the main battle, considering how far both armies had to march in order to meet. Arrian (*Anab.* V.15) explicitly says that Porus drew up on sandy ground to avoid the deep mud present elsewhere, and the subsequent cavalry (and perhaps even chariot) manoeuvres all the way from one flank to another do not chime at all with the bogging down described in the earlier encounter. The scenario below hence begins in overcast conditions, with no restrictions operating at first but with a continuing risk of further wet weather that will asymmetrically handicap Porus's less well-commanded force of chariots and archers.[68]

The size of both armies is a matter of considerable dispute, complicating attempts to use either one as a reliable yardstick against which to measure the other. Arrian (*Anab.* V.14 and 18) says that Alexander crossed the river with 5,000 cavalry and 6,000 infantry, and he repeats the figure of 6,000 foot when discussing casualties after the battle. However, he claims (*Anab.* V.12) that Alexander's infantry force before the crossing consisted of the Hypaspists, archers, Agrianians and 2 phalanx taxeis, which should in theory amount to considerably more troops. Some writers think there really were just 6,000 foot – Lane Fox suggests that only the Hypaspists and light infantry made the crossing, while Bosworth and Daniel argue that the various contingents must have been significantly under strength, perhaps because of the limited capacity of the available boats.[69] Other scholars challenge the figure of 6,000, claiming that it referred only to the heavy infantry or that some of the other troops that Arrian (*Anab.* V.12) says were left at intervals along the bank managed to cross and join up before the main battle. Hammond, Green and Ashley estimate that there were 9–10,000 infantry in the engagement, while Devine and Hamilton suggest 15,000 and Montagu goes as high as 23,000.[70]

Arrian's figure of 5,000 cavalry is less controversial, though there is still debate over contingent sizes. Estimates of the number of Companions range from 1,500 to 2,700, with the rest being horse from the eastern satrapies including 1,000 Dahae mounted archers.[71] Our model allows users to experiment with all these possible variations, but the scenario below takes an intermediate approach, assuming there were 6,000 heavy and 2,000 light infantry, plus 2,000 Companions and 3,000 Asiatic light horse. The Hypaspists were surely by now armed with the sarissae that Curtius (VIII.14.15–16) and Diodorus (XVII.88) describe being put to good use against the elephant line.[72] One could argue that more than just the Hypaspists, Companions and Agrianians should by now be classed as veterans, or conversely that some of the Asiatic horse should count as levies, but the scenario instead uses an average rating throughout. With Coenus as an average leader to reflect his prominent supporting role, the army's fighting value at a multiple of 3 hence comes to 85.

This gives us at least some kind of yardstick against which to judge the varying numbers for the Indian forces. Arrian (*Anab.* V.15) states that Porus fielded 30,000 infantry, 4,000 cavalry, 300 chariots and 200 elephants, while Diodorus (XVII.87) gives him 50,000 foot, 3,000 horse, over 1,000 chariots and

130 pachyderms. Curtius (VIII.13.6) agrees with Arrian on infantry and cavalry numbers but says there were only 85 elephants, and Plutarch (*Alex.* 62) gives the lower totals of 20,000 foot and 2,000 horse. Modern scholars disagree just as much, with Hammond and Lane Fox endorsing Arrian's claims while Devine and Green go with Plutarch's much lower numbers. As regards elephants, Hammond and Hamilton think there were 200, Green opts for 130, Devine and Ashley choose 85, and Bosworth suggests less than 50.[73]

At a multiple of 3, each elephant unit in our model represents 15 beasts with light infantry support or 30 without. The only way 200 pachyderms would be practical would be if we discount the infantry support that these beasts seem to have had. At the other extreme, giving Porus less than 50 beasts would mean a fighting value of only 12 for this key component of Indian strength. Six units representing 85 accompanied elephants seems a much more appropriate total. The Indian cavalry fought bravely and for a long time despite being outnumbered, and must surely be classed as average, but the foot archers were low-status troops who should clearly count as levies like their Persian counterparts, especially as the best 4,000 or so infantry are assumed to be in front with the pachyderms.[74] Even if we have 30,000 foot as well as 3,000 horse and up to 300 of the large chariots, then with Porus as an average commander the army's fighting value comes to 66, which still gives Alexander a clear advantage in what was by all accounts a hard-fought battle.[75] Devine's smaller Indian army would have a value of only around 54, which as usual for him seems overcautious given that the value of his inflated Macedonian force would exceed 100.

This brings us to the vexed issue of army frontages. As I mentioned on p. xii, Arrian's figure of 100 ft between elephants (*Anab.* V.15) would give his infantry line alone a length of over 6 km.[76] Hammond reduces the intervals to the 50 ft claimed by Polyaenus (IV.3.22), while Ashley cuts his elephant numbers to 85 and retains Arrian's spacing, but both these writers still suggest an Indian infantry line around 3.5 km long, dwarfing their 1.0–1.2 km line of Macedonian foot, and with the unengaged majority of the Indians conveniently remaining far more inert than Artaxerxes's right did at Cunaxa.[77] Devine's 85 more closely packed elephants would cover only 1,300 m, short enough to be matched by his force of nearly 15,000 Macedonian infantry, but Bosworth thinks there were only 6,000 such foot, with a frontage of just 700 m, and he makes the Indian line equally narrow because he believes that Alexander trapped Porus's entire deeply arrayed army in a complete double envelopment that (if true) would outshine Hannibal's achievement at Cannae.[78] Reputable scholarly estimates of the length of the Indian infantry line thus differ by a factor of five or more!

Our model strongly suggests that both Hammond and Bosworth are wrong, and that the reality lies somewhere in between these two radically different extremes. With a frontage of 500 m per zone, an Indian deployment of 85 elephants at

50 foot intervals, backed by infantry in around 20 ranks, and with cavalry and chariots split evenly between the wings, makes perfect sense. It is also entirely plausible that Alexander would counter this with his usual oblique attack on his right with the Dahae, Companions, Agrianians and Hypaspists, while holding his 8 rank phalanx and flanking light infantry back in the centre to guard the Hypaspists' left, and while detaching Coenus to tie down the Indian right until the main attack could take effect.[79] Arrian (*Anab.* V.16) makes clear that the majority of the cavalry were with Alexander on the right, but putting all the Asiatic horse there seems rather like overkill given the limited frontage available, and it makes more sense for at least some of them to accompany Coenus, as Bosworth suggests.[80] Our model also shows how the other Asiatic light horse have the flexibility to reinforce the central phalanx if its flank is threatened by the Indian right.[81]

The biggest controversy about the tactical course of the battle concerns Arrian's description (*Anab.* V.16–17) of the Indian right wing cavalry being shifted across to reinforce the left wing horse, and being pursued and attacked from behind by Coenus's men, who then joined up with Alexander's cavalry as the Indian horse withdrew to the shelter of the elephants. Some, like Hammond, think that at least one of these movements took place between the two opposing infantry lines, but others such as Hamilton believe that both forces rode round the back of the Indian line.[82] In our model, the former possibility is best simulated as part of initial deployment, with both sides' cavalry already massed on one flank by the time the main lines get so close together. Given the limited frontage on the right, it would actually make more sense for Coenus to be placed on the other wing regardless, so the scenario in Figure 22 is based on the alternative possibility of movements behind the Indian line. If the Indians get sufficient commands on turn 2, they are indeed able to advance their whole main line and then make a free about turn with some or all of their right wing horse and move them all the way to their left rear or left wing using double moves, relying on the elephants to protect the right against Coenus. He in turn can exploit Alexander's capacity for turn reversal to curve round all the way into the Indian rear, thereby catching the Indian horse between two fires as happened historically. This places the Macedonian cavalry in an ideal position to encircle the left and centre of the Indian line. Meanwhile, the Macedonian pikemen and light infantry will engage the elephants in the bitter frontal struggle that the sources describe, until the crowded mass of infantry, cavalry and pachyderms finally gives way under attack from all sides.[83] Indian casualties were enormous, but the sources put Macedonian losses at up to 280 cavalry and 700 infantry, and the bravery of the wounded Porus in defeat stands in stark contrast to the alleged timidity of Darius.[84]

This battle illustrates perfectly how our model can contribute to a vexed scholarly debate that has produced radically different reconstructions using more traditional approaches to the obscure and often contradictory evidence. Despite the complexity of the engagement, which involved units of every single type and class, we can compare proposed armies according to their overall fighting values rather than just their numbers and presumed frontage, and we can study suggested deployments and manoeuvres dynamically and as the product of rational command choices rather than just through blocks and arrows on a map. The results are not conclusive, and there is plenty of scope to experiment with different hypotheses, but our model casts severe doubt on some of the starkly contrasting ideas put forward by writers like Hammond, Bosworth and Devine, however erudite and impressive their scholarship.

HYDASPES, 326 BC (Figure 22)

M: x3. AL: 3. Overcast.

Indians: 9 LAR (Indian), 4 AHC (Indian), 2 ACH (four-horse), 6 IEL (Indian LI), AC (Porus). FV: 66.

Macedonians: 4 VPH (Hypaspists), 2 APH (Foot Companions), 1 VLI (Agrianian), 1 ALI (Archers), BL + VHC (Alexander + Agema), AL + VHC (Coenus + Companions), 3 VHC (Companions), 4 ALC (1 Dahae, 1 Scythian, 1 Bactrian, 1 Sogdian). FV: 85.

10

The Successors

Alexander's death was followed by decades of fighting among his generals for control of his vast empire, but only a few of the resulting battles are recorded in sufficient detail for us to attempt their reconstruction. In 317 or 316 BC (scholars differ), two of the most talented generals, Antigonus and Eumenes, clashed in successive engagements in Media.[1] In the first battle in Paraitacene, the result was inconclusive, but in Gabiene a few months later, Antigonus won enough of an edge for Eumenes's troops to hand him over for execution. This gave Antigonus control of most of Asia, but the other generals united against him, and in 312 BC, a detachment under his son Demetrius was defeated at Gaza by Ptolemy's army from Egypt. Antigonus was still powerful enough to hold his own for another decade, but in 301 he was killed at the massive but ill-recorded battle of Ipsus, and his territory was carved up among the victors to create the enduring tripartite power structure of the Hellenistic world – the Ptolemies in Egypt, the Seleucids in Asia, and the old kingdom of Macedonia itself, which fell to Demetrius's son Antigonus Gonatas in the wake of the devastating Galatian invasions 2 decades later. Macedon continued to clash with its southern Greek neighbours, and in 222 BC Antigonus Doson defeated Cleomenes of Sparta in a battle at Sellasia. The border between Ptolemies and Seleucids also saw continued friction over control of the Lebanon, and in 217 BC Ptolemy IV beat Antiochus III in a massive engagement at Raphia. These and many other internecine conflicts weakened the Hellenistic powers' ability to counter the inexorably growing threat from Rome.

PARAITACENE, 317/6 BC

After several years of sparring and of indecisive clashes, Antigonus and Eumenes confronted one another in the area of Paraitacene. Our only real source is Diodorus (XIX.27–32), which would normally be a serious problem given his infamous unreliability, but in this case he is presumed to have based his 2,000-word account on the lost eyewitness testimony of Hieronymus of Cardia, a friend and companion of Eumenes and later of Antigonus.[2] Diodorus (XIX.26 and 29) describes Antigonus looking down on Eumenes's array from a range of hills and deploying his own army accordingly, which is best reflected by having Antigonus deploy second. The evidence is confused as to how near the hills were to the battlefield. Diodorus (XIX.27 and 31) says that Eumenes's left was actually in contact with the higher ground, but he later claims that the new line that Antigonus formed along the foothills at dusk was 30 stadia (5.5 km) from the original battle site. This suggests that there should not be hills in all of Antigonus's rear zones, but that there should be a spur of hills running from Antigonus's right rear zone to Eumenes's left wing zone.[3]

Our evidence on the size and composition of the opposing armies is better than for any other battle so far, though still not without its problems. Diodorus (XIX.27–8) says that Eumenes fielded 35,000 infantry, 6,100 cavalry and 114 elephants, though the actual total of the contingents he describes comes to 17,000 heavy infantry, 6,300 horse and 125 pachyderms. It is usually assumed that the 18,000 foot not listed in the battle line were light-armed troops including the 10,000 Persian archers and slingers of Eumenes's ally, Peucestes.[4] The heavy infantry included 6,000 mercenaries, 5,000 pantodapoi (Asiatics armed as phalangites and probably best classed as levies), 3,000 Hypaspists and 3,000 Silver Shields. Scholars are unsure how the latter 2 units related to one another and to Alexander's infantry, with Diodorus's claim (XIX.41) that the Silver Shields were all grizzled veterans in their sixties and seventies being rather hard to believe.[5] However, these units (especially the Silver Shields) certainly seem to have carried all before them, and so they clearly deserve veteran status on the basis of their battlefield performance. The cavalry included 900 of Alexander's Companions, 1,500 light horse, 3,000 colonists and natives accompanying the various satraps, and Eumenes's own 900 bodyguards, retainers and picked horse.[6] At a multiple of 6, and with Eumenes as an inspired leader, this gives the army a fighting value of 73.

Diodorus (XIX.27 and 29) gives Antigonus 28,000 infantry, 8,500 cavalry and 65 elephants, though here again there is a discrepancy with his detailed listings that total 28,000 heavy infantry and 10,600 horse. Scholars think there must also have been some light infantry, and Devine suggests a figure of 10,000.[7] The heavy infantry included 8,000 Macedonians, 8,000 pantodapoi, 3,000 Lycians and Pamphylians and 9,000 mercenaries. It is unclear whether both sides' mercenary infantry were now armed as phalangites or whether they were still peltasts as in Alexander's day. Griffith suggests they were pikemen, and this certainly fits in with the equipping of Asiatics as phalangites, though Head points out that Antigonus did have some peltasts as well as bowmen, slingers and other light-armed troops earlier that year.[8] Scholars usually accept Diodorus's higher aggregate figure for the cavalry, which included 1,000 Companions, 4,300 light horse, 4,700 settlers, allies and mercenaries, and Antigonus's 600 bodyguards and retainers.[9] With Antigonus as an inspired leader, this gives a fighting value of 70, and the difference of just 3 neatly reflects the close-run nature of this engagement.

Scholars differ widely on the proportion of the front occupied by the respective phalanxes – Devine puts this at less than 25 per cent, while Billows suggests a figure of over 60 per cent.[10] Scullard reproduces Kromayer and Kahnes's calculation of a frontage of 1,750 m for the infantry centres and of between 600 and 1,100 m for each cavalry wing, though this is based on lower estimates of the numbers of horsemen present.[11] In 16 ranks, Antigonus's 28,000 heavy infantry would indeed take up something like 1,750 m at an average of 1 m per file, and Eumenes's Hypaspists and Silver Shields probably used just 8 ranks to offset their smaller numbers. It is harder to gauge the length of the cavalry wings, but Antigonus's 10,600 horsemen would fill around 2,400 m using the yardstick in Polybius (XII.18), and the horsemen's generally high quality suggests they may not have used multiple lines. The scenario in Figure 23 hence uses the maximum scale of 1,200 m per zone, with the main forces concentrated in the middle 3 zones, and with the side opposite the hills open for the flanking movements that both sides made with light horse. Both generals led on their right with their best horsemen, and both spread their elephants along the front. Antigonus had only a few elephants with his left, but Eumenes placed 45 beasts on his own left in an enigmatic curved formation. Our model shows how important they must have been in holding off Antigonus's much superior cavalry, and it casts doubt on Devine's suggestion that they were deployed on the extreme wing rather than (as is usually assumed) as a forward screen for the left wing horse.[12]

Antigonus launched a classic oblique attack with his right wing in the lead, but as his left wing cavalry outnumbered their opponents by even more, the horse archers there outflanked and began to bombard the enemy elephants. Eumenes called his own light horse to transfer across from the left (taking just 1 double move in our model), and with their help and that of his pachyderms and light infantry, he outflanked and routed Antigonus's left wing cavalry. Meanwhile, the phalanxes met and Eumenes's men were victorious despite having far fewer heavy troops, because of the valour of the Silver Shields. Antigonus was able to charge into the gap that opened as the enemy phalanx advanced, and so outflank and defeat the troops remaining on Eumenes's left wing, but he then had to pull back to rally his own routed forces on the foothills. This was hence yet another 'revolving door' battle, with Eumenes's advantages in veteran infantry and elephant numbers just managing to offset his inferiority in horsemen and heavy foot.[13] Antigonus succeeded in facing off Eumenes's pursuit, and even in reoccupying the battlefield that night – this is simulated by the real chance of him hanging on in the hills until turn 10. Diodorus (XIX.31) says that Antigonus suffered higher casualties (3,750 killed and 4,000 wounded as against Eumenes's 540 dead and 900 wounded), though Devine suggests that the difference may be exaggerated.[14] This finely balanced engagement reveals Hellenistic combined arms warfare at its peak, and offers an ideal proving ground for our model to bolster its validity in other battles where scholarly controversies are greater.

PARAITACENE, 317/6 BC (Figure 23)

M: x6. AL: 5.

Eumenes: 4 VPH (2 Silver Shields, 2 Hypaspists), 2 APH (Mercenary), 1 LPH (Pantodapoi), 2 LLI (1 Persian, 1 Asiatic), IL + VHC (Eumenes + Agema and Picked Horse), 1 VHC (Companions), 2 AHC (Colonist), 1 ALC (Arachosian, Paropanisadae and Thracian), 4 IEL (Persian LI). FV: 73.

Antigonus: 5 APH (3 Macedonian, 2 Mercenary), 1 AHI (Mercenary), 1 LPH (Pantodapoi), 1 LHI (Lycian and Pamphylian), 1 LLI (Asiatic), IL + VHC (Antigonus + Agema and Retainers), 1 VHC (Companions), 3 AHC (2 Colonist, 1 Allied and Mercenary), 3 ALC (1 Tarentine, 1 Thracian, 1 Median and Parthian), 2 IEL (Mercenary LI). FV: 70.

GABIENE, 316/5 BC

Antigonus tried to reverse his rebuff in Paraitacene by a surprise strike that winter, but Eumenes reacted quickly and the outcome was another pitched battle in the region of Gabiene, probably in early January of 316 or 315 BC. Our main source is again Diodorus's 1,500-word summary of Hieronymus (XIX.39–43), which is somewhat less detailed than for Paraitacene but we can supplement it with information from that earlier contest. We also have shorter accounts by Plutarch (*Eum.* 16–17) and Polyaenus (IV.6.13). Apart from a river some way off to Eumenes's rear, the battlefield was apparently a broad and uncultivated salt-plain, and the only impact of the terrain was that the movement of troops stirred up huge clouds of dust that obscured vision.[15] As I discussed on pp. 65 and 69, this poor visibility may be simulated by halving command die rolls and by rolling dice at the start of each turn to see which army goes first, thereby making it much more difficult to plan and to carry out the careful and subtle tactics for which both generals were renowned. A scale of 1,000 m per zone gives the arena the same scale width as the unobstructed part of the Paraitacene battlefield. The camps were some 40 stadia (7.3 km) apart, but Eumenes's baggage was only 5 stadia (900 m) from the fighting line, so deserves placement in his rear zone.[16] Diodorus (XIX.40) describes Eumenes hearing that Antigonus was again leading his right, and this time deciding to confront him head-on. This suggests that Eumenes should deploy second, and that both key zones should be on the same side of the field.

For this battle, Diodorus (XIX.40) only gives summary totals for the two armies, and we have already seen that his totals do not necessarily match his more detailed contingent figures that this time are absent. He says that Antigonus fielded 22,000 foot (presumably again just the heavy infantry), 9,000 cavalry and 65 elephants (one more than in Paraitacene). The reduced infantry total fits fairly well with Diodorus's casualty figures for the earlier battle (XIX.31), as the losses had been overwhelmingly among the foot troops. The cavalry number is more problematic, because it is probably to be compared with his earlier overall figure of 8,500 rather than his aggregated total of 10,600, and because scholars differ over whether the new number did or did not include the additional Median troopers mentioned by Diodorus. Writers nevertheless tend to fall back on the figure of 9,000 for lack of anything else, but as only 54 cavalrymen are said to have died in Paraitacene, and because Antigonus's horsemen played such a significant role in his eventual triumph, it is probably worth pushing overall cavalry numbers to at least 10,000 to take account of a possible underestimate.[17] If we shift to a multiple of 5 to offset the shrinkage of the army and the increased number of unobstructed zones, this gives Antigonus's force a fighting value of 70.

What makes Eumenes's defeat harder to understand is that Diodorus (XIX.40) says he had the same number of elephants (114) as in Paraitacene, and an even larger number of infantry (36,700). Only his cavalry (6,000) were apparently less numerous, and then only by a very small margin. Devine thinks that both sides' elephant figures at this battle are rather suspect, but other scholars accept them as given – we can allow for possible losses by rounding the number of elephant units down rather than up for both armies.[18] The Silver Shields continued to enjoy overwhelming psychological dominance over Antigonus's foot, as shown by Diodorus's tale (XIX.40) of their commander's intimidation of the hostile phalanx just before the battle. However, there is no mention of Eumenes's other infantry playing any significant role, so any accretion of strength probably took the form of yet more Asiatic light infantry, with the Macedonian and mercenary foot numbering even less than the 12,000 recorded in Paraitacene. The real change is that the cavalry, which had performed so well against great odds in the earlier battle, collapsed dismally in this one, with Peucestes fleeing early on along with over 1,500 troopers. If we downgrade the horsemen's status to average and levy accordingly, and also reclassify Eumenes himself as an average leader as he was clearly unable to inspire his men or to counter Antigonus's demoralizing raid on his baggage, then even at a multiple of 5, Eumenes's army has a fighting value of only 64, which puts him at a slightly greater marginal disadvantage than that suffered by Antigonus in Paraitacene.

We know much less than in the earlier battle about both sides' deployments. Antigonus is simply said to have placed his foot in the centre, his cavalry on the wings with himself and his son Demetrius on the right, and his elephants and light infantry spread across the entire front.[19] Billows suggests that his left

wing contained mostly light horse, as it was from here that the Medes and some
Tarentines rode around to seize the baggage.[20] Diodorus (XIX.40) says that
Eumenes deployed his best cavalry including most of the satrapal contingents
on his left together with his 60 strongest elephants. His centre consisted (from
left to right) of the Hypaspists, the Silver Shields, the mercenaries and the
pantodapoi, with elephants and light infantry in front, while the weaker of the
elephants and cavalry were placed on the right and ordered to avoid battle.
Writers usually suppose a fairly even division of horse between the two wings,
but the Companions can hardly be described as 'weak' and so were presumably
on the left along with the colonists, which suggests that not much more than the
light horse started out on the right.[21] As in Paraitacene, scholars differ widely over
the relative frontages occupied by the infantry and cavalry, and Devine makes the
same suggestion that the 60 elephants were deployed beyond the left wing as an
angled flank guard rather than in front of the wing itself.[22] The diversion of at
least some of the pachyderms to provide such a flank guard would help to explain
the reverses suffered by the cavalry and elephants with Eumenes himself, so in
this case it makes rather more sense than in the earlier battle where the left was
refused and was shielded by the neighbouring hills. The scenario in Figure 24 has
Eumenes hoping to get in the first blow on his left thanks to turn reversal, and
then to follow this up with his strong central phalanx before Antigonus's light
horse can overwhelm his refused right.

Antigonus began by using the cover of the dust to send some light cavalry
to seize Eumenes's baggage (that may well be exposed if Eumenes's right
advances to cover the charge of his strong centre). Diodorus (XIX.42) then
describes how the large numbers of Antigonus's cavalry prompted Peucestes
to flee with over 1,500 horse, and how Eumenes's leading elephant fell to an
enemy pachyderm. Eumenes at first charged Antigonus with the few horsemen
left to him on the extreme left, but as the tide turned against him, he led what
remained of his cavalry (probably including the Companions if they were next
to the Hypaspists) round to the other wing – in our model, such redeployments
may well occur after turn reversal, as units cannot attack twice in succession
from the same zone. Meanwhile, Diodorus (XIX.43) tells how the Silver Shields
routed the entire enemy phalanx, killing 5,000 of them for no loss.[23] Eumenes
tried in vain to rally his cavalry to renew the fight, but Antigonus calmly used
some horsemen to 'mark' him while sending the rest to attack the Silver Shields,
who formed a hollow square and withdrew off the field. Our model shows that,
despite Diodorus's hyperbole, Eumenes's other infantry must have played a
very significant part in this action, and it also clearly demonstrates how spent
his foot troops must have become during the phalanx confrontation and hence
how encircling enemy horsemen could indeed turn the tide. Unlike Antigonus
in Paraitacene, it will be hard for any of Eumenes's forces to remain on the board

for 10 turns if the superior enemy cavalry get the advantage, so this battle is less likely to have an indecisive result. In reality, the demoralization caused by losing their baggage and being forced to withdraw prompted the Silver Shields to betray Eumenes to Antigonus that very night.

GABIENE, 316/5 BC (Figure 24)

M: x5. AL: 4. Dust.

Antigonus: 4 APH (2 Macedonian, 2 Mercenary), 1 AHI (Mercenary), 1 LPH (Pantodapoi), 1 LHI (Lycian and Pamphylian), 1 LLI (Asiatic), IL + VHC (Antigonus + Agema and Retainers), 1 VHC (Companions), 3 AHC (2 Colonist, 1 Allied and Mercenary), 4 ALC (2 Tarentine, 1 Median, 1 Thracian and Parthian), 2 IEL (Mercenary LI). FV: 70.

Eumenes: 4 VPH (2 Silver Shields, 2 Hypaspists), 2 APH (Mercenary), 1 LPH (Pantodapoi), 3 LLI (2 Asiatic, 1 Persian), AL + VHC (Eumenes + Agema and Picked Horse), 1 AHC (Companions), 1 LHC (Colonist), 1 ALC (Arachosian, Paropanisadae and Thracian), 4 IEL (Persian LI). FV: 64.

GAZA, 312 BC

Threatened on several fronts, Antigonus in 314 BC left Demetrius (now 22) to defend Syria against Ptolemy, and when the latter crossed the Sinai 2 years later accompanied by the fugitive Seleucus, the armies met near Gaza.[24] Diodorus (XIX.80–5) once again has a 2,000-word summary of Hieronymus's lost account. The battlefield has not been located, but was apparently an open and unimpeded plain.[25] Diodorus (XIX.82–3) describes how both sides initially intended to attack with the left of their line (an interesting inversion of the usual emphasis on the right), but he says that when Ptolemy and Seleucus learned from scouts of Demetrius's array, they changed their formation to confront him head-on. This is therefore a very clear case in which Demetrius should move first and in which both key zones should again be on the same side of the battlefield.

Diodorus (XIX.69) claims that Antigonus left Demetrius in 314 with 10,000 mercenary and 2,000 Macedonian infantry, 500 Lycians and Pamphylians, 400 Persian archers and slingers, 5,000 cavalry and 43 elephants. The figures he gives for the battle itself (XIX.82) are the same for the Macedonians and the elephants, but now include 1,000 Lycians and Pamphylians and just 8,000 mercenaries in the phalanx. However, he says there were 1,500 javelinmen, archers and Persian slingers with the 30 elephants on the left wing, and Devine suggests that the light infantry mentioned with the other 13 pachyderms probably numbered another 650 according to the same 1:50 ratio.[26] The skirmishers fit perfectly into mixed elephant units, and the 11,000 other foot should probably all count as average, with most being phalangites but with the Lycians, Pamphylians and some of the mercenaries being ordinary heavy infantry.[27] Diodorus has a more detailed breakdown of the cavalry, which included 500 guards, 800 Companions, 100 Tarentines and 3,000 of mixed origin, for a total of 4,400 horsemen. Both Diodorus (IX.81–2) and Plutarch (*Dem*. 5) emphasize Demetrius's youth and inexperience as a general, but he was accompanied as co-commander by Pithon, a veteran of Alexander's campaigns, so he deserves to be classed as an average leader. At a multiple of 3, his army thus has a fighting value of 67.

As Hieronymus was an intimate of Antigonus, we know much less about Ptolemy's army. Diodorus (XIX.80) says only that he had 18,000 foot and 4,000 horse, and that the army included Macedonians, mercenaries, and a large number of Egyptians, some of whom were armed for battle. Scholars disagree over whether the 18,000 foot was an overall total or whether it included only the heavy infantry or only the Macedonians and mercenaries.[28] Our model suggests that if Ptolemy really had enjoyed a 64 per cent advantage in high-quality heavy infantry, they would have played a more prominent role than appears to have been the case. The scenario below therefore assumes that the 18,000 included both the phalanx and the light infantry who were decisive in countering the elephants, with some of the skirmishers counting as veterans to reflect their use of spiked obstacles connected by chains to defeat the pachyderms.[29] There is also 1 additional unit of levy light infantry to represent the armed Egyptians, on the same basis as for the armed helots at Plataea, which brings the overall total to around 21,000 foot. In the absence of definitive information, the cavalry are given roughly the same mix of veteran and average units and of heavy and light troopers as in Demetrius's force. Although Diodorus refers to Ptolemy and Seleucus as twin generals, they fought together rather than separately, and Seleucus seems to have contributed no troops of his own.[30] As with Demetrius and Pithon, it hence seems preferable to have just 1 general (Ptolemy), but to make him an inspired leader to reflect his well-attested advantage in skill and experience. This gives the army a fighting value of 79, which is enough of a lead to justify the caution that Diodorus (XIX.81) says Demetrius's friends vainly urged.

Demetrius deployed his best 2,900 horsemen on his left with 30 elephants in front, then his heavy infantry with the remaining 13 elephants, and finally 1,500 cavalry on a refused right flank. Ptolemy countered this by placing 3,000 of his 4,000 horse on his right, screened by javelinmen, archers and the elephant obstacles.[31] Devine and Billows again disagree over the proportion of front occupied by the phalanxes, though not by quite as much as in the previous battles.[32] We have no information on unit depths, but Ptolemy's 15,000 or so heavy infantry in 16 ranks might fill around 1 km, while his 4,000 cavalry would cover a similar distance according to Polybius (XII.18). This suggests a scale of 500 m per zone and deployments as shown in Figure 25.

The fighting started on Demetrius's extreme left where the cavalry under his own command at first prevailed, but Ptolemy and Seleucus led reserve horsemen in a flanking manoeuvre and the cavalry battle became a bitter and prolonged close quarter struggle. Our model neatly reflects the ability of both sides to shift more horsemen out onto the flank while still leaving enough units in their key zones to make the maximum number of attacks. The decisive moment came when the elephant charge foundered against the spiked obstacles and Ptolemy's skirmishers, with the mahouts being shot and all of the pachyderms captured. This triggered the panic of Demetrius's cavalry, carrying him away in the rout.[33] Diodorus (XIX.83–5) says nothing about any fighting elsewhere on the front, merely recording that some of the infantry dropped their weapons and fled, and that 500 of Demetrius's troops (mostly horsemen, including Pithon) were killed and 8,000 captured.[34] Our model suggests that there may indeed have been an initial stand-off in the centre, with the opposing phalanxes holding each other in check while the cavalry contest was decided. Thereafter, it would not have taken much to make the morale of Demetrius's infantry collapse in the face of frontal attack and cavalry encirclement, especially as Ptolemy was more willing than Alexander at the Granicus to let the mercenaries change sides (the coincidence of the figures for mercenaries and prisoners is particularly suggestive in this regard). The battle showed that elephants could be defeated fairly quickly through insightful surprise countermeasures, but this did not stop them playing a significant and often victorious role in many later engagements, so clearly the solution to the problem was not as simple as all that.

GAZA, 312 BC (Figure 25)

M: x3. AL: 3.

Demetrius: 5 APH (1 Macedonian, 4 Mercenary), 2 AHI (1 Mercenary, 1 Lycian and Pamphylian), AL + VHC (Demetrius + Guard), 3 VHC (2 Companions, 1 Lancers), 2 AHC (1 Colonist, 1 Allied and Mercenary), 2 ALC (1 Tarentine, 1 Median and Thracian), 3 IEL (2 Mercenary LI, 1 Persian LI). FV: 67.

Ptolemy: 8 APH (3 Macedonian, 5 Mercenary), 2 AHI (Mercenary), 2 VLI (Anti-Elephant Troops), 1 ALI (Mercenary), 1 LLI (Egyptian), IL + VHC (Ptolemy + Guard), 2 VHC (Guard), 2 AHC (1 Colonist, 1 Mercenary), 2 ALC (Mercenary). FV: 79.

SELLASIA, 222 BC

As Diodorus's account of the climactic contest at Ipsus has been lost, it is another 90 years before we again have comparably detailed descriptions of pitched land battles in the eastern Mediterranean.[35] A war between Sparta and the Achaean League provoked Macedonian intervention, and in 222 BC Antigonus Doson invaded Laconia itself and confronted Cleomenes's Spartans near Sellasia. Our main source is now Polybius, the single most important ancient military historian of our entire era, who has around 1,500 words of detailed narrative (II.65–9) on the resulting engagement. Plutarch (*Cleom.* 28 and *Phil.* 6) also adds a few useful snippets. Terrain was crucial in this battle, and Polybius (II.65–6) describes how Cleomenes formed up on two hills (Euas and Olympus) that straddled the road south to Sparta along the River Oenus, with another river (the Gorgylus) running just to the north of Euas. Like Darius at Issus, Cleomenes used fieldworks to strengthen his defences further, but Polybius (II.68–9) makes clear how limited their value was, as the troops on Euas were quickly pushed back away from their initial positions, while those on Olympus had to tear down part of their own defences in order to advance rather than waiting to be defeated in detail. A fortified camp on Olympus should suffice to reflect this marginal feature. The Spartans should clearly move first to reflect their established defensive stance, allowing them to strike the first blow in combat, but permitting Antigonus to tailor his counter-deployment after several days of sparring and jockeying for advantage as Polybius (II.65–6) describes.

It is generally agreed that the Oenus corresponds to the modern Kelephina, but scholars have long debated where exactly along its course the battle took place. Kromayer and Pritchett concur in identifying Olympus as Mount Provatares, but Kromayer placed Euas on Palaeogoulas while Pritchett prefers the Troules summit 1 km northwest and just over 1 km from the Oenus.[36] Pritchett's site has generally been seen as more persuasive, but Morgan points out that there is a ravine on the slopes of Provatares opposite the Dagla ridge that runs down from Troules, so he suggests that the phalanxes actually met on a saddle on the top of Olympus, about 1 km from the river, with light infantry guarding their flanks.[37] The saddle is only some 300 m wide, which Morgan thinks explains Polybius's claim (II.66) that the Macedonians deployed in a double phalanx perhaps 32 deep.[38] As it is hard for heavy infantry to reach the flank zones, this suggests that the 3 Spartan centre zones should span all the way from Euas (Troules) to the top of Olympus, which produces a scale of around 800 m per zone. The Oenus and Gorgylus are represented merely as streams because of their lack of water in the summer, and the pattern of streams and hills in Figure 30 reflects quite well the actual current topography of the area.

Polybius (II.65) gives most detail on Antigonus's forces, which he numbers at around 28,000 foot and 1,200 horse. The infantry included 10,000 Macedonian phalangites and 3,000 'peltasts', who were guardsmen like the earlier Hypaspists, probably also armed with sarissae.[39] In addition there were 3,000 Achaeans, 3,000 mercenaries, 2,000 Boeotians, 1,600 Illyrians, and contingents of Megalopolitans, Gauls, Epirotes, Agrianians and Acarnanians each numbering 1,000, making a detailed total of 27,600 foot. The Megalopolitans are described as fighting in the Macedonian manner, and Head suggests that the Boeotians and Epirotes would also now be pikemen, while the Achaeans and Illyrians would be medium infantry with the oval thureos, and the Agrianians and Acarnanians would be light infantry.[40] The Boeotian and Epirote foot are not mentioned in the battle, and some may perhaps have been guarding the camp, but the scenario includes both contingents on the Macedonian right, combined into 1 levy unit to minimize their impact and to avoid giving Antigonus too great an advantage.[41] We know from Polybius (II.66) that the mercenaries included some Cretan archers, and the use of others as a screen for the phalanx suggests that they too were light armed.[42] The cavalry, far less numerous than in Alexander's day, included 300 Macedonians, 300 mercenaries, 300 Achaeans, and 300 Boeotians, Epirotes and Acarnanians. At a multiple of 3, and with Antigonus as an average commander as he does not seem to have played a front line role, this gives the army a fighting value of 72.

The only figures that Polybius (II.65 and 69) gives for Cleomenes's forces are an overall total of 20,000 men, of whom around 5,000 mercenary infantry fought with the Spartans themselves on Olympus. Plutarch (*Cleom.* 11, 23 and 28) says that Cleomenes raised the number of Spartan citizen troops to 4,000 in 227 by enfranchising selected perioikoi, and later added 2,000 freed helots, also now armed with the sarissa – this fits exactly with his total of 6,000 for the Spartans at Sellasia.[43] Both Plutarch and Polybius (II.69) describe the Spartans fighting with great courage, so the 4,000 should surely all count as veterans despite the widening of the Spartan 'franchise' and the novelty of the new equipment. Kromayer suggested that even more than 11,000 troops were stationed on Olympus, but modern scholars usually assign the remaining 9,000 to the other parts of the line, with up to 2,000 cavalry and mercenaries in the centre by the river and 7,000 or so perioikoi and allies guarding Euas.[44] The mercenary foot should be a mixture of light and heavy infantry, while the perioikoi and allies had probably not adopted the sarissa so are best classed as generic heavy infantry.[45] Cleomenes escaped despite the heavy Spartan casualties, so like Antigonus he should probably count as an average commander, as Polybius (II.66) describes the opposing generals as evenly matched in ability. This gives the army a fighting value of 63, which is 9 less than the Macedonians.

Polybius (II.66 and 69) has Antigonus stationing the Macedonian bronze shields and the Illyrians opposite Euas, with the Acarnanians, Cretans and 2,000

Achaeans behind them. Walbank thinks the bronze shields were the 3,000 guard peltasts, but Head and Le Bohec suggest much more plausibly that they were part of the phalanx, which Livy (XLIV.41) later describes as being divided into bronze shields and white shields, the latter being mentioned by Plutarch (*Cleom.* 23) in the context of Sellasia itself. Le Bohec puts the number of bronze shields at just 2–3,000, but Polybius (IV.64) describes 3,000 bronze shields forming a flying column 3 years later along with just 2,000 peltasts, 300 Cretans and 400 horsemen, so the scenario below follows Head and Connolly in assuming that the bronze shields as a whole made up around half the regular phalanx, making it easier to understand why the Macedonian right won so quickly while the left was pushed back.[46] The other 1,000 Achaeans together with the cavalry and Megalopolitans were in the centre by the Oenus, while Antigonus himself led the remaining Macedonians and 5,000 mercenaries (presumably including the Gauls and Agrianians) against Olympus. Both sides' key zones should be on this flank to encourage a head-on clash of the best antagonists, urged on by the generals themselves. Even though the attack limit in the centre is reduced from 5 to 3 because of the Oenus, the Spartan centre is very thinly held, so some of the mercenaries from Olympus have been placed here to reflect the fact that the hills actually came down close to the river.[47]

Polybius (II.66) says that the Illyrians had secretly occupied the bed of the Gorgylus the previous night, while Plutarch (*Cleom.* 28) claims that the Illyrians and Acarnanians outflanked the Spartan left via dead ground. Figure 30 hence has both these units thrown forward into the Gorgylus, ready to spearhead the attack on Euas. The left flank of the Illyrian advance was threatened by infantry from the Spartan centre, but these were drawn off when Philipoemen led the Achaean horse forward for a hard-fought contest in the narrow streambed, and the outnumbered Spartan left was soon pushed back onto the reverse slope of Euas and routed.[48] Our model reflects this interaction more abstractly by the ability of the skirmishers near the river to make a double move sideways to defend Euas at the expense of weakening the defence of the centre itself. The opposing mercenaries were meanwhile duelling on Olympus, but Cleomenes soon led his Spartans forward to the attack, with Polybius (II.69) claiming that he did so in fear of encirclement once he saw his centre faltering and his left wing giving way. Polybius (II.69) describes the Macedonians falling back for a long distance in the face of the Spartan advance, and Plutarch (*Cleom.* 28) gives a figure of 5 stadia (900 m). Walbank, Lazenby and Morgan all believe that this distance is greatly exaggerated in view of Macedonian numerical superiority, the brittleness of the pike phalanx, and the fact that such a retreat would mean withdrawing right off the hill, but our model suggests that it is not entirely inconceivable that Antigonus (like Hannibal 6 years later at Cannae) would trade space for time in order to limit his casualties and draw the fearsome Spartans into an encirclement.[49] Eventually, the Macedonians rallied in a close formation of serried pikes and turned the tide – Plutarch's claim (*Cleom.* 28) that only 200 of the 6,000 Spartans survived is obviously intended for dramatic effect, but may well reflect the impact of Antigonus's right and centre swinging round to cut off any chance of escape. Once again, comparative dynamic modelling allows these interactions to be explored rather than merely imagined, and so offers insights that no amount of static diagrammatic reconstruction can provide.

SELLASIA, 222 BC (Figure 30)

M: x3. AL: 5.

Spartans: 6 VPH (Spartan), 1 APH (Freed Helots), 7 AHI (3 Allied, 2 Perioikoi, 2 Mercenary), 2 ALI (Mercenary), 1 ALC (Tarentine), AC (Cleomenes). FV: 63.

Macedonians: 4 VPH (Peltasts), 7 APH (3 Bronze Shields, 3 White Shields, 1 Megalopolitan), 4 AHI (2 Achaean, 1 Illyrian, 1 Gallic and Mercenary), 1 LPH (Boeotian and Epirote), 3 ALI (1 Cretan and Acarnanian, 1 Agrianian, 1 Mercenary), 2 AHC (1 Macedonian and Mercenary, 1 Achaean, Boeotian, Epirote and Acarnanian), AC (Antigonus). FV: 72.

RAPHIA, 217 BC

Five years after Sellasia, Ptolemy IV marched through the Sinai to counter Antiochus III's occupation of Palestine and Lebanon, leading to one of the largest ever ancient battles at Raphia, southwest of Gaza. This is perhaps the most famous Hellenistic engagement, and it has been the focus of many refights over the years.[50] Polybius is again our main source, and he has around 3,000 words (V.63–5 and 79–86) on the armies and the fighting. The battlefield seems to have been a flat and open plain. Bar-Kochva suggests that it occupied a pass between the sea dunes and the desert sands, at a point that is just 3.4 km wide today but that he claims was 5.6 km wide in antiquity, giving Ptolemy some flank protection against the expected Seleucid cavalry superiority.[51] However, this is highly speculative, and there are no clear grounds for including any terrain features on our board in view of the outflanking movements that both sides made on their right. Polybius (V.80 and 82) records the two armies as camping unusually close together, just 5 stadia (900 m) apart, so that skirmishes were frequent during the 5 days preceding the battle proper. This is best reflected by the camp placements and deployments in Figure 32, allowing both battle lines to become fully engaged on turn 2, starting on the Ptolemaic left as happened historically.

Polybius (V.79) describes Antiochus as fielding 62,000 foot, 6,000 horse and 102 Indian elephants. The infantry are broken down into 10,000 Silver Shields and 20,000 regular phalangites, 5,000 Greek mercenaries, 2,500 Cretans, 1,000 Thracians, and 23,500 Asiatic troops of diverse origins.[52] The first 3 contingents were almost certainly all pikemen, and as the settler phalanx collapsed quickly when charged, followed shortly by the Silver Shields, they probably deserve only an 'average' classification, with 1 levy unit being included to represent the more faint-hearted of the settlers.[53] Bar-Kochva suggests that both sides' Cretans supported the elephants, and the same may well be true of the Thracians and some Asiatic light troops described as holding a similar position on the wings, despite Bar-Kochva's scepticism on this score.[54] However, the great majority of the Asiatics on the Seleucid left seem to have been deployed in the main battle line rather than as skirmishers, so they should be classified as levy heavy infantry. Antiochus's horsemen probably included two 1,000-strong guard units as at Magnesia, with the rest being settler heavy cavalry.[55] At the maximum multiple of 8, and with Antiochus as an average leader, this gives the Seleucid army a fighting value of 62.

Polybius (V.79) gives a similarly clear total of 70,000 foot, 5,000 horse and 73 African elephants for the Ptolemaic army, but this has aroused much greater scholarly controversy. He earlier (V.65) breaks the infantry down into 25,000 phalangites, 20,000 native Egyptian heavy foot, 8,000 mercenaries, 6,000 Gauls and Thracians, 3,000 Cretans, 3,000 Libyan pikemen, 3,000 royal guards and 2,000 'peltasts'. Bar-Kochva and Head believe these numbers, but many other scholars such as Griffith and Scullard have argued that the Egyptians should actually be included within the 25,000 phalangites, giving Ptolemy just 50,000 infantry in all.[56] Here, our model once again comes into its own. The Ptolemaic horse included 700 guardsmen, 2,300 from Egypt and Libya (probably settlers rather than natives), and 2,000 Greeks and mercenaries whose wide outflanking manoeuvre is more suggestive of light than heavy cavalry.[57] If we treat most of the native Egyptian pikemen as levies like the earlier pantodapoi, then the army described by Polybius has only a barely superior fighting value of 66, even if we classify the infantry and cavalry guards as veterans despite their historical defeat. Conversely, Griffith's army would have a fighting value of just 51, giving Antiochus a decisive and utterly ahistorical edge. The only way of making Griffith's force superior would be to classify all the Egyptians as average and all the Seleucid settlers as levies, which is ridiculous in view of how little use the Successors made of their copious potential reserves of native manpower. Hence, our model clearly endorses Polybius's figures for the Ptolemaic army. As mentioned on p. 69, Ptolemy himself is best treated as a commander rather than a leader to reflect his escape to the central phalanx after the defeat of his left wing.

Ptolemy deployed his guard troops, his settler cavalry, the Cretans, peltasts and Libyans and 40 elephants on the left of his central phalanx, and his Gauls, Thracians, mercenary foot and horse with the remaining 33 pachyderms on the right. Antiochus opted for a more asymmetric deployment, with two-thirds of his cavalry and 60 of his 102 elephants on his right, and with his left held by flimsy Asiatic infantry. This is best reflected by having Ptolemy move first with a central key zone, while Antiochus has his key zone on the right. Polybius (V.82) places the elephants in front of the cavalry, but he later makes clear (V.84–5) that both sides sent horsemen round the outside of the duelling pachyderms and that there were heavy infantry behind the beasts as well, so it is probably best to use wider zones and to concentrate most of the armies in the 3 central zones at first, as in the other Successor battles. Bar-Kochva suggests that the central Ptolemaic phalanx was 32 deep, giving it a frontage of around 1,300 m out of a total army frontage of over 4 km.[58] This fits well with the maximum scale of around 1,200 m per zone. He thinks that the Seleucid phalanx may have formed up 24 deep in response, which seems plausible given the apparent equivalence in frontage of the 2 phalanxes. A depth of 32 ranks for the settlers and 16 ranks for the Silver Shields would have exactly the same effect, and our model allows easy experimention with alternative assumptions such as shallower and more extended phalanx deployments by both sides.

The battle began with an elephant duel on Ptolemy's left, which Polybius (V.84) describes in some detail, and which quickly led to the outnumbered and intimidated African beasts recoiling into the guardsmen and peltasts behind. Antiochus's cavalry and mercenaries attacked on either side of his elephants and drove back Ptolemy's entire left. On the other flank, however, Ptolemy's horsemen and mercenaries did exactly the same thing, surging forward on either side of the dominant Indian elephants and routing the enemy cavalry and Asiatic foot by converging attacks to produce yet another 'revolving door' engagement. The decisive stroke came in the centre, where the fugitive Ptolemy inspired his phalanx to charge, quickly routing the Seleucid pikemen, and prompting the hitherto victorious Antiochus to retire with his horse guards.[59] Although the close proximity of the 2 phalanxes will lead to them engaging almost from the outset in our model, this is easily rationalized as a psychological more than a physical contest at first, mirroring the waves of hope and fear that Polybius (V.85) describes washing over the two forces, and laying the foundations for a rapid decision later on before either side can turn their flanking units in to attack from the side or to seize the enemy camp. Antiochus is said to have had 10,000 foot and 300 horse killed and a further 4,000 captured, whereas Ptolemy's dead came to 1,500 infantry and 700 cavalry. Elephant losses were allegedly the other way round, with 5 Indian and 16 African pachyderms dead and most of the other Africans captured, though it is hard to see how a fugitive army could manage this, and an inscription suggests that it was actually Antiochus's surviving beasts that were captured.[60] Whichever interpretation is correct, our model suggests that Raphia was a finely balanced engagement, and that the many scholars who challenge Polybius's figures for the Ptolemaic phalanx make the historical outcome harder rather than easier to understand.

RAPHIA, 217 BC (Figure 32)

M: x8. AL: 4.

Ptolemies: 1 VPH (Agema), 11 APH (6 Settler, 2 Mercenary, 1 Peltasts, 1 Libyan, 1 Egyptian), 2 LPH (Egyptian), 1 AHI (Galatian), 1 VHC (Guard), 1 AHC (Settler), 1 ALC (Mercenary), 2 AEL (1 Cretan LI, 1 Thracian LI), AC (Ptolemy). FV: 66.

Seleucids: 7 APH (3 Silver Shields, 3 Settler, 1 Mercenary), 1 LPH (Settler), 2 LHI (1 Arab, 1 Asiatic), 1 ALI (Carmanian and Cilician), AL + VHC (Antiochus + Companions), 1 VHC (Agema), 2 AHC (Settler), 3 IEL (1 Cretan LI, 1 Dahae LI, 1 Thracian and Persian LI). FV: 62.

11

Carthage and Rome

In the western Mediterranean, conflict revolved around two great imperial cities – Carthage and Rome. The confrontation between Carthage and the Greeks of Sicily lasted even longer than that between Greece and Persia in the east, with Herodotus (VII.166) recording the tradition that Gelon defeated a Punic invasion force at Himera on the very same day that Xerxes's fleet was beaten at Salamis.[1] The long-running conflict between Carthage and Syracuse contained few set battles and even fewer adequately documented ones, but two engagements are just about possible to explore with our model.[2] In or around 341 BC, Timoleon attacked and defeated a much larger Punic army while it was crossing the River Crimisus in western Sicily, and a generation later in 310 BC, Agathocles sailed out of besieged Syracuse and launched a bold counter-invasion of Africa, beating a large Carthaginian force near Tunis. Meanwhile in Italy, Rome was gradually extending its sway over its neighbours, and the conflict came to a head in 295 BC when it defeated a coalition of Gauls and Samnites at a hard-fought battle near Sentinum in Umbria. Further Roman expansion prompted Tarentum to call for assistance from the Successor king Pyrrhus of Epirus, and after a poorly documented initial clash near Heraclea, he won another of his famously costly 'Pyrrhic victories' at Asculum in Apulia in 279. Rome and Carthage actually formed a loose alliance to frustrate Pyrrhus's attack on them both over the next few years, but in 264 the two empires clashed in the massive and drawn-out attritional contest of sieges and naval engagements that became the First Punic War. In 256 the Romans invaded Africa, but the following year their army was all but annihilated in a set battle somewhere in the plain of the Bagradas River. With characteristic doggedness, Rome weathered this disaster as well as the far more massive naval losses that it suffered in storms, until it was eventually able to seize Sicily and later Sardinia and Corsica from an exhausted Carthage. However, like the First World War, the struggle left a legacy of bitterness that within a generation gave rise to an even more devastating second conflict.

CRIMISUS, 341 BC

When Hamilcar brought a large Punic invasion force to Sicily, the Corinthian general Timoleon, who had recently ejected the tyrant Dionysius II from Syracuse, decided to meet the attack in enemy territory rather than exposing his allies' lands to devastation. The date of the battle is uncertain – the most popular guess is the summer of 341, but some scholars put it as late as 339.[3] Plutarch (*Tim.* 25–9) and Diodorus (XVI.77–80) describe the engagement in over 1,000 words each, and it is generally agreed that their common source was the Sicilian Timaeus who wrote in Athenian exile in the early third century BC.[4] Polybius (XII.23–28a) devoted several thousand words to a diatribe about Timaeus's faults as a historian, notably his military inexperience, analytical weakness, rhetorical invention and hagiographic attitude to Timoleon. Unfortunately, unlike for Issus, Polybius's critique makes hardly any positive contribution to our understanding of the battle at hand.

Modern scholars do not even agree which river corresponds to the ancient Crimisus, let alone where the battle site may have been.[5] We must therefore fall back on the description by Plutarch (*Tim.* 26–8) of the Greeks cresting a hill overlooking the river, with the intervening plain crossed by numerous streams running down from the high ground. The scenario in Figure 17 incorporates these elements in a necessarily generic fashion. Plutarch (*Tim.* 27–8) describes a thick mist that cleared just after noon as the armies came into view, and he later says that a thunderstorm blew in from behind the Greeks in the middle of the battle, placing the Carthaginians at a grave disadvantage as they floundered on the muddy ground. This is easily simulated by starting the engagement in overcast conditions and by making the streams run more through the Punic than the Greek centre zones, though the random elements in combat, command and weather determination will play an equally important role in allowing reflection of the historical reality. An even more decisive asymmetry in the real battle was that the Carthaginians were caught by surprise while crossing the Crimisus, with only their chariots facing the Greeks at first while the mass of other troops straggled up behind.[6] The provisions for surprise outlined on p. 40 are expressly designed to cater for such an eventuality.

Our most credible information concerns Timoleon's army, but there is a serious disagreement between our two main sources. Diodorus (XVI.78–9) says the Greeks fielded 12,000 men, of whom 1,000 mercenaries (having long been without pay) deserted during the march, while Plutarch (*Tim.* 25) mentions only 3,000 Syracusans and 4,000 mercenaries, with the mercenary desertion leaving just 5,000 foot and 1,000 horse. Modern scholars tend to favour Diodorus's total and to ascribe the difference of 5,000 to Plutarch's omission of the Sicilian allied troops that he mentions during deployment (*Tim.* 27) and of the forces (probably mercenaries) of the tyrant Hicetas that Diodorus (XVI.77) says had recently been added to Timoleon's army after a peace was agreed between the two.[7] The Syracusan and allied infantry were presumably hoplites, but Plutarch (*Tim.* 28) contrasts the heavily armed Carthaginians with the more lightly equipped Greeks, so at least some of the mercenaries were surely peltasts. Sicilian citizen troops had an indifferent reputation as fighters, but the mercenaries were better regarded despite their mutinous behaviour, and the defeated Carthaginians allegedly resolved to rely on mercenaries (especially Greeks) in future rather than on their own citizens.[8] Hence, it seems appropriate to class the best 1,000 of the mercenaries as veterans, and the rest of the Greek troops as average. Although we must beware of Timaeus's hagiographic tendencies, Timoleon's achievement in motivating the great majority of his troops to attack the Carthaginians so unexpectedly against high odds and then to hold on through a long and hard-fought battle seems to merit his classification as an inspired leader. At a multiple of 2, this gives the Greeks a fighting value of 53.

Both Diodorus (XVI.77) and Plutarch (*Tim.* 25) put the Punic army at around 70,000 men, while Polyaenus (V.12) gives the slightly more reasonable figure of 50,000.[9] As at Issus, our model offers a means of estimating a more credible total. Diodorus claims that the army included cavalry, chariots and extra teams of horses amounting to 10,000, which can be compared to his earlier figures (XVI.67) of 300 chariots and over 2,000 extra teams of horses in a 50,000 strong army that invaded Sicily a few years before. The heavy four-horse chariots do seem to have predominated over individual horsemen, but it is hard to believe that more than 400 of them (4 units) were present at Crimisus, plus around 1,000 levy cavalry.[10] Plutarch (*Tim.* 27) describes 10,000 Carthaginian infantry with white shields crossing the river behind the chariots, while Diodorus (XVI.79–80) also mentions this force of 10,000 and says that 2,500 formed the elite Sacred Band of Punic citizens. The latter should probably be classed as average, and the remaining 7,500 (most likely Libyans) should be a mixture of average and levy troops. The other infantry included Iberians, Celts, Ligurians and Numidians, and are best classed as levies.[11] Even with this low rating of troop quality, it is hard to push Punic numbers to more than 30,000 foot without making the army too powerful. Plutarch (*Tim.* 25) says the force was under the joint command of Hamilcar and Hasdrubal, so if they are treated as uninspired commanders, the overall fighting value comes to 62 – a clear advantage had it not been offset by the adverse tactical circumstances.

Timoleon sent his cavalry to attack first and put his allies and some mercenaries on each wing while he himself occupied the centre with the Syracusans and the best mercenaries, so the key zones should clearly be in the centre in this case.[12] Plutarch (*Tim.* 28) describes the Punic front rank as containing 400 men, but this seems ridiculously few for an army of 30,000, and may even refer just to the

Sacred Band – a scale of around 400 m per zone gives a reasonable minimum frontage for armies of this size. Plutarch (*Tim.* 27–8) has the Carthaginian chariots holding up the Greek cavalry, which were then shifted to attack from the flanks, and he says that the Punic foot resisted Timoleon's infantry for a long time until the thunderstorm flooded the ground and the Carthaginian front rank was defeated. Diodorus (XVI.79–80) has a rather different account in which the 10,000 leading troops were quickly shattered but the main body of the Punic army then crossed the river and were prevailing thanks to their superior numbers until the thunderstorm turned the tide. He says that the 2,500 members of the Sacred Band were all killed along with over 10,000 others, while a further 15,000 troops and 200 chariots were captured. Plutarch (*Tim.* 28) puts the dead at 10,000, including 3,000 Carthaginians. These numbers are much more in line with the reduced Carthaginian strength suggested by our model, and the system captures very well how Timoleon's men must have raced against time to defeat the leading enemies before more troops could cross the river and the full Punic numerical superiority could be brought to bear.

CRIMISUS, 341 BC (Figure 17)

M: x2. AL: 3. Overcast.

Carthaginians: 6 AHI (3 Sacred Band, 3 Libyan), 10 LHI (4 Iberian, 4 Celtic, 2 Libyan), 2 LLI (1 Ligurian, 1 Numidian), 1 LHC (Iberian and Celtic), 4 ACH (four-horse), 2 UC (Hasdrubal and Hamilcar). FV: 62. Surprised.

Syracusans: IL + VHI (Timoleon + Mercenaries), 1 VHI (Mercenary), 6 AHO (3 Allied, 2 Syracusan, 1 Mercenary), 1 AHI (Mercenary), 2 ALI (Mercenary), 2 AHC (Syracusan). FV: 53.

TUNIS, 310 BC

When yet another Punic army laid siege to Syracuse itself a generation later, the new leader, Agathocles, sailed out of the city and invaded Africa in response! He was confronted somewhere near Tunis by a hastily raised Carthaginian force led by two bitter enemies, Hanno and Bomilcar. Diodorus is our main source, with over 1,000 words (XX.10–13) on the ensuing engagement, but this is a pretty flimsy reed on which to rely, and the battle only barely qualifies as worthy of attempted reconstruction.[13] Nothing is known of the terrain except for Diodorus's statements (XX.10) that the Punic army drew up on a slight rise and that its left was arrayed in great depth as the terrain precluded a broader front. The fact that the Carthaginian chariots and cavalry made a disastrous frontal charge rather than operating on the flanks strengthens the impression that the battlefield was constrained. The terrain in Figure 26 conforms with these vague indications, but the precise layout cannot be other than highly speculative. Diodorus (XX.10–11) describes Agathocles deploying his own forces after viewing the enemy array, so the Carthaginians should clearly get the first move.

Diodorus (XX.11) gives a fairly detailed breakdown of the Greek army and its deployment. Agathocles himself led his guard of 1,000 mercenary hoplites on the left, supported by 3,000 Samnite, Etruscan and Celtic mercenaries. The centre contained 3,000 Greek mercenaries and 3,500 Syracusans, while the left wing was held by 2,500 unspecified infantry that Griffith and Head suggest may have been Sicilian allies.[14] 500 archers and slingers were divided between the wings, and Agathocles also had some of his ships' crews stretch shield covers over sticks to give the impression from a distance of armed men. Diodorus (XX.4 and 38) says that some of the troops were cavalrymen who aimed to seize horses once in Africa, and he credits Agathocles with 800 horsemen 2 years later in 308, but there is no mention of Greek horsemen in this earlier battle, and their failure to play any apparent role either in countering the Punic mounted troops or in inflicting greater damage during the pursuit suggests that their numbers as yet were probably negligible. The mercenary guards and the small contingent of light infantry can be classed as veterans, and the other troops as average. Agathocles, like Timoleon, seems best classified as an inspired leader, given his bold counter-offensive and his alleged use of stratagems like the 'armed' crews to shift the psychological balance.[15] At a multiple of 2, this gives the Greeks a fighting value of 60.

Diodorus (XX.10) says that the Carthaginians fielded 2,000 chariots, 1,000 horsemen and 40,000 foot, drawn from the citizenry themselves as there had not been time to amass troops from the country and the allied cities. Scholars often accept these figures for want of anything else, but our model suggests that they are highly questionable in the absence of the surprise that offset Punic numerical superiority at the Crimisus.[16] The chariot figure is particularly dubious, as this would imply even more war horses (including spares) than the 10,000 that are alleged at that earlier battle, even though their actual effect was no greater than that of the few score scythed vehicles that made similarly ineffective frontal charges at Cunaxa and Gaugamela. Two hundred vehicles seems a much more reasonable total than 2,000, giving the Carthaginians just 2 chariot units and 1 levy cavalry unit. One could also argue for a force of only around 10,000 foot, as this corresponds more with the number of citizen levies at Bagradas and Zama and in the Mercenary war.[17] However, this would be going too far, as it would give the Greeks numerical as well as qualitative superiority, and it seems more likely that some Libyan and perhaps Numidian infantry were present after all, as Diodorus later mentions (XX.12). The best Punic troops were the reconstituted Sacred Band – Tillyard numbers these men at just 1,000 as Agathocles opposed them with his 1,000 guards, but Head compares the force instead with the 2,000 high-ranking Punic citizens whom Diodorus (XIX.106) records as being sent to Sicily the previous year.[18] Their dogged resistance in this battle suggests a mix of veteran and average troops, while the other Punic foot should be primarily levies with a sprinkling of average units. With Hanno as an uninspired leader to reflect his suicidal bravery, and Bomilcar as an uninspired commander in line with his much more circumspect attitude, an intermediate force of 20,000 infantry gives an overall fighting value of 51, which captures exactly the right level of inferiority compared to the Greeks.

Frontages are a matter of guesswork, but a scale of around 500 m per zone allows the Greek line to be 10 deep and the Punic left 15 deep. Both key zones are on Agathocles's left, where he faced the Sacred Band. The rather puzzling frontal charge by the Punic chariots and cavalry was quickly routed with heavy losses, after which the infantry lines engaged. Hanno led the Sacred Band from the front but suffered several wounds from the hail of missiles and soon died. His troops held on despite being disheartened, but when Bomilcar tried to pull his own men on the Punic left back to the high ground, they panicked and fled to Carthage. The Sacred Band fought on bravely until it was threatened with encirclement, and then also withdrew.[19] Diodorus (XX.13) puts the dead at 200 Greeks and 1,000 Carthaginians, though other writers give casualty figures ranging from 2 to 2,000 for the Greeks and 2,000 to 6,000 for the Carthaginians.[20] Tillyard favours Diodorus's remarkably restrained claim, which fits in with the Greeks' lack of cavalry and with Agathocles's apparent decision to break off the pursuit and plunder the enemy camp.[21] The battle seems to have been a frontal slogging match with little tactical finesse, and the main insight that our model provides is once again to suggest more reasonable numbers for the Punic host, and especially to cast doubt on the figure of 2,000 chariots, which does not seem too unreasonable at first glance but is actually the most problematic of all when viewed from our more systematic comparative perspective.

TUNIS, 310 BC (Figure 26)

M: x2. AL: 4.

Carthaginians: UL + VHI (Hanno + Sacred Band), 1 VHI (Sacred Band), 5 AHI (3 Libyan, 1 Carthaginian, 1 Sacred Band), 5 LHI (3 Carthaginian, 2 Libyan), 2 LLI (Numidian), 1 LHC (Libyan and Carthaginian), 2 ACH (four-horse), UC (Bomilcar). FV: 51.

Syracusans: IL + VHO (Agathocles + Mercenary Guard), 1 VHO (Mercenary Guard), 6 AHO (3 Syracusan, 3 Allied), 6 AHI (3 Greek Mercenary, 1 Samnite, 1 Etruscan, 1 Celtic), 1 VLI (Archers and Slingers). FV: 60.

SENTINUM, 295 BC

In 296, the expanding power of Rome faced a grave crisis when the Samnites, Etruscans, Umbrians and Gauls formed a grand coalition. The following year, the Romans met the combined Gallic and Samnite armies in a climactic battle near Sentinum in Umbria. Polybius (II.19) mentions the engagement, but our main source is Livy, who has a fairly detailed battle account of some 2,500 words (X.26–30). The problem is gauging whether his detailed claims are true, or whether they are rhetorical annalistic inventions as his accounts of even earlier battles are usually believed to be.[22] Cornell thinks the present account may well be the first to contain authentic elements (as the early historian Fabius Pictor could have spoken to survivors), and Oakley in his exhaustive recent commentary on Livy's early books suggests that the fame of the victory may have led to special efforts to preserve the details, though he warns that it could equally well have prompted writers to embellish their descriptions if real details were lacking.[23] Other modern scholars treat the account as broadly reliable, so it seems legitimate for us to incorporate the engagement within our model, while acknowledging (as for so many of these battles) that just because a detailed description seems plausible, this does not necessarily mean it is true.[24] Sommella has postulated a battle site just north of Sassoferrato with a stream bisecting the two halves of the field, but this is obviously highly speculative, and there is no indication in Livy of any significant terrain.[25]

Livy (X.26–7) claims that the Romans fielded two combined consular armies – the I and III legions under Fabius and the V and VI under Decius – and that there was in addition a strong contingent of Roman cavalry, a force of allies and Latins that outnumbered the Romans, and 1,000 picked Campanian horsemen. Polybius's description (VI.19–26) of the organization of the mid-Republican army dates from over a century later, and scholars have long debated how, when and through what stages this military system evolved, and what we are to make of Livy's own broadly similar but subtly different account of army organization (VIII.8–10) in the context of a battle against the Latins at Veseris in 340.[26] Although Livy's description is widely felt to be anachronistic, it is generally agreed that, by the time of Sentinum, Roman infantry tactics had evolved away from the previous hoplite phalanx and into the famous manipular system based on successive lines of hastati, principes and triarii, each operating in maniples ('handfuls') of around 100 men. It is uncertain how many troops still used spears rather than javelins, and whether the non-Latin allies employed the same three-line system, but from our more broad-brush perspective, it seems best to class the entire Roman and allied heavy infantry force as average legionaries.

How many such troops there were at Sentinum, and the numbers and quality of supporting light infantry and cavalry, are rather harder to discern. Cornell puts the overall force at over 36,000 men based on Polybius's basic figures (VI.20–1) of 4,200 infantry and 300 cavalry for the later legion, while Head suggests 45,000 men to take account of the higher allied numbers that Livy records. Each Polybian legion included 1,200 or more velite skirmishers. Livy (VIII.8) mentions only 300 'leves' per legion, but Head and Sekunda suggest that his 900 rorarii were also light infantry, and that the main difference between the earlier and later skirmishers lay not in their numbers but in their equipment and general quality.[27] The early light infantry cannot be dismissed altogether like the hordes of 'light armed' servants who accompanied Greek armies, but it seems best to class them as levies in view of their lack of recorded contribution. Cavalry, by contrast, are given surprising prominence in Livy's account of Sentinum and in Plutarch's description (*Pyrrh*. 16–17) of Heraclea 15 years later, considering the low esteem in which Roman horsemen are sometimes held.[28] Polybius (VI.26) describes the allies providing three times as many cavalry as the Romans themselves, and Head thinks the Campanians at Sentinum were over and above the usual cavalry complement.[29] The scenario below assumes an army of around 40,000, with any additional allied infantry being assumed to be guarding the camp, and with 1 veteran horse unit to represent the Campanians whose encirclement of the Gauls proved decisive. At a multiple of 5, and with Decius as an uninspired cavalry leader and Fabius as an average commander to reflect his allegedly more cautious and insightful generalship, this gives the Romans a fighting value of 69.[30] (Their effective fighting value is actually a few points lower than this, because of the differential value of average legionaries – see p. 25.)

   The opposing army, not surprisingly, is harder to reconstruct. Livy (X.27) and Frontinus (*Str.* I.8.3) claim that the Etruscans and Umbrians were also nearby but were drawn away a few days earlier to counter other Roman forces.[31] The only figures we have for the army are corrupt and for the most part ridiculously exaggerated, so it seems best to use our model to suggest more plausible forces based on Livy's description of the course of the engagement and on what we know from elsewhere of Gallic and Samnite fighting methods.[32] Gallic infantry fought with long swords, while Samnites seem to have been more akin to Greek thureophoroi – loose order troops able to engage with javelins or charge to close quarters. Sekunda suggests that the Samnite 'cohorts' used a multiple line system that may have inspired the manipular legion, but Head is more sceptical. Neither Gauls nor Samnites seem to have made much use of dedicated light infantry skirmishers, and both are described as fighting stubbornly rather than breaking into early flight, so they seem best classified under the generic heading of average heavy infantry.[33] Livy (X.28) also mentions Gallic cavalry and chariots (that he strangely says were a novelty to the Romans), but how many of the various troop types were present is impossible to estimate until after we have reviewed the course of the engagement.[34]

Livy (X.27 and 29) says that the armies camped some 6 km apart, that the Gauls held the right wing and were opposed by Decius while the Samnites held the left and were faced by Fabius, and that the retreating Samnites later made a brief stand in front of their fortified camp because not all could get through the gates at once. This suggests that the Gauls and Samnites should deploy first, with their camp assumed to lie just behind their board edge. Sommella proposes a frontage for the armies of around 3 km for the infantry and a further 1.5 km for the cavalry, but this seems a little high, and a scale of 800 m per zone appears more appropriate if we do not postulate an intervening stream.[35] A central key zone seems best for the symmetrical Roman array, whereas the enemy key zone should probably be on their right to reflect the greater aggressiveness displayed by the Gallic contingent (apparently from the Senones). The impetuous Decius drove back the Gallic cavalry with a mounted charge, but the Celtic chariots appeared and panicked the Roman horse, and the Gallic infantry exploited the confusion to overthrow the first line of legionaries on this wing. Livy then claims (X.28–9) that Decius galloped forward in a suicidal 'devotio', inspiring his men at the cost of his own life, as his father had allegedly done at Veseris. This might appear to be classic literary distortion to excuse and glorify the death of a consul, but both Cornell and Oakley give it greater credence due to the fame of the action in later generations.[36] As I discussed on pp. 70–1, the loss of a single uninspired general in our model does not reduce the morale of an army, precisely so as to encourage such self-sacrificial risks.

On the other wing, Fabius was apparently playing for time, holding back so as to exhaust the Samnites. Eventually, he sent his cavalry to outflank their line and pressed forward with his infantry. The tired Samnites fled to their camp, outside which their leader Gellius Egnatius was killed by the Roman pursuit. Fabius had meanwhile sent 500 Campanians and the principes of the III legion to attack the exposed flank and rear of the Gauls, who Livy (X.29) says had formed a close-packed shield wall after the Roman rally prompted by Decius's death, but who eventually succumbed to encirclement. He claims the enemy suffered 25,000 dead and 8,000 captured, whereas Fabius's army had 1,700 casualties and Decius's force 7,000. These are even higher figures than for the subsequent 'Pyrrhic victories', and they may well be exaggerated, as at the Metaurus where Livy's similar casualty totals (XXVII.49) are several times higher than those given by Polybius (XI.3). This was clearly a hard-fought victory, but our model suggests that the bulk of the Roman left must have held on against the Gauls despite Decius's death (as did Caesar's hard-pressed right at the Sambre), as otherwise the reinforcements from Fabius would have been too little and too late to turn the tide. Livy (X.27) emphasizes the evenly matched nature of the first clash and says that the presence of the Etruscans and Umbrians would have spelt disaster for the Romans, but the Gauls and Samnites alone seem to have been at a significant overall disadvantage, despite their initial success against Decius.

The key seems to lie in Livy's stress (X.28–9) on the lack of endurance of the Gauls and Samnites during prolonged fighting. This arouses suspicion as a well-known literary *topos*, but it fits very well with the alleged course of the engagement, not only on Fabius's wing but also on the Roman left where it offers a more plausible explanation than Decius's death for the Gallic failure to capitalize on their early victory.[37] There is thus a strong case for treating the Gauls and Samnites as fatigued, so as to mirror the pattern of events described. The Gallic cavalry seem to have been well matched with Decius's horse, because he was defeated only when the Celtic chariots intervened. There is no mention of Samnite cavalry interfering with the flanking move by Fabius's horsemen, but some were surely present, albeit perhaps in somewhat lesser strength.[38] Head suggests that overall Gallic and Samnite numbers may have been similar to those of the Romans, and with Gellius as an uninspired leader to reflect his outwitting by Fabius, an army of around 40,000 men would have a fighting value of 60.[39] This should allow the coalition to make a strong initial impact, but fatigue and the stubborn resilience of the legionaries will increasingly shift the odds against them. Our model thus suggests that Livy's account does make military sense when compared with other more securely documented engagements, and that (unlike with certain clearly invented battle pieces) it is not implausible that it contains a significant element of truth.

SENTINUM, 295 BC (Figure 27)

M: x5. AL: 4.

Gauls and Samnites: UL + AHI (Gellius + Samnites), 13 AHI (7 Gallic, 6 Samnite), 4 AHC (2 Gallic, 2 Samnite), 1 ACH (two-horse). FV: 60. Fatigued.

Romans: 10 ALE (5 Roman, 5 Allied), 2 LLI (1 Roman, 1 Allied), 1 VHC (Campanian), UL + AHC (Decius + Romans), 3 AHC (Allied), AC (Fabius). FV: 69.

ASCULUM, 279 BC

The first clash between Pyrrhus and the Romans at Heraclea in 280 is recorded by Plutarch (*Pyrrh.* 16–17) in around 1,000 words, but his account is too anecdotal and lacking in deployment details to warrant reconstruction within our model.[40] Plutarch's description of the following battle at Asculum (*Pyrrh.* 21) is even sketchier, with only half as many words, but we also have a much fuller account with over 1,500 words by Dionysius (XX.1–3), and more dubious renderings by authors like Zonaras (VIII.5). Plutarch himself gives a very brief summary of Dionysius's version, but unfortunately he makes it clear that it differs in significant respects from that of other writers such as Hieronymus. The resulting contradictions could easily warrant our passing over Asculum as well, but it would be a shame to include none of Pyrrhus's battles when Livy (XXXV.14) claims that Hannibal rated him second only to Alexander as a general.[41] Dionysius's account includes specific details of the Greek deployment that have led a number of scholars to believe that it is based in part on the lost contemporary testimony of Hieronymus himself.[42] Even if (like Lévèque) one views the rest of Dionysius's claims with enormous scepticism, it is just about possible to combine these deployment details with Plutarch's much vaguer description to create a tentative scenario.[43]

The biggest discrepancy between Plutarch's and Dionysius's accounts is that the former describes 2 days of fighting while the latter mentions only one. This bears most upon the issue of battlefield terrain. Plutarch says that the first day's engagement took place on rough ground and along a wooded riverbank and dragged on until nightfall, but that Pyrrhus seized the difficult ground at dawn the following day so he could fight on more even terrain. Dionysius describes a drawn-out and indecisive battle fought on the plain and later on wooded hills – of those scholars who give this any credence, most equate it with Plutarch's first day, though a few relate it to the second day instead.[44] There has been long debate over whether Plutarch's river corresponds to the River Carapella a few kilometres from Asculum or to the more distant but faster flowing Aufidus – Lévèque prefers the latter, and suggests that the first day consisted of a frustrated cross-river assault by Pyrrhus while the second day's combat was preceded by a surprise crossing at dawn.[45] Dionysius (XX.3), by contrast, mentions a river only as being crossed by the Romans on their way back to camp, and claims that Pyrrhus earlier had to send elephants and cavalry back downhill to his own camp some 20 stadia (3.6 km) away in a vain attempt to save it from 4,400 Daunian raiders who took refuge on yet another steep hill. As the topography of the battle as a whole is so uncertain and controversial, it seems best to focus our reconstruction just on Plutarch's second day, and to set the engagement on an open plain – those who wish to experiment with various possible placements of hills, woods and rivers may easily do so.

Dionysius (XX.1.8) numbers both armies at around 70,000 foot and 8,000 horse. However, these are massive totals, and sit uneasily with his claims that there were just 20,000 Romans and 16,000 infantry from Pyrrhus's original expeditionary force. Most scholars therefore prefer something closer to Frontinus's figures (*Str.* II.3.21) of 40,000 men on each side.[46] As at Sentinum, the Roman force seems to have consisted of the combined consular armies of Decius and Sulpicius, each with 2 legions plus allied contingents – Dionysius (XX.1.4–5) mentions Latins, Campanians, Sabines, Umbrians, Volscians, Marrucini, Paeligni and Ferrentani.[47] The only novelty is his claim (XX.1.6–7) that the Romans had prepared 300 wagons festooned with various contraptions and crewed and accompanied by light infantry in an attempt to counter Pyrrhus's 19 elephants. Some scholars doubt these wagons even existed, and if they did, they seem to have been easily countered or evaded, so they deserve at most to be represented by an average light infantry unit alongside the usual levies.[48] It is claimed in some ancient sources that Pyrrhus had to calm his troops' fears that Decius would doom them by a self-sacrificial 'devotio' like his father at Sentinum, but whether Decius actually died at Asculum is unclear, and the silence of Plutarch and Dionysius on this matter suggests that there is no case for making the consuls anything other than uninspired commanders.[49] At a multiple of 4, an army of 40,000 gives the Romans a fighting value of 77.

Plutarch (*Pyrrh.* 15) says that Pyrrhus crossed from Epirus the previous year with 23,000 infantry, 2,500 archers and slingers, 3,000 cavalry and 20 elephants. Dionysius (XX.1.1–5) makes clear that the infantry included Macedonian, Epirote and Ambraciot troops (probably all pikemen) and mercenary javelinmen from Aetolia and elsewhere.[50] He also lists a variety of Italian foot at Asculum, including Italiot mercenaries, the white-shielded Tarentine phalanx, and allied Bruttians, Lucanians and Samnites. Numbers are unclear apart from his alleged subtotal of 16,000 for the infantry from Greece, though rough estimates can be made based on what contingents he says faced each Roman legion. Plutarch (*Pyrrh.* 16), Dionysius (XX.2.6) and Frontinus (*Str.* II.3.21) all question the fighting spirit of the Tarentines, so it is worth making some of their pikemen levies.[51] The cavalry included Epirotes, Thessalians and Ambraciots together with Tarentines, Bruttians, Lucanians, Samnites and a variety of mercenaries. Dionysius (XX.1.4) claims that Pyrrhus's guard numbered 2,000 horsemen – this is probably at least double the real figure, in line with his exaggerated totals for the infantry and cavalry as a whole, but the Epirote and Thessalian horse deserve classification as veterans to reflect the Greek cavalry superiority.[52] The 19 elephants would normally translate into just 1 unit at this scale, but the sources lay so much stress on their psychological impact that it is appropriate to use 2 units instead, with over 100 archers and slingers per pachyderm in line with the emphasis placed on these accompanying troops.[53] Pyrrhus himself should clearly count as an inspired leader in the Alexandrian mould. This gives an army of nearly 40,000 men a fighting value of 85, which yields the right level of superiority over the Romans when one also takes into account the differential value of average legionaries.

Dionysius (XX.1) describes the Romans putting their 4 legions in line, each with its own allied contingent, and with the light infantry and wagons outside the line and the cavalry on the wings. He says that the I legion on the left faced the Macedonians, Ambraciots and Italiotes, the III legion confronted the Tarentines,

Bruttians and Lucanians, the IV legion opposed the Epirotes, and the II legion on the right faced the Samnites and mercenaries. Pyrrhus put his Samnite, Bruttian and Thessalian horse on his right and his Ambraciot, Lucanian, Tarentine and mercenary cavalry on his left, while holding his elephants and light infantry in reserve behind each wing and keeping his own guard outside the line ready to reinforce any threatened point. This is best reflected in our model by having Pyrrhus move first to reflect his surprise gambit at dawn, and by placing his Epirote horse in the rear whence they and the elephants can move to either side once the Roman deployment becomes clear and the main infantry lines engage. Dionysius (XX.2.3) says that both sides' right was weaker than their left – this makes some sense for the Greeks, but seems anachronistic for the Romans, so the same combination of key zones as at Sentinum appears appropriate. Frontinus (*Str.* II.3.21) has a briefer and somewhat different version of the two battle lines, and most scholars prefer Dionysius's account.[54] Polybius (XVIII.28) praises Pyrrhus for alternating phalanx blocks with more flexible Italian contingents, but still stresses the indecisiveness of his engagements, no doubt because he is trying to show the inferiority of the Greek fighting method.[55] A scale of around 800 m per zone allows the phalangites to be 16 deep and the other infantry 12 deep, which is probably about right.

The actual course of the battle is very hard to discern. Plutarch (*Pyrrh.* 21) says only that there was a bitter and prolonged frontal clash between legionaries and pikemen, with subsequent attacks by the elephants and by Pyrrhus himself finally forcing the Romans to retreat to their nearby camp. Dionysius's battle account (XX.2–3) has some suspiciously stereotypical rhetoric, but broadly argues that the III and IV legions broke through the enemy centre, mounted a wooded hill to hold off counter-attacks by elephants and cavalry, and fought Samnites and mercenaries sent from the Greek left until nightfall. It is difficult to reconcile these two accounts, and most scholars favour Plutarch's version, despite its brevity.[56] Plutarch records Hieronymus's claim (based on the king's own journal) that Pyrrhus lost 3,505 men and the Romans 6,000, whereas Frontinus (*Str.* II.3.21) says that 5,000 Romans and 20,000 of the enemy fell, in line with the later fiction that Rome actually prevailed.[57] Hieronymus's casualty figures are not much greater proportionally than for Greek hoplite battles, even with armies only half as large as Dionysius claims, but Plutarch famously describes Pyrrhus's despair at the loss of his officers and the lack of reinforcements to face the seemingly inexhaustible tide of Roman recruits.[58]

Our model cannot hope to resolve the many detailed uncertainties about this battle, but it does contribute a very important sense of perspective. Despite the sources' sensationalist preoccupation with the elephants, their numbers were so low relative to the armies as a whole that the more 'conventional' struggle between the infantry and cavalry surely played a greater role than is usually acknowledged. Refighting this obscure battle gives very useful insights into a clash between the early legions and a well-led Hellenistic combined arms force, and so offers an intriguing counterpoint to the better-documented Roman defeats of Greek armies a century later.

ASCULUM, 279 BC (Figure 28)

M: x4. AL: 4.

Greeks: 7 APH (2 Macedonian, 1 Molossian, 1 Thesprotian, 1 Chaonian, 1 Ambraciot, 1 Tarentine), 1 LPH (Tarentine), 7 AHI (3 Samnite, 1 Bruttian, 1 Lucanian, 1 Italiot Mercenary, 1 Greek Mercenary), IL + VHC (Pyrrhus + Agema), 2 VHC (1 Epirote, 1 Thessalian), 2 AHC (1 Samnite and Bruttian, 1 Ambraciot, Lucanian and Mercenary), 1 ALC (Tarentine and Mercenary), 2 IEL (Mercenary LI). FV: 85.

Romans: 13 ALE (7 Roman, 6 Allied), 1 ALI (Anti-Elephant Troops), 2 LLI (1 Roman, 1 Allied), 4 AHC (1 Roman, 3 Allied), 2 UC (Decius and Sulpicius). FV: 77.

BAGRADAS, 255 BC

Rome's invasion of Africa to try to win its drawn-out war with Carthage initially met with great success, but the consul Regulus presented unacceptable peace terms, and the newly arrived Spartan mercenary Xanthippus inspired the Carthaginians to take the field once again to reverse their earlier defeats. Our main source on the ensuing battle is Polybius (I.32–4), who describes the engagement in several hundred words, probably based on an earlier work by Philinus.[59] The battlefield is impossible to locate, as Polybius (I.33) says only that it was on flat, level ground and that the two armies camped 10 stadia (1.8 km) apart. The engagement is often referred to as the battle of Tunis, which the Romans had just captured, but to avoid confusion with Agathocles's victory in 310, I have instead followed Head in naming it after the Bagradas, the main river of the region.[60]

It is easiest to begin with the Punic army, as Polybius (I.32) numbers it at 12,000 foot, 4,000 horse and nearly 100 African elephants (these had replaced chariots as Carthage's exotic weapon, perhaps after the encounter with Pyrrhus's beasts).[61] Some have suggested that Polybius's figures are an underestimate, intended to glorify the Punic victory, but most scholars accept them as reliable.[62] The infantry was a mixture of Carthaginian citizens and mercenaries, presumably including those recently arrived from Greece as well as the survivors of the 5,000 brought back from Sicily by Hamilcar when the Romans first landed in Africa.[63] Griffith suggests that the majority of the foot were mercenaries, but this is dubious as Polybius (I.33) records their presence only on the right wing and with the cavalry.[64] Those accompanying the horsemen were presumably light armed, while the others would be heavier infantry.[65] The Carthaginians are described as a phalanx, but there is no indication that Punic armies ever used sarissae rather than spears.[66] It might be thought that the inexperienced Carthaginian infantry should be rated lower than the mercenaries, but in fact it was the latter who fled while the Punic spearmen cut to pieces those Romans who made it through the elephant screen, so an average rating seems appropriate throughout.[67]

The 4,000 horse were presumably also a mixture of citizens and mercenaries – Hamilcar brought 500 cavalry back from Sicily, and there were perhaps also some loyal Numidians as at Zama.[68] The solid contribution of the horsemen again warrants an average rating. The proportion of elephants to men was 12 times higher than in Pyrrhus's army at Asculum, but the pachyderms still did not cover the entire Punic infantry line, so (as discussed on p. 26) they must have been deployed in an unusually close-packed array, without the normal light infantry accompaniment – this means each unit will represent twice as many beasts as usual. It is unclear what the precise relationship of Xanthippus to the native Carthaginian generals was during the battle itself, and we should beware Philinus's excessive adulation of a fellow Greek – Xanthippus certainly seems to have inspired renewed confidence and been the author of the successful Punic tactics, but Diodorus (XXIII.14) records the difficulty he had in rallying his own mercenaries, so it is probably best to class him as an average rather than an inspired commander, and to include Hasdrubal also as an uninspired commander to represent the Carthaginian generals themselves.[69] At a multiple of 2, this gives the Punic army a fighting value of 84.

Polybius's only indication of the size of the Roman army is when he says (I. 29) that Regulus was left with 15,000 infantry and 500 cavalry when the fleet returned home. He later (I.31) refers to the first legion, so the force was presumably an understrength consular army, especially weak in cavalry because of the difficulty of transporting horses by sea.[70] Some other ancient writers claim that Regulus had 30,000 or more troops at the battle itself, but Polybius makes no mention of Libyan recruits, and Lazenby suggests that Roman infantry numbers cannot have been much greater than Carthaginian after allowing for losses and garrisons.[71] We can perhaps allow a small increment of Numidian horse to at least allow the Romans to contest both flanks, but despite the hostilities that Polybius records (I.31) between Carthage and the Numidians, he makes clear (I.33) that (unlike Scipio at Zama) Regulus was still greatly outnumbered in cavalry.[72] If we represent such a small Roman army on the same basis as at Asculum and Sentinum, it would have a fighting value of only around 50, making its earlier dominance over the Carthaginians impossible to comprehend. Hence, the quality of the Roman infantry needs to be increased by adding a proportion of average light and veteran heavy infantry to reflect the growing maturity of the legionary system and the more select and experienced nature of the troops concerned. With Regulus as an average commander in deference to his earlier successes, a force of 13,000 foot and 1,000 horse can hence have a fighting value of 72, close enough to the Punic value of 84 to tempt the Roman infantry to push forward away from the safety of their camp in the hope of achieving a frontal breakthrough, as they actually did on their left.

Polybius (I.33) describes how the Carthaginian phalanx was deployed behind the elephant line, with some of the mercenaries on its right and the rest accompanying the cavalry on the wings, and he tells how Regulus responded by placing his velites in front, his heavy infantry behind and his horsemen on the flanks. This is easily reflected by having the Carthaginians move first and putting both key zones in the centre, in accordance with the broad symmetry of the battle lines. The biggest enigma of the engagement is Polybius's claim that the legions were many maniples deep, covering a narrower front than before, and that this was a good means of countering the elephants though it exposed the infantry more to cavalry encirclement. Lazenby suggests that the Romans formed up 6 maniples deep rather than the usual 3, and with no gaps between them – he cannot explain Polybius's failure to draw an unfavourable contrast with Scipio's more open anti-elephant formation at Zama.[73] However, Goldsworthy points out that, to break through on the left, the Roman heavy infantry must still have covered the same frontage as the equally numerous Punic heavy foot, so the formation cannot have been as deep as all that.[74] A scale of around 400 m per zone allows the elephants to be at 10 m intervals and the Carthaginian infantry to be 8–10 deep, while yielding the minimum attack limit of 3 units per zone and putting the two camps just behind the respective board edges.[75] The scenario in Figure 29 squares the circle of Polybius's comments by massing the legions in the centre and left centre, leaving only half their units able to engage frontally, but giving them plenty of maniples in reserve to turn round and face the cavalry as Polybius (I.34) describes. Here again, our model casts very useful new light on serious contradictions of force and space that are hardly even recognized in more conventional scholarship.[76]

This battle very much set the pattern for later engagements between Rome and Carthage, with one side's infantry seeking to break through before it was encircled by the superior enemy horsemen. Two thousand troops on the Roman left achieved this by evading the elephants, breaking the mercenaries, killing 800 of them during the pursuit to the camp, and escaping to the Roman base at Aspis. Elsewhere, Polybius (I.34) describes how the legionaries were trampled by the elephants, cut down by the Punic spearmen, and shot by the encircling cavalry who had quickly shattered the outnumbered Roman horse. The few Romans who tried to escape the massacre were quickly caught, with 500 (including Regulus) being captured and the rest killed. Our model portrays the associated grand tactical dynamics very well, and reproduces the Roman dilemma of whether to hang back just outside their camp at the risk of being demoralized and defeated in detail or to seize the initiative and charge forward at the risk of being completely surrounded. It also recreates the related conundrum of whether to form a normal or a deeper and narrower line. Although the asymmetry in casualties was far greater than in Pyrrhus's battles, this seems to have stemmed mainly from the disproportionate impact of victorious cavalry in catching fugitives and cutting off their retreat once resistance had collapsed. The enemy infantry still had to be broken in the first place, and it was here where this battle was more finely balanced – hence Regulus's earlier dominance until the Punic foot and their generals gained the confidence to stand up to him on the plain, and hence the ability of the 10,000 to escape from Persia despite even greater inferiority in mounted strength.[77]

BAGRADAS, 255 BC (Figure 29)

M: x2. AL: 3.

Carthaginians: 10 AHI (7 Carthaginian, 3 Mercenary), 2 ALI (Mercenary), 6 AHC (3 Carthaginian, 3 Mercenary), 2 ALC (Numidian), 5 AEL (Unaccompanied), AC (Xanthippus), UC (Hasdrubal). FV: 84.

Romans: 8 VLE (Roman), 5 ALE (Allied), 2 ALI (Roman), 1 LLI (Allied), 1 AHC (Roman and Allied), 1 ALC (Numidian), AC (Regulus). FV: 72.

12

Hannibal and Scipio

The Second Punic War, unlike its predecessor, saw many land engagements; so much so that my first article on ancient battle mechanics focused purely on this particular conflict.[1] Montagu identifies over 50 different clashes that took place on land (excluding sieges) during the course of the war.[2] However, as with the rest of his 600 or so land battles across our period as a whole, the great majority were only minor engagements on which the source material is so thin and unreliable that it would be hopeless to try to reconstruct them within our model. Even some of the larger battles are difficult to incorporate because of poor documentation (as at Ibera, Beneventum and the Great Plains), often compounded by unusual conditions associated with the forcing of battle on an unwilling opponent (as at Lake Trasimene, Baecula and the Metaurus).[3] Only four set-piece engagements are really well enough recorded for our purposes, thanks to detailed parallel accounts by Polybius and Livy. At the River Trebia south of the Po in 218 BC, Hannibal won his first major victory on Roman soil soon after his epic march across the Alps from Spain. Two years later at Cannae in Apulia, he smashed an even larger Roman army in what has become probably the most famous ancient battle of all. However, the Romans returned to the cautious strategy of Fabius, and used their superior manpower reserves to harass and wear down Hannibal in Italy while taking the offensive elsewhere. This strategy really bore fruit when Scipio the younger conquered Punic Spain using the same brilliant generalship displayed by Hannibal, winning a classic victory over superior numbers at Ilipa in 206. Scipio then invaded Africa, and in a fitting climax he faced and defeated Hannibal himself at Zama in 202, just as Wellington beat Napoleon at Waterloo 2 millennia later. Rome thus gained dominance within the western Mediterranean, and it soon turned its armies east to achieve similar hegemony over the Hellenistic world.

TREBIA, 218 BC

After descending from the Alps, Hannibal won a cavalry battle at the River Ticinus, and then followed the Romans across the Po to the River Trebia, where they were reinforced by Sempronius's army from the south and sufficiently emboldened that judicious Punic provocation prompted them to accept a full-scale engagement. Polybius (III.70–4) is our main source, with around 2,000 words, and he is supplemented by an account of similar length from Livy (XXI.53–6), based heavily on Polybius himself.[4] Polybius (III.68 and 71–2) says that the two armies camped around 40 stadia (7.3 km) apart on opposite sides of the Trebia, and he describes the battle site itself as a flat and treeless area with an overgrown watercourse in which Hannibal concealed an ambush force while he drew up his main line 8 stadia (1.5 km) in front of his camp. Scholars generally agree in placing the battlefield west of the Trebia some 14 km southwest of Placentia (Piacenza), with the Punic camp to the west, the Roman camp several kilometres to the southeast, the battle lines running north–south, and the ambushers hidden 2 km or so south-east of the Roman left flank.[5]

As discussed on pp. 68–9, the ambush is handled abstractly in our model by Hannibal's capacity for turn reversal, so the board need only cover the battle lines themselves. These are generally thought to have been around 4 km long, which translates into a scale of 800 m per zone and allows for an 8 deep line of Punic heavy infantry. Goldsworthy suggests in his text (though not on his map) that the Roman infantry line may have been as much as 2 miles (3.2 km) long, and this possibility may easily be explored in our model by raising the scale to 1,000 m per zone, thereby increasing the attack limit from 3 units to 4.[6] There is some disagreement over the precise location of Hannibal's camp, and hence over how far from the Trebia the battle was fought. However, even those like Kromayer and Goldsworthy who propose a more easterly Punic camp suggest that the river was far enough in the Roman rear that it can be assumed to lie just behind the Roman board edge.[7] This is appropriate because Polybius (III.72–4) makes clear that the battle was fought amid snowstorms and driving rain on a bitterly cold December day, with javelins soaked and the river already swollen due to earlier downpours. Defending the river fords would have been counterproductive for Hannibal in these circumstances as the wet weather would have created an indecisive stand-off, so instead the Carthaginians held back so as to draw the Romans forward past the ambush force – Polybius (III.72) says that the Punic troops did not even deploy from their camp until the river had been crossed.

Polybius (III.71–2) numbers the Punic army at 20,000 heavy infantry, 8,000 light infantry and over 10,000 cavalry, in addition to the picked force of 1,000 horse and 1,000 foot placed in ambush under Hannibal's brother Mago. When it entered Italy, Polybius (III.56) says that the army had contained just 12,000 African and 8,000 Spanish infantry and 6,000 cavalry, so the Celts who had joined Hannibal after his victory at the Ticinus seem to have numbered around 9,000 foot and 5,000 horse.[8] Celts generally lacked skirmishers, a weakness that the Romans had exploited recently at Telamon, so the majority of the light infantry must have been African and Spanish (including the famous Balearic slingers).[9]

Daly has recently revived an earlier claim by Delbrück that the 8,000 skirmishers were *all* invaders and were a distinct contingent not included in the figure of 20,000 infantry for the initial invasion force, but most scholars reject this idea, not least because it would leave hardly any room for Celtic foot in the army at the Trebia when it was in fact their bloody defeat that let 10,000 Romans escape.[10] It is not known how many of the 37 elephants recorded by Polybius (III.42) at the Rhone had been lost during the Alpine crossing, but as they played a smaller role than at Asculum a single elephant unit with accompanying skirmishers seems appropriate in this case.[11] Mago's picked troops are described by Polybius (III.74) as Numidians, and although they were a mixture of horse and foot, they are probably best represented as 2 veteran light cavalry units with Mago as an average leader, to give them the necessary mobility to strike quickly into the Roman rear. The rest of the Punic army was still weak from its recent exertions and had not yet established its superiority over the Romans, so seems best classed as average.[12] At a multiple of 6, and with Hannibal as a brilliant commander, this gives the Carthaginians a fighting value of 83.

According to Polybius (III.72), Sempronius's battle line contained 16,000 Roman and 20,000 allied infantry, plus 4,000 cavalry. Livy (XXI.55) increases the Roman figure to 18,000 and says that there was also a loyal Gallic contingent from the Cenomani, but his claims have been viewed with some scepticism. Particular confusion has been caused by Polybius's statement (III.72) that Sempronius sent out 6,000 javelinmen against the harassing Numidian cavalry while his main force marched to the battlefield, because it is not clear whether these were the only Roman skirmishers present, and it is also uncertain whether they were included in the broader infantry totals.[13] The scenario below assumes a total of about 40,000 infantry including a few thousand Cenomani and the 6,000 light troops (the rest presumably having been lost at the Ticinus), but users are encouraged to experiment with different interpretations.[14] The skirmishers are classed as levies because their missiles had been expended against the Numidians, but the legionaries are classed as a mixture of average and veteran troops as at the Bagradas as otherwise the odds against them would be far too great.[15] Sempronius deserves only to be an uninspired commander, and the other consul (Scipio the elder) had not yet recovered from a wound suffered at the Ticinus, so the fighting value of the army still comes to only 73.[16] What handicapped the Romans just as much as this 10-point inferiority was that they had left camp without breakfast and had become drenched, freezing and exhausted on their long approach march across the river, while the Punic forces girded themselves around their camp fires – there is thus the clearest possible case for treating the Roman army as fatigued.[17]

Polybius (III.72–3) says that both sides formed up in the conventional symmetrical way, with a heavy infantry line screened by light troops, and with the cavalry split between the two flanks after drawn-out and indecisive skirmishing between the Roman and Numidian horse.[18] He says that the elephants were in front of the wings, and does not mention them again until the pursuit, whereas Livy (XXI.55–6) has a ridiculous tale of the pachyderms starting off beyond the ends of the cavalry line, frightening the Roman horses, somehow shifting to the centre where they were roughly handled by Roman skirmishers, and finally being moved to the left where they panicked the Cenomani.[19] In Polybius's much more plausible account, the Romans came off worse in the light infantry duel, and when both sides' skirmishers were withdrawn through the line the Punic cavalry drove back their outnumbered opponents and the Numidians and some of the Carthaginian light troops curved round to attack the Roman flanks. Mago's force now emerged from hiding to assail the Roman rear, but despite this encirclement, the heavy infantry fought on, and 10,000 legionaries actually broke through the Celts and some of the Africans in the enemy centre and escaped to Placentia along with most of the cavalry. Polybius (III.74) says that the remaining Romans were massacred while the Africans and Spanish lost very few troops, although many men and horses and all but one of the elephants perished later because of the terrible weather.

Rather counterintuitively (given the scale of the Roman defeat), the main insight that our model provides in this case is to show how *good* Roman heavy infantry had become relative to their adversaries. Despite being comprehensively outgeneralled and finding themselves ambushed, encircled by superior cavalry, soaked, frozen, exhausted and famished, the central legions still managed to defeat formidable opponents in a frontal infantry contest with only a small advantage in numbers. Even though legionaries already have superior fighting value to other troops, a Roman army limited purely to average legionaries as at Sentinum and Asculum would have a total fighting value of just 57, making the historical breakthrough almost inconceivable even without the added penalty for being fatigued. Goldsworthy describes the Roman army at the Trebia as inexperienced and ill-coordinated, but Hannibal's victory was already over-determined by other factors, and it is a measure of the tactical and psychological strength of the Roman military system that even such a large and ill-led army should have the kind of qualitative edge at the unit level hitherto only achieved by small elites such as Spartan hoplites.[20]

TREBIA, 218 BC (Figure 31)

M: x6. AL: 3. Wet.

Romans: 8 VLE (Roman), 6 ALE (Allied), 1 AHI (Cenomani), 1 LLI (Roman and Allied), 3 AHC (1 Roman, 2 Allied), UC (Sempronius). FV: 73. Fatigued.

Carthaginians: 7 AHI (3 African, 2 Celtic, 2 Spanish), 2 ALI (1 African and

HANNIBAL AND SCIPIO

Balearic, 1 Spanish and Celtic), 5 AHC (3 Celtic, 2 Spanish), AL + VLC (Mago + Picked Numidians), 1 VLC (Picked Numidians), 2 ALC (Numidian), 1 AEL (Moorish LI), BC (Hannibal). FV: 83.

CANNAE, 216 BC

The disaster at the Trebia and the loss of another army to ambush at Lake Trasimene the following year prompted the Romans to adopt Fabius's more cautious strategy of harassment, but this rankled with many, and so the consuls for 216 instead chose to confront Hannibal with massive force. Our main source is again 2,000 words by Polybius (III.112–17) and a broadly parallel account by Livy (XXII.44–9). As I mentioned on p. 6, Appian's similarly lengthy battle piece (*Hann.* 19–26) is a worthless farrago by comparison. I also discussed on p. 7 the lack of scholarly consensus about where along the Aufidus (Ofanto) the battle was fought, and showed on p. 78 how we could evade this disagreement by using a generic battlefield bordered on one flank by the river as both Polybius (III.113 and 115) and Livy (XXII.46–7) describe.[21] Orientation is uncertain apart from Polybius's claim (III.113–4) that the Romans faced south and the Carthaginians north, as broadly indicated in Figure 33. The main camps of the two sides were on the far bank of the river, but the smaller Roman fortified camp was somewhere to their rear. Kromayer and his modern followers such as Lancel and Daly suggest that this smaller camp was so near the fighting line that it would have to be placed in the Roman right rear zone, but this is dubious in the extreme as there is no mention of it interfering with Hasdrubal's cavalry manoeuvre, and its presence in such a position would have made concentrating all the Gallic and Spanish horse on this flank utterly perverse.[22]

I argued on pp. 78 and 86–7 that this same Carthaginian deployment creates a strong circumstantial case for the presence of rough ground on the Punic right wing.[23] This raises the issue of how wide the battlefield actually was. Lazenby, Connolly and Goldsworthy estimate the width of the Roman infantry line at 1.5 km or less, while Kromayer, Lancel and Daly put it at 2 km or so. The cavalry are assumed to take up the same frontage again, or a little more.[24] A significant factor is that Connolly and Goldsworthy are striving to fit the armies into a site that is not much more than 2 km wide in a perpendicular direction between the hills around Cannae and a presumed more northerly course of the Aufidus, while Kromayer suggests a much more open and extensive battlefield further to the east. The sites northwest of Cannae do look very constrained, and our comparative model suggests that Goldsworthy's lower estimate of a 2 km overall battlefront with 1 km infantry lines is ridiculously small for armies of this size (once one realizes that the scale on his more detailed maps is out by a factor of 2).[25] By contrast, Kromayer's battle lines rest not on the river as the sources describe but on the top of a small escarpment several hundred metres away, while Monte Altino on the other wing is really too distant to provide the obstruction I hypothesized.[26] The scenario in Figure 33 is hence based on the Aufidus following a more northerly course than it does today, with the armies arrayed as in Connolly's reconstruction or (perhaps more likely) further to the north-east between the presumed course of the river and the *bottom* of the escarpment that runs north-east from Cannae.[27] Kromayer's alternative may easily be explored by removing the hill and increasing the scale to 1,000 m per zone, thereby boosting the attack limit from 3 units to 4.

I outlined on p. 24 how Polybius's figures (III.114) of 10,000 cavalry and 40,000 infantry in the Punic army may be converted into units within our model. Connolly, Lancel and Daly suggest that the horse consisted of 2,000 Spaniards, 4,000 Celts and 4,000 Numidians, while Lazenby and Goldsworthy put the proportion of Numidians slightly lower.[28] Daly and Lazenby think there were 10,000 Libyan heavy infantry, but this is because Daly believes the initial figure of 12,000 in 218 BC did not include skirmishers and because Lazenby suggests any African skirmishers had been re-equipped as spearmen – both assumptions are highly questionable, and Connolly's and Goldsworthy's figures of around 8,000 for the Libyan phalanx seem far more likely. Similarly, the estimates by Connolly and Lazenby of around 12,000 light infantry are based simply on maintaining the same ratio as at the Trebia, and Daly's and Goldsworthy's guesses of 8,000 fit in far better with the paucity of Celtic skirmishers. This leaves around 24,000 other heavy infantry, of whom 4–6,000 are estimated to be Spanish and the rest Celts.[29] Daly makes the very dubious claims that the infantry total of 40,000 excluded the 8,000 skirmishers mentioned at the Trebia but that it included around 8,000 troops left to guard the Punic camp – fortunately these notions entirely cancel one another out, so there is little net disagreement with other scholars.[30] I discussed on p. 21 how troop classifications may need to shift from battle to battle, and Cannae is a case in point. The Numidians' delaying action against the Roman allied horse gives no sense of the disproportionate contribution that Mago's picked ambushers made at the Trebia, but Hasdrubal's Spanish cavalry fought magnificently, as did the Libyan spearmen now they had been re-equipped with the best captured Roman arms and deployed in the famous flanking columns rather than just as part of the battle line.[31] Now that successive victories had smashed the idea of Roman superiority, this surely justifies giving veteran status to the troops concerned. As outlined on pp. 24 and 67–8, this gives the Punic army as a whole a fighting value of 84.

Polybius (III.107 and 113) claims that Rome fielded the unprecedented total of 8 legions, each with the increased strength of 5,000 Roman and 5,000 allied infantry as well as 300 Roman and even more allied cavalry, making a total force of 80,000 foot and over 6,000 horse. Some scholars have questioned these figures, with Brunt preferring Livy's variant account (XXII.36) that only 10,000 extra troops were raised rather than 4 new legions, and Caven even going so far as to suggest that the Romans had no more infantry than the Carthaginians, but most writers think that there were indeed nearly 70,000 Roman foot on the field, and another 10,000 in their main camp as Polybius (III.117) says.[32] Lazenby and Goldsworthy estimate that 15,000 of the 70,000 were skirmishers, but this presumes that the allies supplied fewer light infantry than the Romans themselves – if not, then a figure of 20,000 seems more reasonable, especially when one includes the 1,000 archers and slingers that Livy (XXII.37) says were provided by Syracuse. Connolly thinks there were 1,600 Roman and 4,800 allied horse, but other scholars prefer figures of 2,400 and 3,600 respectively.[33] Samuels's argument that the Roman army of this period was inherently inflexible is exaggerated in view of its performance earlier in the century, but the loss of so many good troops and officers over the past 2 years must surely have had some effect on the quality of this massive and hastily raised force, however robust its morale.[34] Hence, it seems justified to return to the same mix of average legionaries and levy light infantry as at Sentinum and Asculum. With Paullus as an uninspired commander and Varro as an uninspired leader to reflect his loss with the allied horse, this gives the Romans a fighting value of 70, placing them at a roughly similar overall disadvantage as at Trebia when one takes into account the differential value of average legionaries.

I already illustrated the famous deployments and manoeuvres at this battle on pp. 78–86, and there is no need to repeat the discussion here. As at the Trebia, Polybius (III.113–6) is our most reliable source, with Livy (XXII.45–9) adding dubious details such as the pretended desertion of 500 Numidians with swords hidden under their tunics.[35] In terms of casualties, however, Livy's scattered figures (XXII.49–54) suggesting that around 48,200 Romans were killed, 19,300 were captured and 14,500 eventually escaped are usually seen as preferable, whereas Polybius is trusted for his claims (III.117) that Hannibal lost 4,000 Celts, 1,500 Spanish and Africans, and 200 cavalry.[36] As I have shown on pp. 86–8 and in my remarks above, our broad-brush model allows us to gain significant new insights into the engagement even though scholars like Daly and Goldsworthy have written entire books focused on this single battle – nothing could more clearly demonstrate the value of comparative dynamic modelling as a supplement to more traditional scholarship.[37]

CANNAE, 216 BC (Figure 33)

M: x8. AL: 3.
Romans: 12 ALE (6 Roman, 6 Allied), 1 ALI (Roman and Syracusan), 2 LLI (1

Roman, 1 Allied), UL + AHC (Varro + Allies), 2 AHC (1 Roman, 1 Allied), UC
(Paullus). FV: 70.

Carthaginians: 4 VHI (African), 6 AHI (5 Celtic, 1 Spanish), 2 ALI (1 African
and Balearic, 1 Spanish and Celtic), AL + VHC (Hasdrubal + Spanish), 1 VHC
(Spanish), 2 AHC (Celtic), 2 ALC (Numidian), BC (Hannibal). FV: 84.

ILIPA, 206 BC

Scipio the younger's conquest of Spain after the betrayal and death of his father
and uncle in 211 took a long time despite his military genius, and even after
Hannibal's brother Hasdrubal left for Italy and defeat at the Metaurus, Scipio
still had to face a large Punic army under Hasdrubal Gisgo near modern Seville.
Our main sources are again Polybius (XI.21–4) and Livy (XXVIII.13–15), who
each have around 1,500 words on the engagement. Polybius (V.20) says that the
Carthaginians camped on the edge of some hills with a level plain in front, and
that Scipio made his camp on some low hills opposite. Scullard identified Ilipa
with the modern Alcala del Rio, and in 1935 he found what he believed to be the
hills concerned, with the Roman camp to the north-east of the Punic one and
the intervening plain being up to 6 km across.[38] Other scholars have generally
accepted this identification.[39] The Punic army deployed not far from the foot of
its hill, so both hill and camp can be assumed to lie just behind the Carthaginian
board edge. Polybius (XI.24) and Livy (XXVIII.15) both claim that a violent
rainstorm stopped the pursuing Romans from taking Hasdrubal's camp, so the
battle should clearly begin in overcast conditions to reflect the continuing chance
of such a cloudburst.

Polybius (XI.20) gives Scipio 45,000 infantry and 3,000 cavalry, including
significant numbers of Spanish allies.[40] Scholars generally suggest that the Spanish
made up somewhat under half of the total force, and this tallies with the figures
of 25,000 foot and 2,500 horse that Polybius (X.9) gives for Scipio's Italian field
army at New Carthage in 209.[41] The Roman legionaries should clearly count once
more as veterans given their extensive training and experience over the past few
years, and it is also appropriate to make all of the velites average and some of the
cavalry veterans, to reflect the impact of improvements to their equipment and
training that seem to have happened in 211 if not earlier.[42] Samuels places too
much emphasis on the alleged reforms of 211, but it is surely true that extensive
and sometimes bitter practical experience during this protracted conflict
eventually forged the Roman army into a more effective fighting instrument,
just as the Red Army was transformed by the defeats and hard-won victories of
1941–42 into a force that matched the professionalism of its German adversaries
in 1943–45.[43] The real transformation had come in generalship, and this can be

reflected by including Scipio as a brilliant commander and his lieutenant Silanus, who led the other wing, as an average commander. At the maximum multiple of 8, this gives the Romans a fighting value of 76.

Polybius (XI.20) gives Hasdrubal 70,000 infantry, 4,000 cavalry and 32 elephants, while Livy (XXVIII.12) says that there were 4,500 horse and that some writers put the Punic foot at 70,000 but others suggested 50,000. Scullard and Walbank prefer the lower infantry figure on the grounds that Polybius may have exaggerated to please his Scipionic patrons, while Lazenby supports the higher total because he thinks that otherwise there would have been no need for the elaborate Roman flanking manoeuvres.[44] Our model suggests that the lower figure would make the contest ridiculously imbalanced unless the Libyans, whom Polybius (XI.24) describes as the best troops in the Punic army, are classed as veterans. However, if they are so classified, it is hard to see them playing such an ineffective role as they did historically, whereas the 'weaker' Spanish did resist for some time on the wings.[45] Hence, it seems preferable to go with Polybius's figures after all and to class the whole Carthaginian army as average. Livy (XXVIII.12) describes Hasdrubal as the best Punic general of the war after Hannibal and his brothers, but his mistakes and inertia during this engagement make it difficult to see him as anything other than uninspired. This gives the army a fighting value of 63, which is 13 less than the Romans. To compound the asymmetry, Scipio panicked the Carthaginians into deploying without breakfast and then prolonged the skirmishing for hours while the heat and hunger took its toll, so the Punic army should count as fatigued.[46] Ilipa thus has similarities to both Cannae and the Trebia, but with Scipio relying not on cavalry superiority or on 'expendable' allies but on his better-trained citizen infantry to win the day.

Hasdrubal deployed in the same order as he had over the past few days, with his Libyans in the centre and his elephants in front of the Spanish on the wings. As I mentioned on p. 62, Scipio's dawn advance served not only to deny the enemy breakfast but also to conceal until it was too late his shift of his best Italian troops from the centre to the wings – a stratagem neatly simulated in our model by his ability as a brilliant general to deploy second but to reverse the turn order thereafter. The key zones should clearly be in the centre for these highly symmetrical battle lines. Veith suggests a frontage of over 5 km for Hasdrubal's infantry and elephants alone, but this seems excessive, especially as his reconstruction creates a yawning gap of over 2 km between the Roman infantry wings.[47] Our maximum scale of 1,200 m per zone still allows for a 16 deep Punic heavy infantry line, and it may even be that a scale of 1,000 m per zone would suffice.

Polybius (XI.23) describes the complex columnar and wheeling manoeuvres that Scipio used on both wings to extend his front to match or exceed that of the enemy, and modern scholars have focused their analyses on trying to reconstruct the fine detail of these evolutions.[48] From our broader grand tactical perspective, what stands out just as much is the stalemate in the centre, where Polybius (XI.24) and Livy (XXVIII.14) say that the Libyans were unable either to reinforce the wings or to come to grips with the Spanish facing them. The opposing lines had apparently been only 750 m or so apart when the Roman wings began their manoeuvres, and Scipio's Spanish centre continued to advance (albeit at a slower pace), so there is no case for holding the Spanish forces back behind the Roman key zone.[49] Instead, the Romans can use their far superior command to deploy all the Italians forward by double moves on turn 1, and can then reverse the turn order and attack at once so as to gain the edge in the cavalry duels and perhaps quickly seize the Punic left and right centre zones. The central battle will proceed more slowly as a psychological as much as a physical contest, with the Libyan morale collapsing as their flanks are threatened so that eventually they are likely to flee to their camp as happened historically.[50] This battle is a fascinating case study of the impact of greatly superior generalship on a contest in which both the infantry and the cavalry of the two sides were fairly evenly matched – by using our model to refight the engagement with only Silanus in command of the Romans and with the Carthaginians not being fatigued, one may clearly appreciate how much of a difference Scipio's contribution made.

ILIPA, 206 BC (Figure 34)

M: x8. AL: 4. Overcast.

Carthaginians: 14 AHI (8 Spanish, 6 Libyan), 3 ALI (1 Spanish, 1 Balearic, 1 African), 1 AHC (Spanish), 1 ALC (Numidian), 1 AEL (Moorish LI). UC (Hasdrubal). FV: 63. Fatigued.

Romans: 4 VLE (Roman), 2 ALE (Allied), 4 AHI (Spanish), 3 ALI (1 Roman, 1 Allied, 1 Spanish), 1 VHC (Roman and Italian), 1 AHC (Italian and Spanish), BC (Scipio), AC (Silanus). FV: 76.

ZAMA, 202 BC

Despite the caution of Fabius, Scipio took an army including the survivors of Cannae to Africa in 204, and his victories there prompted peace negotiations and the recall of Hannibal from his Bruttian stronghold to confront the invaders. Polybius (XV.9–16) and Livy (XXX.32–5) are as usual our main sources, with around 2,000 words each, but neither gives any clear idea of the size of the opposing armies. The battlefield is also hard to locate, but this is less important for our purposes as Polybius (XV.5–6 and 13–14) says that it was a flat and level plain with the respective camps some 30 stadia (5.5 km) apart. Veith's suggested site on the plain of Draa el Meinan with Hannibal encamped on a hill to the east-south-east of Scipio has won significant scholarly assent.[51] Both key zones should be in the centre, as usual for these nations.

Appian (*Pun.* 41) says that Scipio had about 23,000 foot and 1,500 Roman and Italian horse, plus large numbers of Numidian cavalry under Masinissa and 600 other Numidians under Dacamas. However, his account of the fighting (centring on a personal duel between Hannibal and Scipio) is largely fantasy, casting grave doubt on his reliability.[52] Polybius (XV.5) and Livy (XXX.29) put Masinissa's force at 4,000 horse and 6,000 foot, but there is no specific mention of Numidian infantry in the battle. Goldsworthy has suggested that the 6,000 foot may have included the legionaries that Polybius (XIV.9 and XV.4) says were sent with Masinissa earlier to help pursue his rival Syphax, while Brunt thinks the 6,000 were included within Appian's figure of 23,000 foot, leaving only 17,000 Italian infantry.[53] However, most scholars add the 10,000 Numidians to Appian's numbers (that they see as in tune with earlier figures for the Roman expeditionary force) to get an army of around 29,000 infantry and 6,000 cavalry.[54] The scenario below uses these numbers, but makes the Numidian light infantry levies to stop them having an undue impact. Of the Roman and Italian forces, the velites should be average, but there is a strong case for making all of the legionaries and heavy cavalry veterans as they were highly experienced and displayed enormous discipline and tactical flexibility, leading Goldsworthy to describe them as 'one of the best trained forces ever produced by the Roman militia system'.[55] At a multiple of 6, and with Scipio as a brilliant commander and Masinissa as an average leader, this gives the Roman army a fighting value of 93.

Appian (*Pun.* 40) gives Hannibal 50,000 men, while Polybius (XV.3, 11 and 14) says that his cavalry included 2,000 Numidians, that his first line numbered 12,000, and that his losses included 20,000 killed and nearly as many prisoners, with only a few escaping. Both authors claim that he fielded 80 elephants. Scholars usually suggest that there were around 4,000 Punic cavalry in all, but there is greater controversy over infantry numbers. Most writers propose that all three of the lines were roughly the same strength, giving around 36,000 foot, but Goldsworthy and Lancel argue that the third line must have contained 15–20,000 troops, based on Polybius's claim (XV.15) that the two infantry forces were nearly equal in numbers after the first two Punic lines had mostly fled.[56] The cavalry and the first line of mercenaries from Mago's army should probably count as average, with the Balearic and Moorish troops integrated as skirmishers within the elephant units.[57] The second line of Carthaginian and Libyan recruits performed dismally and should clearly be classed as levies – as I mentioned on p. 6, Livy's propagandist tale (XXX.33) of a 'legion' of Macedonians being present in this line is almost universally disbelieved.[58] The third line was certainly highly motivated (despite Livy's claim to the contrary), but the more men it contained, the higher the likely proportion of Bruttians rather than real old-timers from Hannibal's early campaigns.[59] The scenario below uses an intermediate force of 15,000 troops, over half of them veterans, but users may easily experiment with the numbers and the quality of this contingent. The army's fighting value comes to 79, which ensures a bitter contest but should allow Scipio to prevail as he did historically without any part of his line giving way altogether.

Polybius (XV.9 and 11) tells us that Hannibal deployed with his elephants in front of his army, his Numidian horse on his left, and his Carthaginian horse on his right, while Scipio put his Italian cavalry under Laelius on his left and Masinissa with all his Numidians on the right. Veith suggests a frontage of just over 4 km for the two armies, which translates into a scale of around 800 m per zone, and means that the elephants will be at roughly 30 m intervals.[60] However, modern diagrams tend to show the cavalry wings as of equal length, making no allowance for the far greater numbers of Numidian than Italian horse in Scipio's army.[61] The infantry may also (at least initially) have covered only 2 km or less, to give each successive Punic line a reasonable depth.[62] To reflect these factors, and to mirror what Polybius (XV.12) says about the retreat of the leftmost elephants panicking the nearby cavalry, the deployment in Figure 35 has the Punic left centre and Roman right centre zones occupied by Numidian horse as much as by infantry. The elephant charge is best simulated by having the Carthaginians move first, while Scipio's famous counter-tactic of leaving lanes between his maniples is reflected abstractly by his command bonus and by the universally high quality of the legionary troops. With both sides having brilliant generals, there is no turn reversal as there was in the other engagements in this chapter.

As I discussed on pp. 46 and 51, a distinctive aspect of this battle is Hannibal's use of multiple lines, with the elephants and the first and second lines being fought to destruction in order to weaken the Romans before the final confrontation with his fresh veterans, held back more than a stade (180 m) to the rear.[63] Such a sacrificial approach makes some sense in our model, as each zone at first contains more units than will fit within the attack limit, and because Hannibal's morale boost should keep his third line from fleeing despite the penalties for being surrounded and having multiple units shattered.[64] Polybius (XV.13–14) describes how the hastati and principes worked together in classic fashion, and how Scipio reorganized his infantry and moved the principes and triarii onto the flanks of the hastati to form a single line for the final contest – precisely the tactic that our treble move for veteran legionaries makes possible. Connolly suggests that the new Roman line outflanked Hannibal's veterans as happened to the 4,000 recalcitrant Celtiberians at the Great Plains the year before, while other scholars believe that the hastati shortened their own front to make room – our model allows dynamic experimentation with both possibilities.[65] Polybius (XV.12 and 14) tells how the Roman cavalry on both wings quickly broke the Punic horse and pursued them off the field, returning in the nick of time to charge into Hannibal's rear and decide the battle. As I discussed on p. 46, our model uses simpler, more abstract restrictions to simulate such off-board pursuits, but what it does clearly show is that Scipio's horsemen represented only a quarter of the total fighting value of his combat units at Zama, compared to a third for the Carthaginian cavalry at the Bagradas and Cannae and almost half at the Trebia, so the Roman infantry were always going to have to do proportionally more of the 'heavy lifting'. Polybius (XV.14) and Livy (XXX.35) put Roman losses at 1,500 dead, while Appian (*Pun.* 48) claims that 2,500 Romans and even more Numidians died. Either way, the complete destruction of Hannibal's army represented a tactical triumph as resounding as any of his own earlier victories, but now with much more decisive strategic effects. This classic and in some ways unusual battle offers a valuable test of the validity of our model, and the central dynamic of a gradual 'wearing out fight' is exactly in tune with the ancient accounts.

ZAMA, 202 BC (Figure 35)

M: x6. AL: 3.

Carthaginians: 6 VHI (Hannibal's Veterans), 5 AHI (2 Bruttian, 2 Celtic, 1 Ligurian), 2 LHI (1 Carthaginian, 1 Libyan), 1 AHC (Carthaginian), 2 ALC (Numidian), 3 AEL (2 Balearic LI, 1 Moorish LI), BC (Hannibal). FV: 79.

Romans: 11 VLE (5 Roman, 6 Allied), 2 ALI (1 Roman, 1 Allied), 1 LLI (Numidian), 2 VHC (1 Roman, 1 Allied), AL + ALC (Masinissa + Numidians), 2 ALC (Numidian), BC (Scipio). FV: 93.

13

Rome Moves East

Compared to its drawn-out conquest of Italy and the western Mediterranean, Rome's subjugation of the Hellenistic east was remarkably rapid. This was partly because of the continuing divisions among the Greek states, and partly because Greek and Macedonian manpower was so scarce and thinly spread that it took only one major battlefield defeat to force even large states to come to terms. Philip V of Macedon had allied himself with Hannibal after Cannae, but he was contained by Roman naval power until Carthage was defeated and soon found himself in a new conflict with Rome (the Second Macedonian War). After 3 years of indecisive campaigning, the two armies clashed at Cynoscephalae in Thessaly in 197 BC, and Rome was victorious. A similar conflict soon developed with the Seleucid kingdom, with Antiochus III being driven out of Greece and then defeated at Magnesia in Ionia at the end of 190. Both rulers were left in power, but in 171, tensions with Philip's son and successor Perseus triggered the Third Macedonian War, and when his army in turn was smashed at Pydna in southern Macedonia in 168 the monarchy was ended, and 2 decades later Macedon became a Roman province. Rome's attention then turned back to western conflicts, but in the following century a long series of wars began with Mithridates of Pontus, including battles such as 2nd Chaeronea, Orchomenus and Tigranocerta that are too ill-documented to be modelled effectively within our system.[1] Power in Rome was passing increasingly to strongmen like Pompey, and when his rival Crassus sought military glory by attacking the Parthians who had overrun the Seleucid dominions, the resulting defeat at Carrhae in Mesopotamia in 53 BC became as infamous in Roman annals as the Allia, Cannae and later the Teutoburg forest. Crassus's death helped to clear the way for open civil war between the two remaining triumvirs – Pompey and Caesar.

CYNOSCEPHALAE, 197 BC

Philip V and the Romans under Flamininus were camped to the north and south of an intervening range of hills called Cynoscephalae ('Dog Heads'), but their covering forces on the ridge came into conflict and the clash escalated into a full-scale engagement. Polybius (XVIII.20–7) is our main source with some 2,500 words, and his account is followed by his famous disquisition (XVIII.28–32) on the inferiority of the phalanx to the legionary fighting system. Livy (XXIII.6–10) has a lengthy but somewhat shaky paraphrase of Polybius, while Plutarch (*Flam.* 7–9) has a shorter description. Modern scholars have focused mainly on trying to identify the battle site. Pritchett rejected Kromayer's suggested location in favour of a point 6 km to the east, but Hammond proposed a different site again, nearly 5 km west of Kromayer's battlefield.[2] Given these disagreements, it seems best to base our terrain more on what the sources actually describe than on any specific site. Polybius (XVIII.21–6) makes clear that the fighting took place on the Roman side of the ridge, with the Macedonian right alternately forced back to the summit and pursuing down the slope until it neared the Roman camp, while the Macedonian left was caught with some of its forces straggling down the slope and others halted on the heights behind. This suggests that hills should run across the Macedonian half of the board as shown in Figure 36, being further advanced in the right centre to reflect the spur of high ground on which the initial fighting seems to have focused (as is evident in Hammond's reconstruction).[3] Low cloud initially shrouded the hills after an overnight thunderstorm, with the poor visibility contributing to the unplanned clash, but the mist cleared as the first major reinforcements were deployed, so it is probably best to start the battle in overcast rather than wet conditions.[4]

Livy (XXXIII.4), presumably drawing on a lost passage by Polybius, gives the Macedonian forces as 16,000 phalangites, 2,000 'peltasts', 2,000 Thracians, 2,000 Illyrians, 1,500 mercenaries and 2,000 cavalry.[5] Head points out that Polybius (II.65 and IV.37) records 3,000 peltast guardsmen at Sellasia and 5,000 under Philip himself in 219, and that Livy (XLII.51) describes Perseus's forces in 171 as containing a picked 'agema' of 2,000 peltasts plus a further 3,000 such troops. He therefore suggests that there were 3,000 extra peltasts at Cynoscephalae who have either been omitted altogether or included in the phalanx total.[6] However, the remaining peltasts may have been detached elsewhere, as 2,000 were during the battle of Pydna, so these seem to be insufficient grounds for amending Livy's explicit figures.[7] At a multiple of 4, and with Philip as an average commander, the Macedonian army thus only has a fighting value of 53.

Plutarch (*Flam.* 7) gives the Romans 26,000 men, including 400 horse and 6,000 foot from Aetolia.[8] Livy (XXXIII.3–4) says that the Romans had about the same number of troops as the Macedonians and were only superior in cavalry thanks to the Aetolians. He also claims that Flamininus had been joined by 1,200 Athamanian infantry and 800 Cretan and Apollonian skirmishers in addition to the Aetolians, whom he numbers at 400 horse but just 600 foot.[9] Kromayer and Pritchett believe the lower figure for the Aetolians, but other scholars prefer the higher total, with Head and Santosuosso reducing Italian infantry numbers to 16,000 in consequence while Hammond uses Livy's reference (XXXIII.1) to

1 legion having 2,000 hastati earlier that year to argue that the legions must have been overstrength and hence that there were some 30,000 foot in all.[10] Walbank and Briscoe also endorse this figure, though they suggest that several thousand men may have been absent in garrisons, bringing the force at the battle back within Plutarch's total.[11]

Polybius (XVIII.22) lauds the bravery of the Aetolian cavalry but highlights the unsteadiness of the Aetolian infantry – as the latter played no clear role in the engagement, it seems appropriate to class the horse as veterans but most of the foot as levies.[12] The Roman and Italian cavalry are usually numbered at 2,000, and there seems no case for making them anything other than average. The Romans also had some elephants sent by Masinissa that made a significant contribution on the right, so 1 unit of pachyderms is clearly warranted.[13] Our model hence suggests that the lower total of 16,000 Roman and Italian infantry is much more credible, not only because it accords with what both Plutarch and Livy say about the equality in overall numbers but also because it reduces the asymmetry between the armies. With Flamininus as an average commander, this gives the Romans a fighting value of 65, which is still 12 more than Philip's total. Hammond's army would have a fighting value of 80, which would yield far too overwhelming an advantage.

Polybius (XVIII.20–4) describes how the Macedonian covering force at first drove back Flamininus's 300 horse and 1,000 skirmishers, and how the successive arrival of 500 more cavalry and 2,000 infantry (mainly Aetolians), then of Philip's cavalry and non-Thracian mercenaries, and then of the Roman legionaries themselves turned the tide in each case in that side's favour. This back and forth contest is well simulated in our model by treating both sides as surprised, and giving the Romans the first move as they were the first to reinforce the initial clash and to bring their heavy troops into play. Putting the Macedonian key zone on the spur of high ground in their right centre encourages them to emphasize this flank, as happened historically. Polybius (XVIII.24) tells how Philip led up his peltasts and part of his phalanx, sent the retreating cavalry and mercenaries to the right wing, and had his pikemen double their depth and close up to the right before charging the approaching legionaries. Kromayer and Pritchett suggest that the doubling was from 8 to 16 deep, while Hammond thinks that it was from 16 to 32 deep and that Philip had with him only some 5,000 phalangites plus the 2,000 peltasts, giving his heavy troops a frontage of just 220 m that fits within the small 'flat areas' that Hammond identifies on the ground.[14] He puts the length of the entire Roman infantry line at about 1 km (once one realizes that the scale on his detailed map is out by a factor of 2), whereas Kromayer, Keppie and Connolly estimate the infantry frontage at around 2 km, with Connolly adding a further 3 km for the cavalry on the wings.[15] As at the Hydaspes, our comparative model suggests that both extremes are highly questionable, and that a scale of around

600 m per zone fits better with the pattern from other engagements. The Roman fortified camp could be assumed to lie just behind their board edge, but it may be better to place it in their rear zone given Polybius's comments (XVIII.24) about the Macedonian light troops advancing almost to the camp before the legionaries intervened.

Philip's men drove the Roman left down the hill, but on the other wing, Nicanor's troops were still strung out on the way down from the summit. Flamininus moved to this wing, and a charge spearheaded by his elephants caused the disorganized Macedonians to flee. There followed the most famous episode of the battle, when an unnamed tribune took 20 maniples from the pursuing Roman right and wheeled them round into the rear of Philip's men, triggering their flight.[16] Our model shows very clearly how vulnerable the Macedonians may become if they advance into the Roman left centre and then lose their own centre zone, and it also captures how hard it is for the Macedonians to get their average phalangites forward as fast as the veteran legionaries, given the higher command cost for double movement. Polybius (XVIII.26) describes how those phalangites who had only just reached the summit held up their pikes in the Greek token of surrender, but says that the uncomprehending Romans cut them down despite Flamininus's efforts to save them. He goes on to claim (XVIII.27) that the dead amounted to 700 Romans and 8,000 Macedonians, with a further 5,000 Macedonians captured. Our model once again casts new light on the significant differences among modern scholars about the battle site and about army frontages and Roman troop numbers, and it gives a better sense of the dynamics of the fighting without tying that interpretation to a single, inevitably dubious location as Hammond's reconstruction tends to do.

CYNOSCEPHALAE, 197 BC (Figure 36)

M: x4. AL: 3. Overcast.

Romans: 5 VLE (Roman), 3 ALE (Allied), 1 LHI (Aetolian), 4 ALI (1 Roman, 1 Roman and Athamanian, 1 Allied, 1 Aetolian), 1 VHC (Aetolian), 2 AHC (1 Roman, 1 Allied), 1 AEL (Cretan and Apollonian LI), AC (Flamininus). FV: 65. Surprised.

Macedonians: 2 VPH (Peltasts), 8 APH (4 Bronze Shields, 4 White Shields), 1 AHI (Thracian), 2 ALI (1 Illyrian, 1 Mercenary), 2 AHC (1 Macedonian, 1 Thessalian), AC (Philip). FV: 53. Surprised.

MAGNESIA, 190 BC

With Hannibal advising Antiochus III and Scipio Africanus accompanying his consular brother Lucius Scipio, the final contest of the Syrian War might have turned into a replay of their confrontation at Zama, but in the event, Africanus was away ill and Hannibal was also absent after a naval defeat.[17] Polybius's account of the battle near Magnesia on the River Hermus has unfortunately been lost, so we have to rely on the derivative versions by Livy (XXXVII.38–44) and Appian (*Syr.* 30–6), each containing 2–3,000 words. Unlike at Cynoscephalae, modern scholars generally accept Kromayer's suggestion that the battlefield lay in the plain between the Hermus to the south and its tributary the Phrygius to the east and north. Livy (XXXVII.38–9) and Appian (*Syr.* 30) describe the Romans crossing the Phrygius, camping some 20 stadia (3.7 km) from Antiochus, and when he held back near his own camp, moving their camp even closer (perhaps 2 km away) until the king finally accepted battle. The earlier Roman position may have allowed them to rest both flanks on the rivers (if one assumes less of a gap than exists today), but the new position left only the Phrygius guarding their left, as shown in Figure 37.[18] Livy (XXXVII.41) says that the battle was fought in foggy conditions that limited visibility and soaked the missiles of the light troops, so it is probably worth starting the scenario in wet weather.

Appian (*Syr.* 31) claims that the Roman army was some 30,000 strong including 10,000 Roman and 10,000 Italian infantry, 3,000 peltasts and 3,000 horse, while Livy (XXXVII.39) says that there were 2 Roman and 2 allied legions each containing 5,400 men, as well as 3,000 Pergamene and Achaean peltasts, 3,000 Italian and Pergamene cavalry, 1,000 Cretan and Trallian skirmishers, 16 African elephants, and 2,000 Macedonians and Thracians who were initially left to guard the camp. Most modern scholars accept these figures as broadly accurate, but Grainger has recently rejected them utterly and argued that the real total was more like 50,000.[19] His arguments are basically that Rome would never have sent such an outnumbered force against a civilized opponent, that Livy may have deliberately exaggerated the odds so as to glorify the Roman victory, and that Livy earlier mentions substantial extra drafts of recruits and reinforcements that are absent from his account of the battle itself.[20] The issue is whether these drafts fought as formed units or served only to keep the legions and alae up to Livy's high paper strengths despite losses and garrisons.

Our model can best contribute to this debate by giving a clearer sense of how the respective interpretations compare when the opposing armies are modelled using the same classification principles as have worked so effectively in capturing other Roman and Hellenistic battles. The legions can be represented with veteran Romans and average allies and velites, as in other cases. Livy (XXXVII.39 and 41–2) says that the 16 elephants were held uselessly in the rear out of fear of

Antiochus's more numerous Indian pachyderms, but that the archers, slingers and cavalry led by Eumenes of Pergamum played a major role in routing the whole Seleucid left. This suggests that we omit the Roman elephants altogether, but classify the Cretans and some of the cavalry as veterans. Lucius Scipio seems to have been lost without his brother, but Appian (*Syr.* 30–1) suggests that the ex-consul Domitius Ahenobarbus was in effective charge, so it is probably best to have Scipio as an average commander because of this experienced support and to include Eumenes as an average leader to reflect his success on the right.[21] At a multiple of 6, this gives the 30,000 strong army a fighting value of 71, whereas Grainger's 50,000 strong force would have a much higher value of around 100.

Livy (XXXVII.37) credits Antiochus with 60,000 foot and 12,000 horse, while Appian (*Syr.* 32) says there were 70,000 troops in all. Livy (XXXVII.40) says the infantry included 16,000 phalangites, an unspecified number of Silver Shields, 3,000 Galatians, 4,700 Cappadocians and mercenaries and 21,500 assorted skirmishers, while the cavalry included 6,000 cataphracts, 2,500 Galatians, 1,200 Dahae horse archers, a contingent of Tarentines and 2 units each of 1,000 horse guards; there were also 54 Indian elephants and some camels and scythed chariots.[22] Bar-Kochva and Grainger both argue that the Silver Shields numbered 10,000 as at Raphia, but whereas Bar-Kochva broadly accepts the other figures, Grainger dismisses the skirmishers altogether, leaving Antiochus with just 45,000 men – less than he thinks the Romans fielded.[23] However, it is not necessary to deprive the Seleucids of numerical superiority to reflect their historical weakness. As I discussed on pp. 157–60, the quality of Antiochus's army left much to be desired even at Raphia, with 40 per cent of his infantry being classed as levies and none as veterans. At Magnesia, the army seems to have been even more cowed and fragile, to judge by Livy's descriptions (XXXVII.39 and 42) of Roman contempt for the enemy and of the whole Seleucid left wing giving way in panic before serious fighting had even begun. If we downgrade the class of those units accordingly, and also include just 1 elephant unit as over half the herd seems to have remained uselessly in reserve like the Roman beasts, then the army's fighting value including the skirmishers and a few thousand camp guards comes to just 61, which is 10 lower even than the value of Livy's 30,000 Romans. To see whether this shortfall is enough, we must review the historical course of the engagement.

Livy (XXXVII.39) describes the Romans forming up with the legions in the centre, the allies on either side, and the cavalry and Greek troops concentrated on the right away from the river – Kromayer and Bar-Kochva estimate their total frontage at over 3 km.[24] Livy (XXXVII.40–1) says that the Seleucids had the phalanx 32 deep in the centre with elephants in the intervals and Galatians to either side, while the wings were held by a mixture of cavalry and infantry, Antiochus himself and the Silver Shields being on the right. His claim that the mass of light infantry were on the extreme wings is very problematic – it leads Kromayer to postulate a 5 km long Seleucid line with a huge overlap on the left, while Montagu shows the phalanx opposite Eumenes rather than the legions and has both sides charging at a ridiculously oblique angle.[25] Our model instead strongly supports Bar-Kochva's argument that Polybius in fact described the light infantry forming a skirmish line in front of the heavy troops, and that the Seleucid line, though very deep, was actually not much longer than that of the Romans.[26] This suggests a scale of around 1,000 m per zone, with the new Roman camp in their rear zone, the Seleucid camp in their right rear, both sides' key zones in front of their camps, and the Romans moving first to reflect Eumenes's seizure of the initiative.

Livy (XXXVII.41–2) describes Eumenes panicking the scythed chariots and quickly routing the entire Seleucid left, while the legions forced back the phalanx despite the flat terrain. Appian (*Syr.* 35) has a longer description of the beleaguered phalanx retiring step by step under missile fire from front and flank before the elephants in the intervals went berserk and caused the troops to flee. However, on the other wing, the Romans faced a crisis. Livy (XXXVII.42–3) focuses patriotically on the defeat of the paltry 120 horse who could not maintain contact between the infantry and the river, but it is clear that at least the Italian ala and perhaps the left hand legion were defeated by frontal and flank attacks from Antiochus's stronger wing.[27] Livy goes on to laud the camp commandant Lepidus, who managed to stem the tide with his Macedonians and Thracians until the collapse elsewhere forced Antiochus to give up his pursuit. Both Livy (XXXVII.44) and Appian (*Syr.* 36) still give hugely asymmetric casualty figures of around 50,000 Seleucid dead after the seizure of the camp compared to only 350 on the Roman side, though Livy does say that many Romans were wounded.

Antiochus's initial success suggests that a margin of 10 points is perfectly adequate to reflect the balance of this engagement. The negation of Seleucid numbers by moral fragility and Roman qualitative superiority is fully in line with Livy's account and with patterns that our model has captured repeatedly elsewhere. Grainger's radical revisionism is like a specific revival of Delbrück's more pervasive scepticism that I discussed on pp. 13–14. If we take such liberties with what seem to be garbled but essentially faithful derivatives of Polybius's lost account, we really are discrediting the ancient sources to the point where modern supposition becomes a more important element of any reconstruction. It would be perfectly possible to model this battle using Grainger's alternative assumptions of a numerically inferior but qualitatively less dissimilar Seleucid army, but the resulting slogging match would bear little resemblance to the contest that the sources actually describe. Rather than assuming that we know better than the ancients themselves about the relative importance of numbers and troop quality, I prefer to explore what common patterns there are in their own claims, and

Magnesia, with consistent and fairly credible numbers for both sides, offers a very important yardstick in this regard.

MAGNESIA, 190 BC (Figure 37)

M: x6. AL: 4. Wet.

Romans: 6 VLE (Roman), 2 ALE (Allied), 2 AHI (1 Pergamene and Achaean, 1 Macedonian and Thracian), 1 VLI (Cretan and Trallian), 2 ALI (1 Roman, 1 Allied), AL + VHC (Eumenes + Pergamenes), 1 VHC (Roman), 1 AHC (Allied), AC (Scipio). FV: 71.

Seleucids: 6 APH (3 Silver Shields, 3 Settler), 1 LPH (Settler), 2 LHI (1 Cappadocian and Mercenary, 1 Galatian and Asiatic), 3 LLI (1 Cyrtian and Elymaean, 1 Trallian and Mysian, 1 Asiatic), 2 ACA (Settler), 1 LCA (Settler), AL + VHC (Antiochus + Agema), 1 AHC (Guard), 1 LHC (Galatian), 1 ALC (Dahae and Tarentine), 1 IEL (Cretan LI), 1 SCH. FV: 61.

PYDNA, 168 BC

As at Cynoscephalae, the decisive battle of the Third Macedonian War came only after 3 years of cautious campaigning. Polybius's account has once more been lost, as have two leaves of the manuscript of Livy, so we are reliant on Livy's 1,200 or so surviving words (XLIV.40–2) as well as an unusually lengthy battle piece by Plutarch (*Aem.* 16–22) totalling around twice that. Both seem to derive partly from Polybius (who became a Roman hostage after this engagement), though Plutarch (*Aem.* 18–19) also refers to the eyewitness testimony of Scipio Nasica and to a contemporary history of Perseus by Posidonius.[28] Plutarch (*Aem.* 16 and 20–1) describes the battlefield as a plain crossed by the Aeson and Leucus streams, with the Romans withdrawing towards Mount Olocrus when the phalanx attacked. Livy (XLIV.40–2) claims that the fighting started on the Roman right between detachments on opposite banks of a knee-deep stream nearer to Perseus's camp, and he says that many Macedonian fugitives were later trapped against the coast. Existing reconstructions of the engagement show conventional battle lines, but the sources' frequent references to troops leaving camp to reinforce an unplanned clash, and their neglect of developments elsewhere than in the Roman centre and right centre, fit more with the kind of escalating confrontation seen at Cynoscephalae, so it seems better to treat both armies as surprised and to place the key zones in the Roman centre and the Macedonian left centre. Those who believe that the battle lines were already formed may easily explore this interpretation by removing the surprise restriction.[29]

Kromayer, Pritchett and others have suggested that the battle was fought across the Mavroneri stream southwest of Katerini and around 20 km from Pydna (whose precise location is itself uncertain), but Hammond argued in 1984 for a radically different site much closer to Pydna, with the Romans facing south-east rather than north-east, and with two smaller streams running through the opposing battle lines to the coast nearby.[30] Both these specific suggestions are problematic, and possible changes to the coastline and watercourses since antiquity mean that the actual site will remain elusive.[31] The scenario below is based on a more generic terrain, with the battle lines running roughly north–south in accordance with Plutarch's statement (*Aem.* 17) that Aemilius waited until the afternoon before precipitating a clash so the sun would not be in his men's eyes – this fits with the overall pattern of the hills being behind the Romans and the coast behind the Macedonians.[32] The location of the streams is highly speculative, but their general course in this region is from north-west to south-east, so the scenario includes two streams with such a course, one of which fits Livy's description and also accords with Plutarch's famous reference (*Aem.* 21) to the Leucus still running red with blood when the Romans crossed it the following day.[33] Scholars do agree that the opposing camps were close together, as Plutarch (*Aem.* 18) claims that the first deaths occurred just 2 stadia (370 m) from the Roman camp after the swift Macedonian advance – Kromayer and Connolly place the camps around 2 km apart, while Hammond has only 1 km between them.[34] Hence, we should place fortified camps in both rear zones and have the Macedonians move first.

Plutarch (*Aem.* 13) says that Perseus had 4,000 horse and nearly 40,000 foot, and this tallies with Livy's more detailed breakdown from 171 BC (XLII.51) of 3,000 Macedonian and 1,000 Odrysian cavalry, around 21,000 phalangites, 5,000 'peltasts' including the 2,000 strong guard, 3,000 Paeonians and Agrianians, 3,000 Thracians, 3,000 Cretans, 2,000 Gauls, 1,000 Greeks and 1,000 Odrysian infantry.[35] However, some of Livy's troops, including 2,000 peltasts, had to be detached to guard against the Roman fleet, and Plutarch (*Aem.* 21) mentions only 3,000 peltasts at the battle itself – the shortfall was presumably made up by extra drafts of allies and mercenaries.[36] This is a far larger force than Philip V had been able to field, but there is no clear case for downgrading any of the troops to levies, so it seems best to class the peltasts as veterans and all the rest as average. Livy (XLIV.42) says that Perseus led the flight at the head of his horse guards, while Plutarch (*Aem.* 19) reports Polybius's claim that Perseus rode off to Pydna as soon as the battle began, as well as Posidonius's contrary testimony that the king joined the phalanx despite being in pain from a horse's kick the day before.[37] The truth is hard to discern from these propagandistic claims, but it seems best on balance to make Perseus a timid leader so that he facilitates the historically swift deployment of the Macedonians but will be wary of going in harm's way. Livy (XLIV.41) says that the 'anti-elephant corps' described by Zonaras (IX.22) was an utter failure, so this can be disregarded.[38] At a multiple of 6, the army thus has a fighting value of only 56.

The Roman army is harder to reconstruct, and we are even more dependent on piecing together scattered references to contingent sizes from earlier in the war. The force was built around a standard 2 legion consular army as at Cynoscephalae and Magnesia, but Livy (XLIV.21) records the legions being increased to 6,000 Roman infantry each for this campaign. Hammond suggests an army of 39,000 infantry and 4,000 cavalry, including 26,000 foot and 1,200 horse from Italy itself, whereas other scholars propose the slightly lower totals of 37–40,000 troops. The non-Italian forces seem to have included Numidians, Ligurians, Pergamenes and Greeks, and there were also some Numidian elephants that Livy (XLII.62) numbers at 22 in 171 BC.[39] With the consul Aemilius Paullus as an average commander, and the young Scipio Nasica as an uninspired cavalry leader to reflect his impetuous nature, an army of nearly 40,000 has a fighting value of 72, which gives the clear superiority warranted by the historical outcome.[40] Lendon portrays this whole engagement as the triumph of the eager *virtus* of Romans like Nasica over the more cerebral *disciplina* of Paullus, who earlier had to restrain his troops' desire for an immediate attack.[41] As discussed in Part I, our model tries to capture both of these key dimensions of ancient battle, by reflecting tactical considerations such as the relative advantages of legion and phalanx and the greater defensibility of Mount Olocrus, but by giving even greater weight to moral factors like the imperative to dominate the battlefield and like the decisive edge that Roman ferocity brought.[42]

The initial clash on the Roman right seems to have involved light covering forces – there are mentions of Thracians, Ligurians, Samnite horse, and several cohorts of Italians including the Paeligni and Marrucini.[43] Plutarch (*Aem.* 18) describes Scipio riding to the front and seeing the enemy advance, led by the Thracians, after whom came mercenaries and Paeonians, then the guard peltasts, and then the bronze shielded phalangites. The peltasts drove back the Paeligni and Marrucini, while in the centre the first legion under Aemilius himself faced the bronze shields and the second legion the white shields.[44] Kromayer and Pritchett suggest that the pikemen were 32 deep because of Frontinus's mention (*Str.* II.3.20) of a double phalanx, but Hammond thinks this referred to the earlier confrontation, and he instead proposes a 16 deep line some 1.5 km long. This is more persuasive in the light of Plutarch's remark (*Aem.* 22) about the unmanageable length of the phalanx, but both Kromayer and Hammond seem to exaggerate when they allow a further 2 km for the other Macedonian infantry – our model suggests that a scale of 1,000 m per zone is perfectly adequate.[45] Kromayer portrayed all of both sides' cavalry as being on the Macedonian right, but Hammond follows Livy (XLIV.42) who suggests that the Royal Guard and the Odrysian horse were on the right and the other Macedonian cavalry

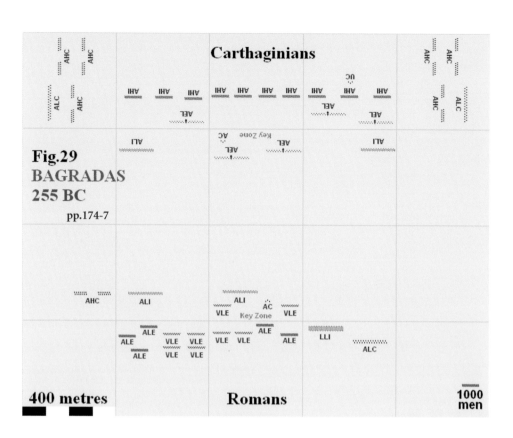

Carthaginians

AHC AHC

ALC AHC

AHI IHA IHA

IHA IHA IHA IHA

IHA IHA IHA

UC

AEL

AEL

AEL AEL

Fig.29
BAGRADAS
255 BC
pp.174-7

ALI

AC Key Zone

AEL AEL

ALI

AHC ALI

ALI AC

VLE Key Zone VLE

ALE

ALE VLE VLE

ALE VLE VLE

ALE

VLE VLE

ALE

ALE

LLI

ALC

400 metres

Romans

1000
men

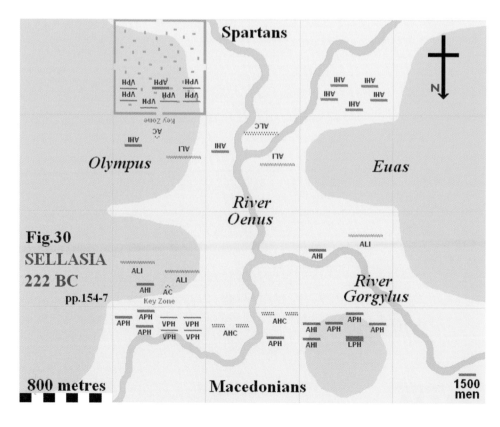

Spartans

VPH VPH VPH

VPH VPH VPH

Key Zone

AHI

AC

ALI

N

IHA IHA

IHA IHA

IHA

ALC

AHI

ALI

Olympus

Euas

River
Oenus

Fig.30
SELLASIA
222 BC
pp.154-7

ALI

AHI

ALI

AHI AC

Key Zone

ALI

AHI

River
Gorgylus

APH APH

APH APH

VPH VPH

VPH VPH

AHC

AHC

APH

AHI APH APH

AHI APH

LPH

800 metres

Macedonians

1500
men

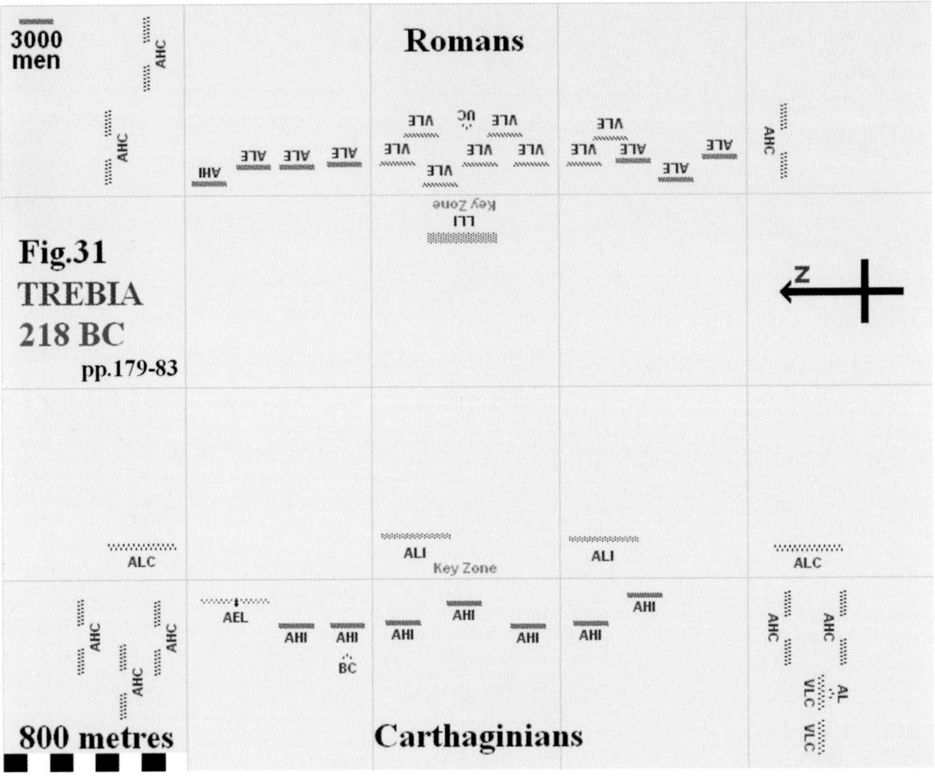

Fig.31 TREBIA 218 BC
pp.179-83

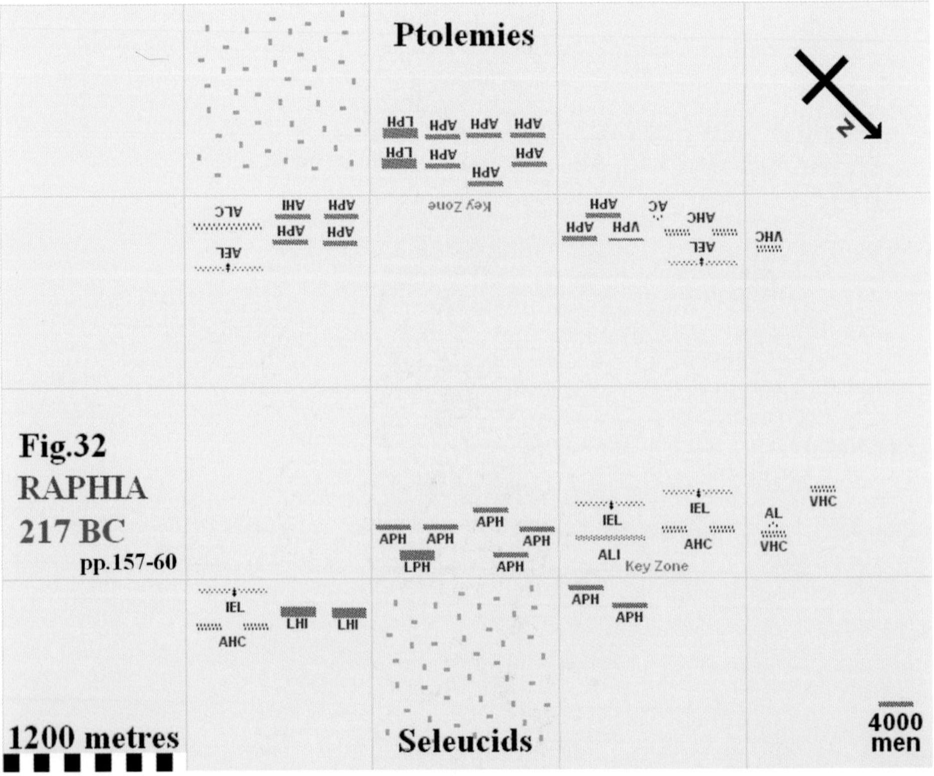

3000 men

Romans

AHC AHC AHC

AHI ALE ALE ALE VLE VLE OC VLE VLE VLE VLE ALE VLE ALE VLE AHC

LLI
Key Zone

N

ALC ALI Key Zone ALI ALC

AEL AHI AHI AHI AHI AHI AHI
BC
AHC AHC AHC AHC AHC AL VLC VLC

800 metres

Carthaginians

Fig.32 RAPHIA 217 BC
pp.157-60

Ptolemies

LPH APH APH APH
LPH APH APH
APH

ALC AHI APH APH AHC AC APH VHC
APH APH APH AHC
AEL AEL
Key Zone

N

IEL VHC
IEL
AHC AL
ALI Key Zone VHC

IEL LHI LHI APH
AHC APH

1200 metres

Seleucids

4000 men

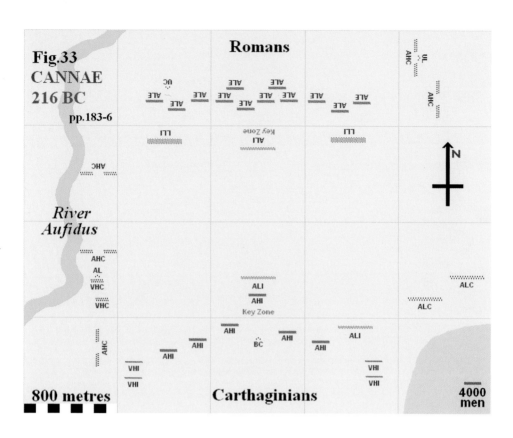

Fig.33
CANNAE
216 BC
pp.183-6

Romans

River
Aufidus

N

800 metres

Carthaginians

4000
men

Fig.34
ILIPA
206 BC
pp.186-8

Carthaginians

N

1200 metres

Romans

4000
men

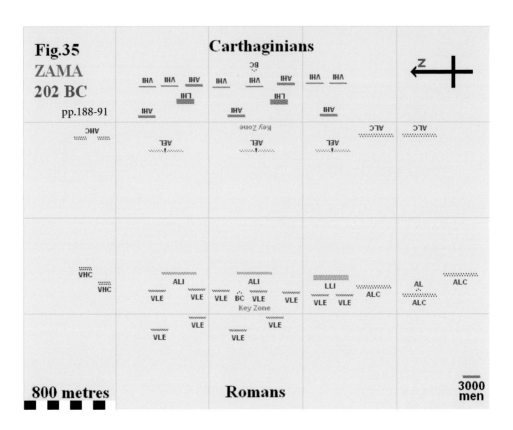

Fig.35
ZAMA
202 BC
pp.188-91

Carthaginians

Romans

800 metres

3000 men

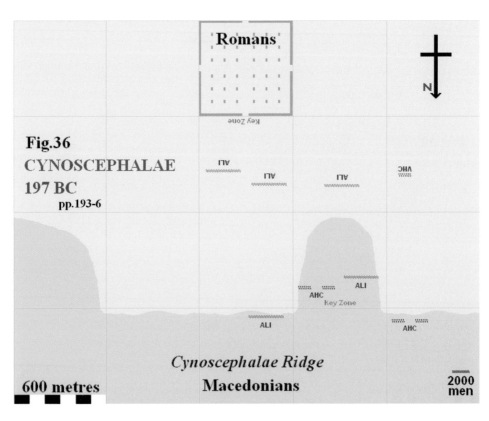

Fig.36
CYNOSCEPHALAE
197 BC
pp.193-6

Romans

Cynoscephalae Ridge

Macedonians

600 metres

2000 men

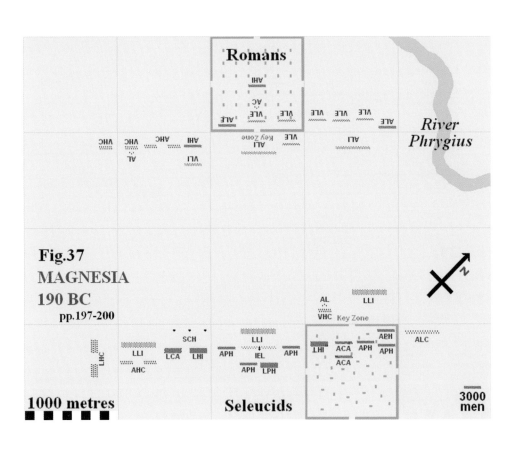

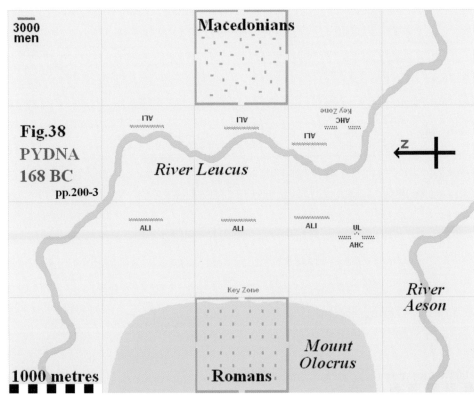

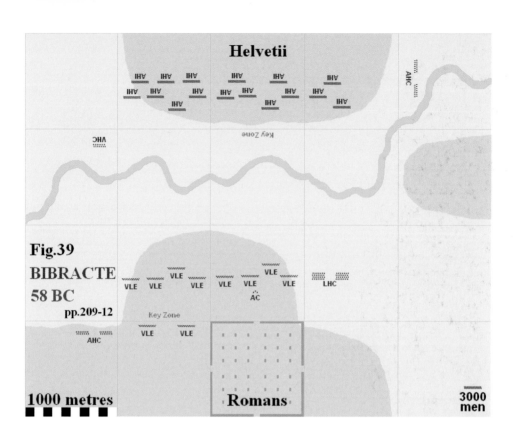

Helvetii

Key Zone

**Fig.39
BIBRACTE
58 BC**
pp.209-12

Key Zone

Romans

1000 metres

3000 men

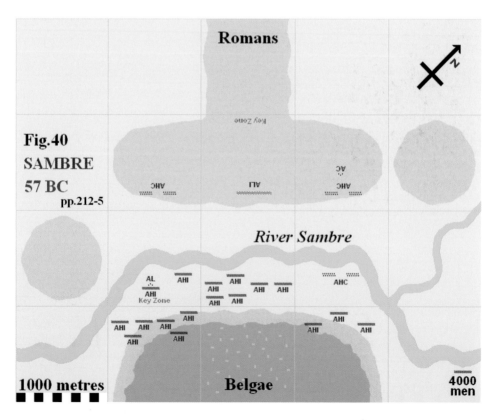

Romans

Key Zone

**Fig.40
SAMBRE
57 BC**
pp.212-5

River Sambre

Key Zone

Belgae

1000 metres

4000 men

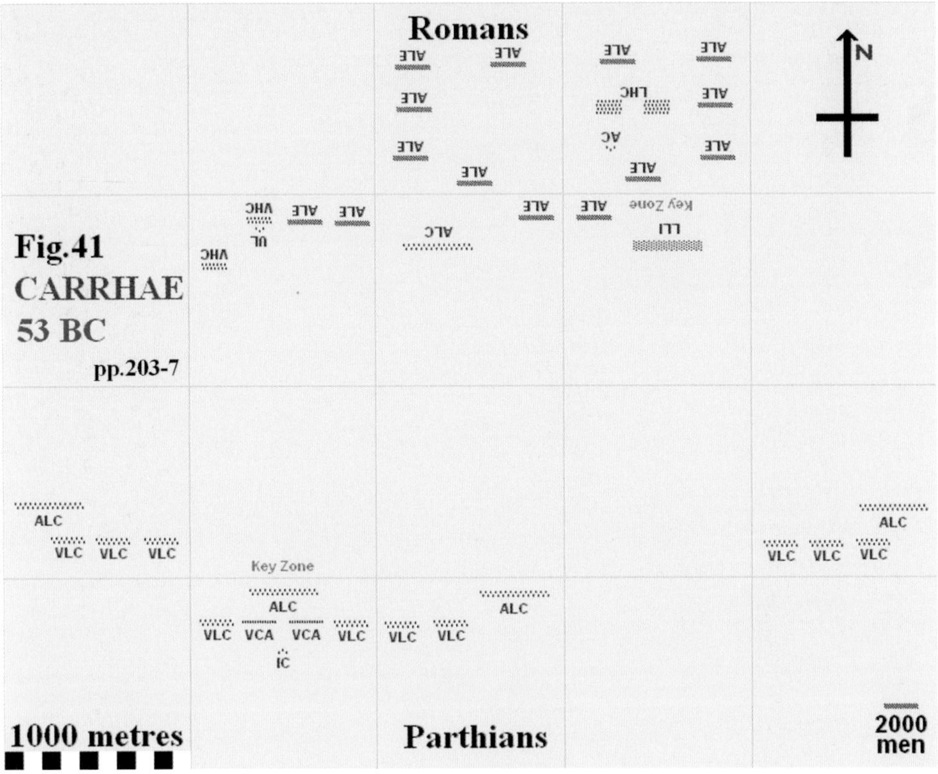

Romans

N

ALE ALE   ALE ALE
ALE   LHC ALE
ALE   AC
ALE   ALE

VHC ALE ALE   ALE ALE Key Zone
VHC   UL   ALC   LTI
LLI

Fig.41
CARRHAE
53 BC
pp.203-7

ALC   ALC
VLC VLC VLC   VLC VLC VLC

Key Zone

ALC   ALC
VLC VCA VCA VLC   VLC VLC
IC

1000 metres   **Parthians**   2000 men

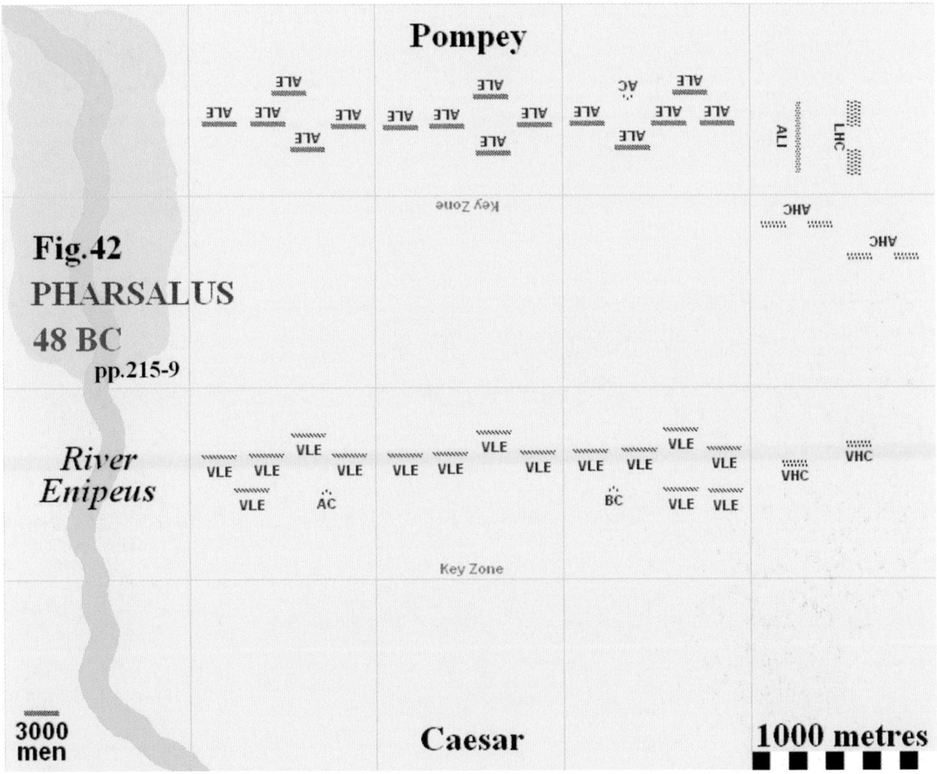

Pompey

ALE
ALE ALE ALE   ALE ALE ALE   ALE   AC   ALE
ALE   ALE ALE   ALE ALE   ALE   ALI   LHC
ALE

Key Zone   AHC
LHC   AHC

Fig.42
PHARSALUS
48 BC
pp.215-9

*River
Enipeus*

VLE   VLE
VLE VLE   VLE   VLE VLE   VLE   VLE VLE   VLE VLE   VHC
VLE   VLE   VLE AC   BC   VLE VLE   VHC

Key Zone

3000 men   **Caesar**   1000 metres

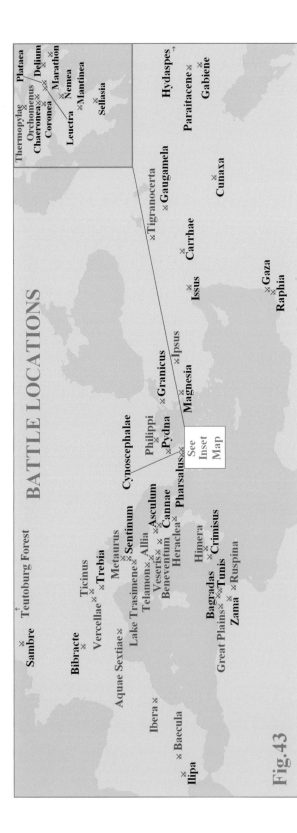

Figure 43: This map shows the approximate locations of all the 35 battles covered in Part II (the black names), as well as of the other engagements mentioned in the book (the blue names). The concentration of recorded engagements in Greece is actually even greater than the map suggests, since Chaeronea, Coronea and Mantinea all witnessed 2 or 3 different battles during this period. Appendix 3 on pp. 249–51 gives the dates of all the battles, as well as brief descriptions or page references as appropriate.

on the left, as their flight north was shielded by the infantry line.[46]

Hammond as usual emphasizes the impact of terrain on this battle, arguing that it was the tangled slopes he discovered at his preferred site that disrupted the advancing phalanx 'like a roller breaking on an uneven coast'.[47] Livy (XLIV.41) does not actually mention this factor, and even Plutarch (*Aem.* 20) touches on it only in passing – both lay much greater stress on the natural tendency of a long line to fragment as parts of it enjoy greater success than others. Our scenario already removes the phalangites' lead unit bonus due to the presence of the Leucus, and the historical Roman withdrawal in the face of the intact phalanx is as likely to be reflected abstractly by units becoming spent as it is through a physical retreat of several hundred metres onto the hill proper. Livy (XLIV.41) says that the Macedonian flight started on their (hitherto victorious) left, when the Romans committed their elephants, backed up by what may well have been both Italian alae. The peltasts stood firm and were cut down, while in the centre the legionaries carved their way into the gaps in the phalanx.[48] Plutarch (*Aem.* 22) says that the battle was decided quickly in only an hour's fighting (3 turns), which is just about feasible in our model if one starts counting when the legions and phalanx first engage.[49] Both Plutarch (*Aem.* 21) and Livy (XLIV.42) give incredibly asymmetric casualty figures – 20,000 Macedonians killed and 11,000 captured during the subsequent pursuit, compared to just 100 Roman dead (mostly from the Paeligni). Our model allows us to finesse the significant uncertainties about army composition, deployment and terrain, and to get a better feel for the dynamic process that produced this highly one-sided outcome.

PYDNA, 168 BC (Figure 38)

M: x6. AL: 4.

Macedonians: 2 VPH (Peltasts), 7 APH (3 Bronze Shields, 4 White Shields), 2 AHI (1 Thracian, 1 Gallic), 3 ALI (1 Cretan, 1 Paeonian and Agrianian, 1 Mercenary), TL + AHC (Perseus + Royal Guard), 1 AHC (Macedonian), 1 ALC (Odrysian). FV: 56. Surprised.

Romans: 6 VLE (Roman), 3 ALE (Allied), 1 AHI (Pergamene), 4 ALI (1 Roman, 1 Allied, 1 Allied and Ligurian, 1 Cretan and Achaean), UL + AHC (Scipio + Romans and Italians), 1 AHC (Pergamene and Greek), 1 ALC (Numidian), 1 AEL (Numidian LI), AC (Aemilius). FV: 72. Surprised.

CARRHAE, 53 BC

Roman dominance over Eastern adversaries was so pervasive that some states even took to creating 'imitation legionaries', as if the problem lay in equipment rather than human factors.[50] Such measures did not save Tigranes of Armenia from defeat by a greatly outnumbered Roman force led by Lucullus at Tigranocerta in 69 BC, but when Crassus invaded Parthia 16 years later, even a significant *superiority* in numbers did not save him from an insightful application of the enemy's own highly asymmetric fighting methods.[51] Plutarch (*Crass.* 20–8) is our main source, with around 4,000 words just on the crucial first day of battle, but the length is deceptive as tactical details take second place to colourful anecdotes. Cassius Dio (XL.21–4) has a much shorter and rather divergent account. Plutarch (*Crass.* 23) says that the Romans had just come to the Balissus stream (almost certainly the modern Belik), but that instead of camping there for the night as his officers urged, Crassus marched off again in pursuit of the Parthians. The only terrain feature mentioned by Plutarch during the battle itself (*Crass.* 25) is a sandy rise on which Publius's detachment vainly took refuge, but this hardly warrants representation as a hill as would the ridge on which the main army found greater (albeit temporary) security 2 days later (*Crass.* 29–31). Dio's claim (XL.21) that uneven and wooded ground allowed the enemy to hide their numbers is highly dubious, and Plutarch (*Crass.* 23) explains this instead by the Parthians massing in depth and wearing cloaks to hide the sheen of their armour. Scholars have sought the battle site somewhere between Carrhae and Ichnae, but for our purposes it should surely be just an open plain.[52]

The Roman army had by now moved from the previous militia system to a more professional and much less differentiated force. There were no more Italian allies, as Roman citizenship had been extended throughout Italy after the Social War. Velites and legionary cavalry had also disappeared with the abolition of the property qualification for service, and the maniples had been permanently merged into 10 larger cohorts per legion.[53] Plutarch (*Crass.* 20 and 23) says that Crassus began his invasion with 7 legions, nearly 4,000 horse and the same number of light infantry, but he claims that during the march to the Balissus, the army formed a square with 12 cohorts per side, which amounts to only 48 cohorts rather than the 70 one might expect. Scholars have suggested that the others may have been in reserve inside the square or may have been detached to form the 7,000 strong garrison that Crassus left in the cities of Mesopotamia, though Brunt thinks these garrisons came mainly from an additional eighth legion.[54] Estimates of the actual number of legionaries at the battle range from 28,000 to 32,000 or more – the scenario below uses the more popular lower figure.[55] Although legions of this era were in theory more professional than those of the mid-Republic, their actual quality was highly variable, and depended greatly on who was in command. Plutarch's descriptions (*Crass.* 16–23) of the ill luck and poor omens that had attended the expedition obviously owe a great deal to 20:20 hindsight, but some of the legionaries were newly recruited, and their performance compares poorly with that of Caesar's troops (many also raw) when faced by skirmishing Numidian horse at Ruspina 6 years later.[56] Their flexibility was also heavily constrained by the need to guard the baggage within the square, so it seems best to class all the legionaries as average.

The best of the cavalry were the 1,000 Gauls that Crassus's son Publius had led during Caesar's campaigns, and these surely deserve veteran status given their heroic sortie against great odds.[57] The other horsemen (probably local allies and mercenaries) were far less effective, and they should be a mixture of average and levy troops. The light infantry should in theory have been an ideal counter to the Parthian horse archers, as shown by the difference that just 800 Athenian archers made against similar Persian cavalry at Plataea.[58] However, Plutarch (*Crass.* 24) describes the light troops' dismal performance in practice, fleeing back to the shelter of the legions in the face of Parthian arrows, so they clearly deserve a levy rating. Crassus himself should probably count as an average commander (as he had eventually managed to defeat Spartacus's slave revolt 2 decades earlier), and Publius should be an uninspired leader of the Gauls (as a higher rating would make it too dangerous to risk him as happened historically).[59] At a multiple of 4, this gives the Roman army a fighting value of 80 (though the differential value of average legionaries reduces this by a few points in reality).

The Parthians were led by a noble called the Surena (more a title than a name), and all we know of the army's size is that Plutarch (*Crass.* 21) describes him as travelling with 1,000 baggage camels, 200 wagons full of concubines, 1,000 mailed horsemen and a larger number of light cavalry, with the total of horsemen, clients and slaves coming to 10,000. It is interesting that the figures are so low given the pro-Roman nature of our sources, and this battle (like Cannae and Leuctra) offers powerful evidence that the idea of small armies triumphing against the odds was not simply a victors' conceit. Some modern writers elevate the number of horse archers alone to 10,000, but it is probably better to stick with 9,000, as Plutarch's statement suggests that the figure could have been even less.[60] The armoured cavalry seem to have been cataphract lancers like those of the Seleucids, and they should surely count as veterans given the damage they did relative to their limited numbers.[61] The horse archers would normally be classed as average, but here the Surena's foresight in loading his camels with spare arrows becomes key. As discussed on pp. 44–5, a significant reason for missile troops losing their combat effectiveness over time was ammunition depletion – Plutarch (*Crass.* 25) captures this very well when he says that the Romans were quite sanguine at first until they realized that the enemy were not withdrawing as usual after emptying their quivers but instead were returning to the fray after visiting the camel train. In our broad-brush and generic model, the simplest way of capturing this increased endurance and hitting power is to make some of the horse archers veterans. If the Surena is classed as an inspired commander, then making half of the light cavalry veterans gives the Parthians a fighting value of 72. This is slightly lower than the Romans, but the first day's fighting left the main Roman force bloodied but intact, so an exhausted stand-off after 10 turns is exactly what we want to create.

Deployment details are very obscure, so diagrammatic reconstructions of this 'lost battle' are almost non-existent.[62] However, Plutarch (*Crass.* 23) does make the interesting point that, before changing his mind and forming square earlier that day, Crassus stretched his legionaries in a long thin line with cavalry at either end, to prevent outflanking. Caesar used exactly such an extended single line to good effect against the Numidian horse at Ruspina, even after being surrounded, and our model allows experimentation with this alternative approach.[63] In the event, Crassus seems instead to have used a square, commanding the centre himself while leaving Publius and Cassius in charge of the two 'wings'.[64] It has been suggested that they actually commanded separate and symmetrical 'wing columns', but the evidence is too sketchy to say.[65] Dio (XL.21) claims that Publius charged out through overeagerness, but Plutarch (*Crass.* 25) says that Crassus ordered him to do so after the Parthians threatened to surround Publius's wing. Whatever the truth, the Parthians withdrew in a classic feigned flight, and then surrounded Publius with his 1,300 cavalry, 8 cohorts and 500 archers at some distance from the main force, where they were shot down by the archers and trampled by the cataphracts despite heroic resistance by the Gauls.[66] The Parthians returned to the main Roman force with Publius's head on a lance, and continued their attacks with both arrows and cataphract charges until darkness fell. They then withdrew and camped nearby, allowing the exhausted Romans to march to Carrhae under cover of darkness, leaving behind 4,000 wounded who were massacred the next day.[67]

Our model neatly captures the virtues of a 4-zone square in protecting its occupants from the multiple penalties for having adjacent enemies to left and right or front and rear, while giving all the Romans the space to fight if engaged. However, the Parthians can launch concentrated attacks on any corner of the square from two sides at once, often getting in the first blow by galloping up from a distance, and if the Romans move their other troops out to even the odds, then the tremendous Parthian mobility advantage with well-commanded veteran light horse will probably allow those forces to be surrounded as happened to Publius.[68] The Roman cavalry will have to take the lead anyway at first because of the vulnerability of heavy infantry stacked with fresh horsemen, and Crassus will have to take the offensive to some extent to offset his marginal points superiority, so the tactical dilemmas for both sides are acute. Having the Parthians move second allows them to react to the Roman deployment, and using the maximum ground scale for these armies of 1,000 m per zone gives the Parthians the space to carry out their preferred tactics of evasion and concentration. Key zones can be placed in both sides' left centre, to avoid unrealistically privileging the centre of the board. The deployments in Figure 41 try to capture what little we know of the historical situation at the time of Publius's attack, but it is in this scenario where our dynamic model with its free deployment option really comes into its own compared to static diagrams, as it allows active experimentation with different possible tactics against a reactive opponent. The engagement's outcome in terms of casualties may have been ridiculously one-sided, but that was equally true of some more 'conventional' battles such as Pydna.[69] Horse archers were no more of an unbeatable wonder weapon than were legionaries (as the Parthians found in many later campaigns against the Romans), and our model offers some very useful insights into this famously asymmetric contest.

CARRHAE, 53 BC (Figure 41)

M: x4. AL: 5.

Romans: 14 ALE (7 Legions), 1 LLI (Archers and Slingers), UL + VHC (Publius + Gauls), 1 VHC (Gallic), 1 ALC (Mercenary), 1 LHC (Allied), AC (Crassus). FV: 80.

Parthians: 2 VCA (Cataphracts), 10 VLC (Horse Archers), 4 ALC (Horse Archers), IC (Surena). FV: 72.

14

Julius Caesar

Crassus's disastrous invasion of Parthia was an attempt to win the same kind of military glory as Julius Caesar was achieving through his conquest of Gaul. Caesar was an 'old man in a hurry', and fought many battles and sieges in the 15 years after he at last achieved senior military command at the age of 41. Three of these engagements are particularly suitable for reconstruction within our model. Caesar's campaigns in Gaul began in 58 BC, when he confronted and defeated the migrating Helvetii at Bibracte 100 km southwest of modern Dijon. The following year, he was ambushed by the Nervii and their allies while making camp on the River Sambre southwest of Maubeuge, and had to fight a desperate defensive action. His subsequent campaigns in Gaul, Germany and Britain revolved more around guerrilla resistance and sieges like those at Avaricum, Gergovia and Alesia, but in 49 BC he famously crossed the Rubicon into Italy and began open hostilities against his political enemies led by Pompey. The decisive clash came at Pharsalus in Thessaly the following year, with Pompey being routed and later assassinated when he fled to Egypt. Caesar's campaigns continued against Eastern adversaries and against the sons of Pompey in Africa and Spain, and he was about to depart on a new campaign against Parthia when he himself fell to assassins' daggers in 44 BC. This sparked off a new round of civil wars that finally destroyed the Republic and concentrated power in the hands of the first Emperor, Augustus.

BIBRACTE, 58 BC

When Caesar broke off his shadowing of the Helvetii to obtain corn supplies from the allied Gallic town of Bibracte, the tribes took this as a sign of weakness and turned to attack him. For the first time, our main source is an eyewitness account by the general himself, who describes the engagement rather sparely in around 1,000 words (*B Gall.* I.23–6). Much has been written about the potential problems of having such a self-interested observer, especially as the commentaries were published just a few years later for political effect, but it is generally felt that the first-hand perspective is preferable in this case to the uncertainties, misunderstandings and inventions too often associated with the more usual second- and third-hand accounts.[1] Caesar (*B Gall*. I.24–5) says that he formed up on a hill, with his recruits, auxiliaries and baggage on the top and his veterans in three lines halfway down, and that when the Helvetii were repulsed, they retired to a hill of their own about 1,000 paces (1.5 km) away. It is usually suggested that the Roman line faced south-west from the hill of Armecy, and that the enemy attacked and then retreated across the Auzon stream that runs into the River Arroux at Toulon 4 km to the southeast, but Goldsworthy and Le Bohec have recently disclaimed such efforts at localization in favour of a more schematic approach because the evidence is so thin.[2] As at Pydna, we too will use a more generic terrain that fits best with the known course of the battle.

Caesar (*B Gall*. I.10 and 24) had 6 legions, including 2 he had recently raised – we know their numbers (VII to XII) from his account of the Sambre the following year (*B Gall*. II.23). Goldsworthy estimates their strength at 25–30,000 men.[3] The 4 experienced legions are best classed as veterans, given their evident professionalism and staying power. However, the new legions had been ordered to entrench the camp on top of the ridge, and do not seem to have been called on to fight in the battle. This is probably best reflected by treating the Roman camp as fortified but representing the new legions by just 1 average unit each and leaving these units undeployed at first in order to get the veterans into position as quickly as possible.[4] Caesar also had an unknown number of auxiliary light infantry (also initially stationed on the hilltop), and 4,000 Gallic allied cavalry, who were not too reliable as they had recently been routed by just 500 Helvetian horse and one of their leaders was under observation for potential treachery (*B Gall*. I.15 and 18–19) – this suggests that some should be classed as levies.[5] Caesar does not say much about his own role in the battle, apart from his gesture of sending away his own horse and those of his officers to show that the commanders shared the same danger as the men (*B Gall*. I.25). This must have reduced the officers' vision and mobility, and it suggests that Caesar should be rated as only an average commander at this stage – he does not seem to have repeated the gesture in future.[6] At a multiple of 6, this gives the Roman army a fighting value of 70.

The biggest uncertainty of the battle concerns the numbers of the opposing force. Caesar (*B Gall*. I.29) claims to have found records in the enemy camp showing that the various tribes numbered 368,000 men, women and children including 92,000 able to bear arms. The proportion of combatants is broadly in line with Caesar's figure of 15,000 warriors for the Boii and Tulingi during the engagement (*B Gall*. I.25), as he listed these tribes as containing 68,000 people in all. As mentioned on p. 13, Delbrück is so dismissive of these figures that he thinks Caesar outnumbered the Helvetii by 3:1 rather than the other way around![7] Goldsworthy does not reject Caesar's overall numbers out of hand, but he does suggest that there was rough numerical parity between the armies when the Helvetii attacked.[8] Once again, our model offers a more systematic approach to this issue, based on comparative evidence from elsewhere. Caesar's description (*B Gall.* I.25–6) of the Helvetii fighting hard for many hours without ever breaking into a panic rout does not sound at all like levy troops, so (as at Sentinum) it seems best to class all the tribesmen as average, apart from 1 unit of veteran horse to represent the 500 cavalry who earlier panicked the Gallic troopers. The army should have a lower overall fighting value than Caesar's men in view of its defeat by the 4 veteran legions alone, but not so much lower a value as to make its initial uphill attack irrational. If we assume that only around 50,000 effective warriors were present, the resulting fighting value of 55 seems to give an appropriate balance between these conflicting imperatives.

Caesar (*B Gall.* I.24–6) describes the Helvetii charging forward in mass formation, brushing aside the Roman cavalry screen, but then being disrupted by a volley of pila from the waiting legionaries. Our model captures well the asymmetry of this contest, as the lead units of tribesmen will have a net combat modifier of −1 while the lead Roman units will have a net modifier of +2 including their cheaper attack bonus. After some time, the Helvetii, many of them wounded, retired to their own hill, but when the legions followed up, their right flank was threatened by the Boii and Tulingi. Some have suggested that the initial attack was a feint to draw the Romans into this ambush, but Goldsworthy follows Caesar in arguing that these tribes had only just arrived at the rear of the column.[9] The famous triplex acies now came into its own, as the legions were able to continue fighting the Helvetii with their first and second lines while wheeling their third line to form a separate front against the newcomers. (The treble movement capability of veteran legionaries is obviously useful here.) After another fierce and prolonged engagement, the Helvetii retired further up the hill while the others fell back to the wagon laager, where resistance continued until well after nightfall.

The best way of simulating this pattern of events is to limit the initial legionary front to just 2 zones, leaving the third column free for the outflanking movement and the consequent redeployment. This is probably best achieved by placing the lower slopes of the hill only in the Roman centre and left centre zones, putting their key zone in their left centre, and giving the Helvetii the first move. The Romans will thus be encouraged to rush veterans forward by double moves to get in the first blow in the defence of the hill, even at the expense of leaving some units undeployed as I discussed earlier. Scholars usually estimate the length of the Roman front at around 1.5 km, but our model suggests that 2 km is a better fit for the more open Roman formations, leading to a scale of 1,000 m per zone, and allowing the first two lines (4 units per zone) to fight effectively while the remaining 2 units are free to be moved elsewhere if required.[10] There is a case for putting the wagon laager in the Helvetian left rear zone, but this would make it less likely for that column to be neglected at first and would lead to the laager falling earlier than it did historically, so it is probably better to assume that it is just off the board edge. Caesar (*B Gall.* I.26) says that the battle lasted from the seventh hour until the evening, and our refight is indeed likely to last for most or all of the 10 half-hour turns, as the already slow pace of heavy infantry combat will be further retarded by the hills and by the crowding of units. The tribes' losses were massive, but Caesar's troops were unable to pursue, and had to halt for 3 days to tend their own wounded and bury the dead (*B Gall.* I.26). Our model casts some useful comparative light on this engagement, and suggests that Caesar's figures for the enemy do indeed seem to be inflated, but not by anything like as much as some scholars have alleged.

BIBRACTE, 58 BC (Figure 39)

M: x6. AL: 4.

Helvetii: 16 AHI (11 Helvetii, 2 Tulingi, 1 Boii, 1 Latobrigi, 1 Rauraci), 1 VHC (Helvetii), 1 AHC (Helvetii and Allies). FV: 55.

Romans: 12 VLE (VII, VIII, IX and X Legions), 2 ALE (XI and XII Legions), 1 ALI (Cretan, Balearic and Numidian), 1 AHC (Gallic), 1 LHC (Gallic), 1 AC (Caesar). FV: 70. (2 VLE, 2 ALE and 1 ALI undeployed.)

SAMBRE, 57 BC

Caesar displayed great generalship the following year when he held off a massive combined army of Belgic tribes at the River Aisne until it dispersed through lack of supply, but as he marched around subduing each of the tribal territories individually, he blundered into an ambush by the Nervii and their allies on the River Sambre. At around 2,500 words, Caesar's account of the action (*B Gall.* II. 16–28) is much fuller than for Bibracte, and is among the most important eyewitness battle narratives of the ancient world.[11] It is widely agreed that the engagement took place near Neuf-Mesnil southwest of Maubeuge, based on Caesar's description of his camp site (*B Gall.* II.18 and 27) as on a hill sloping evenly down to the broad, high-banked and waist-deep river, with a similar slope on the far bank rising into extensive woods after 200 paces (300 m).[12] The scenario in Figure 40 is based on this specific site, though certainty is obviously impossible. Caesar (*B Gall.* II.17 and 22) describes the hillside as being partitioned by thick hedges that limited visibility and impeded cavalry, but hills in our system are already a major obstacle to horsemen, and as I said on p. 34, it is impractical to reflect such smaller scale terrain features directly within our broad-brush model. One of the greatest mysteries of this battle is why Caesar did not carry out more active scouting or take the standard precaution (as at Pydna and in his own confrontation with Ariovistus) of keeping part of his army in battle line to protect those working on the camp, especially as the Romans had long associated woods with Celtic ambushes, and because Caesar actually tells us (*B Gall.* II.16) that he had learnt when he was 10 miles away that the Nervii and their allies were waiting on the other side of the river![13] He did change his march formation so that the veteran legions were all at the front rather than having each one accompanied by its own baggage (*B Gall.* II.17 and 19), but when the head of the baggage train finally appeared and the Gauls attacked, the troops were scattered widely across the hillside preparing the fortifications, a degree of confusion best simulated in our model by treating the Roman army as surprised.[14]

Caesar had much the same army as at Bibracte, but with the XI and XII legions now more experienced and with 2 further newly recruited legions (perhaps the XIII and XIV) bringing up the rear of the column, behind the baggage train.[15] Goldsworthy estimates the army's strength as 30–40,000 legionaries, supported by several thousand cavalry and as many light troops, which Caesar (*B Gall.* II.7) says included Numidians, Cretan archers and Balearic slingers.[16] The XI and XII legions were perhaps not quite yet as good as the others, as Caesar (*B Gall.* II.25) records the men of the XII huddling too closely together and starting to slip away in the face of prolonged attack, so it is worth representing these legions as a mixture of veteran and average units. Conversely, Caesar's favoured X legion made a significant contribution to success, a factor best represented by including as an average commander his lieutenant Labienus, who directed the legion while Caesar was on the other wing (*B Gall.* II.23 and 26). Unlike at Bibracte, Caesar (*B Gall.* II.20–6) portrays himself as playing a major role in directing and motivating his men (especially the beleaguered XII), so he should now be upgraded to an inspired commander. At a multiple of 8, this gives an army of around 42,000 men a fighting value of 83. The central key zone itself in this case represents the uncompleted camp, though it does not count as a camp for the purposes of the model.

In the earlier confrontation at the Aisne, Caesar (*B Gall.* II.4) gave the fighting strength of the relevant Belgic tribes as 50,000 for the Nervii, 15,000 for the Atrebates and less than 10,000 for the Viromandui, and he later says (*B Gall.* II.28) that the Nervii had 60,000 warriors in all. This raises the serious problem that, at the Sambre, Caesar (*B Gall.* II.23) portrays each tribe as facing 2 legions, despite the huge asymmetry in numbers between them. This would certainly help to explain why the Atrebates and Viromandui were so much more easily repulsed, but our model suggests that there cannot have been such a neat equivalence in frontage, and that the Nervii must have occupied around half the total battlefront, as shown in the reconstruction by Rice Holmes.[17] As at Bibracte, Caesar (*B Gall.* II.27) portrays the Nervii as fighting stubbornly to the bitter end, while even the many fewer Atrebates and Viromandui conducted a fighting retreat rather than routing altogether, so there is no case for making any of the tribesmen levies. Caesar (*B Gall*. II.17, 19 and 23) says that the tribes did have some horsemen but very few, and it is worth including their chief, Boduognatus, as an average leader given the guile and energy that the Belgae displayed. Goldsworthy guesses that the Gauls had at least parity of numbers and probably a significant advantage, though not as much as double Caesar's strength, while Delbrück characteristically suggests that it was the Romans who outnumbered the Belgae by 2:1.[18] In our model, around 70,000 Gauls have a fighting value of 60, which is low enough that they are likely to lose in the end despite the initial surprise, and suggests that, in this case, Caesar's figures are entirely credible. The key zone should be in the left centre where the Nervii themselves attacked (though, as at Issus, this matters less in river zones). The Gallic camp was in the woods, and if we make this unfortified, the boost that it gives to deployment will mirror Caesar's remarks (*B Gall*. II.19) about the amazing speed of the Belgic advance.

The charging Gauls brushed aside Caesar's cavalry and light troops that had been skirmishing with the few Belgic horsemen on the far side of the river, and raced up the hill as the legionaries quickly fell in under the nearest standard. The disjointed 6 legion line is usually shown as stretching for around 3 km, which is exactly what our model would predict, and which corresponds to a scale of 1,000 m per zone.[19] On the Roman left, the fully veteran IX and X legions soon gained the advantage over the breathless Atrebates, and followed up as they pulled back across the river and into the wood. In the centre, the VIII and XI legions similarly pushed the Viromandui back to the river, but in so doing they allowed some of the Nervii to get round their right flank and penetrate the camp site itself, spreading panic among the light troops and camp followers (*B Gall*. II.23–4). In our broad-brush model, these differential fortunes are simulated more abstractly by a bitter overall contest between the 2 centre zones. On the Roman right, the VII and XII legions were very hard-pressed by the deep mass of Nervii, and it took Caesar's personal intervention to save them from being overwhelmed. He says (*B Gall*. II.25–6) that the enemy were outflanking the legions on both sides, and our model does indeed allow some of the Belgic infantry to try to move physically into the Roman right flank zone to make their numbers felt, but the cost in time and commands is prohibitive, and it is better to pursue a more localized flanking movement, represented abstractly in our model through the use of commands to provide attack bonuses.

What saved Caesar's wing in the end is that Labienus seized the Belgic camp and sent the X legion hurrying back to help, as well as that the two newly recruited legions finally arrived from the back of the marching column (*B Gall*. II.26–7). Our model clearly shows how capturing the camp would allow the Nervii to be taken in the rear, and it also allows the new legions to arrive on turn 5 and attack on turn 6, having marched from up to 10 km away.[20] Caesar's claim (*B Gall*. II.28) that only 500 Nervii warriors survived out of 60,000 is patently exaggerated, but his own losses had clearly been significant, as indicated by his admission (*B Gall*. II.25) that almost all the centurions of the XII legion had been wounded or killed. Our dynamic model comes into its own in this battle in capturing the conflicting grand tactical pressures of time and terrain. It would normally have been utterly irrational for an inferior army like the Belgae to attack rather than defend when mutual hill positions like those at Bibracte were compounded by an intervening river as at Issus, but in this case the need to capitalize on the temporary Roman disorganization overrode normal tactical wisdom. Both sides face very difficult choices as the contest proceeds – the Belgae over when to pull their right and perhaps even their centre back to the more defensible woods as Roman fighting capability recovers, and the Romans over which parts of the line to reinforce first and how to balance direct defence against counter-attack and envelopment. Nothing could better illustrate the value of our model as a dynamic articulation of the real tactical dilemmas facing the ancient forces.

SAMBRE, 57 BC (Figure 40)

M: x8. AL: 4.

Romans: 11 VLE (VII, VIII, IX, X, XI Legions), 3 ALE (XII, XIII, XIV Legions), 1 ALI (Cretan, Balearic and Numidian), 2 AHC (Gallic), IC (Caesar), AC (Labienus). FV: 83. Surprised.

Belgae: AL + AHI (Boduognatus + Nervii), 16 AHI (11 Nervii, 3 Atrebates, 2 Viromandui), 1 AHC (Belgae). FV: 60.

PHARSALUS, 48 BC

Pompey's triumph in the engineering contest at Dyrrachium had left Caesar on the back foot and short of supplies, but when the two armies confronted one another again at Pharsalus, Pompey's officers and allies persuaded him against his better judgement to complete his victory by accepting Caesar's offer of open battle. Caesar's own 2,000-word account (*B Civ*. III.85–95) is once more our main source, but we also have other descriptions that offer some alternative perspectives, notably the short accounts by Plutarch (*Caes*. 40–6, *Pomp*. 67–72 and *Brut*. 4–6) and over 4,000 words by Appian (*B Civ*. II.65–82), which also draw on other sources including the eyewitness Asinius Pollio.[21] As mentioned on p. 7, a major preoccupation of scholars over the past century and more has been trying to identify the precise battlefield, with many different locations being proposed on either side of a 20 km stretch of the River Enipeus, and no consensus being in sight.[22] Our model cannot hope to resolve this vexed debate, but fortunately it does not really need to. The only terrain feature that played any role in the battle itself was the river, on which rested Pompey's right and Caesar's left flank.[23] Caesar (*B Civ*. III.85) does say that Pompey's camp was on a hill and that he at first deployed his line on the lower slopes, but it was only when he advanced further away from the camp that Caesar decided to engage. The various reconstructions differ significantly over the distance and direction of the hill and camp from the eventual Pompeian line, but for our purposes, all that matters is that these can be considered to lie somewhere just behind the Pompeian board edge.[24] Similarly, several reconstructions have hills on the opposite edge of the battlefield from the river, but there is no suggestion that they impinged on the extensive cavalry operations on that flank, and they mainly affect the overall army frontage that I will discuss shortly. Appian (*B Civ*. II.65) says that the two camps were 30 stadia (5.5 km) apart, so Caesar's camp too can be considered to lie behind his board edge.

Caesar (*B Civ*. III.84 and 89) says that he fielded 80 legionary cohorts totalling just 22,000 men because of earlier losses and attrition, and that he also had 1,000 Gallic cavalry. Appian (*B Civ*. II.70) repeats these numbers and adds a force of Aetolian and Acarnanian light infantry, but says that some writers gave Caesar either one third or two-fifths of a total of 60,000 or 70,000 Italian infantry engaged. Eutropius (VI.20) and Orosius (VI.15) put Caesar's army at 1,000 horse and less than 30,000 foot. Delbrück preferred these higher estimates, but most scholars reject them in favour of Caesar's own figures.[25] The legions seem all to have been highly experienced, and their performance certainly warrants a veteran classification.[26] Caesar also claims (*B Civ*. 84) that his 1,000 cavalry were able to get the better of the 7,000 Pompeian horse in earlier skirmishes, with the assistance of picked light-armed legionaries. He does not mention such integrated support at the battle itself, nor does he say anything about the Greek light troops ascribed to him by Appian, but his cavalry clearly deserve veteran status, and the number of units should be rounded up rather than down to account for the possibility of some accompanying infantry as Frontinus (*Str*. II.3.22) claims. Caesar's famous stratagem of detaching several legionary cohorts to surprise the Pompeian horse warrants his own classification as a brilliant commander, and Mark Antony can also be included as an average commander on the left wing (Labienus having defected to Pompey). At a multiple of 6, this gives Caesar's army a fighting value of 92.

Besides his 7,000 cavalry, Pompey is said by Caesar (*B Civ*. III.88) to have fielded 110 cohorts containing 45,000 men and 2,000 recalled veterans, as well as a contingent of archers and slingers. Appian (*B Civ*. II.70) and Plutarch (*Caes*. 42) broadly agree, while Eutropius (VI.20) and Orosius (VI.15) reduce the total to 88 cohorts with 40,000 foot, and just 1,100 horse. The figure of 88 cohorts surely comes from reducing Caesar's figure of 110 by the 15 cohorts that Plutarch (*Cat. Min.* 55) says were left at Dyrrachium and the 7 that Caesar himself (*B Civ.* III.88) says were guarding the camp – the issue is whether these cohorts were part of the 11 legions or in addition to them (perhaps including non-Italian troops). Delbrück thinks that Pompey fielded only 40,000 legionaries and 3,000 cavalry (compared to the 2,000 horse he suggests Caesar really had), while Brunt suggests 38,000 legionaries, and Greenhalgh goes for 5,500 cavalry and around 15,000 auxiliaries but less than 36,000 legionaries.[27] Most writers prefer Caesar's figures, though they do often express some reservations about the figure of 45,000.[28]

As usual, our model can best shed light on this issue through a comparison of overall fighting values. Caesar (*B Civ.* III.4) earlier says that Pompey's 7,000 horse included 900 Galatians, 500 Cappadocians, 500 Thracians, 200 Macedonians, 500 Gauls and Germans, 800 slaves and herdsmen, 200 Syrians, and others from Illyria, Macedonia, Thessaly and elsewhere, and that his skirmishers consisted of 3,000 archers and 1,200 slingers. We should model these contingents as a mixture of average and levy troops to reflect their historical fragility while still allowing them to beat Caesar's unsupported horse. Command was a key weakness of the Pompeian army, as Labienus badly mishandled the left wing and Pompey was a shadow of his former self, retiring disconsolately to the camp rather than trying to reverse his men's defeat.[29] This suggests that he should be classed as only an average commander, with no effective subordinate. The legions were a mixed bag, including some veterans from Spain, Cilicia and elsewhere, but many more new recruits who had served for only a year, and 2 legions that had previously fought for Caesar in Gaul.[30] Caesar also said (*B Civ.* III.4) that the legions included as 'supplements' large numbers of Greeks, who are perhaps even included within his total of 45,000. If we class all the legions as average because of this qualitative shortfall, then Caesar's figures produce a fighting value of 77 for the Pompeian army, which is low enough to reflect its historical inferiority when one also takes into account the differential value of average legionaries. If any of the better legions are classed as veterans like Caesar's men, then it will require a significant offsetting cut in troop numbers to avoid giving Pompey an unrealistically high chance of outright victory. (This is yet another good example of the trade-off between quality and quantity that I outlined on p. 15 as a key means of addressing the frequent uncertainties about numbers alone.)

Caesar (*B Civ.* III. 86–8) says that Pompey put all his cavalry and skirmishers on his left flank for what he hoped would be a decisive outflanking movement. Frontinus (*Str.* II.3.22) claims that Pompey put 600 horse on the opposite wing by the Enipeus but that Caesar relied on the marshy ground to secure his left flank.[31] Plutarch (*Brut.* 4 and 6) also refers to marshes somewhere near Pompey's camp, so it is probably worth making 2 of the river zones marshy to deter Pompey from placing serious cavalry forces there, as Hannibal did along the Aufidus at Cannae. Both sides deployed their legions in the usual three lines, and Frontinus says that each of Pompey's lines was 10 deep. Despite this specific information, modern estimates of the army frontage still differ widely because of varying assumptions about the spacing of the legionaries and the gaps between cohorts (as well as about the number of Pompeian troops). Some reconstructions make the lines less than 2 km long to fit into a narrow gap between river and hills at the most easterly suggested site, while Veith has the legions alone taking up 3.6 km, leaving a ridiculously short 400 m for the cavalry if the line is to fit into the 4 km between the river and Pharsalus.[32] Morgan suggests 3.3 km for the legions in his own site north of the river, but the popular site near Mount Dogandzis allows less room than this for the entire lines.[33] In our model, the choice is really between a constrained 800 m per zone and a more accommodating 1,000 m per zone – the scenario opts for the latter, but users may easily experiment with the former by reducing the attack limit from 4 to 3 (and also putting a hill in the Roman right wing zone to represent the protruding Kaloyiros feature if testing the Mount Dogandzis site). The sources are confused over whether Pompey commanded his right or left wing, but most scholars follow Caesar (*B.Civ.* III.88–9) and believe the latter.[34]

Pompey's cavalry charged and drove back Caesar's heavily outnumbered horse, but they were suddenly confronted and routed by the cohorts Caesar had withdrawn from his third line to counter them. Appian (*B Civ.* II.76) and Plutarch (*Pomp.* 71) put this force at 3,000 legionaries, which has caused some debate over the number of cohorts and their average strength, but the principle is clear enough.[35] Meanwhile, the infantry lines met, and Pompey's ruse of telling his men not to charge fell flat when the Caesarians halted to redress their own ranks and then charged home themselves. Caesar's turn reversal capability in our model allows a good simulation of these events, as his men can attack from the 2 leftmost zones on turn 2 with multiple attack bonuses while Caesar uses his command exemption to shift 2 legionary units into his right flank zone using treble movement, after which on turn 3 every unit in the two rightmost zones can attack straight away with multiple bonuses using the new set of commands. Once the cavalry and light troops had been shattered, it was actually Pompey's legions that found themselves outflanked, and when Caesar sent in the fresh troops of his third line in addition to the onslaught from the rear, the Pompeians fled. Caesar (*B Civ.* 99) claims that 15,000 of the enemy were killed and 24,000 surrendered, while he lost just 200 troops and 30 centurions. Appian (*B Civ.* II.82) says that some writers increased Caesar's loss to 1,200, and that Asinius Pollio put the Pompeian dead at only 6,000. Whatever the truth, this battle gives the clearest possible illustration of how better troops and commanders could overcome greatly superior numbers of identically equipped and organized adversaries. The engagement vindicates the overwhelming focus of our model on quality and on human factors, and this aspect of the battle gives far more useful wider insights than are ever likely to arise from the intriguing but inconclusive scholarly debate over the precise location of the battlefield.

PHARSALUS, 48 BC (Figure 42)

M: x6. AL: 4.

Pompey: 15 ALE (110 Cohorts), 1 ALI (Archers and Slingers), 2 AHC (1 Gallic, Galatian and German, 1 Cappadocian, Thracian and Slave), 1 LHC (Macedonian, Thessalian, Illyrian and Syrian), AC (Pompey). FV: 77.

Caesar: 15 VLE (80 Cohorts), 2 VHC (Gallic), BC (Caesar), AC (Antony). FV: 92.

Conclusion

As I have shown in Part II, one major contribution that this volume makes to our understanding of ancient battle is to cast new light on long-running scholarly controversies such as those over the size of the Spartan army, the details of Alexander's engagements, the shadowy evolution of the Roman army into the sophisticated military system that Polybius describes in the second century BC and the veracity of Caesar's numerical claims. Even the mere construction of the various scenarios throws up many important insights, but when one actually refights the engagements and considers alternative tactical options to those pursued historically, a whole new set of questions and ideas is generated, as illustrated in Chapter 6 with regard to the Battle of Cannae. However, these are all the detailed fruits of a much more fundamental contribution of this volume, namely to give a better sense of the grand tactical dynamics of ancient battle as a generic phenomenon, and of how factors such as terrain, numbers, troop types, troop quality and generalship interacted to shape the course and outcome of the many different engagements. I will close by summarizing in more traditional qualitative terms the key features of the model, which essentially involve the complex and multidimensional interrelationship of four constituent elements – force, space, time and command.

FORCE

Victory in ancient battle did not go to the 'big battalions', as the processes of combat were very different to the mutually devastating firepower duels of the nineteenth and early twentieth centuries. Fatalities from missile fire or *mêlée* seem to have been remarkably light until one force turned tail and exposed itself to one-sided slaughter. When victorious armies did suffer significant losses, these were usually concentrated in parts of their force that had given way before the eventual triumph. Hence, raw numbers were much less important than fighting spirit and a fearsome reputation, as good troops could stand firm even against great odds and could sometimes panic less-resolute adversaries into flight even before physical combat was joined. By far the most important variable in the model is troop quality, to reflect this psychological factor and also to show

how good troops like Spartan hoplites and Roman legionaries could use their superiority in drill and discipline to achieve tactical advantage.

The interaction of different troop types was a less significant but still an important variable. Each form of armament had its own strengths and weaknesses, and even the eventual dominance of the legionary system owed as much to Roman manpower reserves and to the quality of the troops themselves as it did to inherent tactical superiority. Cavalry were able to increase greatly the losses of a broken opponent by riding down fugitives or cutting off their retreat, but it was almost always one's own infantry that had to play the major role in breaking the enemy foot in the first place. Although combat did not involve heavy mutual fatalities, it does seem to have revolved around shorter-term attritional mechanisms such as wounds, exhaustion, psychological strain and ammunition depletion, so the distinction between fresh troops and those who have become 'spent' becomes a key means of tracking the progressive loss of resilience.

SPACE

Ancient armies faced a perennial tension between breadth and depth of deployment to avoid the twin perils of penetration and encirclement. However, even small armies used many more ranks than would allow the men at the back to fight directly, and depths increased greatly in larger forces. This was a key reason why raw numbers were less important than other factors, and it also meant that battle line frontages did not vary anything like as much as the size of armies themselves. There were some cases in which one or both sides were caught by surprise and deployed their forces piecemeal, but most big ancient engagements involved the prior arraying of the opposing lines in a remarkably formalized fashion. The standard battle array placed the heavy infantry in the centre, with light infantry and perhaps elephants in front, and cavalry on the flanks. Each army would usually attack with some parts of its line, while resisting enemy superiority elsewhere. Offensive elements that achieved a breakthrough might turn against the flank or rear of other enemy contingents. Defensive sections of the line might be held back in an oblique order to delay combat, or they might retire in the face of enemy pressure in order to trade space for time and perhaps draw the enemy forward into an encirclement. Greek and Hellenistic armies tended to attack on one flank and defend on the other (producing either a head-on clash or a 'revolving door' engagement), while Roman and Punic deployments tended to involve a more even balance between the two wings, leading to more symmetrical double envelopments by the side with cavalry superiority.

Most battles were fought on relatively flat and open plains, with terrain used (if at all) only to shield one's flanks. This is partly because of the unwieldiness of the formations involved, and partly because the enemy could always choose not to attack a strong defensive position, so battles tended to occur mostly by mutual consent when both sides were willing to fight in the open. On the battlefield, defensive features like river lines could be a double-edged sword, as the enemy could focus his attack wherever he chose, and you would have to attack across the river yourself to exploit his weakness elsewhere. Adopting too cautious and defensive an approach could also shift the psychological balance between the armies, and so prove counter-productive in terms of overall combat effectiveness. Without this moral pressure to come down onto the plain or move away from the safety of one's camp and take the risk of engaging on equal terms, many confrontations would have ended in indecisive stand-offs, given the enormously high stakes involved when the losing army was likely to be completely shattered and have its troops massacred in the pursuit.

TIME

Time is the most neglected dimension in existing battle reconstructions, focusing as they do on static diagrams of force dispositions. Our more dynamic model shows that time was just as important as force and space in shaping the battles concerned. The great majority of the engagements involved some form of 'race against time', be it a surprised army rushing up reinforcements before the forward troops were overwhelmed, an army in a 'revolving door' battle striving to break through and roll up the enemy line before its opponents did the same, or a Roman or Punic army trying to win the infantry contest before the enemy cavalry encirclement took effect. Deployment may have taken many hours, and we know that cavalry and light infantry skirmishing could continue almost indefinitely as long as the troops had a safe place of refuge where they could recover before sallying forth once again, but once both sides' heavy forces came into action, the pace of events quickened and battles could reach a decision with remarkable speed.

The 'battlefield clock' created by wide-ranging grand tactical manoeuvres gives us some idea of how long it might take for combat to be resolved. In large battles, it would obviously take longer for troops to cover the greater distances, but combat itself also seems to have lasted longer because of increased formation depth, so the two factors largely cancelled one another out. Heavy cavalry and Greek hoplite combat were usually much quicker than clashes between other troop types, and it was rare for such contests to remain undecided until other contingents intervened. Roman legionaries, by contrast, could hold out for a lot longer thanks to their stubborn resilience and their multiple line system. It was always possible for shaky or disordered troops to collapse at the first shock, but the generally longer duration of Roman infantry combat helps to explain why cavalry double envelopments became such a characteristic feature of battles during the Punic Wars.

COMMAND

Command in ancient armies was a collective as much as an individual endeavour, because the primitive communications made it hard for one man to exercise control even over the relatively short distances involved. Indeed, command limitations seem to have been a major reason why large armies formed up in greater depth, rather than trying to coordinate operations across an impractically long front. Pre-planning and delegation of authority to local subordinates were the norm, and some forces did not even have a single overall general. It was because command was so problematic that most ancient armies achieved so much less than the troops themselves were theoretically capable of, as inertia and confusion reduced movement rates and inhibited decisive attacks. This meant that asymmetries in command, which allowed one army to suffer less than its opponents from the restrictions involved, could have a major impact on fighting performance.

Perhaps paradoxically, given the difficulties for any single individual of maintaining real-time control of anything more than a small segment of the battle line, this was the golden age of 'great captains' like Alexander, Hannibal, Scipio and Caesar whose generalship was a very significant determinant of victory. The explanation seems to be that there were many other ways in which such individuals contributed to success besides their personal influence during the battle itself. Training and motivating their troops and building up capable subordinates in the months and years beforehand could significantly improve the quality of the army as a whole. Winning the intelligence contest could allow novel pre-planned deployments and manoeuvres precisely tailored to counter the enemy battle line, and seizing the initiative could panic or provoke the enemy into hurried reactions that left their army vulnerable and unprepared. The actual fighting was thus only the culmination of an overall process that stacked the odds heavily in favour of the better-commanded side.

A NEW PERSPECTIVE

When expressed in such generic qualitative terms, there is little here that is really new. What is unique about the model developed in this book is that it tries to gauge the relative weighting of the many individual factors I have just described, based on the evidence from dozens of different engagements. These relative weightings can only ever be very approximate, but bringing together numbers, troop types, troop quality and generalship within a single overall 'fighting value' gives us a whole new angle for comparative study in addition to the measures of army frontage and raw army size. Not only that, but the system allows a broad-brush recreation of the actual force-space-time-command dynamics of each contest, making traditional battle diagrams 'come to life' and generating a host of new questions and insights about the grand tactical choices made in reality. The model comes into its own as a vehicle for user experimentation with different ideas and interpretations, including through tweaks to the system itself. It should thus advance our understanding considerably more than would the expression of yet another set of individualistic personal 'hunches' about the engagements concerned. If it also happens to be quite fun to study the battles in this way, so much the better!

Appendix 1: Rules

1: THE ARMIES

1.1: UNIT TYPES AND CLASSES

Each army consists of around 20 'units'. Each unit has a particular type and class. There are 6 basic unit types, namely heavy infantry (HI), light infantry (LI), heavy cavalry (HC), light cavalry (LC), elephants (EL) and chariots (CH). There are 3 unit classes for infantry and cavalry, namely veteran (V), average (A) and levy (L). Chariot units are always considered average, but elephant units are instead categorized as African (A) or Indian (I). Certain units may consist of specific subtypes such as hoplites or legionaries, as noted in 9.1.

1.2: TROOP RATIOS

Each scenario lists a multiple (M) from 1 to 8. The rough number of actual troops represented by each unit depends on this multiple and on the unit's type and class, as follows:

- Levy infantry unit: $1,000 \times M$ foot soldiers
- Average infantry or levy cavalry unit: $500 \times M$ foot soldiers or horsemen
- Veteran infantry or average cavalry unit: $250 \times M$ foot soldiers or horsemen
- Veteran cavalry unit: $125 \times M$ horsemen
- Chariot unit: $100 \times M$ two-horse or $50 \times M$ four-horse vehicles (except as noted in 9.5)
- Elephant unit: $10 \times M$ unaccompanied beasts, or $5 \times M$ beasts with the usual guard of 50 skirmishers per elephant

1.3: GENERALS

Besides its combat units, each army will have 0, 1 or 2 named generals. Each general is rated for his ability as either uninspired (U), average (A), inspired (I) or brilliant (B). Each general is also categorized as a leader (L), who is permanently attached to a specific guard unit, or as a commander (C) who may move across the battlefield independently. Some average leaders are further categorized as timid (T).

1.4: FIGHTING VALUES

Each army has a fighting value (FV), made up of 2 points for each levy unit, 3 points for each average unit or African elephant unit (except as noted in 9.3 or 9.5), and 4 points for each veteran unit or Indian elephant unit. Each general contributes 3 points if uninspired or timid, 6 points if average, 12 points if inspired, and 18 points if brilliant.

1.5: FRESH AND SPENT STATUS

All units begin the battle fresh. When a fresh unit is hit, it becomes spent. Spent units never recover, and suffer certain combat and morale penalties, but otherwise they continue to operate normally. However, if a spent unit receives a further hit, it is 'shattered' and is immediately removed from play.

2: THE BATTLEFIELD

2.1: ZONES

The battlefield consists of a 5 × 4 array of square 'zones' similar to the squares on a chessboard, each representing an area between 300 and 1,200 m across as shown on the scenario map. Each zone is defined in terms of which army's half of the field it occupies, and what its position is in relation to that army's deployment, as shown in Figure 2. Once on the field, units occupy a specific zone at all times. All actions are on a zone-to-zone basis, and the position of units within each zone has no effect on play (except as noted in 6.4). Units may freely enter or attack into the enemy's half of the field, except as noted in 3.4. Zones never adjoin one another diagonally, and diagonal movement or attacks are not allowed. All distances are measured orthogonally, so a diagonally connected zone counts as 2 zones away.

2.2: TERRAIN

Some battlefields will contain terrain features, in the shape of hills, woods, marshes, streams, rivers, shorelines or impassable terrain such as open water. Each terrain feature occupies 1 or more specific zones, as shown on the scenario map. Streams and rivers may run diagonally between zones, without affecting the other two neighbouring zones. Towns on the board edge have no effect on play. Terrain symbology is illustrated in Figure 7. Zones may contain more than one terrain type, and the effects of each apply individually (though penalties do not double up). Units may never enter or deploy into impassable zones. Terrain affects movement as noted in 5.4, stacking as noted in 5.5, and combat as noted in 6.1, 6.3 and 6.5.

2.3: CAMPS AND KEY ZONES

Each army will have a key zone in 1 of its 3 centre zones. Some armies may have an unfortified or fortified camp in 1 of their 3 rear zones. Camp symbology is illustrated in Figure 7. Camps affect deployment as noted in 3.3 and 3.4, movement as noted in 5.4, and combat as noted in 6.1 and 6.5. Enemy occupation of key zones and camps affects undeployed units as noted in 3.4, morale as noted in 7.1 and victory points as noted in 11.2.

3: SEQUENCE OF PLAY

3.1: TURNS

Battles are refought in up to 10 successive turns. Each turn represents around 3 min for every 100 m of scale distance across each of that scenario's zones (see 2.1).

3.2: TURN SEQUENCE

Each turn consists of 2 player turns, starting with the army listed first in that scenario (except as noted in 8.9 or 10.3). In each of your player turns, you start by dicing for commands for your army. You then activate a group of 1 or more friendly units of your choice, which begin in the same zone or are all undeployed, and you use them to move and/or attack. Once a group has finished its activation, another friendly group may be activated, and so on until all desired units have been activated. You may activate your units in any order you wish. Attacks take place at the end of each group's activation, so you may move other units later to exploit the results of an attack or to reinforce units that have attacked. At the end of your player turn, you must designate a lead unit in each friendly occupied zone not already containing such a unit.

3.3: DEPLOYMENT

On turn 1, both armies start off undeployed. You may activate an undeployed unit or group of units on any turn, and then place it facing forwards in your left rear, rear or right rear zone, as shown by the solid arrows on Figure 2. This costs 1 move (even if the initial zone would normally cost 2 moves to enter). A unit or group consisting entirely of cavalry and/or chariots may instead use 1 move to deploy in your left rear zone facing left or in your right rear zone facing right, as shown by the outline arrows on Figure 2. Extra moves may be used to change facing and/or proceed further, before the next unit or group is activated. Units deployed in a camp zone need not stop as per 5.4, and those deployed in an unfortified camp zone have the cost of deployment waived, and so may use all of their moves to change facing and/or proceed further. Each scenario map contains historical first turn deployments for each side, allowing refights based more on the actual troop dispositions to begin at the start of turn 2 if you prefer.

3.4: DEPLOYMENT RESTRICTIONS

Units may deploy using double or treble movement as in 4.4 or 9.3. After turn 1, units may only deploy into their (central) rear zone facing forwards unless their army is surprised as in 10.1 (though they may use extra moves to change facing or proceed further). Units may not deploy into an enemy-occupied zone, nor may they enter the enemy half of the field or launch an attack on the turn in which they deploy. Units may deploy into a friendly occupied zone, subject to the stacking and facing constraints in 5.1 and 5.5. They must stop in such a zone, even if they have moves remaining. You may deploy as many activated units per turn as you wish, except as noted in 10.1. Similarly, you may hold units off the field for as long as you wish, but all your undeployed units and generals are treated as withdrawn or lost respectively if an enemy unit ever enters your (central) rear zone or your camp.

4: COMMANDS

4.1: ACQUIRING COMMANDS

The command flexibility of your army is represented by the expenditure of a limited stock of 'commands' for all game actions. At the start of each of your player turns, you must roll a six-sided die and add 1 to the score for every full 10 points of fighting value in your army. Shattered, routed or withdrawn units and lost or killed generals do not count, and their points must be deducted from your army's initial fighting value for this calculation. The result is the number of commands you may expend this player turn. Any commands not expended are lost, and may not be carried over to the next player turn. See also 10.1, 10.3 and 10.4.

4.2: ACTIVATION

The primary use of commands is to activate groups of units for movement and/or attacks. Not all units need be activated each turn, but each unit may be activated only once per turn. To be activated as a group, units must either all begin undeployed, or they must all begin in the same zone. They must then stay together and make exactly the same moves and facing changes, and they must all expend the moves to launch an attack if any do so (though not all of them need advance if the attack succeeds). It costs 1 command to activate a group containing 2 veteran units or a single unit of any type. It costs 2 commands to activate any larger group, though you may activate the group instead at a discount rate of 1 command, in which case it cannot move or deploy (only change facing), and only a single unit (of whatever kind) may attack or advance after combat. See also 8.3.

4.3: GROUP RESTRICTIONS

You need not include all the units in a zone in an activated group. Hence, some units in a zone could form a group and move away, leaving the rest to form separate activation groups and move or attack in different directions later that turn. However, no group may attack from a zone that also contains any friendly unit that is not part of that group. This means that, if any units enter an occupied zone, neither they nor the existing occupants may attack from that zone this turn, as they cannot form a single group. Units that are not activated may not move or attack, but one may become the lead unit in that zone at the end of your player turn (see 6.4).

4.4: MOVEMENT AND COMBAT BONUSES

At any point or points in your player turn, you may activate a single unit for double movement instead of regular movement or attacks, at a cost of 1 command for a veteran unit, or 2 commands for any other unit. The unit then has 2 moves if infantry or elephants, or 4 moves if cavalry or chariots. It otherwise follows all normal movement rules, but (very importantly) *it may not attack that turn*. Units using double movement are always activated individually, and there is no command discount even if several units make exactly the same successive double moves. Any or all elephant or non-veteran light infantry units may make double deployment moves for 1 command each rather than 2, but light infantry are not then entitled to the free turn discussed in 5.3, so may only move straight forward. An alternative use for commands is to give attack bonuses. Just before rolling the dice for a unit's attack as in 6.5, you may give a +1 attack bonus to the dice roll, at a cost of 1 command for a light cavalry unit or a lead unit of veterans or Indian elephants, or 2 commands for any other unit. See also 3.4, 8.3, 8.4, 8.5 and 9.3.

5: MOVEMENT

5.1: UNIT FACING

Units in a zone are always faced in one of four directions – straight ahead, left, right or straight back. Hence, they will always face one neighbouring zone or directly off the field. All units in the same zone must face the same way, at the end of each individual unit's or group's movement. Hence, a group may only enter or deploy into a zone containing friendly units in a different facing if it can immediately change into the same facing (see 5.5), and it may only change facing in its initial zone if it immediately moves out of that zone or if there are no other units in the zone (even if they have yet to move or change facing themselves). See also 4.2.

5.2: MOVE ALLOWANCES

On activation, each unit has 2 moves if it is a cavalry or chariot unit or 1 move if it is an infantry, elephant or cataphract unit (9.4), unless increased as in 4.4 or 9.3. Units may expend less than their maximum moves. It costs 1 move for a unit to enter or attack the zone that it is facing, except as noted in 3.3 or 5.4. A unit may change facing at any point or points in its activation (except after combat), but it must expend 1 move for each 90 or 180 degree change, except as noted in 5.3. Hence, heavy infantry may either move 1 zone forward or change facing, whereas heavy cavalry or chariots may change facing and move, move forward and change facing, or move 2 zones forward. See also 9.5.

5.3: FREE FACING CHANGES

There are three important exceptions to the turning costs in 5.2:
- Units other than hoplites (see 9.2) need not expend a move to make an about turn through 180 degrees in their initial zone if there are no enemy units in the adjacent zones to either side of the way they are facing or in or adjacent to the zone towards which they turn (if it is on the field).
- Units facing off the field or which have no enemy units in the zone they are initially facing need not expend a move to turn to face adjacent enemies before launching an attack from their initial zone.
- Light infantry may make 1 free facing change per turn (except as in 4.4), and light cavalry may make up to 2 free facing changes per turn, in addition to any free initial about turn under the first rule above.

Eligibility for free facing changes is judged at the start of the unit's activation. See also 6.1.

5.4: TERRAIN COSTS

It costs 2 moves rather than 1 for a cavalry or chariot unit to enter or attack into a hill, wood, marsh or fortified camp zone or a zone containing enemy elephants, unless that zone is the first zone of the unit's deployment as noted in 3.3, or unless the troops are cataphracts (9.4). Streams, rivers and shorelines do not affect movement costs, and no terrain affects facing changes or infantry, elephant or cataphract movement costs. However, units that enter a camp zone may not leave or attack out of that zone on the same turn, except when deploying as noted in 3.3. Note that units that deploy into an unfortified camp zone expend no moves at all to do so.

5.5: UNIT STACKING

Units may never enter an enemy-occupied zone. They may freely enter or deploy into a friendly occupied zone, but they may not then leave the zone that turn, and so they must be able to change to the same facing as the existing occupants (see 5.1). Also, there may never be more than 12 units in a zone at any time, counting levy units as 2 units each. The limit falls to 8 units in zones containing rivers, shorelines, marshes or woods, and it applies even if the existing units are about to leave. See also 6.9, 8.2, 8.8 and 9.5.

5.6: MIXED GROUPS

Units activated as a group must make exactly the same movements and facing changes, but the number of moves they possess and the costs to perform a given action are judged on an individual unit basis rather than for the group as a whole. Hence, a mixed group of heavy cavalry and light infantry could turn through 90 degrees (costing the cavalry their first move) and then move forward 1 zone (costing the cavalry their second move and the light infantry their only move). Mixed groups may never split up except through advance after combat (6.9), and so none of their constituent units may continue moving, changing facing or attacking if the cost of this would exceed the moves available to any unit in the group (even if the unit is not itself making an attack). See also 9.5.

5.7: LEAVING THE FIELD

Activated groups that are not in a shoreline zone and that are facing off any edge of the field with at least 1 move remaining for all of their units may leave the field. The units and generals involved may never return to the battle, and they count as withdrawn if they are fresh, routed if they are spent, or lost if they are generals.

6: COMBAT

6.1: COMBAT ELIGIBILITY

Groups may end their activation by attacking into the enemy-occupied zone they are facing, at a cost of 1 move (or 2 moves for non-cataphract cavalry or chariots attacking into hills, woods, marshes, fortified camps or into a zone containing enemy elephants). Any spare moves or free facing changes as in 5.3 may be used to move and/or change facing before the attack, but this incurs an attack penalty, and attacks from any of the 5 enemy flank or rear zones into any of the 3 enemy centre zones are prohibited altogether to units that change facing that turn. Mixed groups may attack only if all of their units (not just those within the attack limits in 6.3) have the necessary moves left to attack – see 5.6. Attacks may also be prohibited as noted in 3.4, 4.4, 5.4, 8.9 and 10.3. Groups may not change facing or expend any further moves after launching an attack, though victorious units may be able to advance as in 6.9.

6.2: MULTIPLE ATTACKS

Attacks may only be launched if every single unit in the zone at that instant is part of the attacking group. Hence, you should move other units away before launching the attack, and move reinforcing units into the zone only after the attack. Enemy-occupied zones may only be attacked once per turn from each adjacent zone because of this restriction, but they may be attacked later from other adjacent zones. Commanders need not be part of the attacking group (though they may be – see 8.2 and 8.4).

6.3: UNIT ATTACK LIMITS

Each unit in the attacking group makes an individual attack, up to a limit of 3, 4 or 5 units per zone as listed in the scenario. The limit is increased by 1 if the attacking group starts its attack adjacent to another enemy-occupied zone without having adjacent enemies to its left and right or front and rear. The modified attack limit is halved (rounding halves up) if both sides occupy stream, river or shoreline zones (in any combination). Except as noted in 6.8, 9.3 or 9.4, veteran heavy infantry count as half a unit each towards this limit, while non-veteran troops other than heavy infantry count as 2 units each. At the cost of an attack penalty, the last attacking unit in a group may count only half as much as normal, to allow the limit to be used up in full. In a group activated at a discount rate as in 4.2, only the single lead unit may attack.

6.4: LEAD UNITS AND ORDER OF ATTACKS

You may decide just before each unit's attack which unit will attack. You may choose the first and all subsequent attacking units freely, except as noted in 6.8 or 9.5. The first attacking unit in each zone becomes the lead unit in that zone. If the unit conducts an all-out attack (see 6.7), it loses its lead status. At the end of each friendly player turn, you must choose a lead unit for all friendly occupied zones not already containing such a unit (including all zones where the lead unit conducted an all-out attack). Units lose their lead status at the start of each friendly player turn, leaving you free to select new lead units (but see 6.8 and 9.5). Lead units receive several special combat modifiers in 6.5, but they will also be the focus of all enemy attacks on that zone, from whatever direction. If your lead unit is hit (or removed due to poor morale) in the enemy player turn, you must immediately select a new lead unit for that zone. Except as constrained by 6.8 and 9.5, you may choose freely which unit to designate as the new lead unit, including leaving the original unit in the lead if it is only spent.

6.5: ATTACK PROCEDURE AND COMBAT MODIFIERS

To attack with a unit, roll two dice, add the scores, and adjust the total according to any relevant tactical modifiers from the list in the table below. All the modifiers are cumulative, but each individual modifier is only applied once, even if multiple qualifying conditions exist. See also 9.5.

+1 for the **lead unit**, unless it is scythed chariots (9.5) or has adjacent enemies to its left and right or to its front and rear

+1 if the unit was given an **attack bonus** (4.4)

+1 for a leader's guard unit given a **second attack bonus** (8.5)

+1 for a non-levy unit attacking a **levy** unit

+1 for heavy infantry (of any kind) attacking **hoplites, phalangites or archers** (9.1 and 9.2) who are not facing the attack

'+1 for **hoplites** attacking a zone containing enemy hoplites which did not all just enter the zone on their own preceding player turn (9.2).

+1 for a lead unit of fresh **hoplites or phalangites** attacking heavy infantry, unless the phalangites have adjacent enemies they are not facing or are attacking into or from a zone containing a camp or any kind of terrain feature (9.2)

+1 for a non-lead unit of fresh average **hoplites or phalangites** attacking heavy infantry, if the attacking unit is accompanied by another fresh average unit of the same subtype that neither attacks nor supports another attack that turn (9.2)

+1 for cavalry or chariots attacking heavy infantry, if both zones are on any **board edge** or the heavy infantry are accompanied by **fresh cavalry, chariots or light infantry** or the attacking unit is in the lead and the infantry are **facing 180 degrees away**

+1 for a lead infantry unit attacking from a **hill** to a non-hill zone

+1 for any lead unit attacking from a non-river to a **river** zone

+1 for **archers** attacking light infantry or light cavalry (9.1)

−1 if the attackers **moved or changed facing** (even at no cost) before attacking (6.1)

−1 for a non-infantry unit, or a lead heavy infantry unit not in its own fortified camp, attacking into or starting its activation in a **wood, marsh, hill or fortified camp** zone

−1 for the **last attacking unit** in a group if it counts at half the normal rate towards the attack limit (6.3)

−1 for any unit attacking **cataphracts** (9.4), a lead unit of cavalry or chariots attacking **elephants**, or a lead unit of infantry attacking fresh **legionaries** (9.3), unless in any of these cases the enemy unit is not facing towards the attack

−1 for an **African elephant** unit attacking a zone containing an Indian elephant unit

−1 for a spent attacking unit in a **fatigued** army (10.2)

−1 for chariots, archers, spent light infantry or light cavalry, or the lead unit in a stream or river zone in **wet weather** (10.4)

6.6: COMBAT RESULTS

Compare the modified dice roll from 6.5 with the figure from the combat table below for that combination of attacking and lead defending units. If the modified score is less than the required total, there is no effect. If the score exceeds the required total, or if it equals the total and the attacker performs an all-out attack (6.7), the lead enemy unit receives a hit and immediately becomes spent or shattered as in 1.5. If the score exceeds the required total by 4 or more, or if it exceeds it by 3 or more and the defender is an elephant unit or the attacker performs an all-out attack, the lead enemy unit receives 2 hits and is shattered outright if it is a fresh levy unit. Any other lead unit receives a single hit and then another defending unit (or perhaps the same one if only spent) must be selected by the opponent as in 6.4 to receive the second hit, unless the zone was emptied by the first hit. See also 6.8 and 8.6.

Attacking unit	Defending unit					
	Heavy infantry	Light infantry	Heavy cavalry	Light cavalry	Elephants	Chariots
Heavy infantry	9	9	8	9	9	8
Light infantry	9	9	8	8	8	8
Heavy cavalry	9	7	7	8	9	8
Light cavalry	10	9	9	9	9	9
Elephants	8	8	7	8	8	7
Chariots	9	8	7	9	9	8

6.7: ALL-OUT ATTACKS

If the modified dice roll exactly equals or is exactly 3 more than the required total, the attacker may have the option of declaring an all-out attack to inflict an extra hit, as noted in 6.6. This is only possible if the attacking unit is fresh, and you choose to make it spent. All-out attacks must be declared before either hit is applied or any rally attempts (8.6) are made. Lead units that make an all-out attack lose their lead status, so a lead unit will have to be chosen at the end of the player turn as in 6.4. Only light infantry or light cavalry may make all-out attacks on light cavalry. See also 9.2 and 9.5.

6.8: LIGHT INFANTRY AND ELEPHANT SCREENS

A first attacking unit of elephants or fresh light infantry counts as 1 unit rather than 2 towards the attack limit, as long as it was also the lead unit at the start of the player turn. Attacks on light infantry who are accompanied by at least 1 heavy infantry unit only ever inflict 1 hit if every unit in the attacked zone is still fresh – in this case, there is no all-out attack option on a differential of +3, and differentials of +4 or more cause just 1 hit rather than two. Spent light infantry may not be selected as the lead unit as in 6.4 unless there is no other choice or unless they are facing 180 degrees away from adjacent enemies who are facing them, in which case they *must* be chosen as the lead unit. However, spent light infantry may never be used as the first attacking unit unless there is no other choice, even if they do have enemies behind, so they should not need to be placed in the lead until the original lead unit is hit.

6.9: ADVANCE AFTER COMBAT

If an attack (and any subsequent removal of units due to a morale test) leaves the attacked zone empty, any or all of the units from that attacking group (only) may be advanced into the empty zone, without changing facing, except as noted in 9.2. This is the only way a group may split up after activation. Which (if any) units to advance is entirely at the attacker's discretion, as long as they belong to the group attacking at that moment (whether or not they actually attacked). Earlier groups that attacked the same zone are not eligible to advance. If the group attacked using a discounted activation as in 4.2, only the single unit that actually attacked is eligible to advance. Morale tests always *precede* advances. Advancing units may not launch any more attacks that turn, even if they have spare moves and their own attack was pre-empted by attack limits or by the collapse of the enemy force. The lead attacking unit must remain the lead unit in whichever zone it occupies, unless it made an all-out attack.

7: MORALE

7.1: ARMY MORALE

You must take an army morale test every time one of your units is shattered and/ or one of your generals is killed. The test occurs as soon as all the hits inflicted by that enemy unit have been applied. You must then roll as many dice as there were units shattered and/or generals killed by that enemy unit, take the lowest individual score, and then halve it, rounding halves up. The cumulative modifiers shown below are now applied to the result to give the overall army morale.

+1 if there are at least twice as many friendly as enemy units currently on the field

−1 for every 4 friendly units that have been shattered (including by this attack)

−1 if at least 2 uninspired or 1 average or better friendly generals have been lost or killed (including through this attack)

−1 if there are at least twice as many enemy as friendly units currently on the field

−1 if at least 2 more friendly centre zones contain enemy units than there are enemy centre zones containing friendly units (counting non-river key zones as 2 zones each and non-key river zones as half a zone each), or if your camp has ever been occupied by the enemy (2.3)

7.2: UNIT MORALE

You must apply the following additional cumulative modifiers to the army morale to work out the morale of each individual friendly unit that might be at risk. As noted in 2.1, distances are never measured diagonally, only orthogonally.

+1 for a veteran unit, an average legionary unit (9.3), or an Indian elephant unit

+1 for a heavy infantry unit, except for hoplites adjacent to enemy hoplites (9.2)

+1 if the unit is 3 or more zones away from the zone under attack

+1 for non-elephant units if there is a brilliant or inspired friendly general in the unit's zone, or a brilliant friendly general in an adjacent zone (except as in 8.6)

−1 for a levy unit, a scythed chariot unit, or the guard of a timid general

−1 for a spent unit

−1 if the adjacent zones to the unit's front and rear and/or to its left and right are both enemy occupied

7.3: MORALE RESULTS

Once every unit's morale has been calculated, all results are applied. First, all units with a morale of −1 or less are removed permanently from the field and counted as withdrawn if they are fresh or routed if they are spent. Then, all units with a morale of 0 suffer a similar fate if they are in the same zone where a unit was just shattered due to the current enemy unit's attack, or where a unit was just removed due to the current morale test. The shattering or panic of a single light infantry unit does not cause accompanying units other than light infantry to flee if their morale is 0. If 2 or more light infantry units in a single zone are shattered and/or panic due to the same unit's attack, that does cause all accompanying units with a morale of 0 to flee. The death of a general does not in itself cause the removal of accompanying units with a morale of 0. Morale levels are not recalculated due to the flight of units or generals until a subsequent morale test. See also 9.5.

7.4: UNDEPLOYED UNITS

Undeployed units do check their morale, but the only unit modifiers that apply are +1 for veterans, average legionaries or Indian elephants, +1 for heavy infantry, and −1 for levies, scythed chariots or the guard of a timid general. Units whose morale is −1 or less are treated as having withdrawn, but units with a morale of 0 remain undeployed.

8: GENERALS

8.1: LEADERS

Generals classed as leaders are permanently attached to a specific guard unit, as noted in the scenario, and are always activated with this unit. If the unit is withdrawn, routed or shattered, they are removed from play and counted as lost. Leaders may also be killed without their guard unit being shattered, as noted in 8.6.

8.2: COMMANDERS

Commanders are either undeployed or occupy a specific zone, but they have no facing or stacking value, and never stop unit movement. They may be activated and move along with any unit or group that begins in the same zone, in which case they remain with that group throughout its movement and may advance after combat if any of the units do so. Alternatively, they may be activated independently at no command cost, and may simply be placed in any passable zone free of enemy units (without tracing a movement path), or else withdraw permanently from the field. Commanders may be activated only once per turn. They never test their morale, but they are removed from play and counted as lost if every unit in their zone becomes shattered, routed or withdrawn, or if they end their player turn in a zone with no friendly units (or with no friendly units undeployed if they are undeployed). See also 8.8.

8.3: ACTIVATION BONUSES

Generals give exemptions from the first commands needed to activate units in their initial zone (see 4.2 and 4.4), as long as the general himself has not completed his own activation. Uninspired generals give a 1 command exemption, average generals give a 2 command exemption, and inspired or brilliant generals give a 4 command exemption. These exemptions are applied to each successive activation in that zone, but when the cumulative total is exhausted, the balance must be paid from ordinary commands. If a general is undeployed, his command exemptions may be applied to undeployed units on the same basis. See also 8.8.

8.4: ATTACK BONUSES

Generals who are activated with an attacking group give exemptions from the first commands needed to provide attack bonuses to that group's units (see 4.4). As with activation, uninspired generals give a 1 command exemption, average generals give a 2 command exemption, and inspired or brilliant generals give a 4 command exemption. These exemptions are separate from and in addition to those for activation costs, so a general could activate a group as in 8.3 and still have his full allowance of exemptions to pay for attack bonuses. The exemptions apply to the first eligible attacking units, and you may not withhold them for use by later units. As noted in 6.2, commanders need not be activated as part of an attacking group, and so may move elsewhere after the attack, but in this case all attack bonuses must be paid for as normal, even if the commander has not used all his exemptions for unit activation. See also 8.8.

8.5: LEADER'S GUARD

If your leader's own guard unit is the first attacking unit in its group, you must give it 2 attack bonuses rather than 1 if you can, as long as both are covered by the exemption discussed in 8.4. Hence, a guard unit of veterans or light cavalry will receive 2 bonuses if it has an average or better leader (see 4.4), and any other guard unit will receive 2 bonuses (normally costing 4 commands) if it has an inspired or brilliant leader. If the guard unit is not in the lead, it is only eligible for a single bonus, whether or not this is covered by the leader's exemption.

8.6: LEADER RALLY ATTEMPTS

Whenever a unit other than levies, light infantry, elephants or scythed chariots is hit in the enemy player turn (not through its own all-out attack), a leader in that zone may try negate the hit by rallying the unit. If the unit is the leader's own guard, he *must* make a rally attempt if possible; otherwise the attempt is optional (except as noted in 9.2). However, timid leaders (see 1.4) may not attempt to rally any units, even their own guard. A leader succeeds in negating the hit by rolling two dice and scoring 10 or more if uninspired, 9 or more if average or inspired, or 8 or more if brilliant. However, if the score is 2 or 3, uninspired or average leaders are killed. Inspired or brilliant leaders die on a roll of 2, while on a score of 3 they have a close shave – until the end of their own next player turn, they give no command exemptions or morale bonuses, and they may make no more rally attempts (even compulsory ones) for the rest of the battle. Lead units that have a hit negated remain in their lead position, and so will suffer any second hit inflicted by that attacker (and be eligible for a second rally attempt). A unit that made an all-out attack as in 6.7 remains spent, even if the hit it inflicted is negated by rallying.

8.7: COMMANDER RALLY ATTEMPTS

Commanders may make rally attempts as in 8.6, but they are never required to do so. In addition to the normal unit prohibitions, commanders may only attempt to rally units that are already spent and at risk of being shattered. The same rules for success as in 8.6 apply, but commanders who attempt a rally always die on a roll of 2 or 3, and uninspired or average commanders also die on a roll of 4.

8.8: MULTIPLE GENERALS

Generals may never be part of the same group, and a general may never enter or be placed in a zone containing another friendly general. If both generals begin undeployed, their activation exemptions for undeployed units are combined and may even be used by the same group. However, if 2 friendly generals begin their own player turn in adjacent zones, only one of them (owner's choice) may provide activation and attack bonus exemptions that player turn.

8.9: BRILLIANT GENERALS

If you have a brilliant general, you will usually start off having the second player turn in each turn, but at the start of any turn except turn 1, you may declare that this order will be reversed on that and all subsequent turns. This will allow you to have 2 player turns in immediate succession. You must make your announcement before any weather or command die rolls for that turn. A reversal cannot take place if *both* armies began the battle with a brilliant general, or if your brilliant general has been lost or killed before your announcement, or in dry and dusty conditions (see 10.3). You may not launch any attacks in the second player turn from any zones from which you attacked in the first player turn. Note that individual units *may* be able to attack in both player turns, as long as they do so from different zones (for example, following an advance after combat).

9: SPECIAL UNIT TYPES

9.1: SUBTYPES AVAILABLE

The scenarios may designate certain units as containing particular subtypes of troops. Within heavy infantry, these subtypes are archers (AR), hoplites (HO), phalangites (PH) and legionaries (LE). In addition, heavy cavalry may be cataphracts (CA), and chariots may be scythed chariots (SCH). The codes shown replace the normal codes, but the units still count as HI, HC or CH for all purposes. Each subtype has one or more special combat modifiers in 6.5 in addition to the normal modifiers they receive for being HI, HC or CH, but there are also other special rules below for all except archers and phalangites.

9.2: HOPLITES

Hoplites must always opt for all-out attacks as in 6.7 if eligible to do so. They are not eligible for the free about turn in 5.3, and they may not advance after combat as in 6.9 if they are adjacent to any enemy heavy infantry units. A leader with a hoplite unit *must* attempt a rally if possible if any hoplite unit in his zone is hit. Hoplites adjacent to enemy hoplites do not receive the usual heavy infantry morale bonus in 7.2.

9.3: LEGIONARIES

Veteran legionaries have an additional option of treble movement (just like double movement in 4.4 but with 3 moves rather than 2) at an activation cost of 2 commands per unit. They also count as 1 unit rather than half a unit each towards the attack limits in 6.3. Average legionaries receive a morale bonus in 7.2 just like veterans, but their fighting value is treated as 4 rather than 3 for all purposes *except* when judging enemy victory point awards for spent, withdrawn, routed or shattered legionary units (11.2).

9.4: CATAPHRACTS

Cataphracts have only 1 move per turn (or 2 if using double movement), and it costs them only 1 move to enter or attack into any zone. They count as only 1 unit (or half a unit if veterans) towards the attack limits in 6.3.

9.5: SCYTHED CHARIOTS

Scythed chariot units represent only around 25 × M four-horse vehicles, and have a fighting value of 1 rather than 3. They are removed from play and counted as withdrawn as soon as they change facing or enter a zone that already contains another friendly unit. Other units in their group may then continue moving or attacking to the limit of their own remaining moves (see 5.6). Scythed chariots are also removed from play and counted as routed as soon as they are attacked, with no need to roll the dice for that unit's attack. Their removal does not in itself trigger a morale test, but if scythed chariots do withdraw due to failing a morale test, this does cause the removal of accompanying units with a morale of 0, as in 7.3. Scythed chariots must always be chosen as the lead or first attacking unit in their zone as in 6.4. They may receive an attack bonus as in 4.4, but they may not make all-out attacks as in 6.7.

10: SCENARIO CONDITIONS

10.1: SURPRISE

Some battles begin with one or both armies surprised. A surprised army may deploy no more than 4 units per turn (plus any attached leaders and any available commanders). On turn 1, heavy infantry and elephants count as 2 units each towards this deployment limit. Units deploying on later turns are not restricted to the rear zone and may use any of the zones and facings available on turn 1, but they must still observe other deployment constraints (see 3.3, 3.4 and 4.4).

A surprised army must deduct the fighting value of its undeployed units and undeployed generals from its overall fighting value when determining how many commands it receives, as in 4.1. Undeployed generals still give exemptions to activation costs as in 8.3.

10.2: FATIGUE

Some battles begin with one or both armies suffering from fatigue. As shown in 6.5, units in a fatigued army suffer a –1 attack modifier once they become spent.

10.3: DUST

Some battles are fought in particularly dry and dusty conditions. Both armies have their command die rolls in 4.1 halved (rounding halves up), and you must also roll a die at the start of every turn after turn 1. If the result is 4, 5 or 6, the player turns that turn occur in the opposite order to that indicated in the scenario. Armies that get 2 player turns in succession may not attack in the second player turn from a zone from which they attacked in the first player turn (the same restriction as in 8.9).

10.4: WET WEATHER

Some battles begin in overcast or wet weather. You must roll a die at the start of every turn after turn 1. If you score a 6, the weather changes from wet to overcast or from overcast to wet. No special rules apply while the weather is overcast. During wet weather, both armies have their command die rolls in 4.1 halved (rounding halves up), and there is also a combat penalty for various units as noted in 6.5.

11: VICTORY

11.1: ENDING THE BATTLE

The battle ends the instant that one army has fewer than 3 units on the field and/or undeployed, counting levies and scythed chariots as half a unit each. At that point, all that side's surviving generals count as lost, all its remaining fresh units count as withdrawn, and all its surviving spent units count as routed. The battle also ends after 10 turns have been completed.

11.2: VICTORY POINTS

Once the battle ends, each player calculates his victory point total by adding up the figures shown in the table below, remembering the special counting rules for average legionaries in 9.3.

The fighting value of all spent, withdrawn and routed enemy units and lost enemy generals

An extra 1 for every routed enemy unit

Twice the fighting value of all shattered enemy units and killed enemy generals

5 if you ever occupied the enemy camp and any enemy are still on the field or undeployed

20 if your army was fatigued

30 if your army was surprised

Twice the difference between the initial fighting values if your army had the lower total

11.3: VICTORY LEVELS

If the victory points are exactly equal, the contest is a draw. Otherwise, the player with most points wins, with the level of victory determined by the difference between the two totals, as follows:

- 1 to 24: Narrow Victory
- 25 to 49: Clear Victory
- 50 to 74: Major Victory
- 75 to 99: Resounding Victory
- 100 or more: Stunning Victory

Note that even an army which flees the field may 'win' in game terms by doing better than it did historically.

12: SUMMARY CHARTS

12.1: ACTIVATION & ATTACK BONUS COSTS

0 Commands:

- commander activated for independent relocation (8.2).

1 Command:

- single unit activated for normal movement/attack.
- group of two veteran units activated for normal movement/attack.

- group activated for facing change and/or single unit attack (4.2).
- veteran unit activated for double movement.
- light infantry or elephant unit activated for a double forward deployment move (4.4).
- attack bonus for a light cavalry unit.
- attack bonus for a lead unit of veterans or Indian elephants.

2 **Commands:**

- any other group activated for normal movement/attack.
- average or levy unit activated for double movement.
- veteran legionary unit activated for treble movement (9.3).
- attack bonus for any other unit.

12.2: MOVEMENT & ATTACK COSTS

0 **Moves:**

- any troops deploying into an unfortified camp zone (3.3).
- light infantry making any one turn.
- light cavalry making any two turns.
- any troops (except hoplites) making an initial 180 degree turn, unless outflanked (5.3).
- troops with no enemy in front making an initial turn to attack.

1 **Move:**

- each 90 or 180 degree turn in other circumstances.
- entering or attacking any zone except as noted below.

2 **Moves:**

- chariots or non-cataphract cavalry entering or attacking a zone containing hills, woods, marshes, a fortified camp or enemy elephants, unless it is their initial deployment zone (5.4).

12.3: UNIT ATTACK EQUIVALENCES

0.5 **Units:**

VHI except VLE; VCA.

1 **Unit:**

VLE; AHI/LHI; VLI; fresh lead ALI/LLI; VHC except CA; ACA/LCA; VLC; lead IEL/AEL (6.8).

2 **Units:**

ALI/LLI; AHC/LHC except CA; ALC/ LLC; IEL/AEL; CH including SCH.

Appendix 2: Using the Model

All you really need to refight any of the battles in Part II is a pencil, some paper, an eraser and two dice. You can then draw out a large version of the board (similar to those shown in the colour plates), mark on any terrain, and write in the position of each unit. When a unit moves or changes facing, you simply erase its previous position and write in the new one. Lead units can be underlined, and spent units put in brackets, making them easy to distinguish. You can easily keep side notes of the turn number, the acquisition and expenditure of commands, the fate of units and generals removed from play, and the fighting value remaining on each side.

A slightly more advanced approach is to create more permanent laminated sheets containing the basic gridded board and boxes to record the various statistics, and then to use differently coloured wax pencils to draw the terrain and the two armies, as these are easier to erase. You can obviously design your own sheets, but I have put some for free download from the book's website at http://www.kcl.ac.uk/schools/sspp/ws/staff/ps-lostbattles.html if you prefer. I have also put there a set of charts and tables that you may print out and use for ready reference, so you have less need to refer constantly to the rules in Appendix 1.

If you want to use a hard copy, but do not wish to be constantly erasing previous unit positions, then you will have to create separate unit counters that can be moved physically across the board. Again, you can design these yourself if you wish, but I have included bitmaps on the website that show a basic board and sheets of counters and terrain tiles like those on the colour plates in this volume, ready for you to print out and assemble at any desired scale. My counters include a reverse side to show the unit as spent, and units may simply be moved to the front of their zone to indicate lead status.

The easiest approach if you are happy to refight the battles on the computer screen is to use Cyberboard. This is a wonderful freeware PC program designed by Dale Larson for the e-mail play of conflict simulations (though sadly it does not run on Macs). You may download the latest version from http://cyberboard.brainiac.com. I have included on my own course website the requisite files for each of the 35 battles, with the units already in place as per the historical deployment option (as shown on the colour figures). You can slide the units over the map, as well as rotating them to change their facing and 'flipping them over' to indicate spent status. I include basic operating instructions, and by tweaking the files you may modify scenarios as desired.

I fear that it would take major reprogramming to integrate my system with the graphics from *Rome: Total War*, but if you already refight ancient battles using miniature figures on a tabletop, then you may use the model in this book just like any other set of rules. Any basing system is fine, and you do not even need to use a gridded board, as just 12 unobtrusive dots or strategically placed trees or rocks will suffice to indicate all the internal corners of the zones. The number of figures per unit should ideally be in proportion to the actual troop ratios shown on p. 27 (so a levy infantry unit would contain 8 times as many figures as a veteran cavalry unit), but all that really matters is that unit types and classes are clearly distinguishable and that you leave gaps to show where one unit ends and another begins. Spent status may be indicated simply by disordering the figures or twisting them at a slight angle.

I have set up an online discussion site: http://groups.yahoo.com/group/lostbattles/, and I encourage you to join this discussion group if you have questions or comments on any aspect of the model or the methodology as a whole. The site now contains several hundred posts and numerous attached files, and offers a very useful supplementary resource and online forum. If any significant errata emerge, or if I come up with further system developments, I will also post these on the book's website along with the other free downloads.

As I mentioned in the Introduction, previous versions of the model as it has evolved over the past 15 years have been published by the Society of Ancients. This is an international society, founded in 1965, for enthusiasts of ancient and medieval military history and wargaming. Among the activities it has organized in recent years have been comparative refights of Gaugamela, Cynoscephalae and the Sambre using a variety of different rules systems (including my own). The Society publishes a bimonthly journal, *Slingshot*, and further information and subscription details may be found on the website at http://www.soa.org.uk.

Finally, Decision Games will hopefully be producing a deluxe board game package including a copy of this book, separate rules and charts for ready reference, full colour card maps and terrain overlays, and full colour die-cut counters for the units. This will look *much* better than my own self-print version, as well as being much easier to construct and to use. Decision Games hope to make a limited number of 'upgrade kits' available by direct mail at a discount price for those who already own a copy of this book. For further details, please visit www.decisiongames.com.

Appendix 3: Directory of Battles

All the battles covered or mentioned in this book are listed below. The battles are also marked on the map in Figure 43 to indicate approximate geographical location of the battleground.

1. **Aquae Sextiae, 102 BC:** The invading Teutones were defeated by the Romans under Marius.
2. **Allia, 390/386 BC:** An invading Gallic force under Brennus scattered the Roman army and went on to sack Rome itself.
3. **Asculum, 279 BC:** See pp. 170–4 and Figure 28.
4. **Baecula, 208 BC:** Scipio the younger successfuly assaulted a hill position held by Hannibal's brother Hasdrubal.
5. **Bagradas, 255 BC:** See pp. 174–7 and Figure 29.
6. **Beneventum, 275 and 214 BC:** The Romans under Curius finally defeated Pyrrhus after his failed night march to surprise them, then in 214 another Roman army led by Gracchus, including freed slaves, shattered a Punic force under Hanno.
7. **Bibracte, 58 BC:** See pp. 209–12 and Figure 39.
8. **Cannae, 216 BC:** See pp. 77–87, 183–6 and Figures 3–6 and 33.
9. **Carrhae, 53 BC:** See pp. 203–7 and Figure 41.
10. **Chaeronea, 338 and 86 BC:** On the first battle, see pp. 125–9 and Figure 18. The second saw the Romans under Sulla beat a Pontic force led by Archelaus.
11. **Coronea, 447 and 394 BC:** On the second battle, see pp. 114–17 and Figure 14. The first was a defeat of the Athenians under Tolmides by the Boeotians during the First Peloponnesian War.
12. **Crimisus, 341 BC:** See pp. 162–4 and Figure 17.
13. **Cunaxa, 401 BC:** See pp. 107–10 and Figure 12.
14. **Cynoscephalae, 197 BC:** See pp. 193–6 and Figure 36.
15. **Delium, 424 BC:** See pp. 99–101 and Figure 10.
16. **Gabiene, 316/5 BC:** See pp. 148–51 and Figure 24.
17. **Gaugamela, 331 BC:** (Also known as Arbela.) See pp. 136–9 and Figure 21.
18. **Gaza, 312 BC:** See pp. 151–3 and Figure 25.
19. **Granicus, 334 BC:** See pp. 129–33 and Figure 19.

20. **Great Plains, 203 BC:** Scipio the younger's Romans defeated a Punic army of Celtiberians and others led by Hasdrubal and Syphax.

21. **Heraclea, 280 BC:** Pyrrhus of Epirus won his first 'Pyrrhic victory' over the Romans under Laevinus.

22. **Himera, 480 BC:** Gelon of Syracuse beat a Punic invasion force led by Hamilcar after using deception to infiltrate his camp.

23. **Hydaspes, 326 BC:** See pp. 139–43 and Figure 22.

24. **Ibera, 215 BC:** Publius and Gnaeus Scipio defeated Hannibal's brother Hasdrubal when his Spanish centre collapsed.

25. **Ilipa, 206 BC:** See pp. 186–8 and Figure 34.

26. **Ipsus, 301 BC:** Antigonus and his son Demetrius were beaten by a coalition force including hundreds of war elephants, led by the other Successor generals Seleucus and Lysimachus.

27. **Issus, 333 BC:** See pp. 133–6 and Figure 20.

28. **Lake Trasimene, 217 BC:** Hannibal ambushed and destroyed a marching Roman army led by Flaminius.

29. **Leuctra, 371 BC:** See pp. 117–21 and Figure 15.

30. **Magnesia, 190 BC:** See pp. 197–200 and Figure 37.

31. **Mantinea, 418, 362 and 207 BC:** On the first and second battles see pp. 101–5, 121–4 and Figures 11 and 16. In the third, the Achaeans under Philipoemen beat a Spartan army led by Machanidas.

32. **Marathon, 490 BC:** See pp. 91–5 and Figure 8.

33. **Metaurus, 207 BC:** Hannibal's brother Hasdrubal tried to escape a reinforced Roman army under Livius and Nero, but was caught, defeated and killed.

34. **Nemea, 394 BC:** See pp. 111–14 and Figure 13.

35. **Orchomenus, 86 BC:** Sulla's Romans again beat Archelaus's Pontic army, as they had recently done at 2nd Chaeronea.

36. **Paraitacene, 317/6 BC:** See pp. 145–8 and Figure 23.

37. **Pharsalus, 48 BC:** See pp. 215–19 and Figure 42.

38. **Philippi, 42 BC:** Octavian and Mark Antony fought an indecisive battle against Republican forces led by Brutus and Cassius, then in a second engagement the Caesarians were victorious.

39. **Plataea, 479 BC:** See pp. 95–9 and Figure 9.

40. **Pydna, 168 BC:** See pp. 200–3 and Figure 38.

41. **Raphia, 217 BC:** See pp. 157–60 and Figure 32.

42. **Ruspina, 46 BC:** A small and inexperienced force led by Caesar was surrounded by Numidian skirmishers led by his former lieutenant Labienus, but managed to extricate itself.

43. **Sambre, 57 BC:** See pp. 212–15 and Figure 40.

44. **Sellasia, 222 BC:** See pp. 154–7 and Figure 30.

45. **Sentinum, 295 BC:** See pp. 167–70 and Figure 27.

46. **Telamon, 225 BC:** An invading Gallic army of Boii and Insubres was sandwiched between two Roman forces led by Aemilius and Atilius, and destroyed after a hard fight.
47. **Teutoburg Forest, AD 9:** Three Roman legions under Varus were ambushed and annihilated in several days of bitter fighting by Arminius's German tribesmen.
48. **Thermopylae, 480 BC:** Leonidas with a small Spartan and allied force held the pass for several days against Xerxes's entire Persian army until outflanked and overwhelmed.
49. **Ticinus, 218 BC:** A cavalry and light infantry force under Publius Scipio was defeated by Hannibal's more numerous horsemen.
50. **Tigranocerta, 69 BC:** A Roman army led by Lucullus beat a much larger host under Tigranes of Armenia, including cataphract cavalry.
51. **Trebia, 218 BC:** See pp. 179–83 and Figure 31.
52. **Tunis, 310 BC:** See pp. 164–6 and Figure 26.
53. **Vercellae, 101 BC:** The Romans under Marius and Catulus defeated the invading Cimbri in a confused battle obscured by clouds of dust.
54. **Veseris, 340 BC:** A battle of dubious historicity in which the Romans beat the similarly organized Latins.
55. **Zama, 202 BC:** See pp. 188–91 and Figure 35.

Appendix 4: Glossary

Achaemenid   The dynasty that ruled Persia from Darius I until the Alexandrian conquest.

Agema   Greek term for a body of guard troops.

Agrianians   Highly capable light infantry from the northern border of Macedonia, employed especially by Alexander the Great.

Alae   The 'wings' of Italian allied troops attached to mid-Republican Roman legions.

Antigonid   The dynasty that ruled Macedon from 277 BC until the monarchy was abolished by the Romans in 168 BC.

Boeotia   The league of neighbouring cities dominated by Thebes.

Brasideioi   The force of freed Spartan helots and mercenaries commanded by Brasidas in northern Greece before his death in 422 BC.

Bronze Shields   One division (probably half) of the Antigonid Macedonian phalanx.

Cardaces   Native Persian infantry of uncertain type who fought in the battleline at Issus in 333 BC.

Cataphracts   Heavy lancers with full armour for man and horse, employed by the later Seleucids and Parthians.

Centurion   Roman junior officer who commanded a 'century', usually of rather less than 100 legionaries.

Cohort   A unit of several hundred infantry, initially made up of Italian allied foot or of 1 maniple from each line of a mid-Republican Roman legion, which became the standard tactical unit of the late Republican legion.

Companions   Elite mounted lancers in Alexandrian and Successor armies (though regular Alexandrian phalangites were called 'Foot Companions').

Cyreans   The Greek mercenaries, originally over 10,000 strong, who served with Cyrus in his ill-fated attempt to seize the Persian throne in 401 BC.

Enomotia   The smallest sub-unit of Spartan armies, containing a few tens of hoplites.

Galatians	Celtic tribes who invaded Greece and settled in central Asia Minor in the early third century BC.
Gerrhophoroi	Persian close-order infantry with large wicker shields, usually armed with bows.
Hastati	The front heavy infantry line of the mid-Republican Roman legion, containing 10 maniples of young men armed with pila.
Hellenistic	The period of Greek history after Alexander the Great.
Helots	Messenian 'serfs' used by the Spartans to farm the land so they themselves could concentrate on military training.
Hippeis	The 300 'knights' who formed the hoplite guard of Spartan kings.
Hoplite	The Greek term for heavy infantry, usually used today to refer specifically to the spearmen of classical Greek poleis with their distinctive round 'hoplon' shields.
Hypaspists	The guard infantry of Philip and Alexander of Macedon and of some Successor armies. Their early armament is uncertain, but they seem later to have adopted the sarissa if they were not already so equipped.
Immortals	The 10,000 strong infantry guard of early Achaemenid kings.
Ionia	The Greek regions of western Asia Minor.
Lacedaemonian	The generic term for troops from the Spartan home region of Laconia.
Legion	A standard unit of a few thousand Roman troops, composed in the mid-Republic of successive lines of velites, hastati, principes and triarii plus a few hundred cavalry, and in the late Republic of 10 cohorts of heavy infantry.
Leves	Livy's term for the light infantry of the mid-Republican legion before the Second Punic War.
Lochos	A unit of a few hundred Spartan hoplites.
Maniple	A 'handful' of Roman heavy infantry, composed of 2 centuries, and forming the main tactical sub-unit of the mid-Republican legion.
Mora	A unit of several hundred, and perhaps even over 1,000, Spartan hoplites.
Pantodapoi	Asiatic troops armed with sarissae to bolster phalanx numbers in Successor armies.
Peltasts	Greek term for javelin-armed light and medium infantry, originally with the distinctive crescent-shaped 'pelte'

shield, but later including any non-phalangite foot (especially mercenaries). The term even became attached to the Antigonid Macedonian and other guard infantry, who were almost certainly sarissa-armed.

Perioikoi Free non-Spartan residents of Laconia and Messenia, who were progressively incorporated into the Spartan army as native manpower declined.

Phalangites Troops (usually Macedonian or Greek) who fought with the sarissa in a pike phalanx.

Phalanx Generic Greek term for the heavy infantry line, usually used today to refer specifically to a formation of hoplites or phalangites.

Pilum The distinctive heavy javelin used by Roman legionaries.

Poleis Classical Greek city states.

Polemarch The overall commander (often titular) in some hoplite armies.

Pontus The Hellenistic kingdom centred in north-eastern Asia Minor that fought a series of wars with Rome in the early first century BC.

Principes The second heavy infantry line of the mid-Republican Roman legion, containing 10 maniples of middle-aged men armed with pila.

Psiloi The Greek term for light-armed infantry skirmishers, ranging from hordes of armed servants to specialist archers and slingers.

Ptolemaic The Successor dynasty established in Egypt by Alexander's general Ptolemy.

Punic The Roman term for the Carthaginians, based on their Phoenician origins.

Rorarii Light troops mentioned by Livy in the legion of the fourth century BC.

Sacred Band Elite infantry formations employed by the Thebans and the early Carthaginians.

Sarissa The long two-handed pike introduced by Philip of Macedon, which came to dominate Hellenistic infantry equipment.

Satrap Asian regional governor in the Achaemenid and Successor periods.

Sciritae Several hundred more flexible hoplites from the hills northwest of Sparta, used to guard the left wing in battle.

Seleucid	The Successor dynasty established in Asia by Alexander's general Seleucus.
Silver Shields (Argyraspides)	Name given to Alexander's Hypaspists when their equipment was upgraded at the end of his reign. These troops fought for Eumenes in the early Successor wars, and the Seleucids later raised a less-impressive infantry force of the same name.
Spartiates	The full Spartan citizens, whose numbers dwindled greatly as time went on.
Stadia (or Stades)	Greek units of distance corresponding to 600 ft (roughly 183 m), but varying significantly between different writers.
Strategos	Greek term for general.
Successors	The military strongmen who fought for power and established their own kingdoms after Alexander's death.
Tarentine	Shielded Greek mercenary light cavalry who skirmished with javelins.
Taxis	Sub-unit of the Alexandrian phalanx, containing around 1,500 troops.
Thureophoroi	Greek medium infantry (often mercenary) equipped with the oval 'thureos' shield.
Triarii	The third heavy infantry line of the mid-Republican Roman legion, containing 10 smaller maniples of older men armed with thrusting spears.
Tribune	Prestigious mid-ranking command appointment within the Roman legion.
Triplex Acies	The three-line formation of the Roman legion, usually referring to the 4–3–3 array of cohorts in late Republican times.
Trireme	The standard war galley of the fifth century BC, with three banks of oars.
Turma	A Roman cavalry squadron with around 30 troopers.
Velites	The light infantry of the mid-Republican legion, recruited from the youngest and poorest troops.
White Shields	One division (probably half) of the Antigonid Macedonian phalanx.

Notes

Notes to Introduction

1   On the very different character of twenty-first-century warfare, see Smith (2005) and Freedman (2006).
2   Livy (XXII.49) says that around 48,200 Romans died at Cannae, compared to the 21,392 British troops killed or missing on the Somme on 1 July 1916. See Lazenby (1978), pp. 84–5, and Middlebrook (2001), p. 263.
3   See, for example, Warry (1980), Connolly (1981), Hackett (1989) and Anglim *et al.* (2002).
4   Manstein (1987).
5   See Kromayer (1903, 1907), Kromayer and Veith (1912, 1922–9, 1924–31), Hanson (1989), Roth (1999) and Austin and Rankov (1995). For a broader overview of recent scholarship, see Hanson (1999b), Sidebottom (2004) and Sabin, van Wees and Whitby (2007).
6   Goldsworthy (1996–2006).
7   Sabin, van Wees and Whitby (2007).
8   See Hammond (1989a), pp. 207–16, Devine (1987) and Bosworth (1995), pp. 262–310.
9   See Scullard (1974), pp. 198–207 and Jones (1988), Chapters 3–4.
10 Ferrill (1985), pp. 215–23.
11 Lloyd (1996), Santosuosso (1997), Lendon (2005) and Kagan (2006).
12 Montagu (2000, 2006).
13 Pritchett (1971), Chapters 11–12 and (1985), Chapter 1, Krentz (1985a), Gabriel and Metz (1991), Chapter 4, Goldsworthy (1996), Daly (2002), Engels (1978).
14 Hammond (1983).
15 Roth (1999).
16 Sabin (1996, 2000).
17 Keegan (1978).
18 Kagan (2006) and Hutchinson (2000).
19 On the development of this technique during World War Two, see Crowther and Whiddington (1947), Part II, Blackett (1962), Part II and Air Ministry (1963). On the famous 'Lanchester equations' that were first developed to model air combat in World War One, see Lanchester (1995), Chapters 5–6 and Lepingwell (1987).
20 Biddle (2004).
21 Dupuy (1979).
22 Freedman (2005), p. 428.

23   Dupuy (1992), Chapter 9. For a fuller analysis of the campaign, see May (2000).

24   See Lendon (2005), Kagan (2006) and Montagu (2006).

25   See Grant (1974, 1977), Barker and Bodley Scott (1993), Priestley (2005), Baggett and Grace (1992), Harrison (2004) and Creative Assembly (2004). For a broader overview of wargaming as a popular hobby, see Sabin (2002a).

26   See Perla (1990) and Allen (1987). A good survey of modelling and simulation theory as applied to the professional study of war is Hausrath (1971).

27   Clausewitz (1976), p. 86.

28   Clausewitz (1976), pp. 84–6.

29   Culham (1989), Kagan (2006), Chapter 4 and Beyerchen (1992).

30   Good generic overviews of the potential of such conflict simulation techniques may be found in Dunnigan (1992) and Perla (1990).

31   For a sense of the ever-increasing range and complexity of these simulations, see the detailed reviews in the journals *Fire & Movement* and *Paper Wars*, and the websites at http://www.consimworld.com, http://www.grognard.com and http://www.wargamer.com.

32   See, for example, Reed (1980), pp. 29–43.

33   See Rohrbaugh (2006), especially p. 3.

34   See the course website at http://www.kcl.ac.uk/schools/sspp/ws/consim.html, from which many past student projects (including some on ancient battles) may be downloaded, in addition to supporting material for this book as outlined in Appendix 2 on pp. 247–8.

35   See Herman and Berg (1991, 1992) and Erudite Software (1999).

36   This series has also extended to early modern battles such as Breitenfeld, for which the level of detail is more defensible. See Herman and Berg (1993).

37   Treating each battle individually does have the offsetting advantage that the simulation can be better tailored to specific details if these are known, as in the recent Alesia game by Berg and Herman (2005), though here, any academic merit is compromised by the complete absence of a bibliography.

38   On the case for less detail but more rigorous documentation in conflict simulations in general, see Haggart (2005–6).

39   See Sabin (1993, 1997, 2003, 2006). On the Society of Ancients, see p. 248.

40   See, for instance, Warry (1980) and Montagu (2000, 2006).

41   Kromayer (1903, 1907), Kromayer and Veith (1912, 1924–31), Tarn (1948) and Delbrück (1920).

42   See David Aaronovitch in *The Times*, 27 December 2006, p. 24, and my own reply on 5 January 2007, p. 16.

43   Some recent software nevertheless achieves very interesting and impressive results in simulating land battles in other periods – see Panther Games (2003) and MadMinute Games (2006).

44   See, for example, Pape (1996), who uses the technique to model the determinants of coercive success in air bombardment.

45   Dupuy (1979) and Biddle (2004).

46   On the importance of validation, see Haggart (2005–6).

47   See Wheeler (2001).

48   See Morrison, Coates and Rankov (2000) and Croom and Griffiths (2000).

49   See Luttwak (1976) and Wheeler (1993).

50   See, for example, Hammond (1989a), Figures 3, 7, 8, 11, 14 and 20.

Notes to Chapter 1: Sources

1   See Edwards (1995), Tatton-Brown (1987), pp. 67–8, Keppie (1984), pp. 46–51 and Yadin (1966).

2   See Fiorato, Boylston and Knüsel (2000) and Foard (1995).

3   See Hammond (1938, 1968).

4   See Snodgrass (1999), Sekunda and McBride (1986), Bishop and Coulston (1993) and Feugère (2002).

5   See Connolly (1981) and Embleton and Graham (1984).

6   See Wheeler (1988) and Campbell (1987).

7   See Hansen (1993). As generals would have to give their address repeatedly at different points along the line – as described in Thucydides (IV.94–6) – only short and down-to-earth speeches like the one he ascribes to Hippocrates, or that Tacitus (*Ann.* XIV.36) later attributes to Suetonius, have anything like the ring of truth.

8   On the modern strategic impact of this media-driven triumph of anecdotalism over statistical judgement, see Sabin (2002b), pp. 96–7.

9   The armies at Philippi also used fieldworks to a significant extent, making it hard to cover this battle without undesirable special rules. For more traditional attempts to reconstruct these engagements, see Bar-Kochva (1976), Chapter 6 and Keppie (1984), pp. 119–21.

10   See Dilke (1985), pp. 28, 32–3 and Lazenby (1978), p. 286, (1985), p. 136 and (1993), p. 55.

11   See Keegan (1978), Chapter 3 and Kagan (2006).

12   See Hornblower (1981).

13   See Briscoe (1973), p. 263.

14   For a slightly different interpretation, see Dorey (1957).

15   See Diodorus (XVII.19–21, 33–4) and Cornell (1995), p. 361.

16   Delbrück (1975), pp. 328–31.

17   Whatley (1964).

18   See Kromayer (1903, 1907) and Kromayer and Veith (1912, 1922–9, 1924–31).

19   Pritchett (1969) and Hammond (1938, 1968, 1980, 1984, 1988).

20   Hammond (1989a), pp. 95–111 and (1992).

21   See Foard (2004).

22   See Rayner (2004), pp. 61–6.

23   Daly (2002), Map 5.

24   Connolly (1981), pp. 183–5 and Goldsworthy (2001), Chapter 4.

25   See Devine (1985d), pp. 45–6 and Hammond (1992), p. 395.

26   Bosworth (1988), p. 60.

27   See the detailed summary in Morgan (1983).

28   Du Picq (1920), Dodge (1890, 1891, 1892), Fuller (1960, 1965), Hackett (1989), Bagnall (1990) and Peddie (1994, 1997).

29 See Walsh (1961).

30 For comparisons based on enduring human characteristics, see Engels (1978), Lloyd (1996) and Sabin (2000).

31 See Whatley (1964), p. 126.

32 See Engels (1978) and Hammond (1983).

33 See Whatley (1964), p. 126 and Donlan and Thompson (1976).

34 See Connolly (1991, 1998), Junkelmann (1986), Gabriel and Metz (1991) and Croom and Griffiths (2000).

35 See Morrison, Coates and Rankov (2000).

36 See, for example, Wheeler (2001), pp. 174–81.

37 See Burn (1984), pp. 246–8, Hammond (1968), pp. 39–41, and the counter-arguments in Lazenby (1993), pp. 59–61.

38 See Green (1991), pp. 489–512, and his later retraction in the new preface on p. xiv in the face of critiques like that of Badian (1977).

39 See Whatley (1964), pp. 129–30 and Hammond (1989a).

40 See Head (1982) for a fine overview from this perspective.

41 Hanson (1989), Lazenby (1985), Head (1992), Spence (1993), McCall (2002), Bar-Kochva (1976), Sekunda and McBride (1994) and Goldsworthy (1996).

42 Samuels (1990). For a more balanced comparison of the Roman and Punic armies at this time, see Daly (2002), Chapters 3–4.

43 Bosworth (1980, 1995) and Walbank (1970, 1967, 1979).

44 Hornblower (1981).

45 Rubincam (1991) and Lendon (1999). Whitby's chapter on 'Reconstructing Ancient Warfare' in Sabin, van Wees & Whitby (2007) vol. 1, Chapter 3 shows how important such historiographical perspectives can be.

46 Loreto (2006) Part VI makes some undeservedly kind remarks about my contribution in this regard.

47 Krentz (1985a).

48 See Devine (1985a).

49 Diodorus (XVII.36, 61, 89).

50 See, for example, Warry (1980).

51 Delbrück (1975), pp. 112–13, 212, 246, 325–7, 399–401, 459–76, 542–9.

52 Dupuy and Dupuy (1993), pp. 829, 833, 840, 910, 913, 963, 970–1.

53 Delbrück (1975), pp. 112–13, 399–401.

54 See Herzog (1982).

55 See pp. 117–24, 179–86, 203–7. On the general issue, see Hammond (1989b), pp. 59–62.

56 See Hammond (1938a).

57 Brunt (1971), pp. 694–7.

58 This philosophy is well articulated in Whatley (1964), p. 139 and Lazenby (1993), Chapter 1.

59 Whatley (1964), pp. 119–20.

Notes to Chapter 2: Armies

1   See Berg and Herman (1999).
2   Bar-Kochva (1976), p. 165 and Map 14.
3   Devine (1987), pp. 112–13.
4   See Tajima (2005), Rinella (2003), Nelson (1976) and the PC simulation by Panther Games (2003).
5   See Lazenby (1985), Daniel (1992) and Aperghis (1997).
6   See Head (1982), pp. 3–43.
7   See Connolly (1981), Rawson (1971), Bell (1965), Sekunda and Northwood (1995) and Sekunda and McBride (1996).
8   See Keppie (1984), Polybius (XI.1, XIV.8, XV.14, XVIII.26), Plutarch (*Mar.* 20, *Sull.* 19, *Luc.* 28) and Caesar (*B Gall.* I.25, *B Civ.* III.89).
9   The loss of detail with only 10 or 12 units per side is illustrated in Sabin (1993) and Barker (2001).
10 Livy (XXXVII.39), Appian (*Syr.* 31).
11 I develop this argument further in Sabin, van Wees and Whitby (2007), Vol. 1, pp. 399–433.
12 Lendon (1999).
13 See Lazenby (1985), Billows (1990), Chapter 3 and Goldsworthy (2006), Chapter 19.
14 Xenophon (*An.* I.8, *Hell.* IV.4.10).
15 See Lazenby (1978, 2004).
16 With much better historical information, one can use conflict simulation techniques to explore the fragility of the actual outcome of contests like Waterloo or the Battle of Britain, and to ask how likely it was that the result might have been reversed. We know so much less about ancient battles that understanding what did really occur is more than enough of a challenge in itself.
17 Diodorus (XIX.27–31, 40–3).
18 Biddle (2004).
19 For existing ideas on the subject, see Lloyd (1996), Goldsworthy (1996) and Lendon (2005).
20 Livy (XXII.47, XXXI.35).
21 See Hyland (1990, 2003), Dixon and Southern (1992), Spence (1993), McCall (2002) and Sidnell (2006).
22 Gaebel (2002).
23 Jones (1988), Chapter 1.
24 See Best (1969) and Griffith (1984).
25 The best overview of these various issues is still Head (1982).
26 See p. 184, for more discussion of these figures.
27 See Daly (2002), pp. 182–4.
28 One system infamously even rated Indian archers, regarded as the lowest status element of the army, as 'superior' because of their large bows and two-handed swords, thereby placing them in the same category as English medieval longbowmen! See Barker and Bodley-Scott (1993), p. 7.

29   See Head (1982), p. 118 and Wilcox (1986), pp. 9–10.

30   See Hanson (1989, 1991) and Head (1992).

31   See Brunt (1971).

32   The entire history of war chariots is surveyed in Cotterell (2004).

33   The standard reference remains Scullard (1974).

34   Bar-Kochva (1976), p. 82 and Devine (1984), pp. 31–5.

35   Bar-Kochva (1976), Chapter 10, and see the scenario on pp. 157–60.

36   See Lazenby (1996), Chapter 7.

Notes to Chapter 3: Movement

1   These two approaches are well illustrated in Connolly (1981), especially pp. 183–6.

2   See Langer (1980), Plate 107 and Foard (2004), Figure 54. On the role of such pitched battles throughout the early modern era, see Weigley (1991).

3   See Hanson (1989, 2001). There was in fact a clear tension in the ancient world as in most societies between this 'chivalric' impulse and the use of trickery and stratagem to inflict one-sided slaughter, a tension well analysed by Wheeler (1988) in terms of the conflicting ethos of Achilles and Odysseus.

4   See, for example, Creasy (1911), Fuller (1954) and Seymour (1988).

5   Source references for all of these battles may be found in Part II.

6   Compare Connolly (1981), pp. 184–7, 203–7 and Devine (1985a), Figure 1 with Lazenby (1978), Map 21, Keppie (1984), Maps 6, 7 and 11 and Billows (1990), Figure 3.

7   See, for example, Pritchett (1971), Chapters 11–12, Krentz (1985b) and Goldsworthy (1996), pp. 176–81 and (1997).

8   See Nosworthy (1992), pp. 80–6.

9   Marsden (1964), p. 39.

10   See Lazenby (1993), p. 64 and Bar-Kochva (1976), Chapter 10, especially notes 9 and 13.

11   Lazenby (1978), p. 80, Connolly (1981), p. 184 and Goldsworthy (2000a), p. 204.

12   Walbank (1967), pp. 369–70.

13   Polybius (XII.19–21), Asclepiodotus (IV.1–4), Vegetius (III.14–15) and Pritchett (1969), p. 74 and (1971), pp. 144–54.

14   Dupuy (1992), Chapter 9.

15   Morgan (1981) and Hammond and Walbank (1988), p. 361.

16   See Hammond (1980).

17   Goldsworthy (2000a), p. 174, and Connolly (1981), pp. 183–5.

18   See Herodotus (IX.69–71), Livy (X.29, XXVIII.15), Caesar (*B Civ.* III.95), Xenophon (*An.* I.10), Arrian (*Anab.* III.14–15), Dionysius (XX.3) and Polybius (III.117).

19   See Xenophon (*Hell.* IV.3.18), Livy (XXXVII.42–3) and Caesar (*B Civ.* II.26).

20   Diodorus (XIX.42–3).

21   See Arrian (*Anab.* II.10) and Polybius (II.65, 69).

22   See Foard (2004), Chapters 7–8 and Adkin (2001), Section 4.

23   Herman and Berg (1991, 1992). See, for comparison, the better-documented simulation of Waterloo by Davis (1983) and the review of it by Haggart (1978).

24 See, for comparison, the more traditional maps in Hammond (1967), pp. 568, 609.

25 See Kagan (2006), Chapter 5, Conliffe (1996) and Berg (2005).

26 See, for example, Baggett and Grace (1992).

27 See Plutarch (*Luc.* 28), Caesar (*B Gall.* II.26), Anderson (1970), Chapter 10 and Devine (1984).

28 See Sabin (1996, 2000).

29 Engels (1978), pp. 153–6.

30 See Peddie (1994), pp. 72–6.

31 See Goldsworthy (1996), pp. 139–40 and Nosworthy (1995).

32 Asclepiodotus (X) has an extensive theoretical discussion of countermarching as well as of the procedures needed to turn units to either side.

33 See pp. 147, 150, 156–7, 199.

34 See Livy (X.29), Polybius (XI.1, XIV.8, XV.14, XVIII.26), Plutarch (*Sull.* 19) and Caesar (*B Gall.* I.25).

35 See Herman and Berg (1992) and Berg (2005).

36 See Baggett and Grace (1992).

37 Buckingham (2002) tellingly devotes the first eight of his 20 chapters to analysing the preparations for this operation, rather than the fighting itself.

38 Polybius (II.69). The advantages and disadvantages of camp fortifications are well discussed in Anderson (1970), pp. 62–6.

39 The detailed mechanics and tactical thinking behind the deployments at Cannae are discussed on pp. 78–81.

40 See pp. 129–31, 142, 147, 149–50, 152–3, 159, 190–1.

41 See Goldsworthy (2000a), pp. 203–8, 281–2 and (2006), pp. 220, 428.

42 See Lazenby (1985), Chapter 8 and (1978), pp. 80–5, 145–50. For additional diagrammatic reconstructions, see Anderson (1970), Figure 6 and Connolly (1981), pp. 186, 200.

Notes to Chapter 4: Fighting

1 Gabriel and Metz (1991), pp. 70–3.

2 Wheeler (2001), pp. 174–81.

3 See Hughes (1974).

4 Gabriel and Metz (1991) went so far as to say, on p. 72, that these factors 'rendered arrows fired in salvo at range almost totally ineffective in generating casualties within an infantry formation'.

5 See Sabin (2000). The insignificance of the bayonet as a cause of casualties (as opposed to a trigger for flight) in Napoleonic battles is discussed in Muir (1998), pp. 86–9.

6 Xenophon (*An.* I.8).

7 Polybius (III.115), Caesar (*B Gall.* I.25, II.23).

8 See Gabriel and Metz (1991), pp. 87–8. Curtius (III.11.27) does give a figure (504) for the Macedonian wounded at Issus, but some think it is 10 times too low due to scribal error! Diodorus's figures (XIX.31) for the wounded on both sides in Paraitacene are only a little more than for the dead (4,900 as against 4,300) but it is unclear whether they include the lightly wounded.

9   The story in Livy (VIII.8–10), though almost certainly apocryphal, nicely illustrates this preoccupation.

10 This assumes that his 80 cohorts had the full complement of 480 centurions, even though they only numbered 22,000 troops – if not, the disproportion would be even greater.

11 See Herman and Berg (1992).

12 See Polybius (XI.21–2).

13 This relatively small battle would last around 50 10-minute turns in our system, giving long periods for regrouping during the intervals between successive Norman attacks. See Lawson (2002), Chapter 6.

14 The Greeks later used the shields and arrows as firewood. See Xenophon (*An.* I.8, II.1).

15 See Plutarch (*Demetr.* 29).

16 See Polybius (XV.12, 14).

17 See Polybius (XV.11).

18 See pp. 87, 94, 104–5, 218.

19 Polybius (II.65–6, III.113–14) and Thucydides (IV.96).

20 See Sabin (2000), p. 10, Pritchett (1971), pp. 144–54 and Goldsworthy (1996), pp. 179–80.

21 See Thucydides (IV.93–6) and Xenophon (*Hell.* IV.2.18, VI.4.12, VII.5.21–5).

22 See Sabin (2000) and Zhmodikov (2000). For ancient references to the use of missiles in protracted close combat, see, for example, Caesar (*B Gall.* II.25, *B Civ.* I.45–6).

23 See Polybius (III.116).

24 See Lazenby (1996), Chapter 7 and Sabin (1996).

25 See Polybius (XI.1) and Caesar (*B Gall.* II.23–7).

26 Livy (XXII.6, XXIII.40, XXIV.15, XXV.19, XXVII.12). The notional length of ancient 'hours' varied with the season, as each one represented one twelfth of the period of daylight.

27 Anderson (1970), Chapter 8.

28 Culham (1989) and Kagan (2006), pp. 99–106.

29 See Daly (2002), pp. 195–6.

30 Livy (XXXVII.40, 42) and Polybius (I.34).

31 See Scullard (1974).

32 *Ibid.* Plutarch (*Pyrrh.* 21) shows how the impact of just 19 elephants at Asculum was magnified into an excuse for the defeat of a Roman army at least 40,000 strong.

33 See Livy (X.28), Plutarch (*Tim.* 27) and Caesar (*B Gall.* IV.33, V.16).

34 See Livy (XXIII.29), Polybius (II.27–30), and (*B Afr.* 13–17).

35 Lazenby (1985), Chapters 7–8.

36 On the strength of the position, see Caesar (*B Gall.* II.23, 27).

37 Arrian (*Anab.* II.10), Herodotus (VII.208–11), Polybius (II.69) and Livy (XXXVII.43).

38 Herodotus (IX.65–8).

39 Plutarch (*Luc.* 28).

40 See Livy (X.28–9, XXVII.48), Polybius (III.72–3, XI.22–4) and Plutarch (*Mar.* 26). Such fatigue became a literary *topos* for Celtic forces, and so should be viewed with some scepticism in that context. See Rawlings (1996).

41 See Arrian (*Anab.* V.14–15), Plutarch (*Tim.* 28) and Livy (XXI.54–6, XXXVII.41).

42 Kagan (2006), pp. 99–106.

43   See, for example, Barker (1980), pp. 23–6, Barker (1986), pp. 22–3 and Barker and Bodley-Scott (1993), p. 25.
44   See Xenophon (*An.* I.8, 10), Arrian (*Anab.* I.16) and Livy (XXXVII.42–3).
45   See Caesar (*B Civ.* III.85–7) and Appian (*B Civ.* II.65–9).
46   See Sabin (1996), pp. 65, 68–9. Vegetius (III.18) makes clear that even the Romans saw the right wing as more prestigious, but this had nothing like as much practical grand tactical impact as in Greek and Hellenistic armies.
47   See pp. 99–105, 111–21, 151–3, 157–60.
48   See Xenophon (*Hell.* IV.3.17). Hoplite fragility might even produce a 'tearless battle' in which one side fled before contact – see Hanson (1989), p. 161.
49   See Sabin (1997).

Notes to Chapter 5: Command

1   There have been several recent studies of battlefield command covering various parts of our era, notably Everett Wheeler, 'The General as Hoplite', in Hanson (1991), pp. 121–70, Pritchett (1994), Chapter 3, Goldsworthy (1996), Chapters 1, 5 and 6, Hutchinson (2000) and Kagan (2006).
2   See van Creveld (1985), pp. 41–57 and Kagan (2006), pp. 192–200.
3   Xenophon (*Hell.* IV.3.18), Arrian (*Anab.* III.14), Polybius (V.85) and Plutarch (*Sull.* 19).
4   Herodotus (IX.52–8) and Thucydides (V.71–2).
5   Xenophon (*Hell.* IV.2.13, 18).
6   See Arrian (*Anab.* I.13–14, III.10–11), Diodorus (XIX.81), Polybius (III.100–5, 110–13), Livy (XLIV.36–40) and Appian (*B Civ.* II.65–9).
7   Herodotus (VI.108–13) and Xenophon (*Hell.* IV.2.13, 18).
8   Daly (2002), Chapter 5 offers an excellent discussion of command in the specific context of Cannae.
9   Livy (XXVII.43–7). The best survey of the tactical intelligence contest is in Austin and Rankov (1995), Chapter 3.
10   Polybius (XI.22).
11   Hammond (1989a), pp. 103–4, 211–14.
12   Lazenby (2004), pp. 123–5.
13   See Livy (XXXIII.9, XXXVII.43).
14   On the mega-game format as a means of simulating ancient warfare, see Grainger (1990).
15   The shortcomings of artificial intelligence are well illustrated in the PC conversion of Herman and Berg's 'Great Battles' system by Erudite Software (1999). For an idea of what can be achieved with better modern processing capabilities, see Mad Minute Games (2006).
16   See Sabin (2002a), pp. 208–9, 227–30.
17   On game theory, see Schelling (1960).
18   See Plutarch (*Tim.* 27–8).
19   See my remarks in Sabin, van Wees and Whitby (2007), Vol. 1, pp. 406–9. Onasander (22)

and Vegetius (III.17) did both strongly advocate the maintenance of reserves, but they seem to have been thinking of the tactical as much as the grand tactical level.

20   Diodorus (XVI.85), Polyaenus (IV.2.2) and Arrian (*Anab.* I.12).
21   See, for example, Barker (1986), pp. 3, 20–1.
22   Adkin (2001), p. 76.
23   Arrian (*Anab.* III.14), Polybius (III.71–4, XI.22–4) and Caesar (*B Civ.* III.89–94).
24   Diodorus (XIX.42) and Plutarch (*Mar.* 26).
25   See Everett Wheeler, 'The General as Hoplite', in Hanson (1991), pp. 121–70, and Goldsworthy (1996), Chapter 4.
26   Arrian (*Anab.* I.15–16), Plutarch (*Pyrrh.* 16, *Sull.* 21) and Caesar (*B Gall.* II.25).
27   Plutarch (*Sull.* 19) and Caesar (*B Gall.* II.21, 25–6).
28   See Polybius (III.116, V.84–5).
29   See Arrian (*Anab.* V.18–19), Livy (X.28–9, XXII.49), Polybius (I.34, XI.2) and Appian (*B Civ.* IV.113).
30   Arrian (*Anab.* I.15) and Plutarch (*Pyrrh.* 16–17).
31   Herodotus (VI.114), Thucydides (V.10–11) and Xenophon (*Hell.* VII.5.24–5).
32   Polybius (III.116, XV.11–14).
33   Herodotus (VI.114), Diodorus (XX.12), Livy (X.28), Polybius (III.116) and Plutarch (*Crass.* 25–6).
34   Arrian (*Anab.* II.11, III.14) and Plutarch, (*Aem.* 19, *Luc.* 28).
35   Schelling (1960).
36   See Crowther and Whiddington (1947), Part II, Blackett (1962), Part II and Air Ministry (1963).
37   See, for example, Barker (2001).

Notes to Chapter 6: The Model in Operation

1   See Walbank (1970), pp. 439–40, Lazenby (1978), pp. 75–6 and Daly (2002), pp. 25–9 for a survey of this debate.
2   See Samuel (1990) and Daly (2002), Chapter 3.
3   See Connolly (1981), pp. 183–5, Goldsworthy (2001), Chapter 4 and Daly (2002), pp. 32–5.
4   Polybius (III.116) does say that Paullus took part in the cavalry fighting on the right before joining the infantry centre, but this nuance is hard to represent in the model without either leaving him too vulnerable or making commanders in general too invulnerable by letting them escape the overrunning of their zone. Incidentally, Connolly (1981), pp. 184–7 suggests that Paullus's position on the more prestigious right wing indicates that he was actually in command on this fateful day, and that Polybius shifted the blame unfairly to Varro because of the historian's unwillingness to criticize his Aemilian patrons.
5   See Billows (1990), Figures 4 and 5.
6   See Polybius (III.74) and Sabin (1996), p. 66.
7   See Healy (1994), Goldsworthy (2001) and especially Daly (2002).
8   See the illustrations in Caven (1980), p. 137 and Goldsworthy (2001), p. 146.

9   See Goldsworthy (2001), pp. 146–51.

10 See, for example, the diagrams in Connolly (1981), p. 186, Santosuosso (1997), pp. 178–9 and Daly (2002), p. 41.

11 Livy (XXIII.29). Polybius (III.116) claims that Hannibal fought personally in the front line just like Paullus, who was killed while doing so, but this may simply reflect the 'heroic' imagery that I discussed on p. 69.

Notes to Chapter 7: Athens and Sparta

1   See, for example, Whatley (1964), Hammond (1968), Lloyd (1973), Burn (1984), Chapter 12, Lazenby (1993), Chapter 3, Evans (1993), Doenges (1998) and Sekunda and Hook (2002).

2   See Hammond (1968), Plan 2 and Lazenby (1993), pp. 65–6.

3   See Pritchett (1969), p. 10, Burn (1984), p. 244, Doenges (1998), pp. 10–11 and Sekunda and Hook (2002), pp. 58–64.

4   See Hammond (1968), p. 18, Lazenby (1993), p. 64, Santosuosso (1997), p. 34 and Sekunda and Hook (2002), pp. 54, 60.

5   See Hammond (1968), 34 and Doenges (1998), pp. 6–7.

6   See Lazenby (1993), p. 64.

7   *Ibid.*, pp. 57–8, 72.

8   See Hammond (1968), pp. 32–3 and Lazenby (1993), pp. 46–7.

9   Doenges (1998), pp. 4–6.

10 Sekunda and Hook (2002), pp. 20–5, 51–2.

11 *Ibid.*, p. 25. Santosuosso (1997), p. 37 also suggests 15–18,000.

12 On the equipment and fighting style of early Achaemenid infantry, see Head (1992), pp. 22–30 and Sekunda and Chew (1992), pp. 16–18.

13 See Hammond (1968), p. 39, Lazenby (1993), p. 46, Sekunda and Hook (2002), p. 25, Evans (1993), pp. 298–9 and Doenges (1998), p. 5.

14 Lazenby (1993), pp. 59–61.

15 For different ancient stories of Datis's fate, see Lazenby (1993), p. 75.

16 *Ibid.*, pp. 31–3.

17 The reversed front interpretation is well illustrated in Sekunda and Hook (2002), pp. 74–5.

18 Hammond (1968), pp. 19, 29–30, 46.

19 Burn (1984), p. 244 and Lazenby (1993), pp. 68–70.

20 Whatley (1964).

21 Hammond (1968), p. 32, suggested that he saw 30,000 as a likelier figure than 25,000 for Persian numbers at Marathon.

22 Herodotus (VI.117).

23 The best modern survey is in Lazenby (1993), Chapter 9. The debate was already in full swing 50 years ago, as illustrated in Pritchett (1957, 1965), Chapter 8.

24 See Delbrück (1975), p. 112 and Lazenby (1993), p. 227.

25 See Hunt (1997), especially pp. 138–9.

26 See Green (1996), pp. 58–60, 211, 249–50, Head (1992), pp. 62–5, Burn (1984), p. 511, Lazenby (1993), pp. 90–2, 228, Santosuosso (1997), p. 59 and Connolly (1981), p. 29.
27 Head (1992), p. 65 and Lazenby (1993), p. 207.
28 See Head (1992), pp. 31–3 and Lazenby (1993), pp. 222–3.
29 See, for example, Pritchett (1957), p. 24 and Green (1996), pp. 248–9.
30 Connolly (1981), pp. 32–4.
31 For a broader survey of recorded phalanx depths, see Pritchett (1971), Chapter 11.
32 See Lazenby (1993), pp. 232–5.
33 Xenophon (*Hell.* VI.4.12).
34 See Lazenby (1993), p. 246.
35 For a further example, see Wallace (1982).
36 Thucydides (IV.90–1). Modern accounts of the campaign include Kagan (1974), pp. 278–87 and Lazenby (2004), pp. 87–91.
37 Pritchett (1969), Chapter 4. See also Kromayer and Veith (1922–9) Griech. Abt. Blatt 3.5.
38 See Lazenby (2004), p. 88 and DeVoto (1992).
39 See Lazenby (2004), pp. 88–90.
40 See Thucydides (II.13) and Spence (1993), pp. 15–16, 124.
41 See Hanson (1989), p. 180.
42 See Woodhouse (1933), pp. 57–65, 106–30, Pritchett (1969), pp. 56–8, 62–3 and Kagan (1981), pp. 122–3.
43 See Lazenby (2004), p. 121 and Sekunda and Hook (1998), p. 49.
44 Anderson (1970), pp. 227–51.
45 On Brasidas's original force, see Thucydides (IV.78–81).
46 Sekunda and Hook (1998), pp. 13–17, Cartledge (1987), pp. 37–43, 429–31, Lazenby (1985), pp. 13–20, 41–4, 128–9 and (2004), pp. 121–2 and van Wees (2004), pp. 83–5, 243–9. Woodhouse (1933), pp. 131–6 gave Agis 3,700 allies, 1,920 Sciritae, Brasideioi and freed helots and 7,040 Spartan hoplites, compared to his estimate of 10,900 enemy hoplites.
47 See Kagan (1981), p. 124 and Lazenby (1985), pp. 42, 126 and (2004), p. 122.
48 See Anderson (1970), pp. 229–30 and Lazenby (1985), pp. 128–9, 198 note 8 and (2004), p. 122.
49 Lazenby (1985), pp. 3–20.
50 Lazenby (2004), pp. 120–1.
51 Cartledge (1987), pp. 37–43, 427–31 and Herodotus (IX.10–11, 28).
52 See Strachan-Davidson's remarks as quoted in Whatley (1964), p. 139.
53 Van Wees (2004), pp. 245–7. For other efforts to explain this attempted redeployment, see Anderson (1970), pp. 231–6, Lazenby (1985), p. 43 and Woodhouse (1933), Chapters 9–10.
54 Van Wees (2004), pp. 83–5.
55 Lazenby (1985), p. 129 and (2004), p. 122.
56 Lazenby (1985), Figures 6–7 and (2004), Map 8 probably exaggerates the degree of overlap on the Spartan right, because of the 3,000 extra Spartan troops he thinks were in the centre.
57 On the general issue of Thucydides's casualty figures, see Rubincam (1991).

Notes to Chapter 8: The Age of Xenophon

1 Hutchinson (2000) provides a useful thematic survey of command in this era, and has sketch plans of all five battles in this chapter on pp. 256–65.
2 This is well summarized in Bigwood (1983).
3 Parke (1933), Chapter 5.
4 Xenophon (*An.* I.6.1, 8.1) and Rahe (1980).
5 Anderson (1974), pp. 99–100 and Bigwood (1983), p. 341.
6 Anderson (1974), p. 100, Bigwood (1983), p. 342 and Cawkwell (1972a), p. 38.
7 Xenophon (*An.* I.8.19–20, II.1.6) and Diodorus (XIV.23).
8 See Head (1992), pp. 22–30, 39–44 and Sekunda and Chew (1992), pp. 16–19, 23–5.
9 Anderson (1974), pp. 100–7 and Nelson (1975), pp. 64–6.
10 Anderson (1974), p. 106.
11 See Kromayer and Veith (1922–9) Griech. Abt. Blatt 4.4, Cawkwell (1972a), pp. 37–8 and Nelson (1975), p. 65.
12 Xenophon's description (*An.* I.10.7–8) of Tissaphernes's horsemen charging through gaps in the peltasts' ranks while leaving them unscathed cannot be reproduced directly in our model, so the best alternative is to deploy the peltasts in the right centre, able to move to the flank zone at a later stage.
13 Bigwood (1983), pp. 351–6.
14 Anderson (1970), p. 143, Pritchett (1969), Chapter 6 and Lazenby (1985), pp. 135–7.
15 Anderson (1970), pp. 148–50, Pritchett (1969), Plate 54 and Hamilton (1979), p. 221.
16 Pritchett (1969), pp. 73–4, Anderson (1970), p. 143, Cartledge (1987), p. 220, Hamilton (1979), p. 221 and Lazenby (1985), p. 136.
17 Lazenby (1985), pp. 5–20, 136–8, Cartledge (1987), pp. 37–43, 220, Anderson (1970), pp. 143, 239–45 and Sekunda and Hook (1998), p. 15.
18 Anderson (1970), pp. 143–4 and Lazenby (1985), pp. 136–8.
19 Diodorus (XIV.82–3) gives both sides a bare 500 cavalry, thereby further weakening the credibility of his numbers.
20 Anderson (1970), pp. 9–12 and Cartledge (1987), Chapter 5.
21 Hammond (1967), p. 457.
22 Pritchett (1969), pp. 74–6 suggests 1,388 yards, but we may be better allowing a metre per file to leave at least some scope for slight intervals between units as discussed on pp. 31–2.
23 See Lazenby (1985), pp. 138–9.
24 Anderson (1970), pp. 144–5, 398–9.
25 Lazenby (1985), pp. 139–42.
26 Xenophon (*Hell.* IV.2.21–3).
27 No distinction is made in our model between shielded and shieldless flanks, as the about-turn of the allied contingents is not represented directly, so such a contrast would here yield the opposite result.
28 Pritchett (1969), pp. 83–4 suggests that the defensibility of the Rachiani's eastern bank would have helped the allies to hold on.
29 See Pritchett (1969), Chapter 7 and Plate 56, Lazenby (1985), pp. 144–7 and Kromayer and Veith (1922–9) Griech. Abt. Blatt 5.3.

30 Lazenby (1985), p. 144.
31 Pritchett (1969), p. 93 and Cartledge (1987), p. 220.
32 Xenophon (*Hell.* IV.3.3–9) and Rahe (1980).
33 Pritchett (1969), p. 93, Cartledge (1987), p. 220, Hamilton (1979), p. 225 and Anderson (1970), p. 151.
34 Lazenby (1985), pp. 143–4.
35 See Cartledge (1987), pp. 208–19.
36 Lazenby (1985), p. 143 and Anderson (1970), p. 151.
37 See Lazenby (1985), p. 146.
38 See Krentz (1985a).
39 See Handel (1996), pp. 229–33.
40 Buckler (1980), pp. 54–61 and Lazenby (1985), pp. 151–4.
41 See Pritchett (1965), Chapter 3, Buckler (1980), pp. 60–1, Cartledge (1987), Figure 12.5 and Anderson (1970), p. 214.
42 Stylianou (1998), pp. 395–7.
43 Lazenby (1985), p. 155.
44 Anderson (1970), pp. 197–8, 321–3, Cartledge (1987), p. 238, Buckler (1980), pp. 55, 63, Hamilton (1991), p. 208 and DeVoto (1992), pp. 11–12.
45 See Plutarch (*Pel.* 18–23), DeVoto (1992) and Cartledge (1987), p. 238.
46 Hanson (1988). For a more balanced portrayal, see Cawkwell (1972b).
47 See Lazenby (1985), p. 155, Anderson (1970), pp. 196–8, Cartledge (1987), p. 238, Buckler (1980), pp. 62–3, Hamilton (1991), p. 208 and DeVoto (1992), p. 11.
48 Hammond (1967), p. 663.
49 Lazenby (1985), pp. 3–20, 152–5.
50 Anderson (1970), pp. 196, 239–49, 320, van Wees (2004), pp. 83–5, 247–9, Stylianou (1998), p. 403 and DeVoto (1992), p. 11. Hammond (1967), p. 663 suggests just 2,100 Spartan hoplites.
51 Cartledge (1987), p. 238.
52 The 1.3 km front of the Spartan infantry in Kromayer and Veith (1922–9) Griech. Abt. Blatt 5.5 is dubious in the extreme.
53 See Lazenby (1985), p. 156 and Anderson (1970), pp. 205–9.
54 See the maps in Anderson (1970), p. 402, Cartledge (1987), p. 237, Warry (1980), p. 60 and DeVoto (1992), p. 13.
55 See Anderson (1970), pp. 209–20, 402–3, Devine (1983), Buckler (1985), Lazenby (1985), pp. 156–60, Hanson (1988), DeVoto (1992), pp. 11–14 and Stylianou (1998), pp. 398–407.
56 Pritchett (1969), pp. 70–2 is highly critical of Diodorus, while Hamilton (1991), pp. 249–51 and Stylianou (1998), especially pp. 510–19, are less dismissive.
57 Cartledge (1987), pp. 235–6.
58 Xenophon (*Hell.* VII.5.14–18), Diodorus (XV.84), Polybius (IX.8) and Stylianou (1998), pp. 510–12.
59 This position is well illustrated in Pritchett (1969), Plates 21–4 and Buckler (1980), pp. 213–17.
60 Hammond (1967), pp. 507–8 and Pritchett (1969), pp. 39, 65.
61 Pritchett (1969), pp. 56–7.

62 Buckler (1980), pp. 212–8, Anderson (1970), p. 222, Lazenby (1985), p. 168, Cartledge (1987), p. 391, Stylianou (1998), p. 513 and Hutchinson (2000), pp. 163–5, 178.
63 See Lazenby (1985), pp. 136–8 and Diodorus (XV.84).
64 Stylianou (1998), p. 513
65 Hammond (1967), p. 508, Pritchett (1969), pp. 64–6, Stylianou (1998), p. 514 and Buckler (1980), p. 217.
66 Diodorus (XV.80, XVI.30) and Hammond (1967), p. 663.
67 Pritchett (1969), p. 65, Buckler (1980), p. 356 note 56 and DeVoto (1992), p. 15 all suggest 7,000 Boeotian hoplites. Lazenby (1985), p. 166, p. 203 note 2, suggests just 6,000 as part of a 30,000-strong army attacking Sparta in 369.
68 Hammond (1967), p. 507.
69 Diodorus (XV.85).
70 Pritchett (1969), pp. 58–9, 66 and Buckler (1980), pp. 218–9, 316–7.
71 Hammond (1967), pp. 508–9 and Stylianou (1998), pp. 515–7.
72 Pritchett (1969), p. 59, Kromayer (1903), pp. 47–76 and Map 2 and Kromayer and Veith (1922–9) Griech. Abt. Blatt 5.8 and (1924–31), pp. 317–23.

Notes to Chapter 9: Alexander the Great

1 Ellis (1976), especially pp. 186–97.
2 Hammond (1938a), pp. 212, 216–18 and Pritchett (1958).
3 Kromayer and Veith (1922–9) Griech. Abt. Blatt 5.10, Hammond (1938a), pp. 186–9, 201–18 and Hammond (1989a), pp. 116–19.
4 Pritchett (1958), DeVoto (1992), pp. 16–18, Ellis (1976), p. 294 and Hammond and Griffith (1979), pp. 596–9. Cawkwell (1978), pp. 145–6 and Ashley (1998), pp. 153–5 proposed a slightly shorter line running north-west.
5 Hammond (1938a), pp. 204–9, Pritchett (1958) and Hammond and Griffith (1979), pp. 601–2.
6 DeVoto (1992), p. 16.
7 Hammond (1994), p. 149, *contra* (1967), p. 567. On the question of Philip's allies, see Ellis (1976), pp. 186–97.
8 Head (1982), pp. 11–12, 102–8, Sekunda and McBride (1984), pp. 27–30 and Hammond (1989a), pp. 100–4.
9 Markle (1978), especially p. 497, Rahe (1981) and Manti (1994).
10 Hammond (1989a), pp. 115–16.
11 Pritchett (1958), p. 310, Head (1982), p. 64 and Ashley (1998), pp. 153–4.
12 DeVoto (1992), pp. 16–17.
13 Hammond (1938a), p. 206, (1967), p. 569, (1989a), pp. 115–17 and (1994), pp. 148–9.
14 Hammond (1994), p. 149.
15 Diodorus (XVI.85) and Polyaenus (IV.2.2).
16 Markle (1978), Rahe (1981), Manti (1983) and Mixter (1992).
17 Hammond (1989a), pp. 117–19 and (1994), pp. 153–4. For a more open perspective, see Hammond and Griffith (1979), pp. 600–3.

18   Montagu (2006), pp. 146–8.
19   Lawson (2002), pp. 198–204.
20   Green (1991), pp. xiv, 173–81, 489–512 and Badian (1977).
21   Badian (1977), Hammond (1989a), pp. 69–77, Devine (1988), Bosworth (1988), pp. 39–44 and Lane Fox (2004), pp. 119–22. The early debate is well summarized in Bosworth (1980), pp. 114–24.
22   Foss (1977), Badian (1977), pp. 277–82 and Hammond (1980), pp. 77–80.
23   Bosworth (1988), p. 40. Hammond (1989a), pp. 71–3 thinks the hills were closer, but he has to postulate a much more easterly course of the river to achieve this.
24   Badian (1977), pp. 283–4, 289–92.
25   On the details, see Bosworth (1980), pp. 98–9.
26   Hammond (1989a), pp. 69–71, 74–6, Devine (1988), pp. 5–6 and Bosworth (1980), p. 119.
27   Hammond (1989a), pp. 73–4, Bosworth (1988), p. 39 and Devine (1988), pp. 6–10.
28   Green (1991), pp. 172–3, Ashley (1998), p. 192 and Badian (1977), pp. 284–6. For counter-arguments, see Parke (1933), pp. 178–81.
29   See Badian (1977), pp. 283–4 and McCoy (1989).
30   Judeich in Kromayer and Veith (1922–9) Griech. Abt. Blatt 6.2 gives both armies a frontage of nearly 4 km, which seems far too long for the Macedonians.
31   Devine (1988), pp. 7–8.
32   Hammond (1980), p. 82, Ashley (1998), pp. 194, 454 note 24 and Devine (1988), p. 10.
33   See Hammond (1980), pp. 83–5, Badian (1977), pp. 289–90 and Devine (1988), pp. 11–13.
34   Grant (1977), Chapter 5.
35   Devine (1985c).
36   Bosworth (1980), pp. 203–4 and (1988), p. 60, Devine (1985d), pp. 45–6 and Hammond (1992), p. 395.
37   Hammond (1989a), pp. 98–102 and Devine (1985d), p. 44.
38   See Bosworth (1980), pp. 212–13 on the reliability of these rather contradictory claims.
39   Hammond (1989a), pp. 98–102 and Devine (1985d), pp. 45–6, 49–55.
40   Hammond (1989a), p. 102 and (1992), p. 396 and Bosworth (1980), pp. 210–11.
41   See Hammond (1989b), p. 63.
42   Head (1992), pp. 42–3, Bosworth (1980), p. 208 and Hammond (1992), p. 404.
43   Devine (1985d), pp. 47–8 and Ashley (1998), pp. 223–5.
44   Hammond (1989a), pp. 101–3, Devine (1985d), pp. 46–9, 58–9 and Bosworth (1988), p. 60.
45   Arrian (Anab. II.8–9) and Hammond (1989a), pp. 103–5.
46   Hammond (1992) and Bosworth (1980), pp. 213–14.
47   Bosworth (1980), pp. 214–16 and Hammond (1989a), pp. 105–7.
48   Devine (1985d), pp. 55–6.
49   Hammond (1989a), p. 102, Devine (1985d), pp. 58–9 and Ashley (1998), pp. 222–30 all show the Persian right wing horse occupying only 650 m or less, despite the explicit strictures of Polybius (XII.18).
50   Devine (1986), pp. 94–6.
51   Hammond (1989a), p. 142, Marsden (1964), p. 39, Judeich in Kromayer and Veith (1922–9) Griech. Abt. Blatt 7.5a and b and Devine (1989), pp. 77–9. Ashley (1998), p. 260 makes the Macedonian frontage 3.6 km and the Persian frontage 5.5 km.

52   See Marsden (1964), Chapter 3 and Parke (1933), Chapter 19.

53   Hammond (1989a), pp. 142–5, Marsden (1964), pp. 65–73 and Devine (1989).

54   Hammond (1989a), pp. 142–5 does not even include them in this battle, instead postulating a larger mercenary component. Marsden (1964), p. 66 and Devine (1989), p. 78 put them in the second line. I have not classed them as hoplites, to avoid unrealistic interactions with Darius's Greeks.

55   Bosworth (1980), pp. 300–4.

56   Marsden (1964), p. 74, Hammond (1989a), p. 142 and Devine (1989).

57   Marsden (1964), pp. 31–7 and Devine (1986), pp. 100–3. Ashley (1998), pp. 258–9 agrees with Marsden.

58   Hammond (1989a), pp. 140–3.

59   Lane Fox (2004), p. 229 and Head (1992), p. 67. Arrian (*Anab*. III.16) puts the number of Greeks fleeing with Darius at 2,000, and Curtius (V.8.3) says 4,000. See also Parke (1933), pp. 184–5.

60   Arrian (*Anab*. III.11).

61   Arrian (*Anab*. III.8, 13) and Head (1982), pp. 86–91 and (1992), pp. 39, 67.

62   Hammond (1989a), pp. 141–3.

63   Arrian (*Anab*. III.14), Curtius (IV.15) and Diodorus (XVII.59). This story is problematic in several respects, as noted in Bosworth (1980), pp. 308–9. Fuller (1960), pp. 175–9 suggests that some of the raiders reached only the first-line transport rather than the camp itself further to the rear, but this is highly speculative and does not justify putting the camp on the board.

64   Griffith (1947), Marsden (1964), Chapter 4, Devine (1986), pp. 103–7, Hammond (1989a), pp. 145–9, Ashley (1998), pp. 261–9 and Bosworth (1980), pp. 304–12 and (1988), pp. 81–4.

65   Bosworth (1980), p. 312 and Devine (1986), pp. 107–8.

66   Arrian (*Anab*. V.11).

67   Bosworth (1995), pp. 265–9 and Devine (1987), p. 96.

68   See Head (1982), p. 136 and Bosworth (1995), pp. 291, 293.

69   Lane Fox (2004), p. 355, Bosworth (1988), pp. 127–8 and (1995), pp. 277–9, and Daniel (1992), p. 52.

70   Hammond (1989a), pp. 210–13, Green (1991), p. 393, Ashley (1998), p. 318, Devine (1987), pp. 98–100, Hamilton (1956), p. 26 and Montagu (2006), p. 151.

71   Hammond (1989a), p. 213, Devine (1987), pp. 98–9, Daniel (1992), p. 51, Bosworth (1995), pp. 293–5 and Aperghis (1997), pp. 143–4.

72   See Bosworth (1995), pp. 59–61 on the debate over the weapon used to kill Cleitus 2 years earlier.

73   Hammond (1989a), pp. 211–13, Lane Fox (2004), pp. 357–8, Hamilton (1956), p. 27, Devine (1987), pp. 101–2, Ashley (1998), p. 318, Green (1991), p. 396 and Bosworth (1995), p. 292.

74   Head (1982), pp. 135–9.

75   Polyaenus (IV.3.22) describes Porus as riding the leftmost elephant of the line, but elephants and levies cannot be rallied by leaders in our model, and Arrian (*Anab*. V.18) makes clear that Porus remained on the field as long as a single unit fought on, so it is more appropriate to treat him as a commander.

76   Hamilton (1956), p. 27.
77   Hammond (1989a), pp. 212–14 and Ashley (1998), pp. 322–6.
78   Devine (1987), pp. 101, 113 and Bosworth (1995), pp. 292–3, 296.
79   Hammond (1996), pp. 27–31 brings some interesting insights from Polyaenus (IV.3.22) to bear on this.
80   Bosworth (1995), pp. 294–5.
81   Arrian (*Anab.* V.18) claims that 200 of his 230 cavalry losses fell among horsemen other than the Companions and Dahae.
82   Hammond (1989a), pp. 211–14, Fuller (1960), pp. 192–7, Judeich in Kromayer and Veith (1922–9) Griech. Abt. Blatt 7.7a,b, Warry (1991), pp. 76–9, Ashley (1998), pp. 323–5, Hamilton (1956), Scullard (1974), pp. 69–70, Green (1991), pp. 397–9, Devine (1987), pp. 102–7 and Bosworth (1995), pp. 299–300.
83   Arrian (*Anab.* V.17–18).
84   Arrian (*Anab.* V.18), Diodorus (XVII.89), Devine (1987), pp. 108–9 and Bosworth (1995), pp. 304–10.

Notes to Chapter 10: The Successors

1   Devine (1985a,b) and others suggest 317, while Billows (1990), Chapter 3 prefers 316.
2   Hornblower (1981).
3   Devine (1985a), pp. 75–6, 84, Billows (1990), pp. 94–6 and Scullard (1974), pp. 87–9.
4   Diodorus (XIX.14, 17), Head (1982), p. 16 and Devine (1985a), pp. 76–9.
5   Devine (1985a), p. 78, Head (1982), p. 16 and Hammond (1978), p. 135.
6   Diodorus (XIX.27–8) and Head (1982), p. 16.
7   Devine (1985a), p. 81.
8   Griffith (1935), pp. 47–50, 317–21, Head (1982), pp. 15–17, 97–8 and Diodorus (XIX.19).
9   Diodorus (XIX.29), Head (1982), p. 17 and Devine (1985a), pp. 79–81.
10 Devine (1985a), p. 84 and Billows (1990), pp. 96–7.
11 Scullard (1974), p. 86 and Kromayer and Veith (1924–31), pp. 408–24.
12 Diodorus (XIX.27–9) and Devine (1985a), p. 77.
13 Diodorus (XIX.29–30) and Devine (1985a), pp. 81–3.
14 Devine (1985a), p. 86, Scullard (1974), p. 89 and Billows (1990), pp. 96–7.
15 Diodorus (XIX.42–3), Plutarch (*Eum.* 16) and Devine (1985b), p. 88.
16 Diodorus (XIX.39, 42).
17 Diodorus (XIX.31, 40), Devine (1985b), pp. 88–9, 94, Scullard (1974), p. 91, Head (1982), p. 69 and Billows (1990), p. 101.
18 Devine (1985b), pp. 88–91, Scullard (1974), p. 90, Head (1982), pp. 68–9 and Billows (1990), p. 101.
19 Diodorus (XIX.40).
20 Billows (1990), pp. 100–2.
21 Scullard (1974), p. 91, Billows (1990), p. 100 and Devine (1985b), p. 94.
22 Devine (1985b), pp. 88–91, 94, Scullard (1974), pp. 91–3 and Billows (1990), p. 100.
23 Polyaenus (IV.6.13) says that 300 of Eumenes's men fell.

24 Diodorus (XIX.69, 80).

25 Diodorus (XIX.84) and Devine (1984), p. 31.

26 Devine (1984), pp. 31–5.

27 Griffith (1935), p. 317 and Head (1982), pp. 120–1.

28 Billows (1990), pp. 125–6, Head (1982), pp. 20, 69, Seibert (1969), pp. 165–7, Scullard (1974), p. 95, Devine (1984), p. 35 and Griffith (1935), pp. 109–10.

29 Diodorus (XIX.83–4).

30 Diodorus (XIX.80–5) and Devine (1984), p. 35.

31 Diodorus (XIX.82–3) and Seibert (1969), pp. 167–73.

32 Devine (1984), p. 32 and Billows (1990), p. 126.

33 Seibert (1969), pp. 173–5.

34 Plutarch (*Dem.* 5) says there were 5,000 dead, but this is universally dismissed as erroneous.

35 For attempts to reconstruct Ipsus from the summary given by Plutarch (*Dem.* 28–9), see Bar-Kochva (1976), Chapter 6, Billows (1990), pp. 181–4 and Montagu (2006), pp. 165–8.

36 Walbank (1970), pp. 276–8 initially followed Kromayer (1903), pp. 215–23 and Map 5, but later in Hammond and Walbank (1988), pp. 358–60 he backed Pritchett (1965), Chapter 4.

37 Morgan (1981).

38 Walbank (1970), p. 281.

39 Walbank (1970), p. 274, Head (1982), pp. 18, 111 and Le Bohec (1993), pp. 290–4.

40 Head (1982), pp. 18–19, 114–15 and Walbank (1970), pp. 273–5.

41 Hammond and Walbank (1988), p. 360.

42 Griffith (1935), p. 70.

43 Griffith (1935), p. 95 and Lazenby (1985), p. 172.

44 Kromayer (1903), pp. 226–7, Walbank (1970), pp. 278–9, Head (1982), pp. 6–7, Pritchett (1965), p. 68, Hammond and Walbank (1988), p. 359 and Le Bohec (1993), p. 431.

45 Head (1982), pp. 6–7.

46 Walbank (1970), pp. 280–2, Hammond and Walbank (1988), p. 360, Le Bohec (1993), pp. 290–4, 426–35, Head (1982), p. 18 and Connolly (1981), p. 77.

47 On the other wing, Walbank, in Hammond and Walbank (1988), pp. 358–9, concentrates the perioikoi and allies too much on the actual summit of Troules, leaving a 1 km gap on the Dagla ridge to be held by just 2,000 cavalry and light troops. Pritchett (1965), p. 68 suggests a more balanced defence of the ridge.

48 Polybius (II.67–9) and Plutarch (*Phil.* 6).

49 Hammond and Walbank (1988), p. 361, Lazenby (1985), p. 172, Morgan (1981) and Le Bohec (1993), pp. 440–2.

50 See Miller (1977) and Boehm (1981).

51 Bar-Kochva (1976), pp. 129–32.

52 Griffith (1935), Chapter 6, Walbank (1970), pp. 607–9 and Bar-Kochva (1976), Chapters 1–3, 10.

53 Polybius (V.85).

54 Bar-Kochva (1976), pp. 82, 134. Polybius (V.79, 82, 84) is very confused about the deployment of the 5,000 Asiatics under Byttacus – see Walbank (1970), p. 611 and Scullard (1974), p. 141.

55 Head (1982), pp. 23–4 and Bar-Kochva (1976), pp. 67–75.
56 Bar-Kochva (1976), pp. 138–41, Head (1982), pp. 20–2, Griffith (1935), pp. 118–25, Scullard (1974), pp. 139–42 and Walbank (1970), pp. 589–92.
57 Polybius (V.65, 79, 85) and Head (1982), pp. 20–1.
58 Bar-Kochva (1976), pp. 131–5, especially notes 9, 13. The accompanying Map 8 purports to have a scale of 1 mm = 60 ft, but appears to understate the claimed frontages by 20 per cent – an object lesson in the perils of attempting such scale reproduction in books.
59 Polybius (V.84–5) and Bar-Kochva (1976), pp. 135–8.
60 Polybius (V.86) and Scullard (1974), p. 142.

Notes to Chapter 11: Carthage and Rome

 1 Burn (1984), Chapter 22.
 2 Gela in 405 BC might be another candidate, but was closely associated with the siege of the city, just like the battles with the Athenians at Syracuse several years earlier. See Caven (1990), Chapter 5 and Lazenby (2004), Chapters 8–9.
 3 See Talbert (1974), pp. 44–51.
 4 Westlake (1938) and Hammond (1938b).
 5 Talbert (1974), pp. 69–75. He himself favours the River Belice near ancient Selinus on the south-west coast.
 6 Plutarch (*Tim.* 27).
 7 Parke (1933), pp. 173–4, Talbert (1974), pp. 59–61 and Head (1982), pp. 10, 63. Hammond (1938b), p. 147 is more non-committal.
 8 Plutarch (*Tim.* 30), Diodorus (XVI.81), Parke (1933), pp. 174–5 and Head (1982), p. 10.
 9 Talbert (1974), pp. 63–4.
10 Head (1982), pp. 179–80.
11 Diodorus (XVI.73), Plutarch (*Tim.* 28) and Head (1982), pp. 33–5.
12 Plutarch (*Tim.* 27).
13 On the ancient sources for Agathocles, see Tillyard (1908), Chapter 1.
14 Griffith (1935), p. 199 and Head (1982), p. 11.
15 Tillyard (1908), pp. 112–14 is sceptical of this ruse and also of Diodorus's tale (XX.11) of owls (the symbol of Athena) being released to encourage the troops.
16 See Tillyard (1908), p. 111 and Warmington (1960), p. 108. Langher (2000), p. 139 even inflates the cavalry figure to 10,000!
17 See Head (1982), p. 34.
18 Tillyard (1980), p. 112 and Head (1982), pp. 33–4.
19 Diodorus (XX.12).
20 Justin (XXII.6) and Orosius (IV.6.25).
21 Tillyard (1908), p. 115.
22 Walsh (1961), pp. 197–204.
23 Cornell (1995), p. 361 and Oakley (2005), pp. 288–91.
24 Salmon (1967), pp. 265–8 and Head (1982), pp. 70–1. There is even a recent 750-page book entitled *La Battaglia del Sentino*, but this ranges over broadly associated cultural, historical

and archaeological topics rather than focusing on the battle itself – see Poli (2002).

25 Sommella (1967), pp. 35–47.

26 See Sumner (1970), Rawson (1971), Connolly (1981), pp. 126–8, Head (1982), pp. 38–40, Keppie (1984), pp. 19–23, Miller (1992) and Sekunda and Northwood (1995), pp. 33–41.

27 Cornell (1995), p. 361. Head (1982), pp. 39, 159–60 and Sekunda and Northwood (1995), pp. 40–1.

28 McCall (2002) argues strongly against this critical view.

29 Head (1982), p. 70. Brunt (1971), p. 683 challenges the 3:1 ratio.

30 Oakley (2005), pp. 290, 326 suggests that the contrast between Decius and Fabius is suspiciously stereotypical.

31 Oakley (2005), pp. 288–9.

32 On the various readings of the ancient figures, see Oakley (2005), pp. 330–2.

33 Connolly (1981), pp. 105–26, Head (1982), pp. 41–2, 57–8, 61–2, 150–5, 163–7, Sekunda and Northwood (1995), pp. 33–9 and Cunliffe (1999), Chapter 5.

34 On the chariots, see Oakley (2005), pp. 319–20 and Connolly (1981), pp. 125–6.

35 Sommella (1967), p. 43.

36 Cornell (1995), pp. 348, 362 and Oakley (2005), pp. 290–1. See also Garoufalias (1979), pp. 363–5.

37 Oakley (2005), pp. 317–19, Rawlings (1996) and Cunliffe (1999), Chapter 5.

38 Livy (X.28–9) and Head (1982), p. 42.

39 Head (1982), p. 70.

40 More conventional scholarship on the battle is summarized in Garoufalias (1979), pp. 69–77, 334–47.

41 Lancel (1998), pp. 110–11.

42 See Hornblower (1981), pp. 71–2, 128, 141–2, Lévèque (1957), pp. 379–80 and Garoufalias (1979), p. 368.

43 Lévèque (1957).

44 Garoufalias (1979), pp. 92–3, 374 and Head (1982), p. 72.

45 Lévèque (1957), pp. 380–7 and Garoufalias (1979), pp. 89, 363.

46 Lévèque (1957), pp. 377–9, Garoufalias (1979), pp. 88–9, 361–2 and Head (1982), pp. 19–20, 72.

47 Garoufalias (1979), pp. 89, 362–3 and Lévèque (1957), pp. 376–7.

48 Lévèque (1957), pp. 388–9, Scullard (1974), pp. 107–9, Garoufalias (1979), pp. 90–2, 365–6, 372 and Head (1982), p. 181.

49 Garoufalias (1979), pp. 89–90, 363–5 and Lévèque (1957), pp. 395–8.

50 Head (1982), p. 19.

51 Head (1982), p. 10.

52 Head (1982), p. 19.

53 Plutarch (*Pyrrh.* 21), Dionysius (XX.1–3) and Scullard (1974), pp. 106–10.

54 Lévèque (1957), pp. 390–4 and Garoufalias (1979), pp. 91–2, 368–70.

55 Garoufalias (1979), pp. 91, 366–8 and Walbank (1967), p. 586.

56 Lévèque (1957), pp. 384–90, Scullard (1974), pp. 106–10 and Garoufalias (1979), pp. 91–3, 370–5.

57 Lévèque (1957), pp. 394–5 and Garoufalias (1979), pp. 92–3, 373–5.

58   Krentz (1985a).

59   Walbank (1970), p. 89.

60   Lazenby (1996), p. 104, Le Bohec (1996), p. 89 and Head (1982), pp. 73–4. The general topography of the campaign is discussed in Fantar (1989).

61   Scullard (1974), pp. 146–9 and Head (1982), pp. 35–6.

62   Walbank (1970), pp. 91–2, Lazenby (1996), p. 103 and Goldsworthy (2000a), p. 88.

63   Polybius (I.30, 32) and Goldsworthy (2000a), p. 88.

64   Griffith (1935), p. 213.

65   Caven (1980), pp. 38–9.

66   Head (1982), pp. 33–4, 140–5, *contra* Connolly (1981), p. 148.

67   Polybius (I.34).

68   Polybius (I.30–1, XV.9–11) and Head (1982), p. 34.

69   Polybius (I.30–4), Walbank (1970), pp. 89–94, Lazenby (1996), pp. 102–6 and Goldsworthy (2000a), pp. 88–91.

70   Lazenby (1996), p. 98 and Goldsworthy (2000a), p. 85.

71   Walbank (1970), p. 92 and Lazenby (1996), p. 103.

72   Goldsworthy (2000a), p. 90 suggests odds of at least 4:1, which is the ratio used in the scenario.

73   Lazenby (1996), pp. 104–5. Griffith (1935), p. 214 can only suggest that Polybius did not really understand elephant tactics.

74   Goldsworthy (2000a), p. 89.

75   This tallies with Kromayer and Veith (1922–9) Röm. Abt. Blatt 1.6, which gives the infantry a front of 1.25 km.

76   Le Bohec (1996), p. 90 even has a reconstruction in which the entire Roman line has a significantly *wider* frontage than that of the Carthaginians, despite the depth problem and the enormous cavalry imbalance.

77   Polybius (I.30–3) and Xenophon (*An*. I–IV).

Notes to Chapter 12: Hannibal and Scipio

1   Sabin (1996).

2   Montagu (2000), pp. 177–95.

3   On these battles, see Lazenby (1978), pp. 62–6, 102, 128, 141–2, 187–90, 208–11.

4   On the sources and reliability of these writers for this conflict, see Lazenby (1978), pp. 258–60.

5   See the maps in Walbank (1970), p. 398, Scullard (1974), p. 160, Lazenby (1978), Map 5, Caven (1980), p. 112, Connolly (1981), p. 169 and Goldsworthy (2000a), p. 174.

6   Goldsworthy (2000a), pp. 174, 177.

7   Kromayer and Veith (1922–9) Röm. Abt. Blatt 3.6 and Goldsworthy (2000a), p. 174.

8   Polybius (III.56, 66–8), Walbank (1970), pp. 404–5, Lazenby (1978), pp. 53–6, Caven (1980), pp. 105–6, 110 and Goldsworthy (2000a), pp. 167, 178.

9   Polybius (II.30), Head (1982), pp. 34–7, 55–8, 145–54 and Connolly (1981), pp. 113–26, 148–52.

10 Daly (2002), pp. 30–2, 106–11, Walbank (1970), p. 366 and Polybius (III.74). Delbrück (1975), pp. 361–2 argues that Hannibal had at most 2,000 Celtic infantry in this battle, and perhaps none at all. Santosuosso (1997), p. 173 makes the strange suggestion that Hannibal had only 19,000 infantry in all.

11 Scullard (1974), pp. 159–61.

12 Polybius (III.60).

13 Walbank (1970), pp. 405–6, Lazenby (1978), p. 56, Caven (1980), p. 111, Connolly (1981), p. 170, Head (1982), pp. 40, 76 and Goldsworthy (2000a), pp. 178–9.

14 On the Ticinus losses, see Polybius (III.65) and Livy (XXI.46).

15 Polybius (III.73).

16 Polybius (III.66, 70).

17 Polybius (III.72).

18 Connolly (1981), p. 169 shows the Africans in column on each wing as at Cannae, despite Polybius's clear statement that they formed a single line with the Celts and Spaniards.

19 Walbank (1970), p. 406. Goldsworthy (2000a), p. 174 shows the elephants in the line itself between the infantry and cavalry, but most scholars much more plausibly place them in front of the infantry wings.

20 Goldsworthy (2000a), p. 177. The roots of early Roman qualitative superiority are explored in Lendon (2005), pp. 163–211.

21 Daly (2002), pp. 32–5.

22 See the diagrams in Kromayer and Veith (1922–9) Röm. Abt. Blatt 6, Lancel (1998), p. 106 and Daly (2002), p. 34.

23 Lazenby (1978), pp. 78–9 highlights the more broken terrain south of the river as a possible incentive for the Romans to fight there, despite their declining battle to the north.

24 Lazenby (1978), p. 80, Connolly (1981), pp. 184–7, Goldsworthy (2000a), pp. 204–5, Kromayer and Veith (1922–9) Röm. Abt. Blatt 6, Lancel (1998), p. 106 and Daly (2002), pp. 34–7.

25 Goldsworthy (2001), pp. 96–102. His reconstruction would require even Hannibal's Celtic and Spanish centre to be an average of 24 deep, and would squeeze the 70,000 Roman infantry into roughly the same frontage as the 15,000 Romans at the Bagradas, whose formation Polybius (I.33) already described as unusually deep!

26 Kromayer and Veith (1922–9) Röm. Abt. Blatt 6.

27 Goldsworthy (2000a), p. 201 at first hinted at such a site, before opting in (2001) Chapter 4 for his implausibly compressed lines north-west of Cannae.

28 Connolly (1981), p. 187, Lancel (1998), pp. 106–7, Daly (2002), p. 32, Lazenby (1978), p. 82 and Goldsworthy (2000a), pp. 204, 207.

29 Daly (2002), pp. 29–32, Lazenby (1978), p. 81, Connolly (1981), p. 187 and Goldsworthy (2000a), p. 207.

30 Daly (2002), pp. 29–30, following Dodge (1891), p. 359.

31 Polybius (III.113–14).

32 Brunt (1971), pp. 648, 671–2, Caven (1980), pp. 137–8, Walbank (1970), pp. 439–40, Lazenby (1978), pp. 75–6, Seibert (1993a), pp. 191–2, Santosuosso (1997), p. 176 and Daly (2002), pp. 25–9.

33   Lazenby (1978), pp. 79–80, Goldsworthy (2000a), p. 204, Connolly (1981), pp. 184–7 and Daly (2002), pp. 27, 56–7, 76–9.

34   Samuels (1990), Goldsworthy (2000a), pp. 198–206 and Daly (2002), Chapter 3.

35   The fighting is exhaustively analysed in Daly (2002), Chapters 2, 5 and 6.

36   Walbank (1970), p. 440, Lazenby (1978), pp. 84–5, Goldsworthy (2000a), p. 213 and Daly (2002), p. 202.

37   Daly (2002) and Goldsworthy (2001).

38   Scullard (1936) and (1970), pp. 89, 262–3.

39   Walbank (1967), p. 296, Lazenby (1978), pp. 145–6 and Goldsworthy (2000a), p. 279.

40   Livy's claim (XXVIII.13) that the total came to 45,000 altogether is usually dismissed as a mistake – see Lazenby (1978), p. 145.

41   Lazenby (1978), pp. 148, 294, Head (1982), p. 40 and Goldsworthy (2000a), p. 279. Connolly (1981), p. 199 thinks that less than half of the army was Italian.

42   Livy (XXVI.4), Polybius (VI.22, 25), Scullard (1970), Chapters 2–4, Head (1982), pp. 39, 159–61, McCall (2002), Chapter 3 and Daly (2002), pp. 70–6.

43   Samuels (1990) and Glantz and House (1995).

44   Scullard (1970), pp. 88, 262, Walbank (1967), pp. 296–7 and Lazenby (1978), p. 145. Head (1982), pp. 79–80, Le Bohec (1996), pp. 235–7 and Goldsworthy (2000a), p. 279 are all non-committal.

45   Polybius (XI.24).

46   Polybius (XI.22, 24) and Livy (XXVIII.15).

47   Kromayer and Veith (1922–9) Röm. Abt. Blatt 8.2.

48   Walbank (1967), pp. 299–304, Lazenby (1978), pp. 147–50 and Map 17, and Connolly (1981), pp. 200–1.

49   Livy (XXVIII.14) says 500 paces (750 m), while the manuscripts of Polybius (XI.22) say just 1 stade (180 m), but this is usually seen as an error and corrected to 4 stadia – see Walbank (1967), p. 300 and Lazenby (1978), pp. 147, 294.

50   Polybius (XI.24) and Goldsworthy (2000a), pp. 282–3. Le Bohec (1996), p. 236 has a much more dubious reconstruction in which the Roman cavalry redeploy and attack in the centre.

51   Kromayer and Veith (1922–9) Röm. Abt. Blatt 8.6, Walbank (1967), pp. 446–9, Scullard (1970), pp. 271–4, Lazenby (1978), pp. 218–19 and Connolly (1981), pp. 203–4.

52   Appian (*Pun.* 40–7).

53   Goldsworthy (2000a), p. 301 and Brunt (1971), pp. 672–4.

54   Walbank (1967), pp. 450, 454–5, Lazenby (1978), pp. 219–21, Head (1982), p. 80, Connolly (1981), pp. 203–4, Seibert (1993a), p. 467 and Lancel (1998), p. 175. Santosuosso (1997), p. 191 thinks Scipio had as many as 34,000 foot.

55   Goldsworthy (2000a), p. 203.

56   Walbank (1967), pp. 449–50, Scullard (1970), p. 143, Lazenby (1978), pp. 220–1, Caven (1980), p. 250, Head (1982), p. 80, Seibert (1993a), pp. 467–8, Lancel (1998), pp. 171, 175 and Goldsworthy (2000a), pp. 302–3.

57   Our comparative model suggests that this is far more likely than the ideas in Walbank (1967), pp. 456–7 and Scullard (1970), pp. 143, 274–5 that the mercenaries were all heavy troops and that light infantry were either absent altogether or present but unmentioned.

58   Polybius (XV.13, 16) and Dorey (1957).

59 Livy (XXX.20, 33–4) and Lazenby (1978), pp. 215, 222.

60 Kromayer and Veith (1922–9) Röm. Abt. Blatt 8.6.

61 See, for example, Goldsworthy (2000a), p. 301.

62 Connolly (1981), p. 205 goes rather too far in this regard, by showing both sides' foot occupying only one third of the entire battlefront.

63 Polybius (XV.11, 13–16).

64 The veterans will probably be used to conduct supporting attacks from an early stage because of their concentration bonus, but this does not necessarily represent physical involvement at the front line, and is an unavoidable abstraction in this case because of the broad-brush nature of the zone system.

65 Polybius (XIV.7–8), Connolly (1981), pp. 203–5, Kromayer and Veith (1922–9) Röm. Abt. Blatt 8.6, Walbank (1967), pp. 460–3 and Lazenby (1978), p. 225.

Notes to Chapter 13: Rome Moves East

1   On 2nd Chaeronea, see Hammond (1938a).

2   Kromayer (1907), pp. 60–78, Kromayer and Veith (1922–9) Röm. Abt. Blatt 9.3, 4, Walbank (1967), pp. 576–9, Pritchett (1969), Chapter 11, Connolly (1981), pp. 205–7 and Hammond (1988).

3   Hammond (1988), Figure 3.

4   Polybius (XVIII.20–3) and Livy (XXXIII.6–7).

5   Walbank (1967), pp. 584–5 and Hammond (1988), p. 65.

6   Head (1982), p. 18.

7   Hammond (1989c), pp. 347–9, 369–74.

8   On the details of Roman armies in this century, see Sekunda and McBride (1996).

9   Briscoe (1973), pp. 251–3.

10 Kromayer (1907), pp. 102–5, Pritchett (1969), p. 135, Head (1982), p. 81, Santosuosso (1997), p. 161 and Hammond (1988), pp. 65–6.

11 Walbank (1967), pp. 572, 585 and Briscoe (1973), pp. 249, 251, 253–4.

12 Head (1982), pp. 8–9.

13 Scullard (1974), pp. 178–9.

14 Kromayer (1907), p. 81, Walbank (1967), p. 582 and Hammond (1988), p. 74.

15 Hammond (1988), Figure 3, Kromayer and Veith (1922–9) Röm. Abt. Blatt 9.4, Keppie (1984), p. 42 and Connolly (1981), p. 207. One must always watch out for such errors in scale – see the various maps in Goldsworthy (2001), Chapter 4 and Glantz and House (1995).

16 Polybius (XVIII.25–6), Walbank (1967), pp. 583–4 and Hammond (1988), pp. 74–6.

17 Grainger (2002), pp. 318, 320.

18 Kromayer (1907), pp. 163–79, Kromayer and Veith (1922–9) Röm. Abt. Blatt 9.7 and 9.8, Bar-Kochva (1976), pp. 163–5 and Grainger (2002), p. 324.

19 Kromayer (1907), pp. 180–1, Scullard (1974), p. 180, Bar-Kochva (1976), pp. 165–6, Head (1982), pp. 81–2, Montagu (2006), p. 215 and Grainger (2002), pp. 320–2, 359–61.

20 See especially Livy (XXXVI.14) and (XXXVII.2, 4).

21 Grainger (2002), pp. 323–4.

22   Head (1982), pp. 23–6. Griffith (1935), pp. 144–6 is hopelessly confused on these numbers.
23   Bar-Kochva (1976), pp. 8–9, 60–5, 166–9 and Grainger (2002), pp. 318–23.
24   Kromayer and Veith (1922–9) Röm. Abt. Blatt 9.8 and Bar-Kochva (1976), p. 166.
25   Kromayer and Veith (1922–9) Röm. Abt. Blatt 9.8 and Montagu (2006), pp. 215–18.
26   Bar-Kochva (1976), pp. 166–9 and Map 14. Briscoe (1981), p. 350 does not like the challenge to Livy, but experience elsewhere suggests it is sometimes justified!
27   Appian (*Syr.* 34), Justin (XXXVI.8) and Bar-Kochva (1976), pp. 169–73. Briscoe (1981), p. 355 again defends Livy's reliability.
28   Walbank (1979), p. 378.
29   Plutarch (*Aem.* 18), Walbank (1979), pp. 387–8 and Hammond (1984), pp. 44–6.
30   Kromayer (1907), pp. 310–16, Kromayer and Veith (1922–9) Röm. Abt. Blatt 10.1, 10.3, Fuller (1954), Chapter 5, Pritchett (1969), Chapter 12, Walbank (1979), pp. 384–6 and Hammond (1984).
31   Among recent writers, Goldsworthy (2004), p. 99 follows Hammond, while Connolly (1998), pp. 39–40 sticks with the Katerini site.
32   Hammond (1984), pp. 35–7.
33   Pritchett (1969), p. 147.
34   Kromayer and Veith (1922–9) Röm. Abt. Blatt 10.3, Connolly (1998), p. 40 and Hammond (1984), p. 40.
35   Griffith (1935), pp. 74–7 and Head (1982), pp. 18–19.
36   Hammond (1989c), pp. 372–4.
37   Walbank (1979), pp. 389–90.
38   Scullard (1974), p. 184.
39   Kromayer (1907), pp. 340–8, Pritchett (1969), p. 158, Head (1982), pp. 39–41, 83 and Hammond (1984), p. 46 and (1989c), p. 373.
40   Plutarch (*Aem.* 17–18, 22).
41   Livy (XLIV.36–40) and Lendon (2005), pp. 203–11.
42   See Livy (XXXI.34–5) and my own remarks in Sabin, van Wees and Whitby (2007), Vol. 1, Chapter 13A.
43   Plutarch (*Aem.* 18) and Livy (XLIV.40–1).
44   Plutarch (*Aem.*20) and Livy (XLIV.41).
45   Kromayer (1907), pp. 322–3, Kromayer and Veith (1922–9) Röm. Abt. Blatt 10.3, Pritchett (1969), p. 162, Hammond (1984), pp. 39–40, Connolly (1998), p. 40 and Goldsworthy (2004), p. 99.
46   Kromayer and Veith (1922–9) Röm. Abt. Blatt 10.3, Walbank (1979), p. 388, Hammond (1984), p. 46 and Santosuosso (1997), pp. 164–6.
47   Hammond (1984), p. 46.
48   Plutarch (*Aem.*20–1) and Goldsworthy (2004), pp. 97–104.
49   Each of the 12 'hours' in a June day would be around 90 min long.
50   Sekunda and McBride (1994).
51   Plutarch (*Luc.* 25–8).
52   Rice Holmes (1923) Vol. II, pp. 312–13.
53   Parker (1923), Chapter 1, Smith (1958), Bell (1965), Keppie (1984), Chapter 2 and McCall (2002), Chapters 1, 6 and 7.

54 Rice Holmes (1923) Vol. II, pp. 313–14 and Brunt (1971), pp. 461–3.

55 Delbrück (1975), p. 441, Rice Holmes (1923) Vol. II, p. 160, Cook, Adcock and Charlesworth (1932), p. 608, Marshall (1976), p. 144, Barker (1981), p. 47, Wilcox and McBride (1986), p. 22 and Montagu (2006), p. 231.

56 Caesar (B Afr.12–18) and Brunt (1971), pp. 460–1.

57 There is an entertaining historical novel by Duggan (1956) about these Gallic horsemen.

58 Herodotus (IX.22, 60) and Jones (1988), pp. 35–41.

59 Marshall (1976), pp. 25–34.

60 Cook, Adcock and Charlesworth (1932), p. 608, Barker (1981), p. 47 and Wilcox and McBride (1986), p. 22.

61 Wilcox and McBride (1986), pp. 6–10.

62 Warry (1980), p. 156 is a rare exception, and even he just shows a square under symmetrical attack from all sides.

63 Caesar (B Afr. 13–17).

64 Plutarch (Crass. 23).

65 Rice Holmes (1923) Vol. II, pp. 313–15 and Montagu (2006), pp. 229–30.

66 Plutarch (Crass. 25).

67 Plutarch (Crass. 26–8).

68 Dio (XL.23) has a rhetorical and deeply unconvincing tale of an Arab traitor bringing his force to attack the Romans from the rear, thereby catching them between two fires.

69 Montagu (2006), pp. 225–7, 229–31.

Notes to Chapter 14: Julius Caesar

1 Rice Holmes (1911), pp. 201–56, Welch and Powell (1998) and Kagan (2006), Chapters 5–6.

2 Kromayer and Veith (1922–9) Röm. Abt. Blatt 15.1, Rice Holmes (1911), pp. 53–4, 624–8, Fuller (1965), pp. 103–4, Keppie (1984), pp. 82–3, Le Bohec (2001), pp. 160–1 and Goldsworthy (2006), pp. 220–1.

3 Goldsworthy (2006), p. 213. On the problem of judging the strength of legions in this era, see Rice Holmes (1911), pp. 559–63 and Brunt (1971), pp. 687–93.

4 Goldsworthy (2006), pp. 219–22.

5 Rice Holmes (1911), pp. 579–81.

6 Kagan (2006), pp. 119–25 and Goldsworthy (2006), pp. 220–1.

7 Delbrück (1975), pp. 460–3, 470–5.

8 Goldsworthy (2006), pp. 209–10, 220.

9 Rice Holmes (1911), pp. 55, 629–31 and Goldsworthy (2006), pp. 221–2.

10 Kromayer and Veith (1922–9) Röm. Abt. Blatt 15.1, Rice Holmes (1911), p. 53 and Fuller (1965), p. 104.

11 Kagan (2006), pp. 128–36.

12 Kromayer and Veith (1922–9) Röm. Abt. Blatt 15.7, Rice Holmes (1911), pp. 75–6, 671–5, Fuller (1965), pp. 112–13 and Goldsworthy (2006), pp. 244–5.

13 Polybius (III.71), Livy (XLIV.37), Caesar (B Gall. I.49) and Goldsworthy (2006), pp. 246–7.

14   Peddie (1994), pp. 68–75.

15   Le Bohec (2001), pp. 186–7 and Goldsworthy (2006), p. 233.

16   Goldsworthy (2006), p. 244.

17   Kromayer and Veith (1922–9) Röm. Abt. Blatt 15.7 and Rice Holmes (1911), p. 75.

18   Goldsworthy (2006), p. 244 and Delbrück (1975), pp. 491–3.

19   Kromayer and Veith (1922–9) Röm. Abt. Blatt 15.7 and Rice Holmes (1911), p. 75.

20   Peddie (1994), pp. 72–5 suggests that the baggage train would have been even longer, but this depends on one's assumptions about the width of the column.

21   Gwatkin (1956), 109–11.

22   Kromayer (1907), pp. 401–25, Rice Holmes (1908) and (1923) Vol. III, pp. 163, 452–67, Kromayer and Veith (1924–31), pp. 637–46 and Gwatkin (1956) are just a few of the many contributions, which are well summarized and analysed in Morgan (1983).

23   Goldsworthy (2006), pp. 425–8 has a generic reconstruction showing just this feature.

24   Some reconstructions show the battlelines much closer to a proposed Pompeian camp on Mount Dogandzis, but this site is compatible with a more advanced position of Pompey's line in tune with Caesar's statement. See Rice Holmes (1923) Vol. III, p. 163, Fuller (1965), p. 232 and cf Gwatkin (1956), p. 113.

25   Delbrück (1975), pp. 542–5, Rice Holmes (1923) Vol. III, pp. 472–6, Fuller (1965), p. 234, Morgan (1983), p. 25, Le Bohec (2001), p. 386, Montagu (2006), p. 234 and Goldsworthy (2006), p. 427.

26   Rice Holmes (1923) Vol. III, pp. 433–4, 469.

27   Delbrück (1975), pp. 545–9, Brunt (1971), pp. 691–2 and Greenhalgh (1981), pp. 299–303.

28   Rice Holmes (1923) Vol. III, pp. 472–6 and Goldsworthy (2006), p. 425.

29   Caesar (B Civ. III.94), Plutarch (Pomp. 71–2) and Fuller (1965), pp. 236–9.

30   Rice Holmes (1923) Vol. III, p. 167.

31   Eutropius (VI.20) and Orosius (VI.15) say 500 horse, but the deployment is negligible within our model in any case.

32   Rice Holmes (1923) Vol. III, p. 163 and Kromayer and Veith (1922–9) Röm. Abt. Blatt 20.4, 20.5.

33   Morgan (1983), pp. 37, 42.

34   Gwatkin (1956), pp. 109–11 advances the contrary view.

35   Rice Holmes (1923) Vol. III, pp. 470–4.

Bibliography

ANCIENT AUTHORS

Aelian: First to second century AD author of a derivative account of Hellenistic tactics.

Appian: Second century AD Greek historian who wrote a history of Rome's wars focusing on each successive conquered people.

Aristobulus: A Greek engineer who travelled with Alexander's army and later wrote a history of him (now lost).

Arrian: Second century AD Greek general who wrote a treatise on Hellenistic tactics and a history of Alexander's campaigns.

Asclepiodotus: First century BC Greek philosopher who produced a rather arcane handbook of Hellenistic military theory.

Asinius Pollio: One of Caesar's lieutenants who wrote a history of events from 60 to 42 BC (now lost).

Caesar: Produced commentaries on his own campaigns, with the work being continued from the Alexandrian war onwards by other anonymous hands after he was assassinated.

Callisthenes: Aristotle's nephew, who wrote the official history of the first few years of Alexander's campaigns (now lost) before his execution in 327 BC.

Cassius Dio: Third century AD Greek senator who wrote a history of Rome from its foundation.

Cleitarchus: A sensationalist (and now lost) writer on Alexander who lived at the time but had no personal knowledge of the campaign and no compunction about inventing fantastic tales.

Ctesias: Greek doctor at the court of Artaxerxes, who wrote a romantic history of Persia (now lost).

Curtius Rufus: First to second century AD author of a history of Alexander.

Diodorus: First century BC Sicilian Greek writer of a universal history of very variable reliability.

Dionysius: First century AD Greek historian from Halicarnassus who produced a rhetorical account of Rome's past.

Ephorus: Fourth century BC Greek author of the first universal history (now lost), whose military reliability attracted criticism from Polybius.

Eutropius: Fourth century AD writer of a survey of Roman history.

Fabius Pictor: The first Roman historian, who wrote a lost account in Greek of events in living memory at the end of the third century BC.

Frontinus: Roman governor of Britain in the late first century AD, who produced a thematic collection of historical stratagems that preserve some interesting nuggets of information.

Hellenica Oxyrhynchia: Second century BC papyrus fragments from Egypt that contain some useful independent insights on the period covered by Xenophon.

Herodotus: The first Greek historian, a native of Halicarnassus, who wrote a highly discursive account of the Persian invasions of Greece sometime in the mid-fifth century BC.

Hieronymus: A Greek statesman from Cardia who was an eyewitness of the early Successor period and the author of an impressively detailed survey (now lost) of the 50 years after Alexander's death.

Justin: Produced a Latin epitome of the lost universal history by the first century AD writer Pompeius Trogus.

Livy: A leading Roman historian in the reign of Augustus, whose history of Rome from its foundation is wonderfully written but not always entirely reliable.

Nepos: First century BC Roman biographer of dubious quality, only a few of whose works survive.

Onasander: First century AD Greek philosopher who wrote a treatise on generalship that is much more practical than Asclepiodotus's theoretical work.

Orosius: Fifth century AD theologian who produced a history aimed at rebutting pagan claims that Christianity was to blame for current disasters.

Pausanias: Second century AD author of a guide to the monuments and historical sites of Greece, with some obvious relevance for battlefield geography.

Philinus: Pro-Carthaginian historian of the First Punic War, whose lost work was used by Polybius.

Plutarch: First to second century AD Greek writer from Chaeronea who penned 23 sets of 'parallel lives' of famous Greeks and Romans. These are intended for moralistic rather than historical purposes and so rarely contain as much detail as other writers, but they are a very useful supplement when other sources fail.

Polyaenus: Second century AD Macedonian rhetorician, who compiled a collection of historical stratagems that is far less well organized than that of Frontinus but contains a few useful nuggets of information.

Polybius: Second century BC Achaean statesman who became a Roman hostage and part of the 'Scipionic Circle'. His history of Rome's rise to world dominion is dry and often pedantic, but is based on detailed and critical research. Its main shortcoming is that so much of the work after Cannae has been lost, but at least it was able to inform the work of later historians such as Livy.

Posidonius: Wrote a lost account of the reign of Perseus in Macedon.

Ptolemy: One of Alexander's generals, who founded the Ptolemaic dynasty in Egypt and who later wrote a history of Alexander (now lost) based on his recollections and the king's own journal.

Tacitus: First century AD Roman historian whose work is of high quality but does not cover our period.

Thucydides: An Athenian general who was exiled during the Peloponnesian War but who wrote a detailed account of the conflict based on clear analysis and careful historical method.

Timaeus: Fourth to third century BC Sicilian Greek historian who wrote lost accounts of Sicilian history and of Rome's war with Pyrrhus, but whose methodology is criticized by Polybius.

Vegetius: Fourth to fifth century AD Roman writer who produced a book on military theory to try to revive the discipline and success of the past.

Xenophon: Greek mercenary general who wrote an eyewitness account of the 10,000's campaign in Persia and who continued Thucydides's history of Greece from 411 to 362 BC, but who tended to rely more on his own memory than on detailed research.

Zonaras: Twelfth century AD Byzantine writer who compiled a universal history and who preserves a few ancient sources that have been lost since then.

MODERN SOURCES

Adcock, F. (1940) *The Roman Art of War under the Republic*. Cambridge: Harvard University Press.

Adcock, F. (1962) *The Greek and Macedonian Art of War*. Berkeley: University of California Press.

Adkin, M. (2001) *The Waterloo Companion*. London: Aurum.

Air Ministry (1963) *The Origins and Development of Operational Research in the Royal Air Force*. London: HMSO, Air Publication 3368.

Allen, T. (1987) *War Games*. London: Heinemann.

Anderson, J.K. (1970) *Military Theory and Practice in the Age of Xenophon*. Berkeley: University of California Press.

Anderson, J.K. (1974) *Xenophon*. London: Duckworth.

Anglim, S., Jestice, P., Rice, R., Rusch, S. and Serrati, J. (2002) *Fighting Techniques of the Ancient World, 3000 BC–AD 500*. London: Greenhill.

Aperghis, G.G. (1997) 'Alexander's Hipparchies', *Ancient World*, 28, 133–48.

Ashley, J. (1998) *The Macedonian Empire*. Jefferson: McFarland & Co.

Austin, N. and Rankov, B. (1995) *Exploratio*. London: Routledge.

Badian, E. (1997) 'The battle of the Granicus: a new look', in *Ancient Macedonia II*. Thessalonika, Institute for Balkan Studies, pp. 271–93.

Baggett, L. and Grace, W. (1992) *Four Battles of the Ancient World*. Lancaster: Decision Games/ Overlord Games.

Bagnall, N. (1990) *The Punic Wars*. London: Pimlico.

Barker, P. (1979) *Alexander the Great's Campaigns*. Cambridge: Patrick Stephens.

Barker, P. (1980) *War Games Rules 3000 BC to 1485 AD*, 6th edn. Goring-by-Sea: Wargames Research Group.

Barker, P. (1981) *The Armies and Enemies of Imperial Rome*, 4th edn. Wargames Research Group.

Barker, P. (1986) *War Games Rules 3000 BC to 1485 AD*, 7th edn. Devizes: Wargames Research Group.

Barker, P. (2001) *De Bellis Antiquitatis*, Version 2. Devizes: Wargames Research Group.

Barker, P. and Bodley Scott, R. (1993) *De Bellis Multitudinis*. Devizes: Wargames Research Group.

Bar-Kochva, B. (1976) *The Seleucid Army*. Cambridge: Cambridge University Press.

Bath, T. *Hannibal's Campaigns*. Cambridge: Patrick Stephens.

Bell, M.J.V. (1965) 'Tactical Reform in the Roman Republican Army', *Historia*, 14, 404–22.

Berg, R. *et al.* (1977) *Wargame Design*. New York: Simulations Publications Incorporated.

Berg, R. (2005) *Men of Iron*. Hanford: GMT Games.

Berg, R. and Herman, M. (1999) *War Galley*. Hanford: GMT Games.

Berg, R. and Herman, M. (2005) *The Siege of Alesia*. Hanford: GMT Games.

Best, J.G.P. (1969) *Thracian Peltasts and their Influence on Greek Warfare*. Groningen: Wolters-Noordhoff.

Beyerchen, A. (1992) 'Clausewitz, nonlinearity and the unpredictability of war', *International Security*, 17(3), 59–90.

Biddle, S. (2004) *Military Power: Explaining Victory and Defeat in Modern Battle*. Princeton: Princeton University Press.

Bigwood, J.M. (1983) 'The ancient accounts of the battle of Cunaxa', *American Journal of Philology*, 104, 340–57.

Billows, R. (1990) *Antigonos the One-Eyed and the Creation of the Hellenistic State*. Berkeley: University of California Press.

Bishop, M.C. and Coulston, J.C.N. (1993) *Roman Military Equipment*. London: Batsford.

Blackett, P.M.S. (1962) *Studies of War*. London: Oliver & Boyd.

Boehm, J. (1981) 'A rematch at Raphia', *Slingshot*, 95, 34–6 and 96, 31–4.

Bosworth, A.B. (1980) *A Historical Commentary on Arrian's History of Alexander*, Vol. I. Oxford: Clarendon Press.

Bosworth, A.B. (1988) *Conquest and Empire*. Cambridge: Cambridge University Press.

Bosworth, A.B. (1995) *A Historical Commentary on Arrian's History of Alexander*, Vol. II. Oxford: Clarendon Press.

Briscoe, J. (1973) *A Commentary on Livy, Books XXXI–XXXIII*. Oxford: Clarendon Press.

Briscoe, J. (1981) *A Commentary on Livy, Books XXXIV–XXXVII*. Oxford: Clarendon Press.

Brun, P. (ed.) (1999) *Guerres et Sociétés dans les Mondes Grecs (490–322)*. Paris: Éditions du Temps.

Brunt, P.A. (1962) 'Persian accounts of Alexander's campaigns', *Classical Quarterly*, 12, 141–55.

Brunt, P.A. (1971) *Italian Manpower, 225 BC–AD 14*. Oxford: Clarendon Press.

Buckingham, W. (2002) *Arnhem 1944*. Stroud: Tempus.

Buckler, J. (1980) *The Theban Hegemony, 371–362 BC*. Cambridge: Harvard University Press.

Buckler, J. (1985) 'Epameinondas and the *Embolon*', *Phoenix*, 39, 134–43.

Burn, A.R. (1965) 'The generalship of Alexander', *Greece & Rome*, 12, 140–54.

Burn, A.R. (1984) *Persia and the Greeks*, 2nd edn. London: Duckworth.

Bury, J.B., Cook, S.A. and Adcock, F.E. (eds), (1927) *The Cambridge Ancient History*, Vol. 6. Cambridge: Cambridge University Press.

Cagniart, P. (1992) 'Studies on Caesar's use of cavalry during the Gallic war', *Ancient World*, 23, 71–85.

Campbell, B. (1987) 'Teach yourself how to be a general', *Journal of Roman Studies*, 77, 13–29.

Cartledge, P. (1987) *Agesilaos and the Crisis of Sparta*. Baltimore: Johns Hopkins University Press.

Caven, B. (1980) *The Punic Wars*. London: Book Club Associates.

Caven, B. (1990) *Dionysius I: Warlord of Sicily*. New Haven: Yale University Press.

Cawkwell, G. (1972a) 'Introduction', in Xenophon, *The Persian Expedition*. Harmondsworth: Penguin, pp. 9–48.

Cawkwell, G. (1972b) 'Epaminondas and Thebes', *Classical Quarterly*, 22, 254–78.

Cawkwell, G. (1976) 'Agesilaus and Sparta', *Classical Quarterly*, 26, 62–84.

Cawkwell, G. (1978) *Philip of Macedon*. London: Faber & Faber.

von Clausewitz, C. (1976) *On War*, edited and translated by M. Howard and P. Paret. Princeton: Princeton University Press.

Conliffe, A. (1989) *Tactica*. New York: Quantum.

Conliffe, A. (1996) *CrossFire*. New York: Quantum.

Connolly, P. (1981) *Greece and Rome at War*. London: Macdonald.

Connolly, P. (1991) 'The Roman fighting technique deduced from armour and weaponry', in V.A. Maxfield and M.J. Dobson (eds), *Roman Frontier Studies 1989*. Exeter: University of Exeter Press, pp.358–63.

Connolly, P. (1998) 'Legion versus phalanx', *Military Illustrated*, 124, 36–41.

Cook, S.A., Adcock, F.E. and Charlesworth, M.P. (eds) (1932) *The Cambridge Ancient History*, Vol. 9. Cambridge: Cambridge University Press.

Cornell, T. and Matthews, J. (1982) *Atlas of the Roman World*. London: Phaidon.

Cornell, T. (1995) *The Beginnings of Rome*. London: Routledge.

Cotterell, A. *Chariot*. London: Pimlico.

Creasy, E (1911) *The Fifteen Decisive Battles of the World*. London: Cassell.

Creative Assembly (2004) *Rome: Total War* (PC software). Slough: Activision.

van Creveld, M. (1985) *Command in War*. Cambridge: Harvard University Press.

Croom, A.T. and Griffiths, W.B. (eds) (2000) 'Re-enactment as research', *Journal of Roman Military Equipment Studies*, 11.

Crowther, J.G. and Whiddington, R. (1947) *Science at War*. London: HMSO.

Culham, P. (1989) 'Chance, command and chaos in ancient military engagements', *World Futures*, 27, 191–205.

Cunliffe, B. (1999) *The Ancient Celts*. London: Penguin.

Daly, G. (2002) *Cannae: The Experience of Battle in the Second Punic War*. London: Routledge.

Daniel, T. (1992) 'The *taxeis* of Alexander and the change to Chiliarch, the companion cavalry and the change to Hipparchies: a brief assessment', *Ancient World*, 23, 43–57.

Davis, F. (1983) *Wellington's Victory*. Lake Geneva: TSR.

Delbrück, H. (1920) *History of the Art of War*, Vol. I, 3rd edn, translated by W. Renfroe. Reprinted in 1975. Lincoln: University of Nebraska Press.

Dennis, G. (1984) *Maurice's Strategikon* (translated). Philadelphia: University of Pennsylvania Press.

Devine, A.M. (1983) 'Embolon: a study in tactical terminology', *Phoenix*, 37, 201–17.

Devine, A.M. (1984) 'Diodorus' account of the battle of Gaza', *Acta Classica*, 27, 31–40.

Devine, A.M. (1985a) 'Diodorus' account of the battle of Paraitacene (317 BC)', *Ancient World*, 12, 75–86.

Devine, A.M. (1985b) 'Diodorus' account of the battle of Gabiene', *Ancient World*, 12, 87–96.

Devine, A.M. (1985c) 'The strategies of Alexander the Great and Darius III in the Issus campaign', *Ancient World*, 12, 25–38.

Devine, A.M. (1985d) 'Grand tactics at the battle of Issus', *Ancient World*, 12, 39–59.

Devine, A.M. (1986) 'The battle of Gaugamela: a tactical and source-critical study', *Ancient World*, 13, 87–115.

Devine, A.M. (1987) 'The battle of the Hydaspes: a tactical and source-critical study', *Ancient World*, 16, 91–113.

Devine, A.M. (1988) 'A pawn-sacrifice at the battle of the Granicus: the origins of a favorite stratagem of Alexander the Great', *Ancient World*, 18, 3–20.

Devine, A.M. (1989) 'The Macedonian Army at Gaugamela: its strength and the length of its battle-line', *Ancient World*, 19, 77–80.

DeVoto, J. (1992) 'The Theban sacred band', *Ancient World*, 23, 3–19.

Dilke, O.A.W. (1985) *Greek and Roman Maps*. London: Thames & Hudson.

Dodge, T. (1890) *Alexander*, Vols I and II. New York: Houghton Mifflin, republished by Greenhill, 1993.

Dodge, T. (1891) *Hannibal*, Vols I and II. New York: Houghton Mifflin, republished by Greenhill, 1993.

Dodge, T. (1892) *Caesar*. New York: Houghton Mifflin, republished by Da Capo, 1997.

Doenges, N. (1998) 'The campaign and battle of Marathon', *Historia*, 47, 1–17.

Donlan, W. and Thompson, J. (1976) 'The charge at Marathon: Herodotus 6.112', *Classical Journal*, 71, 339–41.

Dorey, T.A. (1957) 'Macedonian troops at the battle of Zama', *American Journal of Philology*, 78, 185–7.

Dorey, T.A. and Dudley, D.R. (1971) *Rome Against Carthage*. London: Secker & Warburg.

Dixon, K. and Southern, P. (1992) *The Roman Cavalry*. London: Routledge.

Ducrey, P. (1986) *Warfare in Ancient Greece*, translated by J. Lloyd. New York: Schocken.

Duggan, A. (1956) *Winter Quarters*. London: Peter Davies.

Dunnigan, J. and Nofi, A. (1990) 'Men at arms', *Strategy & Tactics*, 137, 10–52.

Dunnigan, J. (1992) *The Complete Wargames Handbook*, 2nd edn. New York: William Morrow.

Du Picq, A. (1920) *Battle Studies*, translated by J. Greely and R. Cotton. Republished in *Roots of Strategy*, Book 2. Harrisburg: Stackpole, 1987.

Dupuy, E. and Dupuy, T. (1993) *The Collins Encyclopedia of Military History*, 4th edn. Glasgow: HarperCollins.

Dupuy, T. (1979) *Numbers, Predictions & War*. London: Macdonald & Jane's.

Dupuy, T. (1992) *Understanding War*. London: Leo Cooper.

Edwards, D. (1995) 'The pen and the spade: a siege in Cyprus', *Slingshot*, 179, 6–9.

Ellis, J.R. (1976) *Philip II and Macedonian Imperialism*. London: Thames & Hudson.

Embleton, R. and Graham, F. (1984) *Hadrian's Wall in the Days of the Romans*. Newcastle: Frank Graham.

Engels, D. (1978) *Alexander the Great and the Logistics of the Macedonian Army*. Berkeley: University of California Press.

Erudite Software (1999) *The Great Battles Collector's Edition* (PC software). Bracknell: Interactive Magic.

Evans, J.A.S. (1993) 'Herodotus and the battle of Marathon', *Historia*, 42, 279–307.

Fantar, M. (1989) 'Régulus en Afrique', in H. Devijer and E. Lipinski (eds), *Punic Wars, Studia Phoenicia X*. Leuven: Uitgeverij Peeters, pp. 75–84.

Ferrill, A. (1985) *The Origins of War*. London: Thames & Hudson.

Feugère, M. (2002) *Weapons of the Romans*, translated by D. Smith. Stroud: Tempus.

Fiorato, V., Boylston, A. and Knüsel, C. (eds) (2000) *Blood Red Roses*. Oxford: Oxbow.

Foard, G. (2004) *Naseby: The Decisive Campaign*. Barnsley: Pen & Sword.

Foss, C. (1977) 'The battle of the Granicus: a new look', in *Ancient Macedonia II*. Thessalonika, Institute for Balkan Studies, pp. 495–502.

Frank, T. (1919) 'Placentia and the battle of the Trebia', *Journal of Roman Studies*, 9, 202–7.

Freedman, L. (2005) 'A theory of battle or a theory of war?', *Journal of Strategic Studies*, 28, 425–35.

Freedman, L. (2006) *The Transformation of Strategic Affairs*, Adelphi Paper 379. London: Routledge for IISS.

Fuller, J.F.C. (1954) *The Decisive Battles of the Western World*, Vol.I. London: Eyre & Spottiswoode.

Fuller, J.F.C. (1960) *The Generalship of Alexander the Great*. New Brunswick: Rutgers University Press.

Fuller, J.F.C. (1965) *Julius Caesar: Man, Soldier and Tyrant*. New Brunswick: Rutgers University Press.

Gabriel, R. and Metz, K. (1991) *From Sumer to Rome: The Military Capabilities of Ancient Armies*. Westport: Greenwood.

Gaebel, R. (2002) *Cavalry Operations in the Ancient Greek World*. Norman: University of Oklahoma Press.

Garoufalias, P. (1979) *Pyrrhus, King of Epirus*. London: Stacey International.

Gilliver, K. (1999) *The Roman Art of War*. Stroud: Tempus.

Glantz, D. and House, J. (1995) *When Titans Clashed*. Lawrence: University Press of Kansas.

Glover, R.F. (1948) 'The tactical handling of the elephant', *Greece & Rome*, 17(49), 1–11.

Goldsworthy, A. (1996) *The Roman Army at War, 100 BC–AD 200*. Oxford: Clarendon Press.

Goldsworthy, A. (1997) 'The *othismos*, myths and heresies: the nature of hoplite battle', *War in History*, 4, 1–26.

Goldsworthy, A. (2000a) *The Punic Wars*. London: Cassell.

Goldsworthy, A. (2000b) *Roman Warfare*. London: Cassell.

Goldsworthy, A. (2001) *Cannae*. London: Cassell.

Goldsworthy, A. (2003) *The Complete Roman Army*. London: Thames & Hudson.

Goldsworthy, A. (2004) *In the Name of Rome*. London: Orion.

Goldsworthy, A. (2006) *Caesar*. London: Weidenfeld & Nicolson.

Gowers, W. (1947) 'The African elephant in warfare', *African Affairs*, 46(182), 42–9.

Grainger, A. (1990) 'Clouds in the west', *Slingshot*, 150, 13–20.

Grainger, J. (2002) *The Roman War of Antiochos the Great*. Leiden: Brill.

Grant, C. (1974) *The Ancient War Game*. London: A. & C. Black.

Grant, C. (1977) *Ancient Battles for Wargamers*. Watford: Model & Allied Publications.

Green, P. (1991) *Alexander of Macedon*, 2nd edn. Berkeley: University of California Press.

Green, P. (1996) *The Greco-Persian Wars*, 2nd edn. Berkeley: University of California Press.

Greenhalgh, P. (1981) *Pompey: The Republican Prince*. London: Weidenfeld & Nicolson.

Griffith, G.T. (1935) *The Mercenaries of the Hellenistic World*. Reprinted in 1984. Chicago: Ares.

Griffith, G.T. (1947) 'Alexander's generalship at Gaugamela', *Journal of Hellenic Studies*, 67, 77–89.

Gwatkin, W. (1956) 'Some reflections on the battle of Pharsalus', *Transactions and Proceedings of the American Philological Association*, 87, 109–24.

Gygax, G. (1974) *Alexander the Great*. Baltimore: Avalon Hill Game Company.

Hackett, J. (ed.) (1989) *Warfare in the Ancient World*. London: Sidgwick & Jackson.

Haggart, B. (1978) 'Wellington's victory as history and design', *Fire & Movement*, 11, 52–5 and 58.

Haggart, B. (2005) 'What is a simulation?', *Fire & Movement*, 139, 17–20.

Haggart, B. (2006) 'What is a simulation?', *Fire & Movement*, 140, 29–33.

Haggart, B. (2006) 'What is a simulation?', *Fire & Movement*, 141, 20–1, 29–32.

Hamilton, C. (1979) *Sparta's Bitter Victories*. Ithaca: Cornell University Press.

Hamilton, C. (1991) *Agesilaus and the Failure of Spartan Hegemony*. Ithaca: Cornell University Press.

Hamilton, J.R. (1956) 'The cavalry battle at the Hydaspes', *Journal of Hellenic Studies*, 76, 26–31.

Hammond, N.G.L. (1938a) 'The two battles of Chaeronea (338 BC and 86 BC)', *Klio*, 31, 186–218.

Hammond, N.G.L. (1938b) 'The sources of Diodorus Siculus XVI', *Classical Quarterly*, 32, 137–51.

Hammond, N.G.L. (1967) *A History of Greece to 322 BC*, 2nd edn. Oxford: Oxford University Press.

Hammond, N.G.L. (1968) 'The campaign and the battle of Marathon', *Journal of Hellenic Studies*, 88, 13–57.

Hammond, N.G.L. (1969) 'Strategia and hegemonia in fifth-century Athens', *Classical Quarterly*, 19, 111–44.

Hammond, N.G.L. (1978) 'A cavalry unit in the army of Antigonus Monopthalmus: Asthippoi', *Classical Quarterly*, 28, 128–35.

Hammond, N.G.L. (1980) 'The battle of the Granicus River', *Journal of Hellenic Studies*, 100, 73–88.

Hammond, N.G.L. (1983) 'Army transport in the fifth and fourth centuries', *Greek, Roman & Byzantine Studies*, 24(1), 27–31.

Hammond, N.G.L. (1984) 'The battle of Pydna', *Journal of Hellenic Studies*, 104, 31–47.

Hammond, N.G.L. (1988) 'The campaign and the battle of Cynoscephalae in 197 BC', *Journal of Hellenic Studies*, 108, 60–82.

Hammond, N.G.L. (1989a) *Alexander the Great*, 2nd edn. Bristol: Bristol Press.

Hammond, N.G.L. (1989b) 'Casualties and reinforcements of citizen soldiers in Greece and Macedonia', *Journal of Hellenic Studies*, 109, 56–68.

Hammond, N.G.L. (1989c) *The Macedonian State*. Oxford: Clarendon Press.

Hammond, N.G.L. (1992) 'Alexander's charge at the battle of Issus in 333 BC', *Historia*, 41, 395–406.

Hammond, N.G.L. (1994) *Philip of Macedon*. London: Duckworth.

Hammond, N.G.L. (1996) 'Some passages in Polyaenus' *Stratagems* concerning Alexander', *Greek, Roman & Byzantine Studies*, 37, 23–53.

Hammond, N.G.L. and Griffith, G.T. (1979) *A History of Macedonia*, Vol. II. Oxford: Clarendon Press.

Hammond, N.G.L. and Walbank, F.W. (1988) *A History of Macedonia*, Vol. III. Oxford: Clarendon Press.

Handel, M. (1996) *Masters of War*, 2nd edn. London: Frank Cass.

Hansen, M. (1993) 'The battle exhortation in ancient historiography: fact or fiction?', *Historia*, 42, 161–80.

Hanson, V.D. (1988), 'Epameinondas, the battle of Leuktra (371 BC), and the "revolution" in Greek battle tactics', *Classical Antiquity*, 7, 190–207.

Hanson, V.D. (1989) *The Western Way of War: Infantry Battle in Classical Greece*. London: Hodder & Stoughton.

Hanson, V.D. (ed.) (1991) *Hoplites: The Classical Greek Battle Experience*. London: Routledge.

Hanson, V.D. (1999a) *The Wars of the Ancient Greeks*. London: Cassell.

Hanson, V.D. (1999b) 'The status of ancient military history: traditional work, recent research, and on-going controversies', *Journal of Military History*, 63, 379–413.

Hanson, V.D. (2001) *Why the West has Won*. London: Faber & Faber.

Harrison, P. (2004) *Time Commanders: Great Battles of the Ancient World*. London: Virgin.

Hausrath, A. (1971) *Venture Simulation in War, Business and Politics*. New York: McGraw Hill.

Head, D. (1982) *Armies of the Macedonian and Punic Wars*. Worthing: Wargames Research Group.

Head, D. (1992) *The Achaemenid Persian Army*. Stockport: Montvert.

Healy, M. (1994) *Cannae 216 BC*. London: Osprey.

Herman, M. and Berg, R. (1991) *The Great Battles of Alexander*. Hanford: GMT Games.

Herman, M. and Berg, R. (1992) *SPQR*. Hanford: GMT Games.

Herman, M. and Berg, R. (1993) *Lion of the North*. Hanford: GMT Games.

Herzog, C. (1982) *The Arab-Israeli Wars*. London: Arms & Armour.

Hodge, T. (1975) 'Marathon: the Persians' voyage', *Transactions of the American Philological Association*, 105, 155–73.

Hodkinson, S. and Powell, A. (eds) (2006) *Sparta and War*. Swansea: Classical Press of Wales.

Holladay, A.J. (1982) 'Hoplites and heresies', *Journal of Hellenic Studies*, 102, 94–103.

Holmes, T. (2003) 'Classical Blitzkrieg: the untimely modernity of Schlieffen's Cannae Programme', *Journal of Military History*, 67, 745–71.

Hornblower, J. (1981) *Hieronymus of Cardia*. Oxford: Oxford University Press.

Hornblower, S. and Spawforth, A. (eds) (1996) *The Oxford Classical Dictionary*, 3rd edn. Oxford: Oxford University Press.

Hoyos, B.D. (1983) 'Hannibal: what kind of genius?', *Greece & Rome*, 30, 171–80.

Hughes, B.P. (1974) *Firepower*. London: Arms & Armour.

Humble, R. (1980) *Warfare in the Ancient World*. London: Guild.

Hunt, P. (1997) 'Helots at the battle of Plataea', *Historia*, 46, 129–44.

Hutchinson, G. (2000) *Xenophon and the Art of Command*. London: Greenhill.

Hyland, A. (1990) *Equus: The Horse in the Roman World*. London: Batsford.

Hyland, A. (2003) *The Horse in the Ancient World*. Stroud: Sutton.

Jones, A. (1988) *The Art of War in the Western World*. London: Harrap.

Jung, M. (2006) *Marathon und Plataiai*. Göttingen: Vandenhoech & Ruprecht.

Junkelmann, M. (1986) *Die Legionen des Augustus*. Mainz: Philipp von Zabern.

Kagan, D. (1974) *The Archidamian War*. Ithaca: Cornell University Press.

Kagan, D. (1981) *The Peace of Nicias and the Sicilian Expedition*. Ithaca: Cornell University Press.

Kagan, K. (2006) *The Eye of Command*. Ann Arbor: University of Michigan Press.

Keegan, J. (1978) *The Face of Battle*. Harmondsworth: Penguin.

Keppie, L. (1984) *The Making of the Roman Army*. London: Batsford.

Krentz, P. (1985a) 'Casualties in hoplite battles', *Greek, Roman & Byzantine Studies*, 26(1), 13–20.

Krentz, P. (1985b) 'The nature of hoplite battle', *Classical Antiquity*, 4, 50–61.

Krentz, P. (2002) 'Fighting by the rules: the invention of the hoplite agon', *Hesperia*, 71, 23–39.

Kromayer, J. (1903) *Antike Schlachtfelder in Griechenland*, Vol. I. Berlin: Weidmannsche Buchhandlung.

Kromayer, J. (1907) *Antike Schlachtfelder in Griechenland*, Vol. II. Berlin: Weidmannsche Buchhandlung.

Kromayer, J. and Veith, G. (1912) *Antike Schlachtfelder in Italien und Afrika*, Vols I and II. Berlin: Weidmannsche Buchhandlung.

Kromayer, J. and Veith, G. (1922–9) *Schlachten-Atlas zur Antike Kriegsgeschichte*. Leipzig: H. Wagner & E. Debes.

Kromayer, J., Veith, G. *et al.* (1924–31) *Antike Schlachtfelder*. Berlin: Weidmannsche Buchhandlung.

Lancel, S. (1998) *Hannibal*. Oxford: Blackwell.

Lanchester, F.W. (1916) *Aircraft in Warfare*. Revised edition reprinted in 1995. Sunnyvale: Lanchester Press.

Lane Fox, R. (2004) *Alexander the Great*, updated edn. London: Penguin.

Langer, H. (1980) *The Thirty Years' War*. Poole: Blandford.

Langher, S. (2000) *Agatocle*. Messina: Dipartimento di Scienza dell'Antichita dell Universitad degli Studi di Messina.

Lawson, M.K. (2002) *The Battle of Hastings 1066*. Stroud: Tempus.

Lazenby, J. (1978) *Hannibal's War*. Warminster: Aris & Phillips.

Lazenby, J. (1985) *The Spartan Army*. Warminster: Aris & Phillips.

Lazenby, J. (1993) *The Defence of Greece*. Warminster: Aris & Phillips.

Lazenby, J. (1996) *The First Punic War*. London: UCL Press.

Lazenby, J. (2004) *The Peloponnesian War*. London: Routledge.

Leach, J. (1978) *Pompey the Great*. London: Croom Helm.

Le Bohec, S. (1993) *Antigone Dôsôn*. Nancy: Presses Universitaires de Nancy.

Le Bohec, Y. (1996) *Histoire Militaire des Guerres Puniques*. Monaco: Éditions du Rocher.

Le Bohec, Y. (2001) *César, Chef de Guerre*. Monaco: Éditions du Rocher.

Lendon, E. (1999) 'The rhetoric of combat: Greek military theory and Roman culture in Julius Caesar's battle descriptions', *Classical Antiquity*, 18, 273–329.

Lendon, E. (2005) *Soldiers & Ghosts: A History of Battle in Classical Antiquity*. New Haven: Yale University Press.

Lepingwell, J. (1987) 'The laws of combat? Lanchester reexamined', *International Security*, 12(1), 89–134.

Lévèque, P. (1957) *Pyrrhos*. Paris: de Boccard.

Levi, P. (1984) *Atlas of the Greek World*. Oxford: Phaidon.

Lloyd, A. (1973) *Marathon*. New York: Random House.

Lloyd, A. (ed.) (1996) *Battle in Antiquity*. London: Duckworth.

Loreto, L. (2006) *Per la Storia Militare del Mondo Antico*. Napoli: Jovene editore.

Luginbill, R. (1994) '*Othismos*: the importance of the mass-shove in hoplite warfare', *Phoenix*, 48, 51–61.

Luttwak, E. (1976) *The Grand Strategy of the Roman Empire*. Baltimore: Johns Hopkins University Press.

MadMinute Games (2006) *Take Command: Second Manassas* (PC software). New York: Paradox Interactive.

von Manstein, E. (1987) *Lost Victories*. London: Greenhill.

Manti, P. (1983) 'The sarissa of the Macedonian infantry', *Ancient World*, 8, 73–80.

Manti, P, (1992) 'The sarissa of the Macedonian infantry', *Ancient World*, 23, 31–42.

Manti, P. (1994) 'The Macedonian sarissa, again', *Ancient World*, 25, 77–91.

Markle, M. (1978) 'Use of the sarissa by Philip and Alexander of Macedon', *American Journal of Archaeology*, 82, 483–97.

Marsden, E.W. (1964) *The Campaign of Gaugamela*. Liverpool: Liverpool University Press.

Marshall, B.A. (1976) *Crassus: A Political Biography*. Amsterdam: Adolf M. Hackert.

Martin, S., Monnier, T. and Stratigos, N. (2000) 'Champs de Bataille III', *Vae Victis*, 30, 34–44.

May, E, (2000) *Strange Victory*. London: I.B. Tauris.

McCall, J. (2002) *The Cavalry of the Roman Republic*. London: Routledge.

McCoy, W.J. (1989) 'Memnon of Rhodes at the Granicus', *American Journal of Philology*, 110, 413–33.

Meiklejohn, K.W. (1938) 'Roman strategy and tactics from 509 to 202 BC', *Greece & Rome*, 7(21), 170–8.

Montagu, J.D. (2000) *Battles of the Greek and Roman Worlds*. London: Greenhill.

Montagu, J.D. (2006) *Greek and Roman Warfare*. London: Greenhill.

Morgan, J.D. (1981) 'Sellasia revisited', *American Journal of Archaeology*, 85, 328–30.

Morgan, J. (1983) 'Palaepharsalus – the battle and the town', *American Journal of Archaeology*, 87, 23–54.

Morrison, J., Coates, J. and Rankov, B. (2000) *The Athenian Trireme*, 2nd edn. Cambridge: Cambridge University Press.

Middlebrook, M. (2001) *The First Day on the Somme*. London: Penguin.

Miller, M. (1977) *The Battle of Raphia, 217 BC*. Illinois: Game Designers' Workshop.

Miller, M.C.J. (1992) 'The *Principes* and the so-called Camillan reforms', *Ancient World*, 23, 59–70.

Mixter, J.R. (1992) 'The length of the Macedonian sarissa during the reigns of Philip II and Alexander the Great', *Ancient World*, 23, 21–9.

Muir, R. (1998) *Tactics and the Experience of Battle in the Age of Napoleon*. New Haven: Yale University Press.

Myres, J. (1953) *Herodotus: Father of History*. Oxford: Clarendon Press.

Nelson, J. (1976) *Highway to the Reich*. New York: Simulations Publications Incorporated.

Nelson, R. (1975) *Armies of the Greek and Persian Wars*. Worthing: Wargames Research Group.

Nosworthy, B. (1992) *The Anatomy of Victory*. New York: Hippocrene.

Nosworthy, B. (1995) *Battle Tactics of Napoleon and his Enemies*. London: Constable.

Oakley, S.P. (2005) *A Commentary on Livy, Books VI–X*, Vol. 4. Oxford: Clarendon Press.

Palmer, N. (1977) *The Comprehensive Guide to Board Wargaming*. London: Arthur Barker.

Panther Games (2003) *Airborne Assault: Highway to the Reich* (PC software). Staten Island: Matrix Games.

Pape, R. (1996) *Bombing to Win*. Ithaca: Cornell University Press.

Parke, H.W. (1933) *Greek Mercenary Soldiers*. Reprinted in 1981. Chicago: Ares.

Parker, H.M.D. (1923) *The Roman Legions*. Reprinted in 1980. Chicago: Ares.

Peddie, J. (1994) *The Roman War Machine*. Stroud: Sutton.

Peddie, J. (1997) *Hannibal's War*. Stroud: Sutton.

Perla, P. (1990) *The Art of Wargaming*. Annapolis: Naval Institute Press.

Poli, D. (ed.) (2002) *La Battaglia del Sentino*. Roma: Università degli Studi di Macerata.

Priestley, R. (2005) *Warmaster Ancients*. Nottingham: Games Workshop.

Pritchett, W.K. (1957) 'New light on Plataia', *American Journal of Archaeology*, 61, 9–28.

Pritchett, W.K. (1958) 'Observations on Chaironeia', *American Journal of Achaeology*, 62, 307–11.

Pritchett, W.K. (1965) *Studies in Ancient Greek Topography*, Part I. Berkeley: University of California Press.

Pritchett, W.K. (1969) *Studies in Ancient Greek Topography*, Part II. Berkeley: University of California Press.

Pritchett, W.K. (1971) *The Greek State at War*, Part I. Berkeley: University of California Press.

Pritchett, W.K. (1985) *The Greek State at War*, Part IV. Berkeley: University of California Press.

Pritchett, W.K. (1994) *Essays in Greek History*. Amsterdam: J.C. Gieben.

Rahe, P. (1980) 'The military situation in Western Asia on the eve of Cunaxa', *American Journal of Philology*, 101, 79–96.

Rahe, P. (1981) 'The annihilation of the sacred band at Chaeronea', *American Journal of Archaeology*, 85, 84–7.

Rawlings, L. (1996) 'Celts, Spaniards, and Samnites: warriors in a soldiers' war', in T. Cornell, B. Rankov and P. Sabin (eds), *The Second Punic War: A Reappraisal*. London: Institute of Classical Studies, pp. 81–95 (BICS Supplement 67).

Rawson, E. (1971) 'The literary sources for the pre-Marian army', *Papers of the British School at Rome*, 26, 13–31.

Rayner, M. (2004) *English Battlefields*. Stroud: Tempus.

Reed, R. (1980) *The Longest Day*. Baltimore: Avalon Hill Game Company.

Rice Homes, T. (1908) 'The battle-field of Old Pharsalus', *Classical Quarterly*, 2, 271–92.

Rice Holmes, T. (1911) *Caesar's Conquest of Gaul*, 2nd edn. London: Oxford University Press.

Rice Holmes, T. (1923) *The Roman Republic and the Founder of the Empire*, Vols I–III. Oxford: Clarendon Press.

Rich, J. and Shipley, G. (eds) (1993a) *War and Society in the Greek World*. London: Routledge.

Rich, J. and Shipley, G. (eds) (1993b) *War and Society in the Roman World*. London: Routledge.

Rinella, M. (2003) *Monty's Gamble: Market Garden*. Millersville: Multi-Man Publishing.

Rohrbaugh, P. (2006) 'La Vallée de la Mort', *Against the Odds*, 4(4).

Roth, J. (1999) *The Logistics of the Roman Army at War (264 BC–AD 235)*. Leiden: Brill.

Rubincam, C. (1991) 'Casualty figures in the battle descriptions of Thucydides', *Transactions of the American Philological Association*, 121, 181–98.

Runciman, W.G. (1998) 'Greek hoplites, warrior culture, and indirect bias', *Journal of the Royal Anthropological Institute*, 4, 731–51.

Sabin, P. (1993) 'Phalanx: an ancient battle game', *Slingshot*, 165, 15–24.

Sabin, P. (1996) 'The mechanics of battle in the second Punic war', in T. Cornell, B. Rankov and P. Sabin (eds), *The Second Punic War: A Reappraisal*. London: Institute of Classical Studies, pp. 59–79 (BICS Supplement 67).

Sabin, P. (1997) *Legion*. Bridgend: Society of Ancients.

Sabin, P. (2000) 'The face of Roman battle', *Journal of Roman Studies*, 110, 1–17.

Sabin, P. (2002a) 'Playing at war: the modern hobby of wargaming', in T. Cornell and T. Allen (eds), *War and Games*. Rochester: Boydell, pp. 193–230.

Sabin, P. (2002b) 'Western Strategy in the new era: the apotheosis of air power?', in A. Dorman, M. Smith and M. Uttley (eds), *The Changing Face of Military Power*. Basingstoke: Palgrave.

Sabin, P. (2003) *Strategos*. Bridgend: Society of Ancients.

Sabin, P. (2006) *Strategos II*. Bridgend: Society of Ancients.

Sabin, P., van Wees, H. and Whitby, M. (eds) (2007) *The Cambridge History of Greek and Roman Warfare*, Vols I and II. Cambridge: Cambridge University Press.

Salmon, E.T. (1967) *Samnium and the Samnites*. Cambridge: Cambridge University Press.

Samuels, M. (1990) 'The reality of Cannae', *Militargeschichtliche Mitteilungen*, 47, 7–29.

Santosuosso, A. (1997) *Soldiers, Citizens and the Symbols of War*. Boulder: Westview.

Santosuosso, A. (2001) *Storming the Heavens*. Boulder: Westview.

Schelling, T. (1960) *The Strategy of Conflict*. Cambridge: Harvard University Press.

Scullard, H.H. (1936) 'A note on the battle of Ilipa', *Journal of Roman Studies*, 26, 19–23.

Scullard, H.H. (1970) *Scipio Africanus: Soldier and Politician*. Ithaca: Cornell University Press.

Scullard, H.H. (1974) *The Elephant in the Greek and Roman World*. London: Thames & Hudson.

Seibert, J. (1969) *Untersuchungen zur Geschichte Ptolemaios'I*. Munich: C.H.Beck'sche Verlagsbuchhandlung.

Seibert, J. (1972) *Alexander der Grosse*. Darmstadt: Wissenschaftliche Buchgesellschaft.

Seibert, J. (1993a) *Hannibal*. Darmstadt: Wissenschaftliche Buchgesellschaft.

Seibert, J. (1993b) *Forschungen zu Hannibal*. Darmstadt: Wissenschaftliche Buchgesellschaft.

Sekunda, N. and McBride, A. (1984) *The Army of Alexander the Great*. London: Osprey.

Sekunda, N. and McBride, A. (1986) *The Ancient Greeks*. London: Osprey.

Sekunda, N. and Chew, S. (1992) *The Persian Army 560–330 BC*. London: Osprey.

Sekunda, N. and McBride, A. (1994) *The Seleucid Army*. Stockport: Montvert.

Sekunda, N. and Northwood, S. (1995) *Early Roman Armies*. London: Osprey.

Sekunda, N. and McBride, A. (1996) *Republican Roman Army 200–104 BC*. London: Osprey.

Sekunda, N. and Hook, R. (1998) *The Spartans*. London: Osprey.

Sekunda, N. and Hook, R. (2002) *Marathon 490 BC*. London: Osprey.

Seymour, W. (1988) *Decisive Factors in Twenty Great Battles of the World*. London: Sidgwick & Jackson.

Shipley, G. (2000) *The Greek World after Alexander*. London: Routledge.

Sidebottom, H. (2004) *Ancient Warfare: A Very Short Introduction*. Oxford: Oxford University Press.

Sidnell, P. (2006) *Warhorse: Cavalry in Ancient Warfare*. London: Hambledon Continuum.

Smith, R.E. (1958) *Service in the Post-Marian Roman Army*. Manchester: Manchester University Press.

Smith, R. (2005) *The Utility of Force*. London: Allen Lane.

Snodgrass, A.M. (1999) *Arms & Armor of the Greeks*, new edn. Baltimore: Johns Hopkins University Press.

Sommella, P. (1967) *Antichi Campi di Battaglia in Italia*. Roma: De Luca.

Spence, I. (1993) *The Cavalry of Classical Greece*. Oxford: Clarendon Press.

Stylianou, P.J. (1998) *A Historical Commentary on Diodorus Siculus Book 15*. Oxford: Clarendon Press.

Sumner, G.V. (1970) 'The legion and the centuriate organization', *Journal of Roman Studies*, 60, 67–78.

Tajima, J. (2005) *Target Arnhem*. Millersville: Multi-Man Publishing.

Talbert, R.J.A. (1974) *Timoleon and the Revival of Greek Sicily, 344–317 BC*. Cambridge: Cambridge University Press.

Talbert, R.J.A. (ed.) (1985) *Atlas of Classical History*. London: Guild.

Tarn, W.W. (1948) *Alexander the Great*, Vols I and II. Cambridge: Cambridge University Press.

Tatton-Brown, V. (1987) *Ancient Cyprus*. London: British Museum Publications.

Taylor, J. (1974) 'Solving Lanchester-type equations for "modern warfare" with variable coefficients', *Operations Research*, 22, 756–70.

Tillyard, H.J.W. (1908) *Agathocles*. Cambridge: Cambridge University Press.

Van Wees, H. (ed.) (2000) *War and Violence in Ancient Greece*. London: Duckworth.

Van Wees, H. (2004) *Greek Warfare: Myths and Realities*. London: Duckworth.

Walbank, F.W. (1969) *A Historical Commentary on Polybius*, Vol. II. Oxford: Oxford University Press.

Walbank, F.W. (1970) *A Historical Commentary on Polybius*, Vol. I, new edn. Oxford: Oxford University Press.

Walbank, F.W. (1979) *A Historical Commentary on Polybius*, Vol. III. Oxford: Oxford University Press.

Wallace, P. (1982) 'The final battle at Plataia', *Hesperia Supplements*, 19, 183–92.

Walsh, P.G. (1961) *Livy: His Historical Aims and Methods*. Cambridge: Cambridge University Press.

Warmington, B.H. (1960) *Carthage*. London: Robert Hale.

Warry, J. (1980) *Warfare in the Classical World*. London: Salamander.

Warry, J. (1991) *Alexander 334–323 BC*. London: Osprey.

Weigley, Russell, *The Age of Battles* (Indianapolis: Indiana University Press, 1991).

Welch, K. and Powell, A. (eds) (1998) *Julius Caesar as Artful Reporter*. London: Duckworth.

Westlake, H.D. (1938) 'The sources of Plutarch's Timoleon', *Classical Quarterly*, 32, 65–74.

Whatley, N. (1964) 'On the possibility of reconstructing Marathon and other ancient battles', *Journal of Hellenic Studies*, 84, 119–39.

Wheeler, E. (1979) 'The Legion as Phalanx', *Chiron*, 9, 303–18.

Wheeler, E. (1988) *Stratagem and the Vocabulary of Military Trickery*. Leiden: Brill.

Wheeler, E. (1993) 'Methodological limits and the mirage of Roman strategy', *Journal of Military History*, 57, 7–41 and 215–40.

Wheeler, E. (2001) 'Firepower: missile weapons and the "face of battle"', *Electrum*, 5, 169–84.

Wilcox, P. and McBride, A. (1986) *Rome's Enemies 3: Parthians and Sassanid Persians*. London: Osprey.

Williams, M. (2004) 'Philipoemen's special forces: peltasts and a new kind of Greek light-armed warfare', *Historia*, 53, 257–77.

Woodhouse, W.J. (1933) *King Agis of Sparta and his Campaign in Arkadia in 418 BC*. Oxford: Clarendon Press.

Yadin, Y. (1966) *Masada*. London: Weidenfeld & Nicolson.

Zhmodikov, A. (2000) 'Roman republican heavy infantrymen in battle (IV–II centuries BC)', *Historia*, 49, 67–78.

Zotti, N. (1992) *Zama*. Rome: Proxima.